The Anguish of Tibet

As a free spokesman for my captive countrymen and -women, I feel it is my duty to speak out on their behalf. I speak not with a feeling of anger or hatred towards those who are responsible for the immense suffering of our people and the destruction of our land, homes, and culture. They too are human beings who struggle to find happiness, and deserve our compassion. I speak to inform you of the sad situation in my country today and of the aspirations of my people, because in our struggle for freedom, truth is the only weapon we possess.

Acknowledgments:

Permission to print the following material is gratefully acknowledged:
Map on p. 2 reprinted from *Tibet and Its History*, by Hugh E. Richardson,
© 1962. Reprinted by arrangement with Shambhala Publications,
Inc., 300 Massachusetts Ave., Boston, MA 02115.
Map on p. 32 © copyright Paul Ingram, OPTIMUS. Reprinted by
permission.
"In Exile From the Land of the Snows" excerpted from *In Exile From
the Land of the Snows* © Wylie, Aitken, & Stone. Reprinted by per-
mission.
"Educational Discrimination" from *Merciless Repression: Human Rights
in Tibet.* © Copyright 1990 Human Rights Watch. Reprinted by
permission.
"On the Brink" from *Illusion and Reality*. Dharamsala: Tibetan Youth
Congress, 1989. Reprinted by permission of the author.
One Year under Martial Law. © Copyright 1990 Amnesty Interna-
tional Publications. Reprinted by permission.
"The Agony of Tibet" from Greenpeace Magazine. Reprinted by
permission of the author.
"Unhealed Wound" © Copyright 1990 The Time Inc. Magazine
Company. Reprinted by permission.

THE ANGUISH OF TIBET

Edited by Petra K. Kelly, Gert Bastian,
and Pat Aiello

An "International Year of Tibet" Book

PARALLAX PRESS
BERKELEY, CALIFORNIA

Parallax Press
P.O. Box 7355
Berkeley, CA 94707

Printed in the United States of America

Cover photo of riots in Lhasa by John Ackerly. Cover Design: Gay Reineck. Text layout adapted from a design by Barbara Pope. Composed on a Macintosh IIcx by Lawrence K. Barden, in Altsys Goudy Oldstyle.

Library of Congress Cataloging-in-Publication Data.

Tibet klagt an. English. Selections
   The Anguish of Tibet / edited by Petra K. Kelly, Gert Bastian, and Pat Aiello.
        p.   cm.
Selections from Tibet klagt an and Tibet, ein vergewaltigtes Land,
   translated from the German
   "An International Year of Tibet book."
   Includes bibliographical references.
   ISBN 0-938077-47-3 : $17.00
   1. Tibet (China)--History--1951-   I. Kelly, Petra Karin, 1947- .
II. Bastian, Gert. III. Aiello, Pat, 1950-   . IV. Tibet, ein vergewatigtes Land. English. Selections. 1991. V. Title.
DS786. T49652513 1991   91-2964
951'.505--dc20   CIP

Contents

Preface

Tibet is an occupied country. The political leaders of the world do not acknowledge this, preferring to believe, as the Chinese do, that Tibet is part of China. But, as much of the information in this book reveals, Tibet is a sovereign country that was invaded and remains occupied. Reflecting on the swift retaliation against Iraq for its occupation of Kuwait, Tibet supporters shake their heads and wonder how the world governments can continue to ignore the Chinese occupation of Tibet. Not a single nation has offered diplomatic recognition to Tibet's Government-in-Exile, fearing the potential loss of China's billion-person market.

Despite this, a growing grass roots movement is steadily working for a free Tibet, calling attention to the grave injustices, bordering on genocide, that Tibet's indigenous population is suffering. Buoyed by the Dalai Lama's commitment to nonviolence and reconciliation, the movement aims to liberate this occupied country by using information as its arsenal. This book, we hope, will be a weapon in that struggle, serving as a thorough introduction for those who know little about Tibet and as an essential resource for those already familiar with the situation.

The Anguish of Tibet is based on two books originally compiled in German by Petra K. Kelly, co-founder of the West German Greens party and former member of the German Parliament, and Gert Bastian, also a former Paliamentarian and co-initiator of "Generals for Peace and Disarmament." We have added new articles to reflect the ever-changing situation concerning Tibet. The complete collection includes eyewitness reports, thoroughly researched articles, and vivid accounts of Tibetan life before and after the 1950 invasion. The appendix includes legal documents, guidelines for travel, a list of organizations working on Tibet-related issues, along with other information.

I would like to thank the writers for their generous contributions to this book; Eva Herzer for her help in the initial stages of the book; Will Waters for his excellent translations of the German articles; Lawrence Barden for his editorial expertise; the staff of the International Campaign for Tibet for their help and enthusiastic support; each and every person working for a free Tibet; and especially the Tibetan people, whose courage, tenacity, and good humor continue to inspire me.

The awarding of the 1989 Nobel Peace Prize to His Holiness the Dalai Lama has brought his message of nonviolence and compassion to the attention of the world. That message, which is exemplified by the Tibetan people, will be kept in the public awareness by the many events organized during The International Year of Tibet, 1991. The world is beginning to hear and appreciate the voices of Tibet. Some of the voices speak through this book, and to introduce them is an honor.

Pat Aiello
March 1991
San Geronimo, California

PETRA K. KELLY & GERT BASTIAN

We Must Not Be Silent!

Very little news trickles down from Tibet, the roof of the world. The media in the Free World are not overly interested in up-to-the-minute news coverage of this remote region. The Tibetans' nonviolent resistance against the oppression of the Chinese occupying forces is not dramatic enough, it seems, when compared to more sensational newsbreaks. Only when there are reports of rebellious monks, a police station in flames, or demonstrators killed by security forces, is Tibet granted a few moments of television time or a couple inches of newsprint. Still, the little information that makes its way to the outside world from this land of monks and monasteries is disturbing enough.

With the annexation of Tibet in 1949-50, and particularly after the quelling of the Tibetan popular uprising of March 1959, the People's Republic of China initiated a process whose tragic climax was reached during the Cultural Revolution of the 1960s and 1970s, but whose aim, even today, is clearly the systematic destruction of the rich and sophisticated culture of this last "holy land" and its people. Franz Alt, a German TV journalist, has called the crimes committed against Tibet "an unbelievable tragedy," "a holocaust and an act of barbarism against culture." If the Chinese policy of oppression

vis-a-vis Tibet is allowed to continue unhindered, the Tibetans will
soon become an insignificant minority in their own country, cut off
from their spiritual roots. At that point, little will remain of authentic
Tibetan culture, Tibetan religion, or the Tibetan spiritual tradition.

It is hard to believe that the free world is willing to continue
regarding Tibet's oppression as negligible, and is willing to court the
oppressors instead of practicing solidarity with those deprived of
their rights as human beings.

As a matter of fact, the terrible results of the colonization of Tibet
by the People's Republic of China are sufficient cause for cries of
outrage. More than 1.2 million Tibetans died between 1950 and 1983
under Chinese military rule. This figure includes those who died of
starvation and torture. Tibetan Buddhism was suppressed and more
than 6,000 monasteries, temples, and historical monuments were
systematically plundered and destroyed. Their irreplaceable art
treasures were ravaged or sold on the international antique markets.

Traditional Tibetan agriculture was radically changed and adapted
to the needs of the occupation forces. The yak shepherds were
forcibly collectivized. The cultivation of winter wheat at the expense
of barley—the staple of the Tibetan diet—led to poor harvests and,
in conjunction with extremely high requisitions by the occupation
forces, to famines such as Tibet had never known before. Through
its exploitation of Tibet's natural resources, China has inflicted
immense ecological damage on Tibet's delicate environment.

Under the cover of "brotherly support" for the development of
Tibet, which it considers economically and culturally backward,
Beijing is pursuing a deliberate policy of suppressing the indigenous
culture and of "Sinification." As a result, the six million Tibetans are
already a minority in their own country, facing about eight million
Chinese (including the occupation forces), which further reduces
their chances of regaining their political and cultural autonomy.

One hundred twenty thousand Tibetans—including His Holiness
the Dalai Lama, the political and religious leader of Tibet—were
forced into exile. Most of them live in northern India where the
Tibetan Government-in-Exile is also located, and in the neighboring
Himalayan countries. A few thousand also live in Europe, mainly in
Switzerland.

According to reports dated November 1987 from the Tibetan communities in Europe, several thousand political prisoners are still in jails and forced-labor camps in Tibet. Public executions and gruesome methods of torture have been documented. The Tibetans' fundamental human rights are being persistently violated. The official policy of religious persecution has currently been replaced by a façade of religious freedom. In fact, the essence of Tibetan Buddhism and the teaching or studying of Buddhist philosophy continue to be forbidden.

Where else in the world could similar atrocities occur without at least part of an international public opinion raising its voice in angry protest? But when it is a matter of calling to account the government of the People's Republic of China as the perpetrator of these crimes, other standards apparently apply.

To be sure, the General Assembly of the United Nations did pass three resolutions in 1959, 1961, and 1965 (See Appendix II) condemning China's actions against Tibet. Moreover, China was urged to cease violating human rights in Tibet. However, these resolutions were not complied with to any noticeable extent.

The interest in developing economic and trade relations with China's population of one billion has clearly carried far more weight than the defense, on principle, of international law and human rights, even though Western governments generally do not miss opportunities to point out such violations in areas under communist rule. Thus, Tibet has become a touchstone of morality in international politics.

Chancellor Helmut Kohl of the Federal Republic of Germany stumbled badly over this touchstone in Tibet. During his state visit to the People's Republic in July 1987, he expressly asked to visit Tibet, and thus became the first Western leader to legitimize China's policy on Tibet. The Chancellor ignored all the warnings of the Federal Foreign Minister and the Federal Foreign Office, just as he ignored the protests of the Tibetan Government-in-Exile and Tibetan exile groups. Helmut Kohl dismissed all reservations with the declaration: "Tibet is part of the Chinese polity; this fact is recognized by all the countries in the world."

The Chancellor's opinion is incorrect at any rate, considering the initial attitude of the Western countries towards the annexation of Tibet by troops of the People's Republic of China. Indeed, it was precisely these Western countries which pushed through the above-mentioned UN resolutions condemning China's military intervention and the subsequent violations of human rights in Tibet. As early as 1959 and 1960, in reports of the International Commission of Jurists, China's military invasion of Tibet and its subsequent actions in that country were defined as violations of international law, and China was accused of systematic and deliberate genocide in Tibet. Moreover, the General Assembly endorsed, explicitly in 1961 and implicitly in 1965, the Tibetan people's right to self-determination and expressed the hope that the member states would make every effort to realize the aims of these resolutions.

In a study dated August 12, 1987, dealing with the question: "What considerations speak against an integration, effective in terms of international law, of Tibet into the Chinese polity?" the Reference and Research Services of the German Bundestag came to the unequivocal conclusion that at the time it was first occupied by troops of the People's Republic of China, Tibet met all the requirements, under international law, of an independent state. This study concludes that when China's troops invaded Tibet, it did indeed annex the country by force, but that this did not give it any claim, in terms of international law, that would justify its annexation of territory.

Thus, statements implying *de facto* recognition that Tibet is part of the Chinese polity, such as that made by Chancellor Kohl, are quite welcome to the Chinese government. On July 7, 1987, the Bonn newspaper *General-Anzeiger* commented: "Incidentally, the idea of a trip [to Lhasa] came from Kohl himself. He had his wish communicated to the Chinese. The Beijing government could not have dared to hope that a Western politician would of his own accord promote the idea of Tibet being part of China." The Chancellor was clearly shown how pleased his Chinese hosts were with him—not only through special tokens of friendship and courtesies, but also through a $37.5 million contract for MBB, a German arms company, within the framework of an economic agreement.

He showed his gratitude in his own way: In his speech at the welcoming banquet in Beijing, he did say that respect for human rights was an important criterion, and he explicitly—and rightly—denounced the presence of foreign troops in Afghanistan and Cambodia, but he did not say a word about the presence of Chinese soldiers in Tibet.

This is a shameful omission, of which the Federal Foreign Minister can scarcely have approved. At least not if he meant what he said when he declared on January 24, 1986, during the debate on human rights in the German Bundestag, that in view of the current situation in respect to international law, the principle of non-interference in the internal affairs of other states could not be used to reject demands to respect human rights. Helmut Schäfer, Minister of State at the Federal Foreign Office, supported this position when he declared before the Redoute International Club on June 30, 1987: "No state should reject as interference any criticism of its behavior with regard to the realization of human rights." It is regrettable that the Federal Chancellor, who determines the policy guidelines, does not share this viewpoint.

Just as China's government welcomes statements formally recognizing the annexation of Tibet, it reacts with anger and hostility to criticism of China's policy regarding Tibet. According to China, Tibet has been neither annexed nor militarily-occupied, but liberated from a degrading situation characterized by backwardness, deprivation, and religious repression. Therefore, the policies of the Dalai Lama in particular and the Tibetan Government-in-Exile in general are aimed at solving problems long since overcome.

Unfortunately, similar assessments can often be heard in the West as well. For example, at the height of the political unrest in Tibet, the Bavarian Minister-President, Franz Josef Strauss, declared that a theocratic oligarchy based on the rule of Buddhist monks and their leader did not exactly meet all the requirements of a parliamentary democracy either. Regarding the declaration by Deng Xiaoping that Tibet has long been part of China, Strauss commented, "We must take existing realities into account."

No allegation could be further from the truth. One of the first official acts of the Fourteenth Dalai Lama was to set up a reform commission to implement his plans for the renewal of Tibet. It was not insufficient readiness on the part of the Tibetan government to carry out such reforms that subsequently hindered effective improvements in Tibet, but the policy of the Chinese, who boycotted the work of this very commission. The success of the reform commission would not have fit into the picture of a hopelessly backward Tibet averse to reforms, a picture the Chinese needed in order to justify their occupation.

Despite being forced to flee and go into exile in northern India in 1959, the Dalai Lama continued to be determined to reform Tibetan society. In 1963, from exile, he proclaimed a democratic constitution for a future, self-determined Tibet. In accordance with the constitution, the Tibetan Government-in-Exile was reorganized democratically. The National Assembly was granted the right to forbid the Dalai Lama, by a two-thirds majority, to engage in political activities.

Thus, in a press release responding to Strauss' statement, the representative of His Holiness the Dalai Lama in Europe, Kelsang Gyaltsen, said that it was a "malicious misrepresentation and deliberate falsification of the nature of our struggle for freedom to state, as Herr Strauss has done, that the rebellious Tibetans are seeking to restore the old theocratic system in Tibet."

The Tibetan Government-in-Exile does not deny that, after the Cultural Revolution, a certain relaxation in China's policy regarding Tibet has occurred since about 1980. Chinese politicians admitted having made "mistakes" and a new strategy was announced that was to include negotiations with the Dalai Lama. But this strategy soon foundered on the plebiscite in Tibet demanded by the Tibetan Government-in-Exile. A massive resettlement policy followed, which lured Chinese immigrants to Tibet by promising them three times their normal wages, resettlement allowances, and new homes.

Resettlement measures of this kind have always been one of China's favorite methods of incorporating conquered territory. For example, in Manchuria there are now thirty-five Chinese for every Manchurian and in Mongolia only one in six inhabitants is Mongolian. The Chinese policy of Sinification could well mean the end of Tibet.

Chinese "development aid," intended to improve Tibet's economy, will probably do little to change this. This "aid," in any case, benefits primarily the military infrastructure, the expansion of a strategically important road network, the expensive tourist attractions, and improved living conditions for the Chinese immigrants. Furthermore, the development aid from Western countries—the aid, for example, promised Tibet by Chancellor Helmut Kohl—could be used by China to finance the construction and expansion of an infrastructure intended to facilitate an even greater influx of Chinese into Tibet. The Tibetan Government-in-Exile has drawn attention expressly to this problem.

China's hostile reaction to any defense of Tibetan rights and the embarrassing obsequiousness with which Western statesmen and industrial managers approve of China's policy on Tibet have not, at any rate, been able to alter the fact that many people—especially in the U.S. and Western Europe—continue to stand by the Tibetans in a spirit of solidarity. The activities of Amnesty International, the Society for Endangered Peoples, and the Tibet Information Service are examples of this.

After a "Tibet Forum" in Bonn on June 10, 1987—the first major public discussion of the situation in Tibet with guests from the Federal Republic and abroad—the U.S. House of Representatives unanimously adopted a resolution condemning the human rights violations committed by China in Tibet. Furthermore, this resolution stated that in 1949 the People's Republic of China had subjugated Tibet by means of military force and that it continued to exert power over the Tibetan people through the presence of a large occupation force. On October 6, 1987, a similar resolution was adopted by the U.S. Senate. China responded to these American initiatives with furious tirades. On October 9, 1987, Radio Beijing claimed:

> The resolutions of the U.S. House of Representatives and the Senate were passed at a time when the Dalai Lama was intensifying his political activities intended to create unrest in Tibet and to split the motherland, and when a handful of separatist elements in Lhasa were stirring up political turmoil. Those members of Congress who supported the resolutions may have done so in the name of the defense of

human rights. In fact the resolutions are aimed at destroying China's stability and unity and at dividing the country.

The only correct assertion made in this statement was that the Dalai Lama had visited the U.S. in September 1987, and described Tibet's deplorable situation in an impressive speech before the Congressional Human Rights Caucus on Capitol Hill in Washington. He had also presented a Five-Point Peace Plan, which was imbued with a spirit of reconciliation.

On September 16, 1987, we organized a discussion in Bonn between the Dalai Lama, who was briefly staying in the Federal Republic before his trip to the U.S. and the people concerned about the fate of Tibet. A week later, in a rare show of Bundestag unanimity, a motion submitted jointly by all the parties was passed without any negative votes or abstentions, which called upon the Federal Government to help ensure that the People's Republic of China stops violating human rights in Tibet, responds favorably to the Dalai Lama's efforts for a constructive dialogue, releases all political prisoners in Tibet, and takes the Tibetan people's interests more into account.

The Embassy of the People's Republic of China in Bonn tried, right up to the last minute, to prevent the adoption of this resolution, making vigorous representations to the Federal Foreign Office and to the Parliamentary Secretaries of the German Bundestag. When the resolution passed anyway, the Chinese Ambassador to the Federal Republic protested in a November 3, 1987, letter to the President of the Bundestag. He accused the Bundestag of interfering in the internal affairs of China and of "taking sides with the Dalai Lama clique."

The German Bundestag, however, was by no means alone in its support for Tibet. One day before this initiative, the European Parliament had urged the Chinese government to respect the Tibetans' right to practice their religion freely and to maintain their cultural autonomy.

The parliamentary initiatives on both sides of the Atlantic on behalf of Tibet were accompanied in many countries by a wave of demonstrations in support of Tibet. The largest of these demonstrations took place on November 9, 1987, in Geneva while the United Nations Commission on Human Rights was in session. About 2,000 people, including many exiled Tibetans, participated in this event and demanded that the People's Republic of China stop its oppression of Tibet, withdraw the 300,000 soldiers of the Chinese occupation forces, and make Tibet a demilitarized, non-nuclear, and neutral peace zone. The General Secretary of the United Nations was called upon to order an investigation by the United Nations into the violations of human rights in Tibet, to place the question of Tibet on the agenda of the General Assembly, and to make the Five-Point Peace Plan of the Dalai Lama the basis of this discussion. An independent committee of investigation must be given the opportunity to inform itself at first hand about the situation in Tibet.

We believe that these demands are more urgent today than ever before. They will be met only if the world is made far more aware of the issue of Tibet, and if, in the countries of the free world, governments are forced by a majority of the population to no longer judge questions of international law and human rights by what is expedient but by absolute moral standards.

Human rights are indivisible. Whenever, wherever, and by whomever they are violated, public condemnation by everyone with a voice to raise must be the reaction. Silence is a betrayal of those who are suffering. The aim of this book is to end this disgraceful silence.

This book is dedicated to all Tibetan children and especially to Ms. Kelly's and Mr. Bastian's foster daughter, Nima Chonzon.

The Early History of Tibet

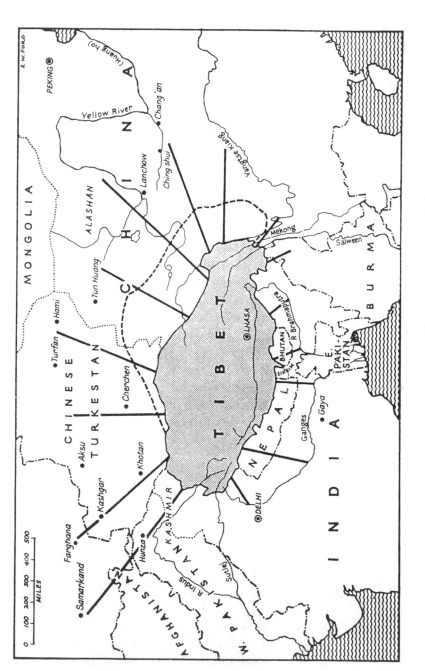

TIBET AND ITS NEIGHBORS: POLITICAL AND ETHNOGRAPHIC

Shaded area: Political Tibet

Broken line: Limits of Ethnographic Tibet

Radiating Lines: Extent of Tibetan influence in 6th to 10th centuries

GYALTSEN GYALTAG

From Monarchy to Democracy: An Historical Overview

To do justice to the problem of Tibet, we need to critically examine conceptions of Tibet that have existed before and after the Chinese annexation. In a word: Tibet must be demystified; we must seek the "truth in the facts," as Deng Xiaoping so excellently formulated it. The idealized image of pre-1950 Tibet as Shangri-la, with its romantic and mystical attributes, corresponds as little to reality as the image of Tibet as "socialist paradise," an image which was, and still is, disseminated by Chinese propaganda and its uncritical Western defenders.

Traditional Tibet before the Chinese occupation was neither a democratic country nor a constitutional state in today's sense. Its social organization can be summed up as a hierarchically constructed society of nomads and farmers with feudal and theocratic structural features that were doubtless in need of reform. A minority ruled over the majority, and the oligarchy of clerics and nobility controlled the decisive means of power. The people lived a hard and simple life, but at the same time a contented one, and above all they led their own life: they were ruled by people of their own language, religion, culture, and ethnicity. Prior to 1950, the Tibetans never experienced a famine, and social injustices never led to an uprising of the people.

Since the middle of the seventeenth century, sovereignty over both the spiritual and the temporal realms of Tibetan society was in the hands of the Dalai Lamas, and government and administration were composed of representatives of the clergy and the nobility. This close alliance of spiritual and temporal authority was the zenith of a long and complex historical process of the mutual accommodation of Buddhist hierarchy and worldly aristocracy. It is this historical process of accommodation that we will first investigate here.

TIBET BEFORE THE SEVENTEENTH CENTURY: KINGSHIP AND FAMILY RULE

In the year 127 B.C. the first Tibetan king, Nyatri Tsenpo, united the different clans of the Tibetan plateau into a single nation. Up until the assassination of the last king, Lang Darma, in 842 A.D., Tibet was ruled for the subsequent almost thousand years by forty-one kings of the Yarlung Dynasty. During this time, Tibet was an important political and military power in Central Asia, whose authority and influence reached far beyond its neighboring countries.

One of the most important rulers of this royal line was King Songtsen Gampo (617-649), who created a particular form of representative government, with one representative at the royal court in Lhasa for every hundred families. These representatives were organized into nine departments, each under the direction of a minister. During his reign Buddhism was brought to Tibet, the Tibetan script was developed, and the first coins were minted. Songtsen Gampo also promulgated a codex consisting of sixteen general guidelines for moral behavior, which Tibetans consider their first book of laws.

The first historically documented social reforms were carried out by the Tibetan King Muni Tsenpo, who ruled from 797 to 804. In his efforts to diminish the great inequalities between rich and poor, he put through a number of land reforms. He appointed special ministers to supervise the just distribution of land and property among the Tibetan populace. But his efforts ended in failure. Discouraged by the failure of his idealistic attempts at reform, the King is said to have consulted the Indian scholar Padmasambhava, who was at that time staying in Tibet. The sage is said to have explained to him that the gap between rich and poor cannot be closed by force, since the conditions of present life are always the consequences of the actions of earlier lives, and therefore the course of things cannot be changed at will.

When Buddhism first appeared in Tibet in the seventh century, it represented a foreign novelty taken up by the royal family and a few families of nobles. It was ignored, or even repudiated, by the adherents of the old animistic Bön religion. Only in the last decades of the eighth century, during the reign of King Tri-song De-tsen (742-797 A.D.), did the new religion really become established in Tibet. During this period Tibetans were ordained as Buddhist monks, and in the year 779 the first Tibetan monastery, Samye, was founded. Buddhism spread rapidly, and by the end of the eighth century Tibetan clergy had secured the highest positions in the administration. The most significant figures in the history of the spread of Buddhism in Tibet were, besides the above-mentioned Tibetan king Tri-song De-tsen, the Indian Tantric master Padmasambhava and the Indian scholars Shantarakshita and Kamalashila. Padmasambhava, whose special achievement was the taming of Tibet's indigenous demons, or the forces of nature they embodied, was the founder of the first sect of Tibetan Buddhism, the Nyingma-pa school.

The last years of the Tibetan kingship, however, were characterized by the persecution and suppression of Buddhism, for the last Tibetan king, Lang Darma, was an adherent of the Bön religion. Lang Darma objected to the large-scale promotion of Buddhism carried out by his brother Ngadhak Tri Ralpachen (815-836), and hired two ministers to assassinate the king, whereupon he himself succeeded to the throne. After a four-year reign, he was in turn assassinated by a Buddhist monk. This marked the end of the Tibetan royal dynasty.

During the reign and after the death of Lang Darma, a dark period for Tibetan Buddhism set in. Only after the arrival in Western Tibet of the famous Indian scholar Atisha (980-1055) in the year 1042, did Buddhism again begin to spread. Atisha had been invited by a king in Western Tibet, Lha Lama Yeshe Oed, to revive the Buddhist teachings there. From the West, Atisha's teaching spread to Central Tibet. Under his influence, ruling nobles throughout Tibet fostered the reawakening of Buddhism, and as the religion grew stronger, so did the political importance of religious leaders. New monasteries were built, and religious orders gained influential positions.

After around four hundred years of political disunity and fragmentation, Tibet was reunited under the Sakya lamas, a lineage of twenty lama-rulers of the Sakya sect of Tibetan Buddhism. This came about when, in 1249, the Mongol prince Godan Khan, grandson of Genghis Khan, appointed the sage Sakya Pandita Kunga Gyaltsen (1182-1251) Vice-Regent of Tibet. With this step he was the first to establish the temporal supremacy of a spiritual leader. The nephew of Sakya Pandita, Sakya Drogön Phagpa (1235-1280), was chosen in 1253 by Kublai Khan, who would later become the Mongolian emperor of China, to be Imperial Tutor and the temporal ruler of all Tibet. This was the real beginning of theocracy in Tibet, the fusion of state and religion in the person of the ruling Lama.

Until 1358 the Sakya lamas exercised political and spiritual rule over Tibet with the support of the Mongols. Ultimately they were deposed by Changchub Gyaltsen, the first of eleven rulers of the noble family of Phagmo-Drupa. He was the leader of a movement for cultural renewal and in 1358 established himself as the sole ruler of all Tibet. He cultivated sentiments of national unity and set about reviving the traditions and the fame of the first Tibetan kings. He and the successors of his lineage were clever in knowing how to turn to their advantage the connection with the Mongols.

Changchub Gyaltsen was also a reformer. He reorganized the administration of Tibet and divided the country into a number of Dzongs, or districts. From among his supporters, he appointed district officials (Dzongpöns) to govern each area. He built roads, bridges, and lodges along pilgrimage routes. And he drew up a codex of thirteen rules for legal process and punishment, based on a contemporary summary of the sixteen guidelines for moral behavior established by King Songtsen Gampo in the seventh century. In this way, he bestowed a historical and ideological legitimation upon his own codex. Furthermore, he divided the land equally among peasants and imposed a tax of one-sixth of the yearly harvest.

Because of internal factionalism, the Phagmo-Drupa family lost their power around the middle of the fifteenth century to the

Ringpung family, which was supported by the influential Karmapa sect. For the next 130 years, Tibet was ruled by four generations of this family. The Kings of Tsang, who followed the Ringpung family in 1566, also based their power on the influence of the Karmapa clergy. During the seventy-six years of their reign, they, therefore, fostered and protected the Karmapa sect above all others.

THE CONCEPT OF REINCARNATION

The influence of this sect, the most important and most powerful branch of Tibetan Buddhism, had a great significance for the later development of Tibet. For it was a lama of the Karmapa sect who founded the religious concept of the reincarnation of a religious leader as a living Bodhisattva. The introduction of this institution, the belief in the living incarnation of a Bodhisattva, proved not only to be a concept with revolutionary consequences within Tibetan Buddhism, but at the same time was of decisive significance for the institution of the Tibetan form of statehood.

In a society permeated by Buddhism and now strongly influenced by the idea of reincarnation, the rulers found themselves without religious support for a biological line of succession. Thus it was this Buddhist notion which made possible the transfer of temporal ruling power to the leading body of monks. It was they who played the deciding role in seeking, selecting, and training the incarnations into whose hands both worldly and religious leadership would be placed.

The leading monks became the actual "king-makers" and, at the same time, the executive organ of the emerging theocratic system, the sole form of state and ruling power in Tibet. Without the monastic establishment, this form of state would have been inconceivable. The main purpose of the monasteries was primarily religious, but they provided the basic doctrines on which the entire political and social order of Tibet rested. The basis of this religious-political system was already laid in the fourteenth century. It reached full development, however, only in the seventeenth century under the rule of the Fifth Dalai Lama. He institutionalized the principle of rulership by reincarnation and set up the unique system of rule of the Ganden-Phodrang, whose basis was the fusion of religious and political leadership in the person of the Dalai Lama.

THE RULE OF THE DALAI LAMAS

From 1642 until March 1959, Tibet stood under the rulership of the Dalai Lamas. To find the origins of the Dalai Lamas, however, we must look back to the fifteenth century, for the Dalai Lamas made their entrance onto Tibet's political stage relatively late. They owed their appearance to the reformer and scholar Tsong Khapa (1357-1419), the founder of the new Gelugpa school of Tibetan Buddhism (Gelugpa means roughly "adherent of the tradition of virtue").

Tsong Khapa's goal was a reform of monastic discipline and a return to greater strictness and intellectuality. His reform movement found great favor among Tibetans and drew increasing numbers of adherents, including certain influential nobles, so that the number of monks and the power of this school grew steadily. Tsong Khapa and his followers founded numerous monasteries, many of which developed into Tibet's most distinguished places of academic learning, with faculties in the various disciplines of Buddhist epistemology.

One of the leading disciples of Tsong Khapa was Gedün Truppa (1391-1474), who posthumously received the title of the First Dalai Lama. After his death, a young monk named Gedün Gyatso was recognized as his reincarnation (1475-1542). He was succeeded by Sonam Gyatso (1543-1588), who was recognized as the third incarnation of Gedün Truppa. Sonam Gyatso, a brilliant scholar and a zealous missionary, traveled to Mongolia in 1577 on the invitation of the Mongol ruler, Altan Khan. He converted Altan Khan and a considerable number of his vassals to Buddhism and created a firm foundation of Buddhist doctrine in the country. Altan Khan bestowed on Sonam Gyatso the title "Tale" (Dalai), a Mongolian word for "Ocean." This honorific title was later retroactively applied to his two predecessors as well. The Mongolian-Tibetan title "Dalai Lama," which all the successors of Gedün Truppa have held up to the present day, means "teacher whose wisdom is as vast as the ocean."

The relations between the ruling house of Altan Khan and the Gelugpa school were deepened when the great-grandson of the Altan Khan, Yönten Gyatso (1589-1617), was recognized by the Tibetans as the Fourth Dalai Lama. Within a short time, the influence of the Gelugpa school stretched over almost all the rival clans of the

Mongols. This base of power was the foundation on which the supremacy of the Dalai Lama in Tibet would finally rest.

In consequence of the repression of the Gelugpa followers by the Tsangpa King Karma Tenkyong Wangpo (1605-1642), the Fifth Dalai Lama turned to the Mongolian prince Gushri Khan for help. Gushri Khan marched with his army into Tibet, overcame the princes in Northeast Tibet, and conquered the Tsangpa King, putting an end to the latter's rule. He made the Gelugpa tradition the state religion and in 1642 made the Fifth Dalai Lama the supreme religious ruler of Tibet. The task of defending the country and the protection of the Dalai Lama he took over himself. Gushri Khan also introduced the office of "Dhe-si," the Regent, who was to be responsible for all political affairs. Only in matters of the greatest importance did he have to consult with the Dalai Lama.

The Fifth Dalai Lama made Lhasa the capital of Tibet, and made it known that the Tibetan government would thenceforth be called "Ganden-Phodrang," after his palace in the Drepung monastery. He enacted laws, revising the codex of Changchub Gyaltsen, appointed district governors, and chose ministers who were charged with constructing a central government. In this way he united both religious and political power in the person of the Dalai Lama.

Tibet's unique system of government was sanctioned by the Dalai Lama's religious authority, which was absolute and rested on his singular position as the highest incarnation, a position subject to question from neither within nor without. During the rules of many of the Dalai Lamas, the actual power of government rested nonetheless in the hands of the regents, since the Dalai Lamas were frequently still underage. Under the Regency, however, the government's power often declined and intrigues and corruption spread.

Despite their power, the Regents never enjoyed the same authority as the Dalai Lamas. They were chosen by the Tibetan National Assembly, the "Tsongdu," and they could, unlike the Dalai Lamas, also be deposed by this body, which occasionally happened. But during the search for the new Dalai Lama and for the period of his minority, the regency remained a weak point of the theocracy.

In comparison with other available forms of succession, such as monarchic primogeniture or selection by an oligarchy of nobles, rulership by incarnation possessed certain advantages. The careful search for the incarnation by specially chosen commissions of monks hindered the intrigues and nepotism of powerful families or nobles, or the enthronement of an incompetent heir. Since the choice of the incarnation lay in the hands of the monastic leadership, the actual power of determining the succession remained in the hands of the clergy, which was recruited from all strata of society.

In this connection it is particularly indicative that, with the exceptions of the Fourth Dalai Lama, who came from a Mongolian princely family, and the Fifth Dalai Lama, who came from a Tibetan noble family, all the other Dalai Lamas were found in humble, non-noble families. Thus the institution of the Dalai Lama was kept free of politically influential connections.

TRADITIONAL GOVERNMENT AND ADMINISTRATION

The spiritual and temporal supremacy of the Dalai Lamas established in Tibet the unequivocal predominance of the clergy in the exercise of power. This was manifest in the filling of government offices, in the judicial administration and in the national assembly, where the abbots of Tibet's three greatest monasteries, Sera, Drepung, and Ganden, had a great influence on the decisions of the government. In the judicial administration, monks were subject to a purely religious judiciary and laypeople to a mixed lay and religious judiciary. Without a doubt, the institution of the Dalai Lamas made an indelible imprint not only on the history and the society of Tibet, but on all of Central Asia.

On the basis of the preeminence and the importance of Buddhist religious and epistemological teachings, the government of the Dalai Lama divided its work into spiritual and worldly affairs. The foundation of their work in both realms was the belief that the primary goal of all their efforts was the spiritual liberation not only of all Tibetans, but of all living beings. Consequently, the spiritual and worldly aspects of Tibet's religious-political structure were so closely interconnected that it is hardly possible to make a clear distinction between them. In the monasteries of all Buddhist sects, monks were educated both for public administration and for the performance of religious services. They formed the connecting link between religious and secular affairs, since the temporal administration was to a great degree occupied by monastic officials as well. Working on all levels of the government, they looked after the cohesiveness of the political structure. It was they who were looked to for the concrete application of ethical and religious precepts in the management of worldly affairs.

Their colleagues, the lay officials, came from the aristocracy. The principal obligation of every noble family consisted in producing at least one son to place at the disposal of the civil service. As remuneration, the family was permitted to keep the income from the landed property in their tenure. The service of the sons for the state was the condition for this privilege, or for the right of usufruct of their estate. Otherwise the family lost their land tenure. The noble families were in this way incorporated as a secondary source of administrative talent into the bureaucracy of the Tibetan state. Their sons were specially educated for this purpose in government schools.

The dualistic character of the Tibetan state also found expression in the administrative organization of the Tibetan government. This consisted of clergy and lay nobles, with the understanding that each group would represent its own interests. Each official government post was doubly occupied, by a monk and a noble simultaneously.

The entire administration, insofar as it could be controlled by the central government in Lhasa, was based on the division of the country into districts, each with a seat of administration, called a "dzong," which was generally a citadel-like fortified construction. Here a temporal and a spiritual governor or district head would officiate together. Their duties were the exercise of justice and the levying of taxes. The populace in the district of the central government elected their own town administration and were subject only to the central government, which was represented by the district heads. The people collected in common the annual taxes that the town had to render. But the land administrations of the nobility and the clergy were subordinate to two different administrative institutions and were represented to the central government, as well as to landlords, usually through a steward or overseer.

The organization of the Tibetan government and administration remained unchanged in its essential features from its establishment two hundred years ago until the annexation of Tibet by the People's

Republic of China in 1951. The Thirteenth Dalai Lama, Thubten Gyatso (1876-1933) did introduce essential modernizations. Under his reign the military and administration were modernized, students were sent abroad, mail and telegraph services were set up, and paper money was printed for the first time. He was also responsible for the entrance of Tibet into international relations, concluding several treaties with Great Britain, Mongolia, and China.

Under the rule of Thubten Gyatso, the Chinese influence in Tibet, which had been steadily growing since 1720, began to diminish sharply. One year after the fall of the Chinese Manchu Dynasty, he proclaimed the independence of Tibet in 1912. In his political testament, he warned the Tibetans of the dangers that could threaten them in the future from their powerful neighbor, and he exhorted them to take preventative measures. But his prophetic warnings could not prevent the Chinese invasion in 1950.

THE FOURTEENTH DALAI LAMA
AND THE TIBETAN GOVERNMENT-IN-EXILE

The present Dalai Lama, His Holiness Tenzin Gyatso, is the fourteenth incarnation in the lineage of succession of the Dalai Lamas. It is in the period of his rule that the Chinese invasion and annexation of Tibet have occurred. Under pressure from the national assembly, he had to take over the full responsibilities of his office as religious and political leader of the Tibetan people at the age of 15, in 1950—shortly after the invasion of Tibet. He strove in vain for a peaceful settlement of the militant confrontation between his people and the invading Chinese.

The current Dalai Lama, a man of liberal views, has tried to advance the modernization process begun by his predecessor. After assuming office, he attempted to implement long overdue changes and reforms. He founded for this purpose a reform commission, consisting of representatives of the Tibetan people, with a cabinet minister presiding. At first the commission was in a position to carry out a series of reform measures, among which was the cancellation of debts and interest payments more than eight years old. Debts that did not date back that far were excused of interest, and only the capital had to be repaid. The administration was centralized, and a regulated system of taxation introduced in all districts of Tibet in order to hinder corruption and misuse of office. The Chinese occupational powers, however, sabotaged the decrees and recommendations of the reform commission, condemning it to impotence.

The failure of his reform measures did not deter the Dalai Lama from pursuing his progressive ideas further, even after his flight into Indian exile. He rallied his despairing countrymen and prepared them for their new life in exile. In 1960, he founded, in the northern Indian hill station of Dharamsala, a Tibetan Government-in-Exile and charged it with the following tasks:

1. Representation of the Tibetan refugees;
2. Guardianship of the Tibetan culture, religion, and language;
3. Care and education of Tibetan children;
4. Preservation of national and cultural identity in exile;
5. Defense of the national sovereignty of the Tibetan people on the basis of a democratic form of state;
6. Continuing the nonviolent Tibetan struggle for freedom in the name of the five million Tibetans in Tibet and in exile.

The Tibetan Government-in-Exile was constructed on the basis of a provisional democratic constitution. This democratic constitution for a future Tibet was proclaimed in 1963 by the Dalai Lama to the Tibetan people. In the preface, he formulated the meaning and purpose of this constitution: "This draft of a constitution should give the Tibetan people new hope and a new idea of how Tibet should be ruled after regaining its independence." The constitution, which relies on principles of Buddhist doctrine as well as on democratic ideas and ideals, should "secure for the Tibetan people a democratic system that is founded on justice and equality, and which ensures the cultural, religious, and economic progress of the Tibetan people." In spite of strong opposition from the people, the Dalai Lama also insisted on a clause stating that a two-thirds majority of the national assembly could revoke his own political mandate.

The present Dalai Lama believes unshakably that the future of Tibet should and must be decided by the Tibetan people. He has repeatedly and expressly presented this conviction in public, and has demanded an internationally supervised plebiscite in Tibet, so that the Tibetan people may avail themselves of their inalienable right to self-determination and fundamental human rights.

JOHN F. AVEDON

In Exile from the Land of Snows

The Thirteenth Dalai Lama died in 1933, soon after his prophetic last words were circulated throughout the land. He seemed to have contracted only a slight cold, and when he died after seven days, his people were left stunned by their loss and filled with worries about the future. According to custom, his body was embalmed, placed in the lotus position, and seated facing south on a throne.

Shortly thereafter, strange things began to happen. Auspicious cloud formations, now and again pierced by rainbows, appeared over the northeastern end of the city. Overnight a giant star-shaped fungus grew on the east side of the northeast pillar of the Dalai Lama's room. A few days later the head of the dead ruler was found no longer facing south; it had turned to the northeast.

In the spring of 1935, Tibet's newly-appointed Regent, joined by members of the national assembly, journeyed to the sacred lake of Lhamo Lhatso, seeking a vision. He hoped to discover the where-abouts of the reincarnated Dalai Lama: the soul of the beloved leader himself, returned in a new body to guide again the fates of his people.

After several days of uninterrupted prayer, the Regent went alone to the edge of the lake. Standing on a high rock, he stared at the water in which, it was believed, the future could be seen. He discerned the image of a great monastery capped by gold and jade rooftops. A white road led east from the monastery to a house before a small hill, its roof strikingly fringed in turquoise-colored tiles, a brown and white spotted dog in the courtyard. Finally there followed a vision of three letters from the Tibetan alphabet, which were later interpreted as pointing to the city and province of the Dalai Lama's rebirth. Later, the Regent dreamed of the same humble farmer's home he had seen in the vision, this time with oddly shaped gutter pipes emerging from the roof and a small boy standing in the yard.

Soon after the Regent's report was submitted to the National Assembly in Lhasa, three search parties were dispatched across eastern Tibet. One group covered over 1,000 miles on its journey to Amdo in the northeast of Tibet. There was a monastery in Amdo famous for its jade and gold roofs. Monks led the group to a house whose walls were inlaid with turquoise-colored tiles. Disguised as merchants, the group appeared at the door of the house and requested the use of the kitchen to make tea—a common practice of Tibetan travelers. When they were granted entry into the court-yard, their leader's gaze was struck by the twisted waterspouts, fashioned of gnarled juniper wood, around the roof, and by the brown and white spotted dog sitting beneath them. Although he was one of the three most important abbots in Tibet, he had chosen the role of a servant and dressed in an old sheepskin coat. Thus it was possible for him to look around undisturbed while the man and woman of the house looked after the group.

It was not long before the abbot found what he was looking for. As he approached the kitchen, a two-year-old boy came running out of it in great excitement. He sat on the abbot's lap and tugged at the rosary that hung around the guest's neck, a rosary that had belonged to the Thirteenth Dalai Lama. "I will give it to you," said the abbot, "if you can guess who I am." "You are a Lama of Sera," the boy said quite correctly and named two other members of the group whom he had not yet seen. Most remarkably of all, the boy addressed the abbot in the dialect of the court at Lhasa, which was completely unknown in his district.

Their interest roused, the delegation stayed the night, planning to leave unnoticed before dawn the next day. But they did not rise early enough. The boy was already up and pleaded with them to take him along. They only calmed him down by promising to return.

When they did, it was to subject the boy to a battery of tests to determine if, in fact, this was the Dalai Lama.

This time the monks wore their robes, offered gifts to the family, and asked to be left alone with the child. Although his parents were poor farmers, they—like all Tibetans—had a small altar in the center of their house. Here the boy was tested. The monks laid before the boy several articles from among the personal possessions of the old Dalai Lama, together with carefully crafted duplicates. In every case, the boy chose the original, while complaining bitterly that all these things belonged to him and they should be given to him at once. Further tests followed, whose climax was the physical inspection. The boy possessed every one of the eight bodily marks traditionally distinguishing the Dalai Lama from all other men.

The monks had already been struck by the boy's large protruding ears, long eyes, and eyebrows curving up at their ends, but they were most astonished when they pulled back the child's clothing. On his legs they found streaks like those of a tiger skin; on the palm of one hand, a print resembling a conch shell; on his shoulders, two rough patches of skin standing for the third and fourth arms of the Bodhisattva Chenrezig, whose incarnation the Dalai Lama is. There was no longer any doubt. Here, halfway through his third year of life, was the Holy One himself, the Fourteenth Dalai Lama of Tibet.

On the morning of October 7, 1939, the Fourteenth Dalai Lama arrived in Lhasa, four and a half years old, to take up his rule. Sitting in a gilded palanquin, he looked out on the enormous crowd which had assembled to see him. "People were crying with joy," he later wrote. "Music and dancing accompanied me everywhere. I felt as though I were in a dream . . . as if I were in a great park covered with beautiful flowers while soft breezes blew across it and peacocks elegantly danced before me."

For the little boy who had been chosen to rule Tibet, dream and reality were not far apart. Their difficult three-month journey through dry, barren Changthang—the vast, uninhabited area of

Central Tibet—was over. The Dalai Lama's caravan had arrived first at a voluminous yellow silk tent, known as the "Great Peacock." Flanked by leopard- and tiger-skin Mongolian yurts arranged in the form of a mandala (a mystical circle), it stood at the heart of a great tent-city which waited to receive the returning "Precious Protector." Behind it rose the Potala, the palace of the Dalai Lama and the seat of Tibetan government.

Within a week, Tenzin Gyatso, as he was now called, was installed on the Lion throne as, pending the attainment of his majority, supreme temporal and spiritual ruler of Tibet.

Tenzin Gyatso's education was exceptional. To ensure behavior worthy of a bodhisattva, numerous teachers and servants surrounded him, while he lived alone in four small rooms at the top of the Potala. More than a quarter mile long, a labyrinth of thousands of chambers, assembly halls, narrow corridors and dark, ancient chapels, the Potala was less a home than a living museum. In winter it was numbingly cold; in summer the stench from the sewers beneath its precipitous walls permeated the building. At its center stood the gold, jewel-encrusted tombs of nine previous Dalai Lamas, before which butter lamps burned and monks prayed.

From the beginning Tenzin Gyatso had to study a great deal and preside over long ceremonies. With the exception of his older brothers he was isolated from all other children. He was referred to as either the "Precious Protector," the "Wish-Fulfilling Gem," or simply the "Presence." But despite the constraints of his position, he seemed at home in the role. "From the earliest age, whatever my brother did, he did perfectly," recalled Thupten Norbu, the Dalai Lama's eldest brother and now head of the Tibetan Studies program at the University of Indiana. "We all saw this. He never complained or rebelled. Everyone was greatly impressed. Being the Dalai Lama seemed to him the most natural thing in the world."

Those in closest contact with him, his teachers Ling and Triyang Rinpoche, were the most impressed. They soon noted their young pupil's remarkable gift for study. In no time he had absorbed the content of 2,500 pages of scripture and grasped difficult metaphysical material with the ease of an experienced scholar. In his free time he worked on subjects that were not included in his study plan, like

English, mathematics, and geography. Heinrich Harrer, an Austrian mountaineer and author who instructed the Dalai Lama in non-religious subjects, was equally impressed by his student. "He continually astonished me by his powers of comprehension, his pertinacity, and his industry," observed Harrer. "When I gave him for homework ten sentences to translate, he usually showed up with twenty."

Perhaps in the isolation of his lonely childhood there was no other choice for the boy than to distinguish himself in this way. If that were so, this negative incentive was more than equalled by his capacity for excitement. As a child, Tenzin Gyatso was fascinated by every Western object that made it over the Himalayas to his palace. He was so entranced with a telescope that he damaged his eyes by looking too long at the busy streets of Lhasa below the Potala. As he became older, his interest in mechanical things turned into a passion. Already as a teenager he had taught himself the basic laws of optical technology by taking apart and reassembling a film projector. He did the same with his watch. Then came Tibet's sole cars, an orange Dodge and two 1927 Austins. These vehicles had been gifts to his predecessor and had lain idle since his death. The Dalai Lama took them apart and repaired them. No one in Tibet knew how these machines functioned. Outside of a handful of people there was no one who even had any idea what they were for.

In the summer, when Tenzin Gyatso left the Potala to travel to the Norbulingka, the Jewel Park, where things were much less formal, people lined the route of his procession six deep. First came a troop of monks, who carried yellow silk bundles containing the personal possessions of the Dalai Lama. His parrots called out from their cages while mounted musicians and more monks followed, bearing ornate religious banners. The entire Tibetan nobility, dressed according to rank, walked along in the procession, and behind them came the regimental band, playing "It's a Long Way to Tipperary," a melody that they had learned from their British teachers.

The Dalai Lama himself sat in his palanquin, which was carried by thirty-six men in green silk coats and round red caps. A monk held a parasol of peacock feathers over him, while his bodyguards—all over six-and-a-half feet tall, with padded shoulders, blackened faces, and long whips—called aloud to clear the path.

Within the Norbulingka, a walled park with many small pavilions, the Dalai Lama spent the happiest times of his childhood. Between study hours he played in the garden (whose fertile earth routinely produced radishes up to twenty pounds), wandered about among the tame musk deer and pheasants, and fed the fish, who rose to the water's surface when they heard the Dalai Lama's footsteps approach. In this seclusion, only in the company of his European teacher Heinrich Harrer, he made for the first time real contact with the outside world.

"He seemed to me like a person who had for years brooded in solitude over different problems, and now that he had at last someone to talk to, wanted to know all the answers at once," wrote Harrer, recalling his first meeting with the then fourteen-year-old Dalai Lama. Through an intermediary, the Dalai Lama had requested Harrer to construct a film hall in the Norbulingka. On its completion, he unexpectedly invited the Austrian to meet with him in person. "I went toward the cinema, but before I could enter, the door opened from the inside and I was standing before the Living Buddha," Harrer recounted. "Come, let us see the capitulation of Japan," said the Dalai Lama, pushing Harrer into the projection booth. Nervously Harrer started to thread the projector, but was "nudged aside" by the Dalai Lama, who completed the task in a moment. Following the film showing, Tenzin Gyatso dismissed his rather distraught abbots, and ushering Harrer into the now sun-filled theater, pulled him down by the sleeve onto the maroon carpet. Confessing that he had long planned a meeting, as he could think of no other way to become acquainted with the outside world, the Dalai Lama poured forth a flood of questions. "Do you like it here in the Holy City? Can you operate an army tank? An airplane? How do jet airplanes fly? Why do you have hair on your hands like a monkey?" Feeling the "attraction of his personality," Harrer stared at the young man. He sat cross-legged before him, hands folded peacefully in his lap, cheeks glowing with excitement, his whole body swaying from side to side. His complexion was considerably lighter than that of most Tibetans. He was tall and well-formed, with "beautiful aristocratic hands" and eyes full of "expression, charm, and vivacity." Rather bashfully, the Dalai

Lama took out his notebook of English words and said, "Heinrich. You will teach me this language. We will start now."

Their lessons continued for months. They included topics ranging from the structure of the atom to why Lhasa was eleven hours behind New York. As their friendship grew, the young Dalai Lama continually brought up the subject closest to his heart: religion. He confided to Harrer that he was practicing techniques by which consciousness could be separated from the body.

But the study of religion went far beyond the "supernatural." Throughout his childhood, the boy's teachers had repeatedly pressed on him the necessity of a selfless attitude. They urged him to practice daily the Six Perfections—the basis for action in the Mahayana way: generosity, moral rectitude, patience, steadfastness, meditative concentration, and deep insight into the nature of all things as empty by nature. These are the six qualities in which a bodhisattva must perfect himself in his striving for enlightenment. For him as Dalai Lama it was essential that he realize their deepest significance. "At every stage of my exercises," he said, "I received the initiations for body and mind in preparation for higher teachings." These initiations—in Tibet called literally "empowerments"—transmitted to him an ever stronger feeling of "peace and happiness" that culminated in a "singular calm of spirit," as he himself described it.

Following his deep belief that people can reach true happiness only through the development of their spiritual powers with the help of religion, he began to hold open lectures in the Jewel Park. Thousands came to his daily talks with picnic baskets filled with eggs, pastries, tea, and meat. Sitting on the lawns, they listened attentively while the young man spoke. His theme was the same then as now: "True love for all creatures can only proceed from a real understanding of the essence of religion. If you do not have peace in your own heart, you can bring no peace to others, and then there will be no peaceful relations, either between individuals or between nations."

On October 7, 1950, eleven years after the beginning of the Dalai Lama's rule, and nearly two decades after the apocalyptic prophecies of the Thirteenth Dalai Lama, China occupied Tibet.

"Tibet is an integral part of Chinese territory. The Tibetan question is exclusively a domestic concern of China. Foreign interference will not be tolerated."

With these statements, the newly-created government in Beijing held the world at bay and marched into Tibet. It was the fulfillment of an ancient Chinese dream. Open conflict between the two countries had been averted until now only through the "priest-patron relationship," under which the Mongol and Manchu emperors recognized the Dalai Lama as the highest religious teacher. Nonetheless China had continually attempted to exercise a kind of feudal tenure or nominal power in Tibet. This had, however, never really succeeded. Although the balance of power tipped back and forth, China had never occupied nor ruled Tibet. When a lasting peace was established in 821 A.D., this occurred rather in the wake of a Tibetan victory and under conditions imposed by the Tibetans.

But there were reasons closer to hand for the Chinese attack. Tibet possessed everything China lacked: land, vast natural resources, and a position that, from the point of view of military strategy, was unassailable. Moreover, until 1950 the "Land of Snows" remained untouched: its mineral, forest, and animal wealth was virtually unexploited.

Since the Chinese seizure of power, coal, borax, copper, lead, iron, and gold have been dug; oil, cement, wood, fertilizer and sugar industries have been established. For the Tibetans themselves, of these only fertilizer is available. All the rest goes to China. One need only look at a map to recognize the strategic value of Tibet. The Tibetan Plateau—in the truest sense of the words, the "roof of the world"—is encircled by the earth's highest mountains. This enormous natural fortress in the heart of the Asian continent is ideally situated from both an offensive and defensive point of view. With Tibet in its sphere of power, China stands at the apex of the Orient.

There was also a political motive that— as it was seen then—lent the greatest urgency to all the others. Still in the first ideological flush of victory, after a twenty-year struggle with the Kuomintang, the Chinese Communist Party regarded it as their mandate to "liberate" all "oppressed" peoples. In Tibet, a nation with a system of government that had remained unchanged since its introduction, they saw a country ripe for revolution. They failed, however, to connect theory with reality in this case.

Without warning, the Chinese crossed the Tibetan border in six places. The first reports of the invasion arrived in Lhasa ten days after the outbreak of hostilities. The invasion was accepted as inescapable. Radio Beijing had been announcing the impending "liberation" of Tibet for more than two months, and the Tibetans had received numerous signs which—so they believed—prophesied impending difficulties.

At the beginning of August, the fifth-largest earthquake in world history had ravaged all of southern Tibet. Thousands died, the Brahmaputra River was completely rerouted, and for hours afterwards the sky over southeastern Tibet glowed with an infernal red light, suffused with the pungent scent of sulfur. A year before, an unusually bright comet appeared in the sky, visible by night and by day. Since the 1910 invasion by China had been preceded by just such a comet, many took it as an indubitable omen of war. The next summer, the unfavorable signs turned from the natural to the uncanny. On a bright, cloudless summer's day, in full view of downtown Lhasa, water poured from one of the golden gargoyles inaccessibly located on the roof of the Central Cathedral. The capital of a tall stone column, erected in 763 A.D. to commemorate Tibet's conquest of China, was found shattered one morning at the foot of the Potala.

As in all times of crisis, the government sent for its oracles. The highest of them was the State Oracle of Nechung: his medium lives today in India and is still regularly consulted. After his arrival in the Jewel Park, the young monk who acted as the medium for the protective deity went into a deep trance. Two assistants set on his head an elaborate headdress weighing nearly a hundred pounds. Under this weight, the medium's body reared up from its seated position, hissing loudly and shuddering with tremendous force. Possessed by the protective deity, he danced wildly through the room. When the time came to submit questions to the deity, the Cabinet ministers humbly sought guidance, a secretary reading their formal request from a scroll. The Oracle came before the Dalai Lama. "Make him King," he clearly said, and collapsed, the trance concluded.

Tenzin Gyatso was filled with anxiety. He was not yet sixteen, still three years short of the accepted point for a Dalai Lama's ascension to secular power. He knew little of government and less of international affairs. Nonetheless, he had no choice. The Red Army could move on Lhasa at any moment. The people themselves had already begged him to lead, posters all over the capital demanding that "the Dalai Lama be given the power." Demurring at first, Tenzin Gyatso finally agreed. "I could not refuse my responsibilities," he later wrote. "I had to shoulder them, put my boyhood behind me, and immediately prepare myself to lead my country."

The seriousness of the situation became apparent when Thupten Norbu, the Dalai Lama's brother, returned to Lhasa from the East. As a prisoner, he had become an immediate witness to the Chinese occupation and had only been released by participating in a Chinese plan. He was either to convince his brother to capitulate or otherwise to murder him. As compensation, the rulership of Tibet was promised him. Thupten Norbu handed the Tibetan government a 3,000-word statement of the Chinese plans, about which—because of propaganda—a good deal remains unclear till today.

Since the beginning of the invasion, the Chinese soldiers had been assuring the Tibetans they had not come to destroy or conquer, but to liberate. Tibetan soldiers captured after the bloody first battle on the upper Yangtse had been called "brothers" by their counterparts, given packets of food and money and then released. Chinese cameras filmed their relieved expressions as evidence of the people's joy on being "liberated." One Khampa warrior summed up the general reaction by observing, "They are strange people, these Chinese. I cut off eight of their heads with my sword and they just let me go."

Stranger still was the content of propaganda pamphlets. The claim that China wished to help Tibet modernize made some sense, but that of "uniting to drive out imperialist forces"—there having been only six Westerners in Tibet prior to the invasion, all of whom had now left—was incomprehensible. Being "welcomed back" to the "big family of the motherland" was considered insolent nonsense. "In the beginning," commented Thupten Norbu, "they put their words like honey on a knife. But we could see, if you lick the honey your tongue will be cut."

The Dalai Lama cherished the wish of avoiding, at all costs, the shedding of blood on both sides. Compared with the modern Chinese army, Tibet's military forces were an anachronism.

But though politically expedient, the course of strict nonviolent resistance was ultimately rooted in the Dalai Lama's religious conviction, shared by the entire clergy. As Kyhongla Rato Rinpoche, a lama of Drepung Monastery and later the founder of the Tibetan Center in New York City, explained: "We could not hate the Chinese because it was their own ignorance that motivated them to harm us. A true practitioner of religion considers his enemy to be his greatest friend, because only he can help you develop patience and compassion."

"Basically everyone exists in the very nature of suffering," the Dalai Lama later wrote of his decision, "so to abuse or mistreat each other is futile." Putting this belief into practice, Tenzin Gyatso decided to negotiate with China.

In the last week of April 1951, a delegation was sent to Beijing. After a courteous reception by China's Prime Minster Zhou Enlai, they were presented with a ten-point plan specifying terms of capitulation or, as it was phrased, Tibet's "peaceful liberation." Because the proposal maintained that Tibet was an "integral" part of China, the delegation refused to sign. A stalemate followed, until a second, Seventeen-Point Agreement was put forth. This time no discussion was allowed. The delegates were cut off from their government and thereafter threatened with both personal violence and large-scale military retaliation against Tibet. On May 25 they yielded—unauthorized by the Dalai Lama and Cabinet. In a formal ceremony later publicized throughout China and the world, they certified the document with duplicate seals of the Tibetan government already forged for the purpose in Beijing.

On the basis of the Seventeen-Point Agreement, Tibet lost its identity as a nation-state. Within three months, 20,000 Chinese troops marched into Lhasa, portraits of Mao and Zhou Enlai held aloft. Setting up camp on Lhasa's cherished picnic grounds near the Norbulingka, the Chinese took over the nobles' larger homes, the roofs of which soon sprouted bright red signboards adorned with colossal black slogans proclaiming the "unity" of all races in "the motherland."

Within nine months of occupation, the first crisis occurred. True to its name, the People's Liberation Army lived off the land, taking from the civilian population whatever it required. On their arrival in Lhasa, the Chinese had demanded a "loan" of two thousand tons of barley from the Tibetan government. When a second order for an additional two thousand tons was issued, the back of the capital's delicate economy broke. The price of grain spiraled to a tenfold increase, that of meat, vegetables, and household goods close behind. For the first time in history, famine hung over Lhasa.

In 1954, the Dalai Lama left his country for the first time and traveled by jeep, airplane, and train to Beijing. Though this was his first experience of the machines that had fascinated him for so long, he felt little joy. Arriving beneath the tall buildings of China's capital, the Dalai Lama strode down the platform to the vigorous applause of hundreds of workers and students marshaled by Prime Minister Zhou Enlai and Vice-Chairman Zhu De, Chief of the Army. That evening a sumptuous banquet was held in the Purple Light Pavilion in central Beijing, officially welcoming the Tibetans "back to the motherland." Two days later the Dalai Lama met Mao Zedong.

The Dalai Lama's reaction to Mao was not unfavorable. He found him forthright, kind, and dedicated. Among other details he observed that the leader of the revolution and Chairman of the Party never wore polished shoes, dressed in frayed cuffs, smoked incessantly, and panted a lot. He seemed to be in poor health, but when he spoke, his unusual powers of analysis shone through. "Chairman Mao did not look too intelligent," noted the Dalai Lama. "Something like an old farmer from the countryside. Yet his bearing indicated a real leader. His self-confidence was firm, he had a sincere feeling for the nation and people, and also, I believe, he demonstrated genuine concern for myself."

Mao, in fact, was quite taken with the nineteen-year-old ruler. He spent long hours offering advice on how to govern, going so far as to admit that Buddhism was a good religion—the Buddha having cared considerably for the common people. Invariably, though, political conviction outweighed personal taste. On one occasion, in the middle of an intimate talk, Mao leaned over and whispered in the Dalai Lama's ear, "I understand you very well, but of course religion is poison." During a New Year's celebration given by the Tibetans, he watched his hosts throw small pieces of pastry in the air as an offering to the Buddha, whereupon, taking two pinches himself, he threw one upward and then, with a mischievous smile, dropped the other onto the floor.

Altogether the Dalai Lama spent a year in China. During his stay he pondered the question of what separated the two nations so profoundly. Basically what had happened was not just the persecution of one people by another, but the collision of two opposed philosophies as to the nature of human beings: the spiritual view on one side, the material on the other. While the Chinese believed that socialism, properly applied, offered a panacea for life's ills, the Tibetans, as Buddhists, felt that earthly existence in any form could never be satisfactory. Liberation, to them, meant freedom gained by enlightenment from the inevitable sufferings of birth, old age, disease, and death. Mere physical well-being had never been an ideal in Tibetan culture.

In recognizing the incompatibility of the two world views Tenzin Gyatso reached the decision to build a bridge between the two. His hope was not unfounded. Through personal negotiation, he had succeeded in awakening in the Chinese sufficient trust in himself to deflect unconditional Chinese military rule. As Mao disclosed, until meeting the Dalai Lama he had intended to govern Tibet directly from Beijing.

But as the Dalai Lama journeyed home to Lhasa, he saw that the situation in his country had greatly deteriorated in a year. The gradual changes China pursued by stealth in Central Tibet, it was choosing to impose by force in Kham and Amdo. In these Eastern Tibetan provinces the Chinese had introduced collective agriculture; they took young Tibetans from their families and placed them in "Minority Institutes" in the Motherland. This was a grave tactical error, since the inhabitants of Kham are known for their implacable will to independence.

Shortly after Tenzin Gyatso had returned to the Potala, the Chinese invited 210 Khampa leaders to a meeting in a centuries-old fortress in the heart of Kham. When they were all inside, 5,000 Chinese troops surrounded the fort. For two weeks the Tibetans were held prisoner. On the fifteenth day of detention, they finally assented to the institution of Chinese "Democratic Reforms" in their territory. After three more days the fortress's guard was relaxed and that same night all 210 men escaped into the mountains. In this manner, Tibet's formal guerrilla resistance was born, the Chinese themselves having turned much of the Khampa establishment into outlaws.

"I was almost despairing," wrote the Dalai Lama. "All my efforts towards a peaceful solution had led to nothing. The worst thing of all was the feeling of losing control over my own people." Pulled back and forth between the growing desire of the Tibetans to strike back and the knowledge that only he would be able to prevent a brutal reprisal against his people, Tenzin Gyatso came to realize that his double role as spiritual and temporal leader was unmanageable. As spiritual leader, he could never endorse killing. "However great the force is that is directed against us, it is never right to answer with force." As political leader, though, he told himself: "Insofar as I restrain the violent instincts of my people, I am helping the Chinese to destroy the people's faith in me."

What made the whole situation even more difficult was the knowledge that he was above all the highest symbol of Tibet, "the kernel of that which the guerrillas wanted to defend." Regardless of which position he took, it would be inadequate to reconcile the competing forces in this conflict.

In the spring of 1959, the situation came to a head. The resistance had spread to the north, east, and south of Tibet. In the most inaccessible mountains of the world, the numbers of the resistance fighters had grown to tens of thousands. The Chinese reacted by bringing in heavy artillery and fighter bombers, leveling hundreds of monasteries, looting priceless antiquities, and killing monks in mass executions. Whole villages were destroyed beyond recognition. The survivors were put onto work crews building roads for the Chinese army. Thousands of refugees streamed into the Lhasa valley to seek protection near the Dalai Lama.

On the first of March of the same year, the Dalai Lama appeared in the Jokhang, the main temple of Lhasa and the location of the holiest artifact in Tibet, an image of the Buddha said to have been created in the Buddha's lifetime. The Dalai Lama was twenty-four years old and stood before the most important event of a Dalai Lama's life: the tests for the Geshé Lharampa, the highest grade of the Doctor of Divinity degree. By all standards, these were the most rigorous tests in Tibet's ancient academic system. As the culmination of twenty-one years of uninterrupted study, this examination remained, even through the Chinese occupation, his greatest personal goal. He was questioned by a rotating team of eighty scholars before 20,000 monks crammed into every niche of the Central Cathedral's inner sanctum. With two breaks only, the test proceeded from early in the morning until ten at night.

"It was extremely remarkable," commented one of his examiners, "that in spite of the demanding duties of his position, he was able to answer every one of our questions correctly, with clarity, precision, and even elegance." Another observer remembers that he "remained relaxed and smiled at the monks in the hall." The Dalai Lama himself found the questions difficult: "Hours of debate seemed like an instant," he recalled, since he was not permitted to hesitate with his answers, which each had to be supported with long memorized quotations from the large canon of Buddhist literature. His performance convinced the assembled abbots and scholars that he was indeed the incarnation of Chenrezig.

Two weeks after the completion of his education, Tenzin Gyatso would be forced to flee Tibet forever.

The Chinese had sent the Dalai Lama an invitation to a theatrical show. It was to take place in the heart of the military encampment, an unprecedented location for the Dalai Lama's presence, and he was asked to appear without bodyguards. The whole event was to remain, in the words of the Chinese general issuing the invitation, "strictly secret." It could not be. Within hours of the meeting, Lhasa was swept by the rumor of a Chinese plan to kidnap the Precious Protector. Similar deceptions had occurred before. In the east, at least four high lamas had been invited to cultural performances without their retinues, whereupon they were imprisoned and all save one executed.

Soon after dawn on March 10, crowds began pouring out of Lhasa. By nine o'clock almost 30,000 people had gathered before the Norbulingka's front gate. Their mood was explosive. Shouting that the Dalai Lama must be protected, they sealed off the Jewel Park. As the morning progressed, seventy of Lhasa's chief citizens were elected to be popular spokesmen. By noon they had obtained the crowd's initial objective: a Cabinet minister announcing over the gate's loudspeakers that the Dalai Lama had decided to forgo the performance as well as to decline—as the leaders had requested—future invitations to the Chinese army headquarters.

When the Dalai Lama sent a letter to the general asking to be released from the invitation, the Chinese answered that he should send precise information about his whereabouts in the Norbulingka so that he might be "liberated." Six days went by. In this time, the Dalai Lama wrote, "I felt as if I were standing between two volcanoes, each likely to erupt at any moment....My most urgent moral duty...was to prevent a totally disastrous clash between my unarmed people and the Chinese army."

In the hopes that both sides would back down if he—the object of contention—were to leave the area, he decided to flee. On March 17, shortly after evening fell, he disguised himself as a soldier and with a gun in his hand, slipped out of a small gate in a remote corner of the park. Accompanied by members of his family and his retinue, all disguised, he fled to the nearby Kyichu River and crossed it in a small coracle. On the opposite shore he was awaited by thirty Khampa warriors with several ponies. Under the protection of darkness, the group rode quickly to the south, past the lights of the giant Chinese army encampment. Undiscovered, they rode for eighteen hours further, almost without stopping, until they reached the mountains beyond Lhasa that were occupied by guerrillas.

Two days later, even before they knew of the Dalai Lama's flight, the Chinese opened fire on the Jewel Park. They bombed Lhasa and the nearby monasteries, which were inhabited by up to 10,000 monks and were the world's largest. The brutal reprisal lasted for six months.

According to conservative estimates, 87,000 Tibetans were killed and 25,000 taken prisoner. But 100,000 Tibetans succeeded in following the Dalai Lama, who within two weeks had crossed the Indian border and established a Government-in-Exile.

The reports of the refugees were beyond all imagining. To degrade Tibet to the status of an enslaved country, the Chinese crucified, dismembered, burned, and buried alive thousands of nuns and monks, forced them to sexual intercourse, or demanded that they accomplish miracles to save themselves. Men and women were publicly tortured to death. Children were forced to execute their parents, and the populations of whole villages were sterilized.

When the International Commission of Jurists investigated these accounts of Chinese atrocities in 1960, it concluded that Red China was guilty of "the gravest crime of which any person or nation can be accused—the intent to destroy, in whole or in part, a national, ethnic, racial or religious group as such"—genocide. Shortly thereafter the General Assembly of the United Nations called "for the cessation of practices which deprive the Tibetan people of their fundamental human rights and freedoms, including most importantly their right to self-determination." In spite of the international resolution, Beijing continued to pursue the extermination of Tibetan culture.

The Dalai Lama himself set to his work: preserving hope for his people. In a statement following his flight, he wrote: "In spite of the atrocious crimes of the Chinese in our country, I hold no hatred in my heart for them. We should not seek revenge on those who have perpetrated crimes against us. All people finally are seeking for peace. My hope rests with the courage of the Tibetans and the love of truth and justice that still lives in the hearts of humanity."

Tibet's Role in the World Community

TIBET UNDER THE COMMUNIST CHINESE RULE

TIBET UNDER THE COMMUNIST CHINESE RULE

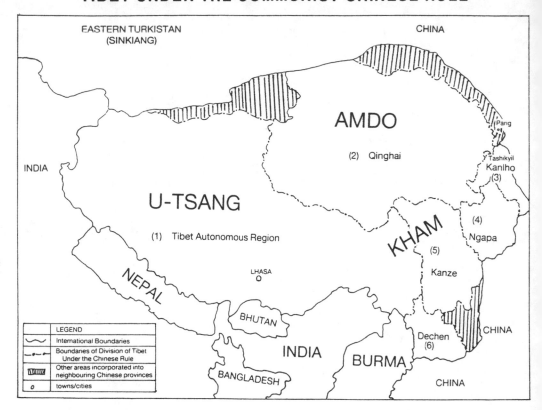

1. **Tibet Autonomous Region:**
Invaded by troops of the People's Liberation Army of China in 1950; proclaimed Autonomous Region of Tibet in 1965.

2. **Qinghai Province:**
Includes most of Amdo region of Tibet. It was claimed as a Chinese province by the Kuomintang regime prior to 1949.

3. **Kanlho Tibetan Autonomous Prefecture:**
Part of Amdo region of Tibet; reorganized as an autonomous Tibetan prefecture under a Chinese province of Kansu during 1958-1964.

4. **Ngapa Tibetan Autonomous Prefecture:**
Part of Amdo region of Tibet; organized as an autonomous Tibetan prefecture under a Chinese province of Szechuan prior to 1950.

5. **Kanze Tibetan Autonomous Prefecture:**
Part of Kham region of Tibet. Occupied by the PLA troops before the Communists came to power in Peking. Organized as part of Sikang province from 1950 to 1954; Sikang dismantled during 1954-1957; and Kanze reorganized as autonomous Tibetan prefecture under Szechuan province.

6. **Dechen Tibetan Autonomous Prefecture:**
Part of Kham region of Tibet. Occupied by PLA troops prior to 1949 and organized as an autonomous Tibetan prefecture under Yunan province. There was widespread fighting in these parts of Tibet even before the PLA troops crossed the Dri-chu (Yangtse) in October 1950.

---

* When the Chinese refer to Tibet they mean the Tibet Autonomous Region. (1) The present Tibet is substantially smaller than in 1950 (before the coming of the Chinese) as the former Tibetan province of Kham has been largely absorbed into the provinces of Szechuan and Yunan (5/6). The huge Amdo region of Eastern Tibet was first claimed by the Chinese Emperor K'ang Hsi in 1720, a claim which was also pursued by the Kuomintang under Chiang Kai Shek when the province was renamed Qinghai. The Communists incorporated this area into China after 1950, but the Tibetans have never accepted such territorial claims deriving from remote imperial dynasties. The Chinese give the population of the TAR as just under two million, although several million Tibetans still live in these eastern provinces outside the TAR.

HUGH RICHARDSON

The Independence of Tibet

Any foreigner living in Tibet before 1950 would have scoffed at a suggestion that the country was not wholly independent. In Lhasa, at the heart of that majestically beautiful country where I went with the British Mission in 1936, our work and our leisure were enjoyed in the company of friendly, cheerful, humorous people dressed in richly colored silk robes, in a city of solid white houses accented by black-framed windows. Our official business was with a government unmistakably managing its own affairs, without any hint of outside influence or interference—shrewd statesmen with long experience in their special world, ready to discuss matters of common interest with quiet, competent thoroughness. In the social sphere we exchanged warm and convivial hospitality with a wide range of friends.

Life in Lhasa, public or private, was conducted at a leisurely pace with calm good humor, openness, and natural good manners. In the villages throughout the country, among people more rugged in appearance and way of living, those same qualities and open manners were pleasantly reflected. These were Tibetan characteristics quite different from the noncommittal, secretive, reserve of the Chinese.

The total devotion of the Tibetans to their religion revealed them further as a different people. Monks in garnet-red robes were to be seen everywhere, and in all towns and villages the most conspicuous and most treasured building was the monastery, temple, or chapel. It was not possible to be present in the Jokhang of Lhasa without feeling intensely the faith of the people who came from all over the country to prostrate themselves in the holy of holies and offer white scarves and butter for the lamps burning before a myriad of Buddhas, Bodhisattvas, saints, and deities. In less formal shrines, even in tiny chapels in remote valleys, some religious duty was always being performed. The house of every layman had, according to its means, an altar or a simple center of worship. The year at Lhasa was marked by a series of day-long religious ceremonies, celebrated with profound seriousness as vital for the well-being of the state.

This was the Tibetan world, self-governing, self-sufficient, apart in race, language, thinking, and behavior from the Chinese. One could travel through the country without seeing any trace of that alien people. Only in Lhasa there was small group of Chinese left surreptitiously in 1934 by General Huang Mu-sung, who had been allowed to visit Lhasa to condole on the death of the Thirteenth Dalai Lama. He also made strenuous efforts to persuade the government to agree that Tibet was part of China, a proposal which the Tibetans firmly resisted. He did, however, succeed in leaving those officials, whose position, as I saw it, was that of uninvited observers of the scene. Their contacts with the Tibetan government appeared to be restricted and generally indirect: and so far as I know they had no personal discussion about such vexed matters as the threatened return of the Panchen Lama with an armed Chinese escort. The Tibetans conducted such negotiations through their officials on the border and in Beijing where they also relied on diplomatic support from the British Ambassador. Unlike those of us in the British Mission, the Chinese in Lhasa were not permitted to travel freely outside the city. When members of their mission wanted to enter Tibet by way of India, they had to get permission from the Tibetan government to do so.

For the first few years, there was little contact between the British Mission and the Chinese, but later, when officials of a rather inferior standard were replaced by men of better quality, we had occasional amicable social meetings. We did not, of course, discuss Tibetan political matters, except in 1944, when Mr. T. L. Shen, an adviser and confidant of Chiang Kai-shek, asked Sir Basil Gould how the Chinese might improve their relations with Tibet. Mr. Shen had no illusions about what he saw, and in his book, *Tibet and the Tibetans*, written together with Mr. S.C. Liu, he said, "Since 1911 Lhasa has to all practical purposes enjoyed full independence."

There were many instances of that independence. No foreigner wanting to visit Lhasa or other places in Tibet would dream of approaching the Chinese, who were incapable of giving that permission; only the Tibetan government could do so. In 1944, when there was a proposal from the Allies to make a route for supplies from India to China across Tibet, the Tibetans declared and maintained their neutrality, even opposing a Chinese survey party with force. An even clearer demonstration of their independence was seen in 1949, when they evicted all the Chinese from Lhasa. There is absolutely no doubt that when the Chinese communists invaded Tibet in 1950, claiming to "bring it back to the fold," and proceeded to occupy it from 1952 onwards, they committed unprovoked aggression against a country that had been free and independent at least since the fall of the Manchu empire in 1911. Unfortunately the world at large knew little about Tibet, and what little it heard came mainly through Chinese propaganda. Until too late, the Tibetans showed no proper understanding of the power of publicity and expressed the ingenuous hope that the truth would surely make itself known. Partly from inexperience and partly from anxiety not to provoke the Chinese, whose designs on their country they had long feared, they relied on others to put their case for them; but there were few people to attempt that.

The one authoritative account, based on practical experience, of Tibet's political status in the twentieth century that was available in 1950 was *Tibet, Past and Present* (1924) by Sir Charles Bell. *Lhasa the Holy City* (1938) by F. Spencer Chapman, who was in Lhasa for some months with the British Mission, describes the independent activity of the Tibetan government but without adding anything significant. The effect of some perceptive articles in the *New York Herald Tribune* by Arch Steele, who visited Lhasa in 1944, was lost in world preoccupation with the closing stages of the war in Europe. And books by two other visitors—*Roof of the World, Key to Asia,* by Amaury de Riencourt and *Out of This World,* by Lowell Thomas—were both published in 1950, too late to be any help to the Tibetans.

So when the blow fell in 1950, there was no generally informed international knowledge of the status of Tibet. Only the British and Indian governments, which had maintained diplomatic relations with the Tibetan government, could have made some positive statement, but the situation was dominated by India's relations—friendly at that time—with China; and the opportunity to speak out before the United Nations was rejected. On the next occasion when the subject of Tibet was considered by the international community at the General Assembly of the United Nations in 1959, the mixture of ignorance, evasion, or prejudice about Tibet's recent past shown by many world statesmen whom I heard speaking or to whom I spoke was disappointing but hardly surprising. And, sadly, the resolution for discussion was not concerned with the violation of Tibet's independence but only about respect for the fundamental human rights of the Tibetan people and for their distinctive cultural and religious life. The seizure of the country and its domination by an alien power were taken as *fait accompli.*

TENZIN GYATSO, THE FOURTEENTH DALAI LAMA

China and the Future of Tibet

During the past decade, I have visited many parts of the world and spoken at universities, colleges, religious institutions, and small centers of learning. I have also had the opportunity to address several organizations concerned with world affairs and foreign policy. In almost every situation, I have taken the liberty to speak on love and compassion. I firmly believe that the promotion of these qualities can contribute to modern society's need for a balance against excessive material preoccupation.

I have spoken at length on these topics not simply as a Buddhist, but from a clear universal recognition that, except for superficial differences, all humans are in essence the same because we all want happiness and do not want suffering. We engage in various techniques to bring this about. Recognition of our fundamental aim and agreement is important.

The press, the general public, and many individuals I have met have shown a keen interest in Tibet, the Tibetan people, and their future. It is obvious that developments in China during the past few years have contributed to this interest and caused speculations of a quick end to my exile. Therefore, I think that I should express my thoughts on the subject and my views on what may possibly lie ahead.

One who is not politically prejudiced can easily see that Tibet is a separate country, different from China. This thought comes quite naturally because Tibet was, and is, different from China—racially, culturally, linguistically, geographically, and historically. No knowledgeable person would, for a moment think, that Tibetans are Chinese.

In the past there existed a special patron-priest relationship between China and Tibet; a relationship that was spiritual rather than temporal. In those times, China, Mongolia, and Tibet were referred to as separate countries. You ask a Tibetan what his nationality is and his answer will be "Tibetan." Similarly, when people discuss something Tibetan, it is always in the sense of something that is different and distinct from Japanese, Indian, or Chinese. For example, when people talk about Tibetan Buddhism, it is never implied that Chinese Buddhism represents Tibetan Buddhism as well.

The word "China" is "Gya-nak" in Tibetan. Since the Tibetan word "Gya-nak" refers to a foreign land, it implies Tibet to be separate from China. The Chinese do not use this word. They use the vague term "our nation" and "motherland" instead of "China" in their official documents and publications in the Tibetan language. They explain to us that Tibet is not a part of Gya-nak (China) but that it is part of Chung Kuo (Middle Kingdom), just as Gya-nak (China) also is! However, Chinese who are not politically oriented do not make this distinction, for they refer to the Chinese language as Chunk Kuo Hua (language of the Middle Kingdom). But politically-motivated Chinese refer to it as Han Hua (language of Han) in order to justify their stand that Tibet is an integral part of the Middle Kingdom. Linguistic concoctions cannot hide the facts of life and history.

Because Tibet as well as Mongolia and East Turkestan are basically and historically different from China, the Chinese have established various autonomous administrative systems in these occupied areas. They also use the language of these countries along with Chinese on their currency notes. Also, in the case of Tibet, because it was independent until 1950, the Chinese signed the

Seventeen-Point Agreement with the Tibetan government. No other Chinese-occupied nationality has any such agreement, pact, or treaty with China. Here again, the Chinese say that this is an "agreement" and not a "treaty," giving the unsatisfactory explanation that "agreements" are made only within a nation between the central and local governments.

It may be of interest that Sun Yat-sen, the father of the Chinese Republic, considered Tibet, Mongolia, and Manchuria as foreign countries. Also, Mao Tse-tung, in the 1930s when he was carrying out his struggle and was not yet in power, supported Tibetan independence. Many years later, in 1954 when I was in China, Mao told me that while we were poor and backward, China would help us, but that after twenty years we Tibetans would be able to help the Chinese. On another occasion he told me that the Chinese personnel then stationed in Tibet would be withdrawn when the Tibetans could manage by themselves.

Even after thirty years of occupation by the People's Republic of China—and in spite of China's worldwide propaganda projecting the picture of Tibet as an inseparable and integral part of China— nobody says that he has been to "China" when he has visited "Tibet" or that the "Chinese" have taken to socialism when he means that the "Tibetans" have.

During these past three decades the Chinese have placed great emphasis on the unity of their nation and have boasted much achievement in that direction. Speeches on this have been made on numerous occasions at public meetings and official receptions. If we are to go by the number of times this theme has been stressed, by now the Chinese should have achieved a rock-like unshakable unity. But his has not happened, for it is an artificial unity that is being imposed unsuccessfully on different nationalities, Tibetans being one of them.

To claim that Tibet is a part of the Chinese nation is both distorted and hypocritical. The Chinese seem to realize this, and one hopes, therefore, that they will change their policy and accept the reality of a Tibetan nation. If the Chinese really want understanding and friendship, Tibetans, Mongolians, and East Turkestanis should be treated according to their real circumstances and should be given their inalienable national rights and fundamental freedoms in their own homelands.

The Chinese claim that they did not come to Tibet as imperialists or colonialists, but as "liberators." What sort of liberation is it that denies the people their birthright and the freedom to determine their own destiny? Having deprived the Tibetan people of freedom, the Chinese talk about an imaginary "state of glorious happiness and progress" said to be existing in Tibet.

I am pointing out these facts not with any antagonism toward the Chinese. If one day all the countries of the world join together as one nation, I would welcome that, and Tibet would become a willing partner in such a movement. But as long as this does not happen, the six million Tibetans are entitled to all the rights that other free peoples have, including the preservation of their separate, unique identity and way of life. As long as the six million Tibetans remain under foreign military occupation, they will continue to struggle for genuine national liberation and for legitimate rights in their own country.

I think it is important that we Tibetans present a clear and factual account of the Tibetan situation. This is particularly necessary now when the present Chinese leadership is reported to be following a more moderate and reasonable path. It remains to be seen whether Chinese leaders are prepared to recognize realities as they really exist, or whether they will continue to direct facts in order to draw conclusions that serve only China's interests.

I have always firmly believed that unless we act according to the real, existing circumstances, we can never achieve our true aspirations. To my great disappointment, ever since the invasion of Tibet by the People's Republic of China, owing both to a lack of understanding of the actual situation and often because the truth was intentionally ignored by the Chinese, there have existed most unfriendly relations between Tibet and China. This is an unfortunate state of affairs between two countries who have been neighbors for centuries. The Chinese have taken advantage of the Tibetans whenever possible, and as a result the Tibetans have grown ever suspicious of them.

Unions or federations can take place only when there is mutual agreement and mutual benefits flow from such arrangements. But they have to be disbanded or discontinued when it is realized that the people do not support them. The future of Tibet is not a matter of determination by the Chinese occupation force. Six million Tibetans obviously cannot be absorbed or integrated with China and their identity cannot be destroyed.

Friendly relations between Tibet and China, which I dearly wish for, can be established only on the basis of equality, mutual respect, and mutual benefit. I, for one, would gladly accept whatever destiny the six million people of Tibet choose for themselves in a climate of genuine freedom and peace. The free will of the Tibetan people is the only true basis for determining their destiny. Until it flourishes, there will be no peace in the hearts and minds of my people. With boundless faith in themselves and in the righteousness of their own cause, they will wait for the day, which must come, when they can fully and freely enjoy their legitimate national rights and at the same time enjoy a relationship with China on a new basis of mutual benefit and respect.

DICKY Y. TENLEY

Tibetan Youth: "The Future Denied to Us."

As the representative of the Tibetan Youth in Europe, and also as a Tibetan woman, I would like to try to explain our current situation and what we hope for in the future. For a long time, we Tibetans in exile hoped, as did the Tibetans in our homeland, that international protest would be raised everywhere if we could only demonstrate that Tibet is an independent state that was forcibly occupied, and how its people have suffered greatly under this occupation. Innumerable letters of appeal and petitions have been sent to the UN and to governments throughout the world. Tibetan and Western scholars have set themselves to the task of documenting historically that Tibet was completely autonomous until the entry of the Chinese troops.

Our entreaty remained, in the eyes of the world powers, the vain hope of a few backward people. In the first years, it is true, we were still good enough to be held up as examples of "victims of Communism." As with so many other peoples and individuals, politicians' and governments' preoccupation with political expediency was our undoing. Caught in their own prejudices and interests, many people even today refuse to recognize the real issue.

This piece is adapted from Tenley's presentation at the Bonn Hearings, April, 1989.

We Tibetans are neither anti-communist nor hostile to democracy or progress. We could even imagine living as good neighbors to the Chinese. We are fighting for our legitimate right to exercise self-determination, freely and in peace. But no notice has been taken of our appeals or our position, even while our countrymen in Tibet have lived through the grimmest period in our history. Up to the unrest in the fall of 1987, a strange mood, something between hope and despair, held sway among Tibetans, particularly among younger Tibetans. After the Cultural Revolution, the so-called politics of liberalization came belatedly into Tibet. A certain relaxation of tension and an improvement in the economic situation in Tibet (which was, however, mostly to the benefit of the Chinese) awakened many false hopes among Tibetans, and their view of the realities of the situation were somewhat distorted. The uprisings from the fall of 1987 to the present have subsequently shown the world that the Tibetans in Tibet, even after thirty years under Chinese foreign rule, have not lost courage, and that the will to regain independence is not corruptible by certain economic improvements. The demonstrations since the fall of 1987 in Lhasa and other parts of Tibet show clearly that we are not seeking an improvement in living conditions, higher wages, or the like, but rather at the risk of our lives we are expressing that we are no longer willing to live under Chinese foreign rule. We must have independence in Tibet.

It is therefore a fundamental misunderstanding when the problem of Tibet, as is occurring more and more in the West, is reduced to the question of human-rights abuses. Our disappointment was great when we had to recognize that our Government-in-Exile was prepared to compromise on this point. We could not imagine living under the Chinese flag. Just at this time the conditions in Tibet seemed more favorable than ever for forming a broad-based resistance movement. Instead, there is a reliance on the readiness of the People's Republic of China to hold talks and on the support of other countries. It is not a single diplomatic move that we are opposed to, but rather the false appraisal of the situation that underlies this initiative. The past has shown that China is not in a position and is not ready to seek a solution to the problem through negotiation. The imposition of martial law in Tibet, which elicited only limited international protest, shows once again the contempt the Chinese occupation force holds for the most fundamental human rights in Tibet. The possibility that international solidarity and political pressure on the Chinese leadership could contribute to the solution of the problem of Tibet seems to us to be ever more illusory. Our greatest hope is the unbroken will to freedom of the Tibetan people themselves. The rallies and demonstrations in Tibet in March 1988 were led by young people. In Beijing last December, Tibetan students demonstrated. These are not "marginal elements," as Chinese propaganda would have us believe, but the Tibetan youth themselves, who are supposed to have been prepared in Chinese elite schools for the tasks of leadership in their own country, and on whom the Chinese have placed such great hopes. Just as the deeply-rooted faith of the older Tibetans in Tibet cannot be extinguished despite all the efforts of Communist indoctrination, so also does the thought of freedom lie very deep in the youth of Tibet who are living in exile.

For the first twenty years, we were exclusively concerned with adapting to a strange environment and trying to preserve our culture. Although this time meant an experience of great privation for us, which we would not have survived without humanitarian support from abroad, we managed to learn a good deal about our new environment during those years. Adjusting to a totally new world brought about far-reaching social changes within our community. These changes moved the Tibetan youth into a completely new role, which would have been unimaginable before then in Tibet. The responsibility of the younger generation grew, both in the family and in the greater community. It is in this context that for the past twenty years the Organization of Tibetan Youth has made it its task to inform the public about the political situation in Tibet, and to convey to young people in exile a political consciousness and a sense of responsibility for the fate of the Tibetan people. The basis of this sense can only be that these young people develop an awareness of their own cultural identity and are moved to preserve it. An essential part of our efforts is the promotion of democratic thinking and behavior in our community.

When anyone speaks about the future of Tibet and possible forms for a future Tibetan society, it can only be the future of the Tibetan youth of today. In this context, the reproaches from many quarters that we Tibetans—especially those in exile—are reactionary and wish to restore the old social order, are completely absurd. We have recognized that the old social order was unjust. Even if the Western system of values and conception of society need not be the measure of all things, we have so deeply internalized values like democracy, the constitutional state, free speech, and social justice that a return to the old theocratic-feudalistic order is no longer thinkable. Young Tibetans in Tibet will never wish to return to the old forms of society. Although their notions and ideals of a future Tibetan nation are certainly more strongly influenced by a society drawn up along socialist lines, there is agreement on the need to work together in democratic competition seeking the best solution for the society of a future, independent Tibet. An important task will be the secularization of political life.

Parallel to the development described above of the Tibetan youth-in-exile, there have been changes in the role of women in our society. Although even in earlier times, Tibetan society adopted a liberal attitude towards women, this was still far removed from equal rights in the Western sense. Unfortunately, even today, it is still true that women encounter more difficulty making their way with the same qualifications as men, a situation that begins in elementary school. We Tibetan women have, although it has not often been noticed, our own tradition in the equal rights movement. The first demonstration of the people of Lhasa against the Chinese occupational powers, in March of 1959, was brought about by women. Throughout the last twenty years it has always been women who have protested openly against the Chinese, often even with arms. In recent months, women and nuns have repeatedly had a leading part in the demonstrations. Maybe we should see it as a sign that the highest tutelary deity of the Tibetan state is female.

In 1983 I had the opportunity to visit Tibet. In the province of Amdo, where my father was born, I visited the cities of Labrang and Xining. On my arrival in Xining, I had to ask myself whether this city had really once been Tibetan territory. I had the impression of being in one of any number of Chinese cities. Nothing could be seen that suggested Tibet or Tibetans. Only a very few nomads, striking in their colorful clothing, were to be seen from time to time along the streets, as if they'd been strewn there randomly. At the sight of my people, who stood wretchedly by the side of the road, having become a dwindling minority in their own country, I was overwhelmed by despair and impotent rage. Many of my relatives told me how, during the Cultural Revolution, they had had to leave their homes to make room for Chinese settlers. Nor did things go better for our people in Lhasa, above all for young people. In conversations with young Tibetans there, I learned that because of the planned colonization of Chinese settlers, predominantly craftsmen and construction workers, many of the young Tibetans were out of work and spent their time hanging out in cheap bars. This had the consequence that these young people were sent to indoctrination camps as "unmotivated workers." A school education was at that time reserved for children of cadre officials. Tibetans had been degraded to second-class citizens in their own country. For me, those few days in Tibet were the saddest and most frustrating I have ever spent.

It is an unhappy and tragic phenomenon on this earth that force draws the attention of governments, media, and the world's people to itself, while quiet and nonviolent actions go virtually unnoticed. It is hardly surprising that people in Tibet are turning more and more towards forceful means. The repressions to which our people have been subjected are becoming more and more brutal and intolerable. The measures that the Chinese security forces are bringing to bear against the civil population are becoming more and more disproportionate. For us, the struggle against the Chinese presence has long since become a struggle for survival. For too long we have indulged in the illusion that the suffering and injustice that have befallen our people would suffice to awaken genuine concern and international solidarity. Time presses, and we are no longer willing to wait; we will make use of all methods at our disposal.

I thank our loyal foreign friends who have tirelessly spoken up for the rights of the Tibetan people, and I hope that we may continue to count on their support. We Tibetans are an optimistic people, and we have never doubted that one day justice will prevail. We Tibetans wish to live in a free and independent Tibet, but the day approaches when we will have no future left to fight for—only the desire for retaliation for the injustice that we have had to suffer, and for the future that has been denied to us.

THOMAS HEBERER

Tibet and the Chinese Concept of Nationhood

In 1911 and again in 1949, Tibet tried to become independent of China. Thus in terms of international law, the status of Tibet was controversial for the community of nations for awhile, even though not a single country ever recognized Tibet as an autonomous state. Today, in terms of international law, Tibet is a part of the People's Republic of China.

This is not sufficient, however, to explain the march of Chinese troops into Tibet in 1950; there are two factors at work here, which have not yet been considered in the Western discussion of the question of Tibet. In determining its boundaries, China clearly proceeded from a different concept of the nation-state than have modern Western countries. In contrast to Europe, where the nations of today have taken shape only in the last 200 years, the Chinese empire has existed for two millennia. The area of the present Chinese state has been Chinese territory for many centuries. What constitutes "belonging to China" in a historical sense is judged by the Chinese, and must be judged differently from the drawing of borders around the young European states. From the Chinese point of view, all

---

This piece is adapted from Heberer's presentation at the Bonn Hearings, April 1989.

peoples who live on the present territory of China are a part of the greater Chinese people.

According to the official interpretation, the Tibetans too have historically belonged to China for a long time. The weaknesses of the Qing Dynasty and the pressure and influence of foreign powers are blamed for the separation of large areas of China in the nineteenth and early twentieth centuries.

On the one hand, there exists this sense that all peoples or groups of peoples who lived within Chinese territory until 1911 are a part of the Chinese nation; on the other hand, there is the fact that China could not prevent the "falling off" of some areas because of its own weakness. This probably amounts to the ideological basis for the "reintegration" of Tibet. The Chinese sense of law, in this case, is proceeding from a territorial principle as the principle of nation-hood, and both the Kuomintang in Taiwan and the Communist Party in Beijing have been in agreement about this principle up to the present.

In 1950, the Communists attempted with the reintegration of Tibet to re-establish the validity of this principle, and at the same time to demonstrate that the era of the "sick man in the East," as China had long been called, was past. China had continually claimed sovereignty over Tibet, even after 1911, and had never given up the claim. China saw itself in the right with the reintegration of a region almost lost because of "imperialist influences."

After the end of the Qing Dynasty in 1911, Chinese power in Tibet was almost nonexistent because of China's inner and outer weaknesses. The struggle between Russia and Britain for hegemony in central Asia had already made Tibet a bone of contention between the two powers in the nineteenth century. In spite of this, the Chinese constitutions after 1912 refer to Tibet as a "neighboring area outside the provincial organization" of the rest of China, and its affairs were assigned to a "Council on Mongolian-Tibetan Affairs." Thereafter, Tibet was called a "Zone of British Interests." Even in 1904, it was a representative of Great Britain who determined who was allowed to enter Tibet. A British journalist wrote in the 1940s:

As in many other places of the world, Great Britain did not at first intend to exploit the riches and possibilities of the country in which it had established a decisive influence. It was sufficient to Britain that no other country could do this. This attitude coincided with the wishes of Tibet's ruling monastic class, who sought to hold all Western influence at a distance so as not to threaten their own rule. In this way, Tibet has remained up to the present a powerful area rich in untapped resources, an area that with the means of modern technology could be transformed into a veritable garden. It has remained an empty desert because this suited the aims of British policy.

And the German diplomatic secret agent Filchner reported on his research into Tibet:

> Tibet has, in the past, played a very particular role in the conflicts of interest between England and Russia, and continues to play that role today.... The eyes of the whole world are therefore turned with justifiable expectation toward the Tibetan plateau, the witch's cauldron of Asia. For the Anglo-Indian government, in its confrontation with Russia, it is of decisive importance to create for itself in Tibet a well-defended bulwark on India's northern border. England has directed its policies in Lhasa entirely from this angle.

It was, first of all, the violation of these interests that alarmed the Western powers in 1950, since with its integration into the Chinese federation, Tibet was really lost to Western interests. The threatening prospect of Western influence in an independent Tibet, from where China (deprived of a natural boundary in the southwest) could be easily harassed, must have made its stamp on the question of Tibet as China saw it.

Of course, all this does not mean that the Tibetans on no account had a right to independence. There is no doubt that they did not enter willingly into the Chinese federation in 1950. The Chinese government carried out their alleged right with force and subordinated the Tibetan efforts toward independence to their own legal claim. Whether they were within their rights in so doing cannot be decided here; very likely there will continue to be controversial views about this well into the future. Here it is much more a question of explaining China's behavior for once from another standpoint, since from the Western point of view it seems difficult to explain.

From the point of view of Western law, it is a question of occupation; from the Chinese point of view, it is the "reestablishment of historically unequivocal rights," which China had, for the reasons mentioned above, been unable to exercise for some time.

If we proceed from international law, then for the problematics of nationhood in general as for the case of Tibet in particular, the problem that emerges concerns the principle of self-determination. The content of this principle is now as ever a subject of international dispute. For a long time, the view was prevalent that self-determination for a people was more a moral or political postulate than a principle of law. In the course of the liberation of colonized peoples, it came to be seen as a basic human right. But there have always been difficulties in the practical implementation of the principle of self-determination. The people, it is said, should be the judges in this matter. But who possesses the identity of a people? And which people has the right to self-determination? If, on the one hand, the dangerous dismemberment of states is to be avoided, but on the other hand this principle is to be put into practice, then there is need of an institution that will judge such matters. A UN declaration from 1970 reads:

> On the basis of the principle of equal rights and of the self-determination of peoples, which is stated in the charter of the United Nations, all peoples have the right to determine their political status freely, without foreign interference, and to pursue their own way in economic, social, and cultural development, and every state is obligated to respect this right in accordance with the decrees of the charter.

As a protective clause, however, for existing nations, UN Resolution 1514 (paragraph XV) established that "every effort which has as its goal a partial or total destruction of the national unity and territorial integrity of a country is incompatible with the goals and principles of the charter of the UN." The UN, therefore, does not promote or support any action which aims at the division or destruction of the territorial integrity or the political unity of sovereign, independent states who "are guided by the principle of equal rights and self-determination." The criterion of "legitimacy" was introduced in order to be able to determine whether a country was, in fact, guided by this principle. According to this criterion, that state possesses "legitimacy" whose government represents its entire people, irrespective of race, religion, or skin color. Conversely, the denial of equal participation in the exercise of national rule (but not the denial of national and cultural autonomy) can constitute a justifiable demand for self-determination. This view is espoused by the Chinese government also. Up to the present, the international community of nations has proceeded from the understanding that China possesses this "legitimacy" and that Tibet is therefore a part of China.

The often-cited "hatred of Tibetans for the Chinese" follows in large part from the Cultural Revolution, in which Tibetan culture was the object of violence and was in part destroyed. Nonetheless, this destruction happened not only to the Tibetans, but to all nationalities in China, even if the storm was particularly savage in Tibet and left this region until today one of the poorest regions in China.

In spite of all liberalization, petty bureaucratic behavior is very widespread among many functionaries in the minority regions, especially among functionaries from the minority groups themselves. Minority functionaries who spoke up for the interests of their nationalities were prime targets of the political campaigns of the 1950s, 1960s, and 1970s. This history has made them cautious and especially bureaucratic. Many centrally-granted freedoms therefore are adopted only slowly and in limited form in Tibet. Criticisms in Beijing very quickly take on the character of persecutions in Tibet. For these reasons, the dissatisfaction with the local bureaucracies is particularly strong. Who will be surprised, then, that many Tibetans see the only possibility of free cultural development in a separate state? Protests and demands for independence may turn the gaze of the world community and of Beijing to the problems of Tibet, and they may bring about long-term improvements. But realistically, China could never allow Tibet independence. This would be not only a security risk, but a terrible loss of face for China which no leadership could afford without the gravest consequences.

Deng Xiaoping stated after the Tibetan protests of March 1989 that China was always and at all times ready for negotiations. *Everything* was open to negotiation, *except the question of the independence of Tibet.* Even the Dalai Lama did not push for Tibetan independence, but—realistically—proposed an autonomous region allied with China, one which would administrate itself along democratic lines, but which would be represented by Beijing in foreign affairs. A limited number of Chinese soldiers would be able to be stationed in Tibet, until it became a neutral peace zone. With this proposal the Dalai Lama was in effect asking to return to a status that Tibet long occupied in its history with China.

Although this position has not yet gained acceptance in the ranks of the exiled Tibetans, it contains significant concessions to the Chinese government. To that extent it could offer a suitable negotiating position to both sides, even if the proposal as it stands represents a maximum demand that would not be accepted by the Chinese regime in this sweeping form.

I hope that an arrangement can be conceded to the Tibetans—as to the other small ethnic minorities threatened by assimilation and extinction—that allows them a greater degree of self-determination.

ERWIN WICKERT

Tibet: A Chinese Territory

The emotional response against China that is awakened when we hear reports about Tibet is understandable. I was raised to consider critically and dispassionately what I hear and to pass no judgment and, above all, no condemnation before hearing the other side as well. While I was Ambassador in China, I often interceded for people whose human rights had been violated, and I was able to help more than a few. In the Tibetan Autonomous Region, thousands, perhaps hundreds of thousands, of human rights violations have occurred.

But what the Chinese suffered in the Cultural Revolution, and even before it, is equally disturbing. That human rights abuses continue to take place today in both China and Tibet, is the judgment not only of critics of the Chinese system, like Fang Lizhi, but also recently of deputies of the National People's Congress and high judicial officers in Beijing.

We in Europe tend to presume that an appreciation of human rights throughout the world goes without saying. But even in our culture, a general consciousness of human rights is only two hundred

This piece is adapted from Wickert's presentation at the Bonn Hearings, April 1989.

years old. In China, where they have been philosophizing about politics for more than two thousand years, they have never spoken of human *rights*, but of human *duties*. Until the flight of the Dalai Lama thirty years ago, there was no talk of human rights in Tibet either, and such rights were denied to the great majority of all Tibetans, the serfs. Today the Dalai Lama demands human rights for his countrymen, who then had none. We should welcome this change. But we should consider critically and dispassionately everything we hear, and pass no judgment or condemnation before hearing the other side as well.

During these hearings the Chinese have been accused of violating human rights, international law, and other standards of justice. "The world power China," Petra Kelly states, "has managed until today, to keep Tibet behind a wall of lies, silence, propaganda, and complicity and so out of the field of view of every other nation, with the intention of annexing Tibet to itself with unrestrained barbarism." I have the impression that things are not quite that way.

When I visited Tibet for the first time, ten years ago, there was not even one proper hotel in Lhasa. And in the last few years, hundreds of thousands, perhaps millions of foreigners have traveled to and in Tibet, although not in times of exceptional circumstances. Many have also seen the barbaric destruction of the monasteries, and many could speak with Tibetans. I have heard so many disturbing reports from the Chinese of Mao's time, but especially of the Cultural Revolution, that corresponding reports by Tibetans can only confirm my views. But I do not know whether the Tibetans who, in early March of 1989, smashed Chinese stores and are said to have set fire to twenty cars, are all angels. Much that we hear about the conditions of Tibet may be correct, but much may also be colored and perhaps not altogether true. I ask you to remember the saying of Confucius:

> Where all praise, there one must look for oneself,
> Where all condemn, there one must look for oneself.

I thank Ms. Kelly and Mr. Bastian for giving me the opportunity to present my views here, and I ask for their indulgence if I may contradict some of their claims with which I cannot agree. Ms. Kelly spoke in January 1989 to the Bundestag of a "holocaust" in Tibet, to which 1.2 million Tibetans fell victim. But in 1953, there were in the Tibetan Autonomous Region, into which Mao's troops had marched in 1951, only 1,207,000 Tibetans. Does this mean that only 7,000 Tibetans were left? How then do we explain that today more than two million Tibetans live in this region?

Ms. Kelly spoke further on October 8, 1987, before the Bundestag of a Chinese infiltration of Tibet, "a mercilessly-pursued policy of Sinification," which has led to the situation that six million Tibetans are facing 7.5 million Han Chinese. But according to the official census, in the whole of China, including the provinces of Qinghai, Gansu, and Sichuan with their Tibetan minorities, there are in total only 3.9 million Tibetans. How does Ms. Kelly arrive at her figures? And why did the Tibetan representative today in the press conference say the Dalai Lama would speak with the Chinese about the fate of the six million Tibetans? Are we speaking of some "Greater Tibet," one which reaches into the Chinese provinces, to Nepal, Bhutan, Ladakh—everywhere Tibetan minorities live? We should observe this juggling of figures very cautiously.

I would also like to address some of the few reproaches directed at the Chinese by the Dalai Lama and his remarkably effective public relations team. It is astonishing how easily many politicians and journalists accept their portrayals. I suggest we study them more critically and, if we are uncertain they are truly accurate, admit the fact. If I may again quote Confucius,

> To know what one knows
> And to know what one does not know,
> That alone is knowledge.

Friends of the Dalai Lama often maintain that the Chinese invaded and occupied the Tibetan state, and Ms. Kelly even compared this to the Soviet march into Afghanistan. This comparison is inadmissible. Occupation by a foreign power, according to international legal criteria, is what happened to, for example, the Baltic states, which had maintained diplomatic relations to many countries of the world, and were in fact members of the League of Nations. Tibet, however, is a part of China, just as Georgia is a part of the Soviet Union. If it is really necessary, it is with this member-republic of the USSR that we may compare Tibet. Tibet had been a part of China for centuries and never maintained diplomatic relations. Every country in the world, without exception, recognizes Tibet as a part of China.

Ms. Kelly even tried to convince the Indian Prime Minister, Rajiv Gandhi, to declare the independence of Tibet before his trip to China. But in China he did exactly the opposite, expressly stating that India recognizes Tibet as a part of China. The Indian government has likewise made it clear that the right to self-determination may not lead to a secession.

The overwhelming majority of the world's nations agree with this view. The examples of Katanga and Biafra provide evidence from the period after World War II that this standpoint is also recognized in practice. The international legal discussion of Tibet can go nowhere. It leads only to accusations. We should have in the foreground the political question: What can one do to bring about a peaceful relationship between Chinese and Tibetans? The German government rightly refuses to place itself against the countries of the world, or to let itself be made into the spearhead of the politics of radical exiled Tibetan politicians who are aiming at the secession of Tibet from China. I am certain that no one at these hearings is holding out hopes that a wedge could be driven between us and the People's Republic of China.

I have already spoken of the barbaric behavior of Chinese troops in Tibet, by which I mean the destruction of the monasteries, the murders, the harassment of the population to the point of the grotesque order to replace the Tibetans' traditional cultivation of barley with the cultivation of the kinds of grains usually grown in Northern China. The Beijing government recognized and admitted its errors in 1980. Since then, it has shown active remorse and has rebuilt many, though I admit far from all, of Tibet's destroyed temples. It has given back, to the extent that they still exist, treasures stolen from temples. Since 1980, Tibet has been freed from the most significant taxes and has received billions in financial and material subsidies from Beijing. In Tibet, where before there were only a few schools, 2,400 elementary schools have been built in the last decades, along with many high schools, vocational schools, and three universities, according to Chinese statements. Hospitals and roads have been constructed.

One cannot, of course, maintain that the Han Chinese and the Tibetans love one another. The Chinese have always had a hard time dealing with religious minorities. They do not understand the total claim a religion can have on a human being because they have never known it themselves. Their suspicion that religious minorities could develop into political powers that could stand in opposition to the state may still be felt, and indeed has often proved itself justified. If riots like those of March 1989 are repeated, it is to be feared that this will also have an effect on the present Chinese course of reparation and relaxation of strictures. One may ask oneself whether there may be certain parties who desire such a tightening up of strictures.

The Dalai Lama fled Tibet in 1959 because he feared, after a failed rebellion, that he would be taken captive by the Chinese. He left his people in the lurch, while the second highest spiritual leader of Tibet, the Panchen Lama, remained in his country despite harsh persecution, including imprisonment for sixteen years. I will not argue whether or not it was the duty of the Dalai Lama to remain with his people and to suffer with them, as I do not know to what extent the advisers of the young Dalai Lama influenced him at that time. It would certainly be good if today he would not listen to advisers who urge a policy of confrontation with China or who believe that pressure could be put on the Chinese government with violent demonstrations. That would only give rise to counter-pressure. It seems as if some of the exiled politicians are overestimating their strength.

It's the same old story: the dog can wag his tail, but the tail should not delude itself that it can wag the dog. The Dalai Lama wrote in a telegram to Petra Kelly which was reproduced in the Bundestag records, "Violence, from any side whatsoever, can never solve a problem." Well said! "From any side whatsoever!"

Should not such a pronouncement by the Dalai Lama be enough to induce the two monasteries principally responsible for the riots in Lhasa to behave peaceably? For it is really only Lhasa we are talking about. Ninety-five percent of Tibetans living outside of Lhasa have never shown any indication of a desire to speak out on political questions. Or have things come to the point, as some have suggested, where the Dalai Lama is no longer able to hold his own against his advisers when it comes to the question of force?

The Chinese government has offered to negotiate with the Dalai Lama about his return, indeed about everything concerning Tibet, but not about Tibet's belonging to Chinese territory or Chinese sovereignty over Tibet. The Dalai Lama's answer to this same last question is unclear and evasive. He has said that he supports the "association" of Tibet with the People's Republic. What does he mean by "association?" He has not defined the word, so that one gets the impression he does, in fact, want to alter the constitutional status of Tibet, to move it to another, looser status, perhaps similar to the position of Hong Kong. This seems to be the policy of the young, radical forces around the Dalai Lama, and perhaps these advisers are really his main problem. The Chinese government has repeatedly acknowledged in recent times that it has made mistakes in Tibet. The new Party Secretary of Tibet, Hu Jintao, is seen as a liberal politician; he was a *protégé* of the late former Party Head Hu Yaobang. The Panchen Lama, in the last speech before his death in early March 1989 referred to the Chinese Communist Party's openness to reform and to its "capacity for self-criticism."

This would, therefore, be a good moment to ask Beijing for as much autonomy and self-determination as possible within the Chinese federation, for absolute religious and cultural freedom, as well as for help in Tibet's economic and technical development. But these goals can only be reached in a long and patient dialogue.

Many of us wish that there may be a dialogue between the Dalai Lama and the Chinese government as well as between the Chinese and Tibetan delegates, and that it may be successful and lead to a decisive improvement of the situation in Tibet. We should do everything we can in the interests of the Tibetan people that eases, rather than heats up, their situation.

In closing, I would like to address the "selective conscience," something one encounters quite often these days. It is good and right to stand up for human rights throughout the world; yet we should remain aware that we Germans did not invent human rights, and in fact that a few decades ago we were, as foreign friends occasionally remark, saying very little indeed about human rights. If today, with our chastened sense of justice, we are speaking up for human rights throughout the world, particularly before humming television cameras, then I would like to offer a warning about the selective conscience. The violation of human rights is not a problem confined to Tibet, Chile, or South Africa, but unfortunately a universal problem. An organization like Amnesty International takes an exemplary stance on this point. It should not become fashionable to fight for human rights in faraway countries at the cost of forgetting our own neighbors and our own countrymen. It was depressing to see how many German politicians were embarrassed until recently to extend a hand to Lech Walesa and support him in his struggle because they did not want to incur the displeasure of the Polish regime.

I witnessed at close range, over many years, the sufferings of the Romanian people, and especially the unspeakable sufferings of the German minorities in Transylvania and Banat. I felt grief and shame when our intercession for their human rights was dismissed by an influential politician with cutting, inhuman coldness as "Germanomania."

In short, I would be grateful if we could consider the human rights not just of the Tibetans, but also of our countrymen, and of the many people in the world to whom human rights remain denied.

MICHAEL VAN WALT VAN PRAAG

Tibet: An Occupied Country

What is "the question of Tibet?" What is really at stake in the matter of Tibet?

One of the reasons the Chinese have not been able to answer the question of Tibet during the last forty years is that they do not understand what the question is really about, in part because they cannot, and in part because they do not want to. There is nothing to indicate that the Chinese, either the officials or the press, have even a faint idea of what the point at issue is. This is also reflected in Dr. Wickert's comments. We have been presented a misunderstanding of the question of Tibet.

What are the main points? First of all, Tibet is an occupied country. It is incontestable that one country has simply been occupied by another. Every objective investigation into the status of Tibet before 1950 shows that Tibet was then an independent state. However the relations between China and Tibet may be judged, there can at the least be no question that, at the time of the invasion, there was no Chinese rule in Tibet, and that the Tibetans, like every other government of the world, were looking after their own affairs.

This piece is adapted from van Walt van Praag's presentation at the Bonn Hearings, April 1989.

In 1960, the Irish ambassador to the United Nations said before the UN plenary session on Tibet: "There are few countries in the United Nations that could claim to have enjoyed as many freedoms in the control of their own affairs as Tibet has." This is an important and true statement. Let us for a moment leave aside the finer judicial points. Tibet was and is a country that has been occupied by the Chinese army. Whether one agrees with this or not is unimportant— the Tibetans, at least, feel this way. They feel that theirs is an occupied country. Anyone who travels to Tibet today, even as a tourist, knowing nothing of the history or background of Tibet, feels that Tibet is an occupied country.

Why are the Chinese in Tibet at all? The government gives two answers to this question. Sometimes they say that Tibet has all along been a region belonging to China. For this argument they rely on a Chinese princess whom a Tibetan king married in the seventh century. In the thirteenth century, the Mongols occupied Tibet; previously they had formed close relations with the Tibetan religious establishment. If China strengthens its claim with facts like these, it is an unequivocally imperialist assertion. Since 1950, the Chinese regimes have proclaimed themselves to be great anti-colonialists and anti-imperialists. No state would dare to justify the occupation of a country by invoking a foreign emperor from the thirteenth century. Nowhere in the world would this be accepted.

The second argument with which the Chinese justify their occupation is the development of the poor Tibetan populace. According to this line of argument, the Tibetans could not develop themselves, but first had to be freed, in 1950, from the imperialists— whoever that may have been. Apparently, though, the Chinese did not fulfill their task very well in the last forty years, otherwise they would not still have to maintain today that the Tibetans are "backward," since with respect to economic development Tibet has not changed since 1950. In the final analysis, the Chinese appeal for the justification of their behavior boils down to imperialist arguments.

If Dr. Wickert maintains that Tibet is a part of China, then I would like to ask him: When and why did Tibet become a part of China? I would like to know the date and the historical event that is supposed to have led to this state of affairs. So far, no one has been able to answer these questions for me.

I agree with Petra Kelly that the Soviet invasion of Afghanistan is very similar. It is a question of the occupation and colonization of a country. Tibet has been made into a colony, not just in the legal and political sense, but in the tradition of the colonial lords of the dim past. Colonialism is not always the same, but the worst form is that which justifies its acts with the development of the subjugated country. I have forgotten the figures on how many hospitals there are today in Tibet, and I would also prefer not to discuss how many schools have been built. Most objective visitors will ascertain that most of the schools are schools in name only. Certainly today there are some schools, but it is not true that before there were none.

In the matter of the statistics on development, some observations are needed. Why do we compare the Tibet of 1949 with the rest of the world in 1989, and then say that Tibet was, in 1950, not as it should be by 1989's standards? We should compare 1949 Tibet with the rest of Asia in 1949. At that time, things were going substantially worse for most Chinese than for the Tibetans. I do not want to create the impression that Tibet was a technically and economically highly-developed country. It was certainly not an ideal system, but look at the rest of Asia and other parts of the world in that era. It would be legitimate to compare Tibet today with what it could have been if the Tibetans could have determined their own fates. Certainly the Tibetans did not, in those days, pursue the most progressive policies of reform. There was no Communist Party and greater reforms were not in sight.

But what kinds of prospects were there then? I agree with Dr. Wickert when he says that the best test is investigating the situation for yourself. I would therefore recommend to Dr. Wickert that he go to see the exile communities and investigate their situation there. The Tibetans live there as refugees; they have no government which can administrate their territory; they cannot appeal to the UN or the World Bank; and they are shunned by most international organizations because people are unwilling to provoke China's displeasure. Finally, they have hardly any contact with the six million Tibetans in their country. I will come back to these six million in a moment, but the Tibetans-in-exile are the crucial test of my theory: Let no one maintain that they are the old aristocrats with lots of money, a good education, and good positions. Go there and see for yourself the people from every level of society. If the Tibetans were today in a position to take their destiny into their own hands, then they would certainly need some time to make a recovery—the gap between Tibet and the rest of Asia has since become greater than in 1949.

But the Tibetans-in-exile have furnished proof that they are able to take their fates into their own hands. They are the best-organized exile nation in the world. They have combined their traditional values with modern education in such a way that they benefit from both. Politically, the exile government is a functioning democratic government. It is not always easy to construct a parliament in exile, but since 1963 the Tibetans have had their exile government, based on a constitution inspired by the Dalai Lama, and it functions very democratically. The Dalai Lama has made it clear—most recently before the European Parliament in Strasbourg—that he bases his demands on principles. He has made it clear, not only with words, but also in the practical administration of the exile communities, that he has no intention of letting feudalism be revived. The people in Tibet also are not nostalgic for undemocratic conditions.

Now let us address the question of the six million Tibetans. When I speak of "Tibet," I mean, as do many Tibetans, the country *before* the Chinese invasion, which encompassed the three territories of Kham, Amdo, and Ü-Tsang. If you ask Tibetans from the Chinese provinces of Qinghai, Gansu, or Sichuan about their identity, they also will say that they are Tibetans. I would rather not speculate about the numbers. Some say there are four million Tibetans in all of China; we think it is six million. We are, of course, not able to conduct a census; otherwise we would have more precise figures. Chinese censuses yielded in 1953 the figure of 6.34 million Tibetans. When we say that 1.2 million Tibetans have been killed by the Chinese, then we are taking as a basis not the two million inhabitants of the so-called autonomous region, but the entire population.

So when we speak about the population of Tibet, we mean the people in all the Tibetan areas, obviously with the exception of the Chinese settlers. I do not know if the number of these settlers is around 7.5 million. With a census we would know this more precisely too. Perhaps we are only one million away from the real number.

Just two more thoughts in closing: One hears again and again that Tibet was never recognized as an independent state or had never maintained international relations. This is a Eurocentric view of things which is, as it happens, incorrect. Even though Tibet conducted no diplomatic relations with the Western powers before 1949—perhaps with the exception of Great Britain—that does not then mean that there was no Tibet. Tibet had relations with all of its neighboring countries on the basis of an independent state entity. Nepal, for example, did not send a mission to the UN before 1949, and yet it existed previously. At that time, Nepal maintained at that time diplomatic relations with Tibet; there was an exchange of ambassadors. Great Britain had an ambassador in Tibet, and when India achieved its independence, it took over the British representation in Lhasa. The English flag was taken down and the Indian flag was raised.

Naturally, Tibet did not maintain diplomatic relations with a great many countries in the world. But consider Bhutan; it maintained until recently practically no diplomatic relations at all, besides with Tibet and India. Nonetheless, no one would call into question Bhutan's independence.

Finally, let us go to the question of negotiations. There was a suggestion in Dr. Wickert's presentation that the Dalai Lama has an interest in inciting violent demonstrations in Tibet. This must be directly refuted. For the past thirty years, even against the criticism of his own ranks, the Dalai Lama has consistently attempted to find a peaceful solution to the problem. Since 1959 he has again and again appealed to his people to practice nonviolence. He has several times been nominated for the Nobel Peace Prize [Ed. note: His Holiness was awarded the Nobel Peace Prize in December 1989]. The discussion in the Council of Europe two or three days ago, and his reception by the General Secretary of the UN Human Rights Commission, document how people value the Dalai Lama. They respect him as someone who is struggling for the improvement of the living conditions of all people, and who is attempting to achieve his goals with all conceivable peaceful means.

DAVID ENNALS

Tibet: A New Colony

I am an old friend of China's, and I traveled to Tibet last year to find out the facts. I do not belong to the so-called public relations team of the Dalai Lama; I speak only for myself. In the 1950s I belonged to the China Advisory Council. I admire China. But I have no respect for what they are now doing in Tibet.

I saw in Tibet an enormous number of Chinese weapons and at least 300,000 soldiers. Everyone knows that there are nuclear weapons in Tibet. It is true that they are not produced there, but they are stationed there. There are troops on the streets and army vehicles in Lhasa.

How do things look with respect to education? Of course there are some schools, but the level of education of Tibetans is very low indeed. Only 30% of all citizens can read and write. It is very difficult for Tibetans to receive an education in their own language.

The Tibetans are in every way poorer and disadvantaged compared to the Chinese. This I can characterize without reservation as colonialism. In Lhasa now there are, quite simply, the poor Tibetans and the much richer Chinese. Moreover, there is an influx of the

---

This piece was adapted from Ennals' presentation at the Bonn Hearings, April 1989.

Chinese, who absolutely dominate the Tibetan culture and society. Before I came to the city, I was told that its population was 5% Chinese. This is utter nonsense: it is well over 50%. The Chinese are changing the nature of a society. This is not only colonialism; it is apartheid. There is no equality between the two peoples who live in Lhasa, and the situation is the same throughout the country. All Tibetans struggle against colonial repression. I found only opposition to China among Tibetans.

In the rest of the country, the situation is equally disturbing. Dr. Wickert was right to warn of further confrontations; but if the Chinese do not speak with or listen to the Tibetans, then it will of necessity come to a confrontation for everyone who believes in peace and liberty. Should the Tibetans accept repression and second-class status? Would we allow others to prescribe for us what we may and may not do? One cannot live this way in a world where human rights exist. Of course it is essential, and urgently necessary, to negotiate, and on these grounds the Dalai Lama has presented proposals for a negotiation. But if the Chinese say that negotiations can only take place on the condition that the Tibetans agree to all their demands and are not permitted even to address the question of independence or self-determination, then there can be no negotiations. If these are the conditions, even if we are told it is for the "unity of the motherland," then there is no common ground to stand on.

We characterize this as colonialism, and we do not accept the Chinese theory of the "unity of the motherland." This is an absolutely absurd concept. The talk of the "motherland" is, with respect to a policy of repression of Tibetan culture and identity, grotesque. Everyone who has seen Tibet can confirm that here a policy of exploitation is in effect. Many expressed their disapproval when martial law was declared, but since then no news has gotten out [Ed. note: Martial law was lifted April 30, 1990]. The Chinese have told us that everything is "quiet," but I fear that this means the quiet of the grave for many people. We do not know how many have been killed or imprisoned there, since it has been impossible for independent observers to enter the country. In the last month Geoffrey Howe, the British Foreign Minister, told me that if the Chinese were put under too much pressure, they would close the door once and for all, and there would be no more dialogue.

The question is, how long is the free world prepared to accept all this without comment? It cannot be tolerated that an iron curtain be dropped before the Tibetan people while people everywhere talk of human rights and perestroika. Is it worse that the Chinese be irritated, perhaps, by a few comments from outside, or that the rights of a peaceful people be trodden underfoot? We must open our mouths now, and this goes for everyone who believes in freedom and human rights. Now, too, the Soviet Union should register what is happening in China. In an open letter this last week, many members of British Parliament and some members of the House of Lords, myself included, asked the governments of the European Economic Community to demand an end to martial law. We appealed, moreover, to the General Secretary of the United Nations to use his office to bring about the recognition of human rights in Tibet and to prevail in having an independent team of observers admitted to Tibet. We demanded that our government send diplomatic representatives to Tibet to find out what is going on there. We called on the Chinese government to enter into dialogue with the Dalai Lama.

I believe this should be our highest priority. If the government in China now lifted martial law and set a date for negotiations, then it might be possible for them to free themselves from this *cul-de-sac*, from this self-inflicted isolation. We have also appealed to the British government and to all governments who are concerned about human rights to take up contact at once with the Dalai Lama and his staff. We wrote a letter to the foreign minister declaring that the time for silence is past. If the British government and other European governments, including that of the U.S., are prepared to speak with the PLO, why can they not speak with the Dalai Lama?

GEORGE FERNANDES

Tibet-India Solidarity

It is my conviction that India failed Tibet at a crucial moment in its history when, in the aftermath of Mao's revolution in China, it became obvious that the Chinese would move in to occupy Tibet. That failure—and I call it a grave mistake—has had disastrous consequences not only for the people of Tibet but also for the people of India. It brought the Chinese armies right on the doorstep of India for the first time ever, and we all know with what results.

What treachery, pusillanimity, naivete, or combination of the three preceded the betrayal of Tibet may never be known. In a letter to Prime Minister Nehru on November 7, 1950, after the Chinese army had overrun Tibet, Sardar Vallabhbhai Patel, then Deputy Prime Minister and Home Minister, observed: "The Chinese government has tried to delude us by professions of peaceful intentions. My own feeling is that at a crucial period they managed to instil into our Ambassador a false sense of confidence in their so-called desire to settle the Tibetan problem by peaceful means. There can be no doubt that during the period covered by this correspondence, the Chinese

This piece is adapted from Fernandes' presentation to the International Convention on Tibet and Peace in South Asia, August 1989.

must have been concentrating for an onslaught on Tibet. The final action of the Chinese, in my judgment, is little short of perfidy. The tragedy of it is that the Tibetans put faith in us; they chose to be guided by us; and we have been unable to get them out of the meshes of Chinese diplomacy or Chinese malevolence."

True, in the immediate aftermath of Chinese occupation of Tibet, Prime Minister Nehru declared in the Indian Parliament on December 7, 1950, that "Tibet is not the same as China. It should ultimately be the wishes of the people of Tibet that should prevail and not any legal or constitutional arguments." He then proceeded to assert, "According to the principles I uphold, the last voice in regard to Tibet should be the voice of the people of Tibet and of nobody else."

There is another very candid statement of Prime Minister Nehru on Tibet made only three days before his death which throws light on what influenced his decisions on Tibet. In a letter to the famous historian, Dr. Gopal Singh, written on May 24, 1964, from Dehra Dun where he was convalescing before the fatal stroke claimed his life on May 27, Nehru says: "It is not clear to me what we can do about Tibet in the present circumstances. To have a resolution in the United Nations about Tibet will not mean much as China is not represented there. *We are not indifferent to what has happened in Tibet.* But we are unable to do anything *effective* about it." (Emphasis added)

This four-sentence letter sums up everything. India acted with a sense of helplessness in formulating its policy on Tibet. There were other factors that influenced that policy. Yet, the belief that India was weak against a China that was perceived as strong clinched it. What Nehru forgot was by acquiescing to China's occupation of Tibet, he provided it with a legitimacy China has used as its card ever since. If in matters of personal relations between people, it is never too late to admit a mistake whenever it may have been committed, there is no reason why in a matter where the freedom of a whole nation is involved India should not have the courage to admit its mistake.

A weak attempt was made by India in 1965 to correct this mistake. Speaking in the United Nations General Assembly on a resolution on Tibet, the official Indian delegate dwelled on the sufferings of the Tibetan people and pointed out, "The naked truth—which all of us must face—is that the Chinese Government is determined to obliterate the Tibetan people." He then proceeded to support the urge for freedom of the Tibetans by declaring that "no people can remain for long suppressed," and said: "I have faith in the world community. I believe it will be able to help restore to the Tibetans all the freedom we have enshrined, with such dedication, in the Universal Declaration of Human Rights." Unfortunately, the faith and the belief were not taken to their logical end.

All the exercises in obfuscation on the part of China cannot hide certain historical facts about Tibet's independent status before the Chinese army marched in in 1950. First, the Communist revolution in China with all its triumph and tragedy of more than two decades including the Long March, which caught the imagination of the world, did not affect the people of Tibet. Second, it was only in January 1950 that Beijing claimed that Tibet was a part of the People's Republic of China and asked Lhasa to send a delegation to Beijing for negotiations. Third, when the Indian government asked for "moderation" by China in dealing with Tibet after announcing that India would not intervene militarily in Tibet, Beijing told India that negotiations would be carried to a peaceful settlement. Fourth, the Tibetan delegation did not go to Beijing. Instead, it came to Delhi in April, where, upon arrival, the leader of the delegation said, "We want to be left alone to pursue our own life." Fifth, during the summer, the Tibetan delegation and the Chinese Communists sounded each other, with India acting as an intermediary. Sixth, on October 23, it was announced from New Delhi that the Tibetan delegation was leaving India for the conference in Beijing. Seventh, on October 24, Radio Peking announced: "People's Army units have been ordered to advance into Tibet to free the three million Tibetans from imperialist aggression and to consolidate national defenses of the western borders of China."

This sequence of events states in loud and clear terms that Tibet was an independent country when the Chinese unleashed the might of the People's Liberation Army against it. In the face of these and other historic facts, for any power in the world to claim that Tibet was a part of China is to negate all known concepts of the nation-state and subscribe to the perverted ideas of imperialist hegemony of a big country over a small and helpless neighbor.

Tibet's independent status in modern history has a special relevance for India and her security. Its vast expanse—over 500,000 square miles which is a little less than half of India's 1,261,000 square miles—has been a perfect buffer between the three great Asian Powers—China, India and Soviet Russia. Even if the nuclear bomb and the Inter-continental Ballistic Missiles (ICBMs) had not given new meaning to the concept of buffer states, the very presence of Chinese ICBMs with nuclear warheads on the soil of Tibet is enough to prove that for India, Tibet still remains crucial to its defense and security.

Of all Indian leaders, it was the Socialist Dr. Rammanohar Lohia who first warned the country of the implications of Chinese occupation of Tibet. When in the immediate aftermath of the triumph of their revolution, the Chinese Communists marched their troops into Amdo in northeastern Tibet bordering on China and engaged a war-weary world and a newly-free India in a debate on the different meanings of sovereignty and suzerainty, it was Dr. Lohia who, at a press conference in London in 1949, held steadfast to his conviction that Tibet was an independent nation and that the government of India headed by Jawaharlal Nehru should have no reservations in saying so and in acting to uphold Tibet's independence. Prime Minister Nehru displayed both a lack of nerve and understanding of India's security interests by surrendering Tibet to China. What followed thereafter is one sordid chapter after another of China's arrogance and aggression, India's cowardice and surrender, and the resultant "baby murder" of the Tibetan people by China's Communist rulers in October 1950.

"Baby murder," in the literal sense, is what the Chinese have been up to in Tibet. The world has been flooded with eyewitness accounts of abortions, sterilizations, and infanticide by the Chinese in Tibet, even while there is a massive population transfer of the Chinese into Tibet. All this obviously is in pursuance of a policy to wipe out the Tibetan identity. The continuing attacks on the human rights of the Tibetans can have few parallels. If the People's Liberation Army can be ordered to massacre protesting Chinese students in Tiananmen

Square in Beijing with the whole world witnessing the incident, one can well imagine the atrocities the Tibetans have been subjected to in the four decades they have been under Chinese occupation.

There are many who believe that it is now too late in the day to speak about the freedom of Tibet. Such people belong to the category of those who have lost faith in themselves and have never understood the indomitable nature of the spirit of the human being. To them history is as static as the Himalayas appear to be, though over the ages, the Himalayas too have kept evolving and changing. To them the Tiananmen Square demonstrations are inconceivable and the ever-growing people's movements in the many republics of the Soviet Union for assertion of their independence are just not visible.

It is time to awaken the international conscience of all those who have come to accept the occupation of Tibet by China as an unalterable fact of history, particularly of the governments that believe that between the human rights of the Tibetan people and the possibilities and opportunities offered by a billion-person market, lucre has to take precedence. The wisdom and farsightedness of His Holiness the Dalai Lama has produced a Five-Point Peace Plan to find a solution to the Tibetan problem. These five points have received universal support from parliaments and parliamentarians. If Tibet should become a zone of peace and be free from Chinese troops and nuclear weapons, there would be no reason for India to maintain a large army on the Himalayan heights. This would immediately enable both India and China to reduce their military expenditure and use the money thus saved for economic development. When countries of Europe are reducing their troops and in the process their military expenditure, why should not India and China follow a similar course? A totally demilitarized Tibet and an India and China living in peace and friendship could trigger changes in South Asia that will end tensions in the region and pave the way for a better life for its people.

The Legal Status of Tibet

1. THE UNCLARIFIED QUESTION OF TIBET'S STATUS

Chancellor Kohl's visit to Tibet has again highlighted the problem of that country's integration into the Chinese state. Prior to his trip, Ms. Petra Kelly, Member of the Bundestag, submitted a written question to the Federal Government of Germany asking whether the Chancellor would raise with the Chinese government the matter of "Tibet's unclarified international status." The reply she received on July 8, 1987, was that "in the opinion of the Federal Government, and of the whole family of nations, Tibet is a part of the Chinese state within the meaning of international law."

Inquiries about this statement show that neither has the Federal Government looked into the problem of Tibet's integration nor can it invoke studies that confirm that such status is indeed valid under international law. For the period since 1950, it simply starts with that premise. This was also obvious from the government answer to a previous question on this subject.

This is a German Federal Government study, prepared on August 12, 1987, by West German Bundestag Reference and Research Services.

Since Chinese troops invaded Tibet in 1950, the problem of that country's international status has been left untouched. The nations of the world accept the *de facto* exercise of sovereignty by China. While not questioning China's claim, practically all of them have refrained from specifically recognizing Tibet as a part of China. But under international law, Tibet is only a part of the Chinese state if it had that status prior to the invasion or if China subsequently acquired a valid title to Tibetan territory.

2. TIBET'S INTERNATIONAL STATUS IN 1950

The crucial question, therefore, in assessing Tibet's present international status is whether it constituted an independent state prior to being occupied by China in 1950. In this context Tibet's previous history is of considerable significance.

After the religious kings of the seventh and eighth centuries had united the heathen Tibetan tribes into one state, the power relationship between Tibet and China underwent several changes. There were periods when Tibet was an independent state and others when it was under more or less lax Chinese suzerainty. When the Dzungars invaded Tibet in 1717, the Chinese emperor intervened at the request of the Tibetans, freed the Dalai Lama in 1720, and made a treaty with him that placed Tibet under the rule of the Manchu emperors. But Tibet retained such a large degree of autonomy that the Thirteenth Dalai Lama ignored the Anglo-Chinese treaty of commerce regarding his country, and not until 1904 was he forced, as the result of an armed British intervention, to grant Britain certain trading rights. The relationship between Tibet and China, which had been fairly good up to 1890, was disrupted by this development.

China continued to base its claim to suzerainty over Tibet on the Treaty of 1720. Tibet, however, argued that the treaty became null and void with the overthrow of the Manchu dynasty in 1911. It is not possible to assess the merits of each side's case because the text of the treaty is not available. To determine Tibet's status, however, such an assessment is not necessary since, after the Chinese revolution of 1911, but from the 1920s at the latest, Tibet had all the features of an independent state under international law. The International

Commission of Jurists spoke of a period of complete *de facto* independence from China.

In 1911 the Tibetans drove out the Chinese garrisons that had been installed in 1910, and at the beginning of 1912 the Thirteenth Dalai Lama proclaimed his country's independence. Although other countries did not formally recognize Tibet's independence, there existed, according to the Commission of Jurists, no legal obstacles to such recognition. At any rate, a state's existence does not depend on its formal recognition by others. According to more recent opinion, such formal recognition has only declaratory value. The main point is that Tibet enjoyed *de facto* recognition. From 1912 Great Britain, the dominant power in that region at the time, treated Tibet as an independent state. In 1943 Tibet became more active in the field of foreign policy and set up its own office for external affairs. Tibetan passports were recognized as valid travel documents.

In July 1949, following the defeat of the Kuomintang Government, the Tibetan Government instructed all Chinese representatives to leave the country in order to make clear that China had no right of suzerainty in Tibet. This act would have severed, with validity under international law, all contractual ties restricting her independence—if such ties had still existed. According to the rules of *clausula sic stantibus*, she was entitled to do so, for a contractual basis ceases to exist in the event of a fundamental change of circumstances that was not foreseeable at the time the treaty was concluded. Such change of circumstances had taken place on each of the occasions when a Chinese Revolutionary Government assumed power (1911 and 1949).

In view of China's claims and her growing strength, Tibet's delay in establishing diplomatic relations and seeking membership of the United Nations was a political error.

3. ACQUISITION OF SOVEREIGN TERRITORY NULL AND VOID

On October 7, 1950, the People's Republic of China, following negotiations with a Tibetan delegation, annexed Tibet by force of arms.[1] But China has not acquired any internationally valid title to Tibetan territory. Her action did not satisfy the requirements for such title under international law.

3.1 ANNEXATION

Under international law, the integration of Tibet into the Chinese state in 1951 was tantamount to annexation. True, relations between the two countries were determined by the treaty of May 25, 1951, which accorded Tibet a certain degree of autonomy whereas China acquired sovereign rights with regard to defense and external affairs, but that treaty merely veiled the unilateral nature of Tibet's annexation. It was the outcome of Tibet's military defeat and was concluded against her will. According to Article 52 of the Vienna Convention on the Law of Treaties, a treaty concluded under duress which confirms a country's occupation is void. Moreover, many of the guarantees given to Tibet were violated by China. Through her "return to the big family of the motherland," in the words of the 1951 treaty, Tibet lost her independence.

The proclamation of Tibet's independence by the Dalai Lama's government on March 11, 1959, and the Dalai Lama's own public repudiation of the treaty with China on June 20, 1959, are proof that Tibet had yielded under the pressure of invasion.

The annexation of Tibet was completed when China, following the suppression of a revolt and the flight of the Fourteenth Dalai Lama in March 1959, dissolved the Tibetan Government and placed the country under China's direct administration, thus depriving Tibet of the remnants of her autonomy. The fact that the Dalai Lama was not formally deposed is immaterial. Under current international law, annexation does not establish any sovereign rights. Under classical international law, the freedom of annexation was derived from the right to wage war. In the meantime that right to wage war has been superseded by the ban on the use of force (Article 2 (4), UN Charter). Thus the freedom of annexation, too, was transformed into a ban on annexation. Even before the United Nations Charter came into effect, it was generally recognized that any annexation of territory, or of a totally occupied country, during war is without validity in international law. The ban on the use of force merely endorsed the legal situation.

In the light of the annexation ban, therefore, China exercises *de facto* sovereignty over Tibet without any valid title in law.

3.2 INTERNATIONAL RECOGNITION

Some authors regard international recognition as a means of removing the contradiction between *de facto* annexation and its *de jure* invalidity. Recognition is a declaration of intent on the part of the organs of a state by which a disputed fact or vague legal position is, in a certain sense, held to exist or to be legitimate. It is bound up in the discrepancy between *de facto* possession and legitimate possession. Its legal significance is contentious. As the question of recognition is governed by political considerations, it is hardly possible to draw up general rules. There are also other reasons why China cannot derive any right to territorial sovereignty from international recognition.[2]

The Stimson Doctrine of non-recognition of forceful changes in territory applies to Tibet. The object of that doctrine, as of the ban on the use of force, is to ensure that territorial changes that oppose that doctrine and therefore have no validity in international law do not ultimately acquire legitimacy through the consolidating effect of recognition by third states. In view of the many contractual and other endorsements of the Stimson Doctrine,[3] it can today be assumed that a rule of international customary law proscribing recognition of territorial changes brought about by force is at least emerging.

Not even outwardly does China's acquisition of Tibet fulfill the prerequisites for legitimacy. The members of the community of nations, in particular the Federal Republic of Germany, do assume that Tibet is a part of China, but few have specifically said so. A declaration to this effect was made by China on April 29, 1954, and by Nepal on September 20, 1956.

The fact that the annexation of Tibet is merely not disputed does not signify recognition of a *de facto* situation under international law. In this connection it is important to note that the annexations ban and the Stimson Doctrine prohibiting recognition of forceful changes of territory, both of which have been endorsed by the United Nations, preclude China's acquisition of sovereign title through explicit recognition.

Recognition may also be tacitly inferred from implied acts. Events in connection with Chancellor Kohl's trip to Tibet may possibly fall into this category, but here, too, there is insufficient substantive evidence.

3.3 USUCAPION

Under international law, territory may also be acquired by usucapion: "The continuous and peaceful display of territorial sovereignty is as good as title."[4] This applies where such sovereignty is effectively exercised and is not interrupted or challenged. The time that has to lapse before usucapion can be deemed effective depends on the circumstances of the case in question.

It is immaterial whether title to a whole state can be acquired by usucapion. This question does not arise in the case of Tibet if only because territories that have been occupied in contravention of international law and in violation of the principles enshrined in the United Nations Charter may not be acquired by usucapion. Such acquisition would contravene this fundamental principle, as reflected in the ban on the annexation of territory, in the Stimson Doctrine based on it, and in the nullity of a state's forced acquiescence in annexations expressed in Article 52 of the Vienna Convention on the Law of Treaties. Such grave violations of international law cannot be made good simply by lapse of time. Hence annexations of conquered territories can never as such constitute the acquisition of sovereign title. The exercise of sovereign rights over a territory cannot establish any title that is not founded in international law.

4. SUMMARY

The community of nations assumes that Tibet is a part of the Chinese state, but Tibet's status has not been clarified.

At the time Tibet was forcefully annexed by China, it was an independent state.

China has not acquired any effective title to sovereign rights over Tibet because such status is incompatible with the fundamental principle of the illegitimacy of annexation deriving from the ban on the use of force. The exercise of sovereign rights over a territory cannot establish any title that is not founded in international law.

1. On November 7, 1950, the Tibetan government appealed to the United Nations, protesting Tibet's [lack of] independence and accusing China of aggression. It also appealed to the Security Council. El Salvador proposed a debate on Tibet in the General Assembly. On a recommendation by Great Britain, supported by India, the matter was postponed indefinitely. (Cf. *International Commission of Jurists: Tibet and the People's Republic of China*, Geneva 1960, p. 161. A detailed account is given by Chanakya Se, *Tibet Disappears*, Bombay 1960, p. 65 *et seq*. - M 505 145). Tibet thus asserted her independence from China before the family of nations and was accepted by China as an autonomous state.

2. Cf. Otto Kimminich, *Einführung in das volkerrecth*, Pullach nr. Munich 1975, p. 99.

3. Cf. Resolution adopted by Assembly of the League of Nations on March 11, 1932, Resolution 2625 (XXV) adopted by the UN General Assembly on October 24, 1970. Article 5 of the third resolution 3314 (XXIX) adopted by the UN. General Assembly on December 14, 1974.

4. Decision on the Palmas case, VN-RIAA, Vol. 2, p. 839.

Human Rights in Tibet: 1950-1991

Left: Lobsang Jinpa, winner of the 1988 Reebok Human Rights Award, speaking at the Bonn Hearing. *Below:* Mrs. Adhi (a Tibetan woman incarcerated by the Chinese) and Michele Bohana (Director for Human Rights at International Campaign for Tibet) listen to testimony at the Bonn Hearing.

photos by Moni Kellermann

MICHELE BOHANA

U.S. Foreign Policy and the Violation of Tibet

I want to thank you for giving me the opportunity to testify today. I would also like to thank the members of the committee for supporting the Tibetan cause and trying, through the legislative process and hearings, to give some sort of redress to the Tibetan people who have suffered under Chinese occupied rule for forty years. In particular, the Campaign wishes to thank Chairman Pell, Senator Helms, and the other Senators of the committee for their assistance in helping to authorize Tibetan-language Voice of America broadcasts as well as fifteen Fulbright scholarships for Tibetan refugees residing in India and Nepal. It cannot be overestimated how valuable a contribution this is for those Tibetans living in Tibet and in exile.

As you know, in 1949 and 1950, at the outset of the Korean War and while America's interest in China lay elsewhere, the Chinese People's Liberation Army marched into Tibet. Tibet has essentially been under military occupation ever since. It can be said that for the

This is a transcript of Bohana's address to the U.S. Senate Foreign Relations Committee, June 6, 1990.

Tibetan people it has been decades—*not eighteen months*—of martial law and colonial rule.

The salient features of colonial domination exist with respect to China's presence in Tibet: forcible occupation of Tibetan territory; the use of armed force to crush resistance to its rule; discrimination against Tibetans based on racial, ethnic, linguistic, and cultural differences; deprivation of human rights including freedom of movement, freedom of speech, freedom of assembly, freedom from arbitrary arrest, due process, and freedom of religion; exploitation of the natural resources of Tibet; colonial administration of the occupied territory, utilizing Tibetans in largely nominal positions; and unmistakable differences in living standards between the colonizers (the Chinese) and the colonized (the Tibetans). The large scale population transfer of Chinese into Tibet, a policy by which China hopes to reduce Tibetans into an insignificant minority in their own country, is colonialism in its worst form.

In addition to the aforementioned human and civil rights, I would stress the political right to participate in one's own government. This is the freedom Tibetans want more than any other. It is the same freedom that has dramatically altered today's geopolitical world, the same freedom that the countries and peoples of Eastern Europe, Southern Africa, the Baltic States and even the Soviet Union's first colony, Mongolia, yearn for. And it is this freedom that is the stumbling block for the Administration.

I find it baffling that the foundations of this nation, the foundation from which this country draws its strength and legitimacy as leader of the free world, can be overshadowed by the sensibilities of a ruthless government. In October 1982, Alexander Solzhenitsyn described the Communist Chinese regime in Tibet as "more brutal and inhuman than any other communist regime in the world."

Why does the Administration believe that the lifting of martial law in Lhasa is a responsive move towards U.S. concern for human rights? Lifting martial law while over 300,000 troops remain stationed in Tibet doesn't stop arrests and torture.

On May 23, the day before President Bush waived Most Favored Nation for the People's Republic of China, granting China preferential trade status, my office received word that two Tibetans were sentenced to death and executed in Lhasa on May 17 for "organizing a prison escape scheme in a planned way." The news of the executions was given on Lhasa TV on Friday, May 18, according to the Monitoring Service of the BBC. The sentences, according to Amnesty International, were announced at a rally held by the Lhasa Intermediate People's Court within the prison compound, apparently in the presence of other prisoners. At the same time, Dhundup Tsering was sentenced to death with a two-year stay of execution. A fourth prisoner, Tashi, was sentenced to nine years' imprisonment and a further three years' deprivation of his political rights.

The Chinese authorities chose to execute these two Tibetans immediately after sentencing and *while* the U.S. Congress, the Administration, and human rights organizations were debating the whole MFN question.

The ending of martial law in Lhasa means that soldiers on the streets will be replaced by armed police known in Chinese as the Wu Jing, a paramilitary force feared for their lack of discipline and restraint. Though martial law was lifted on April 30, many of the provisions denoted in the six martial law decrees remain in effect [See Appendix V]. These include the issuing of identity cards and restrictions on access to the city for Tibetans from other parts of the country.

Two weeks before martial law was lifted, in a clear attempt to avoid unrest, the authorities expelled a number of politically active monks from the major monasteries around Lhasa. The Tibet Information Network, a London-based independent monitoring organization, reported that eyewitness accounts stated that on April 16, thirty-seven monks from Drepung Monastery and eighteen monks from Ganden Monastery were expelled from their monasteries and ordered to return to their home villages.

A number of other events took place that have not received attention:

> On April 28, police paraded forty-three "criminals" in the main street of Lhasa and promised "stern actions...if anyone claimed ignorance."

On *April* 30, a six-point decree announced that the police would "resolutely crackdown on activities that oppose the socialist system." Later that night a senior official announced on television that the organizations of the people must "deal with enemies of the people...with the iron fist of the people's democratic dictatorship."

On *May* 7, the deputy secretary of the Government announced that all foreign visitors would have to apply in advance to the Lhasa government for permission to enter.

On *May* 10, the head of China's Armed Police Force announced that his troops in Tibet would be issued with "the finest riot control equipment."

On *May* 19, one hundred soldiers of the PLA were sent to do unspecified "repairs" to the Potala Palace, furthering long-standing Tibetan fears that unknown damage is being done to their most famous building.

On *May* 20, Xinhua announced that another 1,500 Tibetan school children will be sent to spend their entire secondary school careers in China, hundreds of miles from family and home.

On *May* 23, a new twenty-five clause law was passed in Lhasa prohibiting "any religious or other activities that will endanger the state's unification or destroy...social stability."

These events are not acts of individual officials or rushed responses to a crisis situation. It is important to emphasize that they are all *acts of policy*, the considered decisions of the Central Chinese authorities. The unifying factor of all is the desire to stifle criticism of the Chinese Government and of the Chinese presence in Tibet.

Tibetan Buddhism is the cornerstone of Tibet's unique cultural heritage. Whatever slight improvements that have been gained concerning religious freedom in Tibet since the dark days of the Cultural Revolution are marred when viewed in the context of Chinese motive—to bring in hard currency in the form of tourist dollars—and the treatment generally reserved for monks and nuns who display allegiance to His Holiness the Dalai Lama and/or affiliation with Tibet's independent cause.

There is a new wave of religious persecution sweeping Tibet today, the likes of which has not been seen since the Cultural Revolution when the Chinese tried to literally wipe out all vestiges of Tibetan Buddhism. It is the monks and nuns, who fully embody the Dalai Lama's peaceful, nonviolent approach, who are bearing much of the brunt of the current repression.

The governance of religion in Tibet is similar to other aspects of Tibetan life in that Tibetans have no real power to control their affairs. Religion is being administered by secular, security-oriented officials who are answerable to Beijing. Our study documents how many local officials who are in charge of monasteries are the same officials who oversaw the destruction of those very same monasteries in the Cultural Revolution.

The Chinese claim that they are protecting religion and subsidizing religion by helping to rebuild monasteries. We found that wherever there is Chinese assistance there are many more government controls and political restrictions. It is only in areas where there are few Chinese settlers and administrators that any genuine religious revival is taking place.

The violations perpetrated upon the Tibetans, for decades before the Tiananmen massacre—and since, take various shapes. In our estimation, the most dangerous and insidious may well be termed China's "final solution" for the Tibetan nation. China has imposed a policy of population transfer in Tibet whereby large influxes of Chinese are settling on the Tibetan plateau. Tibetans, though occupied, refuse to be conquered and subjugated. However, by changing the very character and national identity of Tibet and its people through a combination of demographic change and discrimination, Tibet is being destroyed.

On April 2, 1990, *China Daily* published an article which described the functions of an office in Chengdu as "a major transfer post for personnel and freight leaving and entering Tibet." The article reported that the office now handles about 2,000 people each day, in contrast to 278 when it first opened in 1964. This would total, by our estimation, 200,000 Chinese civilians entering Tibet each year.

The influx into Tibet appears to be motivated by a Chinese government policy aimed at reducing Tibetans into a powerless minority in their own country. This strategy proved to be successful in inner Mongolia and Xinjiang (East Turkestan) where the Mongols and Turkish peoples, respectively are outnumbered and, as a result, their culture decimated.

The policy gravely endangers what is left of historical Tibet. If allowed to continue unabated, it will make all other violations pale by comparison. It is for this reason that the Dalai Lama during his last visit to Washington in 1987, when outlining his peace plan, called for the "abandonment of China's population transfer policy which threatens the very existence of the Tibetans as a people."

Racial discrimination has always characterized the Chinese administration of Tibet and has been made worse by the large number of Chinese settlers. A typical example of how the Chinese view the Tibetans was published in the official magazine, *Peking Economic Research Journal*, as stating: "They (Tibetans) lack the capacity to absorb advanced technology and are highly imbued with a character of laziness." The patterns of discrimination have been documented in a written statement by the Minority Rights Group. Their statement was submitted, last January, to the United Nations Human Rights Commission's Forty-sixth Session. Briefly, the discrimination policies outlined to the Commission covered housing, freedom of movement, education, employment, economic development, health care, and the role of official authorities.

With all business being conducted in Chinese, the usefulness of Tibetan language is almost obsolete. Education for Tibetans is principally conducted in Chinese, particularly at high school, college. and graduate levels. Tibetans who do get an education find themselves learning Tibetan as a *second* language.

The health care system primarily serves the Chinese. Of course, the disturbing reports of forced sterilizations and abortions have been widely circulated. As recently as April 20, 1990, the local radio service in Qinghai (formerly Amdo) announced that 87,000 women had been sterilized in the province by the end of last year. In an article that purported to justify population control the *China Population News* reported on December 22, 1989, that "...some of our comrades do not understand that to justify lenient policies (for the minorities) is untenable...human reproduction comprises not only quantitative but qualitative changes in the population. In the minority areas the cultural quality of the population is quite backward, the quality is stagnant...there must not be a reason for relaxing family planning."

We are also very concerned about reports that Tibetans were refused treatment—as a result of wounds sustained during the violent crackdown last March—by Chinese health care workers. The Physicians for Human Rights issued a well-documented report which detailed horrendous and systematic use of torture against Tibetan prisoners.

With respect to housing, racial discrimination is evidenced by segregated housing between Tibetans and Chinese. Tibetan ghettos are common. Now reports are being received from Lhasa that exacerbate the tension between Tibetans and Chinese over housing. Chinese authorities under an "urban renewal plan" are demolishing part of the historic Tibetan quarter of Lhasa. We fear this is designed to provide better access for police and troops. This brings to mind the terror and methods of China's ally, Nicolae Ceausescu. The Tibetan part of the city has now dwindled in size to about 2% of the total area of the town.

The issue of forced labor, or reform through labor, goes to the heart of the Tibetan problem because such a high proportion of Tibetans have suffered and continue to suffer in these camps. Amdo, the birthplace of the Dalai Lama, is oftentimes called the world's largest gulag. Working for the state in order to reform your political, cultural, or religious beliefs cannot be anything less than tortuous, humiliating, and psychologically degrading. These camps, located in historical Tibet have been part of the Chinese Communist system from the outset. They did not go away at the end of the Cultural Revolution. Rather, they continue to thrive today.

How can we offer preferential treatment to a country that seals off vast territorial areas, refuses access to such areas, and makes it legal to do so under their law? Under Chinese law, police have the authority to send people accused of disturbing the peace, "fabricating rumors," hindering government officials, and other offenses to forced labor camps *without* a court ruling. Didn't the leaders in Beijing refer to those Chinese who demonstrated in Beijing accordingly? When we hear news that Tibetans have been taken from their homes and "disappear," the first thing that comes to mind is they have been relocated to a forced labor camp.

Social control in China includes the use of identity cards, the work unit system, the use of political indoctrination, and restrictions on movement. In Tibet's case these controls are more restrictive, more active, and more aggressively enforced. They are also entirely different from those applied in China—they are applied by a foreign civilian administration and enforced by a foreign military power. They therefore resemble not so much the experience of the Soviet Union under Krushchev, but of France under the Germans.

China's handling of Tibet over the last four decades provides a real litmus test of China's human rights policy. A U.S. foreign policy that ignores or minimizes the Tibetan issue is miscast and misrepresentative of American values. I've spoken with Tibetans living in the U.S. and India and without exception they support suspending China's Most Favored Nation status.

We call for the Congress to suspend MFN and overturn the President's waiver. Emigration from Tibet is either impossible or extraordinarily difficult, but moreover the atrocious human rights record justifies suspension. Similarly, the great risks that Tibetans are willing to take in leaving Tibet illegally evidences that these Tibetans believe their application to the Chinese authorities for legal emigration would be useless and, possibly, deadly. Tibetans are willing to risk life and limb to leave Tibet. Reason suggests that they would not do so illegally if there were an easier, legal route out of the country or if conditions were such that they could remain in their homeland.

It is time for Congress to lead on the issue of U.S.-China policy, to take the same kind of clear and resolute stand when the Jackson-Vanik amendment was passed in 1974 and to show, beyond a doubt, not *just sympathy but support* for the Tibetan and Chinese people, whose suffering by the hands of Beijing's leadership is incalculable.

The President, on May 24, did not grant MFN with conditions. The International Campaign for Tibet supports the revocation of MFN status to the People's Republic of China based on their emigration policies, human rights record, and use of forced labor in Tibet and China. Most Favored Nation status will assist the PRC to maintain their costly and large population of military and security personnel in Tibet. Moreover, extending MFN will further entrench the hard-liners in Beijing who are imposing policies that systematically violate the fundamental human rights of the Tibetan people.

We should not forget the horrific events of last June. We should not allow the emotions felt by the American people when seeing a burgeoning democracy movement crushed by the hard line policy of Beijing's leadership become little more than a memory. Moreover, we should not forget the million plus Tibetans who have died as a direct result of China's occupation of Tibet.

After the recent summit with Mikhail Gorbachev, the President stated, when asked about Lithuanian independence, that he hasn't "lessened my view as to people's aspirations for self-determination. And I feel strongly about that. That's a hallmark of American belief and policy. And I haven't changed one bit on that."

I agree with the President, though his statement begs the question: what is the difference between Lithuania and Tibet? Tibetans have died because they held the Tibetan flag. They have been tortured because they refuse to be subjugated by foreign domination. They have held fast to their cultural heritage, religious beliefs, and national identity against indomitable odds. They refuse, categorically, to denounce their beloved leader, the Nobel Peace Laureate, the Dalai Lama. And, it is their hope that some day the U.S. government will respond to *their* aspirations for self-determination, human rights, and democratic freedoms.

PEMA DECHEN

The Oppression and Resistance of Tibetan Women

In the name of the silenced women of Tibet and of their sisters in exile, I wish to speak today about Tibetan women's experiences. Most of you know, I think, that 1,200,000 of us Tibetans have died since 1949 under Chinese occupation. Although fewer women than men are among those dead, for every man who has died in prison, in workcamps, or in battle against the Chinese, there are many women who have grieved: widows, mothers, sisters, and daughters who have waited in vain for news of their men. They have had to live on without hope. Our women have always been strong and courageous. Many believe that we are the most fully-emancipated women in Asia. Since most Tibetans have been farmers and herdsmen, we have worked with our men in the fields and tended the flocks as they did, so that there has hardly been a difference between the work of men and women. We have borne our burdens in common, cheerfully and untroubled. Every task was accompanied with a song. In cities and towns women conducted trade, and many women could assume the

---

This piece is adapted from Dechen's presentation at the Bonn Hearings, April 1989.

work of their husbands when the men were away. We are proud of our 2,500-year history, and we see ourselves as the protectors and custo-dians of our precious religion. Tibetan Buddhist teachings have encouraged us to live selflessly, cheerfully, content, without striving after material gain, and to live companionably with all beings and put the interests of others above our own. But, sadly, the Chinese rule over our homeland has made something quite different out of our peaceful world. Chinese rule has turned that world upside down. The beginnings of this go back to the 1950s, when the Chinese Communists taught our children to despise their parents.

The Chinese were intent on making religion seem laughable, and many children were sent to China to become good Communists with Chinese hearts and Chinese souls. Influential women were compelled to disseminate Chinese propaganda among their less well-educated sisters. But where it was possible, they continued to show resistance. In March of 1959, Lhasa rose in rebellion against the Chinese, and there were some intrepid women who stood on March 12 before the palace of His Holiness the Dalai Lama and cried, "Tibet belongs to Tibetans! Out with the Chinese!" And today they still cry these words at demonstrations in exile, thirty years later. Two of the most fearless women leaders, Galingshar Ani and Kunling Kunsang, were impris-oned, brutally tortured, and ultimately killed. Every year we hold vigils in memory of the Women's Demonstration of 1959. During the dark years of the occupation, the women of Tibet struggled coura-geously against the Chinese, without a thought for their own lives. In the late 1960s, during the nightmare of the Cultural Revolution, when Tibetan men were rounded up into prisons and our monasteries were destroyed, the resistance movement was headed by Nemo Ani. She had to suffer the same fate. Today women are again especially active in the demonstrations. I am sure you have read about the nuns who have been leading demonstrations in Lhasa and proclaiming anti-Chinese slogans.

Their courage is a lesson for us all, but the question is how long we can continue to hold out. Can we survive as a distinct race under a Chinese policy of Sinification which aims to make us a minority in our own country? How can we offer resistance to genocide? Women of every age are being sterilized. Abortions are the rule for women who try to have more than one child, although government policy maintains that Tibetan women may have two children. Since 1987, the one-child-per-family law has been forced upon Tibet also. We have eyewitnesses to testify that fetuses were thrown out in bucketfuls, like garbage. Mrs. Namgyal Lhamo, who came to India in 1988, told me her story about abortions: In June of 1988, she entered the People's Hospital in Lhasa with a friend. Her friend was pregnant, and experiencing pain. The doctors said that the child was positioned badly, and that the mother would have to undergo an operation. But she waited till that evening, and when the pain lessened, she returned home and gave birth to a healthy child without complications. In the ward with her had been seven other Tibetan women in advanced pregnancy, and of them only one was able to bring home her child. The others were all informed that their babies had been stillborn. On the same day, Mrs. Namgyal Lhamo found out about a Chinese woman who had had a miscarriage and had been given one of the Tibetan women's babies.

It is also part of this policy that women with only one child receive economic benefits. For us Buddhists, life is intrinsically valuable. We have never hindered life, and Tibet never had an overpopulation problem until the Chinese began to immigrate and occupy our best plots of land. We hear that healthy children receive injections and subsequently die. In many regions of Tibet it is the law that all mentally and physically handicapped women must be sterilized. I believe you can understand what it means when the Chinese maintain that this law serves the improvement of quality of life. In reality the Chinese are attempting to exterminate the Tibetan people.

Those of us in exile also have experienced restrictions and poor treatment as refugees, but compared with our brothers and sisters in Tibet, things are going much better for us and our children. We receive assistance from abroad, and freedom of opinion, speech, and religion prevail. For these reasons, the responsibility also lies with us to speak out on behalf of our brothers and sisters in Tibet, and to act as the custodians of our culture and tradition. We raise our children in a way that will make them proud of their heritage, and even the youngest know that Tibet is *their* country. All of our children dream of returning to their country.

It is also the task of the Tibetan women's coalition to protect and further nunneries, which are especially in peril today. Since our women have traditionally been very self-reliant, it is not surprising that they have taken important positions in the exile administration as well. Many women are doctors, nurses, teachers, social workers, administrators, and performing artists. But irrespective of our occupations, we all hope passionately that we will one day be able to return to a free Tibet—that we may heal the wounds the Chinese have dealt us.

BLAKE KERR

Tibetans Under the Knife

China's birth control policy can be difficult to ascertain from the literature. The People's Republic of China does not always publish its birth control directives. And statements to Western journalists that laud China's success with population control often conflict with eyewitness accounts of coerced abortion, sterilization, infanticide, and mass sterilization. Nevertheless, a discussion of China's birth control policy in Tibet must be predicated upon some understanding of China's birth control policy in China. With the founding of the People's Republic of China in 1949, Mao espoused the Marxist philosophy that valued a large and growing population. Contraceptives were banned.[4]

In 1953, China's first census put its population at 600 million. By 1956, continued shortages of grain and a steadily growing population prompted the Ministry of Public Health to require local health

This piece is an updated version of testimony presented to hearings at the German Parliament and to the U.S. Congressional Subcommittee on Foreign Operations in April 1989.[1] The author's experiences in Tibet, and subsequent interviews with Tibetan refugees in northern India, form the basis for the conclusions in this article, which includes eight first-hand accounts by Tibetan women who stated that they were coerced to have an abortion and/or sterilization. Excerpts from previous interviews have been published in the *Washington Post* [2] and the *New York Times*.[3]

agencies to actively promote birth control.[5] Although the national and the local authorities insisted that coercive tactics would not be tolerated,[6] "the pressure on the local cadres (work units) to achieve immediate results...induced the cadres to force the masses to conform—as had happened during land reform, collectivization, and other mass campaigns."[7]

During the Great Leap Forward in 1958, proponents of birth control were denounced as rightists and purged. While statistical fabrications led to a doubling of the grain production,[8] food shortages, and widespread famine resulted in an estimated thirty million deaths.[9] Thus the early 1960s saw the re-introduction of local birth control "guidance committees." Local officials were expected to follow a series of new rules: practicing birth control, not having more than two children (a third child was permissible under special circumstances), and waiting three to five years between children.[10]

A peak in the national birth rate in 1963 reflects the effectiveness of China's birth control policies in urban areas, especially when one considers that 80% of China's population is rural.[11] By 1964, the PRC had established a national family planning office.[12] Besides the better organization and new rules, several new contraceptive techniques made the second birth control campaign more effective than the first: the introduction of the IUD, the implementation of abortion by suction (as opposed to D&C), and the promotion of vasectomies. China's birth control policy again fell into disarray with the advent of the Cultural Revolution in 1966. After the failures of the Great Leap Forward, Mao's revolutionary guards purged his enemies. By 1969, when the military regained control of the country, another birth control campaign began.

Under Zhou Enlai's direction, the State Council instituted a two-child limit, instead of the previous three-child limit, and renewed China's national birth control policy with vigor.[13] National statistics report that IUD insertions rose from six million in 1971 to fourteen million in 1973 and seventeen million in 1975. Although the PRC denied that coercive tactics were employed to set nationally established birth rates, it is evident that these birth rates could not be met voluntarily.[14] While China's population increase rate declined from 2.3% in 1971 to 1.2% in 1978, mass sterilizations were emphasized.[15]

In 1979, the PRC instituted its one-child policy for Han couples, whereas minorities and people living in frontier areas could have two children.[16] At this time, severe economic sanctions for an extra child were passed in twenty-seven of twenty-nine provinces to enforce the one-child policy,[17] in addition to emphasizing mandatory abortions for unauthorized pregnancies.[18]

In response to a wave of popular discontent with China's coercive tactics, as evidenced by reports of the sabotaging of family planning cadres' persons, crops, homes, and belongings,[19] the PRC instituted its second "anti-coercion" campaign in 1980.[20] However, relaxing the marriage age[21] resulted in a "tidal wave" of marriages, followed by an increase in first births.[22] Once again, fearing a population explosion, the central authorities renewed their coercive campaign to increase adherence to the one-child policy.[23]

To enforce its one-child policy, the central authorities promoted the "mobilization" of couples with two children for sterilization.[24] Official statistics confirm that three times as many sterilizations (20.8 million) were performed in 1983 as in 1979, the previous peak year, and that 80% of the sterilizations (tubal ligations) were performed on women.[25] In 1984, the *Wall Street Journal* had an editorial that stated that the evidence that China's birth control policy included forced abortions and sterilizations was overwhelming.[26]

While studying in Canada, a Chinese physician, Dr. Bao Fu, published an article in the *China Spring Digest*, "Massacre of the Innocents."[27] The article describes how infanticide is practiced throughout mainland China. The most common method of infanticide is injecting ethanol into the infant's brain through the fontanel as the baby's head appears in the birth canal. According to Dr. Fu, the family planning officials visit the homes of babies born without birth permits and kill the infants. Physicians who refuse to perform infanticide face demotion, fines, and the loss of their jobs.

China's population statistics indicate that the national birth rate began to level off in 1987[28] and decline by 1988.[29] At the same time, the State Family Planning Commission stated that both IUD insertions and sterilizations in 1987 surpassed those in 1986 by at least 40%.[30]

In 1988, despite China's efforts to "educate" the masses to accept its one-child policy, the State Family Planning Commission noted that 72% of urban couples and 90% of rural couples wanted more than one child.[31] Thus it is not surprising that since then there has been a resurgence of articles promoting coerced abortions and sterilization. Individuals must sign contracts with their cadre leaders stating that they will abide by the birth control policy, and local cadre leaders are encouraged to use coercive means to attain family planning targets.[32]

BIRTH CONTROL POLICY IN TIBET

The interviewees unequivocally stated that Tibetan women who lived in cities, where there were likely to be a preponderance of Chinese immigrants, faced the most pressure to conform to China's birth control policy, while Tibetans who lived in small villages and remote nomad areas faced the least pressure. Mobile birth control teams that travel to remote areas in Amdo bear a possible exception to this and are discussed under Mass Sterilization.

In cities, Tibetan women can have two children, while Han women can have only one child. If a Tibetan woman or her husband works in a Chinese cadre, she would have to wait from three to five years before becoming pregnant with her second child. Women who become pregnant outside of these parameters must have an abortion and/or be sterilized or face severe social and economic sanctions.

Dolma, a woman in Lhasa who worked in a Chinese bookshop, explained how not waiting for three years between her first and second pregnancy led to her having two abortions:

> My work unit leader knew that I was pregnant. I went to the People's Hospital, where a doctor gave me an injection in the buttocks twice a day for three days with no result. The doctor said the injection would prevent the formation of the baby. After three days with no result, the doctor told me to return to the hospital in three weeks when the baby was larger. Then I had suction. A tube inserted into my vagina sucked the baby out. This took eight to nine minutes. Both Tibetan and Chinese doctors did this. I was not given anything for pain or medicines of any kind.

> I became pregnant again two years later in 1987. I wrote an application to the work unit leader for an extra child, which was refused. The leader said that if I wanted to have an extra child, I had to wait for three

years. My first child was two years old. So once more, I went to the People's Hospital to have an abortion. I was forty-five days pregnant. The abortion was performed by suction. I had no injection first to induce abortion. The procedure took twenty to twenty-five minutes. I was given no medications of any kind.

The economic fines for couples with extra children were most severe for Tibetans where either one or both parents worked in a Chinese cadre. For these Tibetans, economic sanctions included permanent demotions or the loss of employment, reduction in salary, and fines from 500 to 3,000 yuan (a Tibetan working in a Chinese cadre could make 1,700 yuan per year). For Tibetan farmers who had extra children, fines included having to sell possessions to pay fines ranging from 300 to 5,000 yuan (a Tibetan farmer could make 3,000 yuan a year). Farmers who could not pay the fine would lose part of their land. Nomads who could not pay even a small fee would have to sell their animals or possessions or have them confiscated.

Fines imposed on additional children are more severe than those imposed on the parents. Illegal children are denied legal papers that give them the right to exist, attend school, own property, travel, participate in organized work, or obtain a ration card. A ration card entitles a child to receive monthly allotments of the Tibetan dietary staples at government stores (barley flour and butter). Thousands of children without legal papers or ration cards are said to live in villages. Their economic and social exile may be producing a growing generation of "illegal" children committed to a lifetime of menial jobs such as collecting refuse or dung.

Two types of birth control teams operate in Tibet. Birth control units in Chinese (not Tibetan) hospitals implement birth control policy for Tibetans living near a hospital. Mobile birth control teams implement birth control policy for Tibetans living in small villages and nomadic areas. Both teams were noted to have a monetary incentive to do abortions and sterilizations on as many women as possible. The more names the doctors collect, the more money they get from their government and from women who may be charged for the operation.

ABORTION

A forty-year old woman who stated that she escaped from Lhasa while she was seven months pregnant illustrates the Tibetan fear of being pregnant with an "extra" child. Yangzum had three children when she became pregnant for the fourth time:

Women who are pregnant with extra children are taken to the hospital by the police, if necessary, and forced to have an injection to kill the baby and have it come out. Sometimes women are sterilized after the abortion.

> The Chinese wanted to force me to have an injection to kill my baby when I was five and a half months pregnant. I went to the Military Hospital (near Sera Monastery) to see if I was pregnant. Both the nurse and a Tibetan doctor told me to have an abortion. I refused. The hospital does not have the authority to force me. I went home, then escaped to India to avoid persecution. The Chinese doctors told the police to bring me back, and they would have. This is why I escaped.

Yangzum's case brings up an inconsistency in China's two-child policy for Tibetans. When asked why Yangzum did not have to pay a fine for her third child, she stated that she delivered her first two children in a small village. Her third child was her first child in Lhasa, so she did not have to pay a fine.

A Tibetan policeman from Lhasa denied Yangzum's assertion that the police in Lhasa take women pregnant with extra children to hospitals for abortions and/or sterilizations. Although the policeman stated that Tibetan doctors may automatically perform abortions and sterilizations on pregnant Tibetan women in Chinese hospitals, the policeman also insisted that the local birth control officials, not the police, brought reluctant women to the hospital.

Five of the women interviewed described in detail how they had abortions. The three women from the TAR alleged to have had abortions were all between one and three months pregnant. First, they were given an injection of an abortifactant, followed by suction several days later when the injections did not work. One woman in Amdo had a D&C and suction when she was three months pregnant. And one woman in Kham received an injection to induce abortion at seven months pregnant. Kunsang, a Tibetan physician from Amdo, described the method of abortion in detail:

> When I became pregnant again after my first child, the hospital's birth control official said I had to give up my job or have an abortion. I was three months pregnant. I could not hide this from the official.

> I had an abortion by suction. First, the Chinese doctor used cervical dilators, numbers five, six, seven, eight, and nine. This took five to six minutes. Then the doctor inserted an instrument into my vagina. It was shaped like a spoon and scraped the uterus in all directions. This took five to six minutes and pieces of the fetus came out. Then a tube was inserted. Then the suction was set at negative two hundred. The tube became clogged with fetal parts several times. I was not given any medicines of any kind. Nothing for pain. No antibiotics. Afterwards, I had to rest for one month. I have back pain that continues to this day.

Kunsang's statement gives a precise description of the D&C method of abortion, followed by suction. In the four years that Kunsang had worked in Chinese hospitals, she stated that she had assisted 1,600 to 1,700 abortions by suction, and 400 to 500 abortions by injection. Most of the suctions were performed when the woman was between forty-five and fifty days pregnant. If the women were greater than sixty days pregnant, suction was considered too dangerous. These women had their water broken by needle on the first day. The fetus was taken out by suction on the second day. Women more than six months pregnant had a series of daily injections to induce abortion.

STERILIZATION

Of the five women interviewed who stated that they had been sterilized, all described an operation that, they were told, would prevent them from having any future children. Each woman had a well-healed, vertical, midline scar between her umbilicus and pubic bone (confirmed on physical examination). In each case, the operation described coincided with a tubal ligation.

Three women from Lhasa state that they were sterilized after the birth of their second child. One woman from Lhasa, and another from Kham, claimed to have been sterilized after being given an injection to induce abortion. Another woman from the border region between Tibet and Nepal stated that she was sterilized after her second child. All five of these women were sterilized within the confines of China's two-child limit for Tibetan women.

Tsering, a woman from a small village near the Nepalese border, said that she decided to be sterilized rather than face the social and economic sanctions for having an "extra" child. Tsering thinks that most of the women in her village have been sterilized, but she does not know their names. She says women are not talking about these things, and doing them secretly:

> One year after the birth of my second child, I had an operation to prevent all future children. The main problem was that my family is quite poor, and I had to obey the Chinese rules. My husband also works with the Chinese, so I could have only two children. Before the operation, I had my blood checked to make sure I was healthy. At the hospital, I was lying down, tied at the ankles and wrists. I received an injection at the site of the incision, so I would not feel pain. The procedure took approximately one hour. I stayed in the hospital for one week until the stitches were removed, and I could straighten up.

COERCED ABORTION AND STERILIZATION

All of the Tibetans interviewed felt that the economic and social sanctions in China's birth control policy in Tibet were in themselves sufficient to coerce many Tibetan and Chinese women to have abortions and sterilizations. Another woman named Tsering, from the Chu district in the TAR, near Lhasa, illustrates that pressure for Tibetan women to be sterilized can also come from within the family:

> I was sterilized at Chu district hospital. My husband asked me to have the operation because he works for the Chinese and it would be very bad if I had another child—it was not allowed. I refused. But my husband arranged for me to have an operation. I said that it was sinful, but my husband didn't listen. I finally gave in because my husband kept insisting.
>
> Before the operation, I could climb mountains and look after the animals. After the operation, all of this changed. I sued my husband in court, for forcing me to be sterilized. After I paid 500 yuan, I received the divorce.

Of the eight women interviewed who had abortion and/or sterilization, one woman from Kham reported that Chinese doctors forced
her to be sterilized after an abortion:

> After my first child, I became pregnant again, and the district leader
> said that I would have to pay a 1,500 yuan fine and get no ration card
> if I had a second child. My husband was in the same district but
> working in a field far away. We met once a month. If my husband had
> been present, I could have had my second baby.
>
> I was seven months pregnant when I went to the Markham Hospital.
> First, the doctors felt my belly for a while, then they gave me an
> injection in my abdomen. After two to three hours, the baby came out.
> Before this, I also received white pills. The baby was still alive, and the
> Chinese doctors gave the baby an injection in the head that killed the
> baby.
>
> Then I was taken for sterilization. After one day in the hospital, the
> doctors operated on me. I had no choice. I had an injection in my
> buttocks, then I had a vertical incision in my abdomen below my belly
> button and above the pubic area. The operation took two hours. My
> eyes were covered, but I was breathing, and I could hear. There was a
> tremendous amount of pain. The doctors were Chinese. I received no
> intravenous lines before or after the operation. I got no medicines after
> the operation.

When asked if the police or birth control officials had used physical
force to bring her to the hospital for abortion and sterilization,
Yangzum said that she had the abortion to avoid the social and
economic sanctions and because her husband was not there to
support her. Although Yangzum stated that Chinese doctors sterilized
her against her will, we are unable to confirm this from the interviews.

Besides the economic and social sanctions, the six women in the
TAR who stated that they had an abortion and/or sterilization
attributed these to their husbands' insistence, to not getting along
with their husbands, and to being too poor to pay the fine for an extra
child. In Amdo, a physician who had an abortion said that the head
of the hospital (where she worked) told her that she would lose her
job if she did not have an abortion. In Kham, one woman attributed
having an abortion followed by sterilization to the economic and
social sanctions for having an illegal child.

Although all of the eight women say they were "forced" to have an abortion and/or sterilization, none of the women said they were physically forced by the police or the local birth control officials. While these interviews detail how China's social and economic sanctions against Tibetan couples and illegal children coerce women to have an abortion and/or sterilization, further research must be conducted in order to assess what appears to be a "pressure continuum" inherent in China's two-child policy for Tibetans.[33]

INFANTICIDE

Infanticide is the killing of a newborn. Two of the women interviewed described how Chinese doctors killed their newborn infants. One woman from Kham stated that a Chinese doctor gave her an injection to induce the abortion of her second, legal pregnancy. But when the infant was born alive, the Chinese doctor gave the newborn a lethal injection in the soft spot of his forehead. A 30-year-old woman from Lhasa, Pema, who sold spices to the Chinese Army camp, describes how the Chinese doctors at the military hospital used a different method to kill her illegal newborn:

> In large hospitals, it is rare for extra children to be delivered alive. I knew that if my third (extra) child was born at the hospital, the Chinese doctors would kill it. So I delivered my third child at home. After nineteen days, the baby became sick, and I took her to Sera Hospital. The Chinese doctor ate lunch before he gave the baby oxygen. He then gave the baby a big injection in the heart, and the baby died.

The distinction between infanticide and abortion becomes obfuscated under Chinese law. Several refugees described how women nine months pregnant are injected in the abdomen to induce abortion. If the fetus is delivered alive, it would also be given a lethal injection. Under Chinese law, however, it is legal to inject women nine months pregnant to induce abortion and to give lethal injections to infants while they are still in the birth canal.

MASS STERILIZATION

In mainland China, mass sterilizations are called mass "mobilizations."[34] In Tibet, two monks from Amdo (northeastern Tibet) described what happened when a mobile birth control team came to their village:

> In the Autumn of 1987, a Chinese birth control team set up their tent next to our monastery in Amdo (Northeastern Tibet). The villagers were informed that all women had to report to the tent for abortions and sterilizations or there would be grave consequences. Women who went peacefully to the tents and did not resist received medical care. The women who refused to go were taken by force, operated on, and given no medical care. Women nine months pregnant had their babies taken out.

During the two weeks the birth control tent stood in their village, the monks claimed that *all* pregnant women had abortions followed by sterilization, and *every* woman of childbearing age was sterilized:

> We saw many girls crying, heard their screams as they waited for their turn to go into the tent, and saw the growing pile of fetuses build outside the tent, which smelled horrible. The birth control teams do not round up Chinese women who live in these villages.

The birth control teams were initiated in 1982, but since 1987 there has been a tremendous increase in the number and frequency of the teams that move from town to town and to nomadic areas. Tibetans are outraged that the Chinese are trying to wipe out the Tibetan race. At the same time, Tibetans are helpless to prevent this.

Of the seven Tibetans interviewed from Amdo, all stated that they had seen mobile birth control teams perform mass sterilizations. Two monks stated that the mobile teams sterilized every woman of childbearing age in the village. Five people from Amdo stated that the mobile birth control teams had a list of how many children each woman in the village had and sterilized the women according to China's two-child policy: Tibetan women with two children are sterilized. Although the use of physical force cannot be confirmed from these interviews, it is significant to note that all of the Tibetans from Amdo insisted that the mobile birth control teams, in conjunction with local police, used physical force to make women have abortions and/or sterilization.

CONCLUSION

Eight Tibetan women's accounts of coerced abortion, sterilization, and infanticide refute China's denial that coerced abortion, sterilization, infanticide, and mass sterilization are part of its national birth control policy in Tibet. Eyewitness accounts of mobile birth control teams that conducted mass sterilizations in isolated villages in nomad areas carries a much more serious charge.

In 1961 the World Court ordered China to cease its genocidal policies in Tibet. But neither the World Court nor three United Nations Resolutions stopped an estimated 1.2 million Tibetans (one-sixth of the population) from dying of starvation, execution, and imprisonment.[35] The interviewees confirm the longstanding fear that the Chinese are trying to destroy the Tibetan race. Waves of Chinese immigrants, which threaten to make Tibetans a minority in their own land, exacerbate this fear.[36]

Interviewing indigenous Tibetans is preferable to interviewing refugees. Refugee accounts can be fictitious, biased, or represent aberrations in China's birth control policy. Although the PRC opened Tibet to tourism (and dollars) in 1984, continued demonstrations since the fall of 1987 have made China forbid on-site investigation. Thus confirmed, first-hand accounts by Tibetan refugees provide the best available insight into China's birth control policy in Tibet. The refugees' allegations of coerced abortion, sterilization, infanticide, and mass sterilizations are further strengthened by their distribution throughout the Tibet Autonomous Region, Kham, and Amdo and by their similarity to China's use of forced abortion, sterilization, infanticide, and mass sterilizations in mainland China.

In June of 1989, the Tiananmen Square massacre showed the world how the People's Liberation Army slaughtered their own people. Although governments imposed sanctions against the People's Republic of China, most international lending and investment have quietly resumed. If governments have already forgiven China for atrocities committed against its own people in mainland China, what will happen to the Tibetans, now in their fifth decade of struggle against Chinese military occupation? For Tibetans, the answer to this question is a matter of survival.

1. Blake Kerr, M.D., "Violation of Human Rights in Tibet: Tibetan Refugee Accounts of Torture, Forced Abortion, Sterilization, and Infanticide," presented to the International Hearing on Tibet, German Parliament, Bonn, April 20, 1989; Blake Kerr, M.D., "Tibetan Women Under China's Birth Control Policy: Tibetan Refugee Accounts of Forced Abortion, Sterilization, and Infanticide," presented to the Subcommittee on Foreign Operations, Export Financing, and Related Programs, Washington, D.C., April 24, 1989.

2. Blake Kerr, M.D., "Witness to China's Shame: How Human Rights and Families Suffer in Tibet." *The Washington Post*, February 26, 1988.

3. Blake Kerr, M.D., "Against Their Will." *The New York Times*, Letter to the Editor, October 27, 1990.

4. Stephen W. Mosher, *Broken Earth: The Rural Chinese*, The Free Press, Collier Macmillan Publishers, 1983, p. 231.

5. John S. Aird, *Slaughter of the Innocents: Coercive Birth Control in China*. AEI Press, 1990, p. 21.

6. Sun Jingxia, "Present Problems in the Work of Propaganda on Contraception and Its Technical Guidance," *Guangming ribao* (Bright Daily), Beijing (GMRB), Dec. 9, 1956, Survey of China Mainland Press (SCMP) American Consulate General, Hong Kong, No. 1452, Jan. 17, 1957, p. 9.

7. Aird, *Slaughter of the Innocents*, p. 22.

8. John S. Aird, *The Size, Composition, and Growth of the Population of Mainland China*, International Population Statistics Reports, Series P-90, No. 15 (Washington: U.S. Government Printing Office, 1961), pp. 55-58.

9. Interview with Judith Banister reported in Stephens Broening, "The Death of 30 Million Chinese," *The Baltimore Sun*, April 26, 1984, p. A19.

10. Ye Gongshao, "My Views on Young People's Marriage, Love, and Children," p. 15.

11. Analysis on China's One-per-Thousand-Population Fertility Sampling Survey (Beijing: China Population Information Center, 1984), pp. 159-167.

12. Aird, *Slaughter of the Innocents*, p. 25.

13. *Ibid.*, p. 26.

14. *Ibid.*, p. 27.

15. Mosher, *Op. Cit.*, p. 250-1.

16. Aird, *Slaughter of the Innocents*, p. 29.

17. XINHUA, Beijing, December 22, 1979, FBIS, No. 251, December 28, 1979, p. L7.

18. Fuzhou radio, Fujian Provincial Service, August 18, 1979, FBIS, No. 163,

August 21, 1979, p. O3; Zhengzhou radio, Henan Provincial Service, August 25, 1979, FBIS, No. 169, August 29, 1979, p. P1.

19. Aird, *Slaughter of the Innocents*, p. 30.

20. Xu Dixin, "A Few Problems Concerning Population Science," *Economic Research*, No. 4, April 20, 1981, FBIS, No. 101, May 27, 1981, p. K23.

21. XINHUA, Beijing, December 16, 1980, FBIS, No. 244, December 17, 1980, pp. L15-16.

22. Aird, *Slaughter of the Innocents*, pp. 30-31.

23. "Essential Points of the PRC 1983 Plan for National Economic and Social Development," *People's Daily*, December 20, 1982, FBIS, No. 247, December 23, 1982, p. K18.

24. Aird, *Slaughter of the Innocents*, pp. 33-34.

25. *Ibid.*, p. 33.

26. "Paying for Abortions," *The Wall Street Journal*, April 9, 1984, p. 34.

27. Dr. Bao Fu, "Massacre of the Innocents in China," *China Spring Digest*, January/February 1987.

28. "China Publishes Population Statistics for 1987," *People's Daily*, Beijing, May 14, 1988, FBIS, No. 96, May 18, 1988, p. 39.

29. "Population Growth Slows Slightly," *China Daily*, March 9, 1989, Joint Publications Research Service, Washington, No. 89-030, April 6, 1989, p. 21.

30. Fu, *Op. Cit.*, p. 40.

31. Marlow Hood, "Birth Control Program 'Ineffective' in Provinces," *South China Morning Post*, Hong Kong, November 2, 1988, FBIS, No. 212, November 2, 1988, p. 40.

32. Aird, *Slaughter of the Innocents*, pp. 79-87.

33. A human rights monitor who wishes to remain anonymous coined the phrase "pressure continuum" in reference to China's coercive birth control policies in Tibet.

34. Aird, *Slaughter of the Innocents*, p. 17.

35. John Avedon, *In Exile from the Land of Snows*, Vintage, 1986.

36. "Human Rights in Tibet," *Asia Watch*, February 1988.

JOHN ACKERLY & BLAKE KERR

Torture and Imprisonment in Tibet

In the years following the aborted 1959 uprising, the Chinese put tens
of thousands of Tibetans in prisons and forced labor camps where
many were executed or starved or tortured to death. At the same time,
the Chinese decimated the monastic system by razing over 6,000
monasteries and temples.[1] For the next three decades, the Chinese
effectively closed Tibet off from the rest of the world; the horrors to
which Tibetans were subjected were largely unknown until the 1980s.

A variety of credible sources estimate that thousands of Tibetans
have been arrested in Lhasa since the fall of 1987 and that hundreds
of political prisoners remain in Lhasa area prisons. Precise figures on
the number of political prisoners held in Lhasa area prisons are
impossible to obtain. Clearly, estimates of the number of Tibetan
political prisoners fluctuate. Although many prisoners may be released, some will be imprisoned again following the next demon-

John Ackerly and Blake Kerr happened to be in Lhasa as American tourists when
Chinese occupation forces attacked Tibetan demonstrators in the fall of 1987. When
they began hearing rumors of torture being applied to Tibetan prisoners, they traveled
to Northern India and conducted extensive interviews with 17 Tibetan refugees, eight
of whom were victims of imprisonment and torture. Their subsequent report, *The
Suppression of a People*, published by Physicians for Human Rights in 1989, is the source
for this article.

stration. Therefore, at any given time the number of long-term political prisoners may be only a fraction of the number of Tibetans who have been imprisoned for shorter periods of time.

Estimating the number of political prisoners in Tibet is further complicated by the difficulty of distinguishing between political prisoners and common criminals. Many political prisoners are held on nominal criminal charges; only a fraction are charged as "counterrevolutionaries." Many others are charged with both political and common crimes. For example, Pemba Tsering, thirty years old, was sentenced in August 1989 to three years in prison for "participating in counterrevolutionary riot activities, taking the lead in shouting reactionary slogans and damaging public property."[2]

Asia Watch has reported that many political prisoners are charged solely under criminal statutes that have no political implications, that political beliefs can significantly affect length of imprisonment and conditions of imprisonment (even for common criminals), and that most Tibetan political prisoners are imprisoned because of their involvement in or advocacy of Tibetan independence from China[3] or for proclaiming an allegiance to the Dalai Lama. Given that Lhasa only has 40,000 to 70,000 Tibetans,[4] there are few Tibetans who have not had a family member, relative, or friend detained in prison.

SECURITY FORCES IN TIBET

The exact role and the identities of the various branches of the PRC government and security forces responsible for surveiling, investigating, arresting, interrogating, and torturing Tibetans is outside the scope of this report. However, in Tibet there are few of the ambiguities that exist in some other countries, where it is unclear who is responsible for which atrocity. For example, there are no known private "death squads" such as those in El Salvador. Likewise, a full discussion of the role of Western countries in training and supplying Chinese police forces in Tibet is not possible here. However, it has been reported that Chinese security officials have been trained in recent years in the United States,[5] and anti-riot squads in Lhasa were trained by the Austrian special force "Cobra."[6]

The Public Security Bureau (Gong An Jiu) generally functions as a normal police force, for "investigation, detention and preparatory examination."[7] The Procuratorate (Jian Cha Yuan) is charged with "approving arrest, conducting procuratorial work (including investigation), and initiating public prosecution."[8] Very little information is available on the extent to which the Procuratorate is allowed to, or able to, do its job in Tibet. It appears that in the cases of many prisoners the Procuratorate simply is not involved. Indeed, it appears that whatever "trials" are going on may not follow formal judicial procedures and are very expeditious.

Prison guards and officials also have close working relationships with the Public Security Bureau, which maintains surveillance over released prisoners. Most officials in the PSB, especially those of higher rank, are Chinese, but there are a number of Tibetan police.[9]

Both Tibetan and Chinese guards torture prisoners. Tibetans, ironically, have both the best and the worst reputations among the prisoners. All but one of our interviewees claimed that the Tibetans were the most brutal torturers. The treatment of prisoners varied widely depending upon the guard.

Although Tibetan guards were reputed to be cruel, they were also in a unique position to help prisoners. Since very few Chinese speak or understand Tibetan, interrogation is generally carried out with the help of Tibetan guards, either on their own or as translators. Tibetan guards can thereby confirm where prisoners are being held and what their condition is and communicate this information directly to relatives or friends of the inmate who come to the prisons trying to find a family member, visit, or leave food and blankets.

We were told by one ex-prisoner that torture began to let up toward the end of March 1988 when "guards got bored of torturing so much." Another interview provided by the Tibet Information Network asserted that because of the volume of prisoners in March 1988 guards became upset and irritable at having to work long hours without holidays.[10]

PRISONS AND THEIR CONDITIONS

We received extensive information about Lhasa area prisons, namely Sangyip, Gutsa, and Drapchi.[11] We also received reports about a prison in Shigatse and scanty information about labor camps in isolated areas such as Kong-po. Recent refugees also tell of a new prison facility established at Dechen Dzong in Toelung, twenty kilometers west of Lhasa. And in the fall of 1989 we began to hear reports of the Chokpori detention center, located opposite the Potala, which reportedly is reserved for only a small number of special cases. Tibetans believe that political prisoners are being held in jails or prisons in all of Tibet's main counties and prefectures.[12]

Official Chinese sources contradict this information. According to *Some Basic Facts About Tibet*, a paper distributed by the Chinese Embassy in Washington, D.C., Tibet has only one prison and two labor camps. The names and locations of the prison and camps are not provided. The paper said that Zichang, President of the TAR's Higher People's Court, "laughed at the rumors now circulating abroad about the number of prisons and inmates in Tibet." Zichang said that "97.2% of inmates were convicted on criminal charges and the rest, on charges of counterrevolution." It is possible that these percentages have some basis in reality since many political acts have been criminalized, but this is an area in which Chinese statistics and pronouncements are notoriously unreliable.

We did not gain enough information to include details about the labor camps to which prisoners are often sent after or during a prison sentence. It is known that prisoners have been used in logging and mining operations in eastern Tibet and that both high and low security labor camps exist. The latter sometimes pay workers and allow them to live on their own, but workers must remain under supervision and cannot leave the area.

MAINTENANCE OF PRISONERS

Lobsang Dhondup[†] was beaten and arrested during the March 5 demonstration. First he was taken to Gutsa, where there were no beds or other fixtures in the cell, only a small tin bucket in which to urinate and a thin rug for him and his eleven cell-mates to sleep on. They were given no blankets. One small window provided light for the cell.

Lobsang was moved to Utitod in March 1988. His cell there had two cement platforms covered with a tarpaulin on which to sleep. One blanket was given to every two prisoners to share. Cells were

---

† The names of those interviewed for this article have been changed for publication, at the request of each interviewee, to protect their friends and relatives in Tibet.

not heated, and were bitterly cold during the winter. In some instances, the prison provided an extra blanket.

Few Tibetan homes have indoor plumbing; therefore it is not surprising that most prison cells in Tibet do not have running water. Prisoners are generally not supplied with even a pail of water in their cells. One pail is provided in each cell to use as a toilet and the prisoner is allowed to empty it once a day. Interviewees stated that the stench from these buckets is particularly bad in the summer.

Prisoners are not supplied with soap, and they have only one set of clothes which often are never washed even during a several month stay in prison. We heard of cases where families have been allowed to leave soap for an incarcerated relative at the prison gates. We do not know, however, if the prisoners received packages left by families. Lobsang Dhondup said that he was never allowed an opportunity to wash himself or his clothes properly during his four-month stay in Sangyip and Gutsa.

One man imprisoned in Gutsa from March to April 1988 stated that "sometimes we were let outside twice a day, sometimes only once. It depends on the guard; some guards let us sit in the sun for half an hour. Some guards put us back in the cell immediately after we had been to the toilet." He said that they were always let out "in a group, never alone. Each cell was taken out one at a time."

All of those interviewed stated that the food provided in prison was insufficient and nutritionally inadequate.

Sonam Tsering, a 20-year-old monk from Sera Monastery gave the following account. His day in Sangyip began at 6:00 when the guards woke everyone up. Sometimes they told him that it was an interrogation day, and he would then have little time to get prepared. If it was not an interrogation day, breakfast would come at 8:00, consisting of a half-filled bowl of thin, watery rice porridge that appeared through a hole in the door. At 1:00 the prisoners were served lunch—one ladle of boiled vegetables and steamed bread. Dinner was the same as lunch, except that it did not always arrive. Sonam lost weight rapidly. In Utitod prison, said Lobsang Dhondup, the fixed term prisoners got more food and water and tried to share it with the temporary prisoners but risked severe punishment if they were caught.

Under Chinese law, post-arrest detention without bail is permissible and include pre-arrest detention for up to ten days. The eight Tibetans we interviewed who had been in prison were incarcerated for four days to eight months. Obviously, those held for longer periods were not, and still are not, available for interviews.

The duration of imprisonment is not necessarily arbitrary. All of those interviewed told us that the Chinese are trying to uncover the leaders of the demonstrations and outspoken advocates of Tibetan nationalism, who will be held significantly longer. Prisoners are also released earlier if they do not express any anti-Chinese sentiments during interrogation.

Nima Pasang, a 22-year-old man who shared a cell with a nun, said that he was sure that they would keep her for a long time because she kept yelling "Long live the Dalai Lama" at her interrogators. "Unless you hide your feelings and keep quiet," Nima said, "they will not release you."

Prison is inherently an isolating, lonely environment, made even more so by rules forbidding prisoners to talk among themselves. Lobsang Dhondup reported that in Gutsa all talking was strictly prohibited in the cell. However, at night the prisoners were able to whisper among themselves and find out about each other. One prisoner in Drapchi was reportedly shackled and shown to the prisoners as an example of the punishment meted out for speaking to other prisoners.

Although we received no accounts of prisoners taking their own lives, the literature contains an unconfirmed report of one prisoner who survived an attempted suicide,[13] and another who succeeded.[14]

PATTERNS OF TORTURE

Several of the monks we interviewed explained how their monastic training made them more resistant to torture. First, the discipline required to meditate for long periods of time helped monks endure the rigors of prison. And second, Buddhist doctrines of patience and compassion for all living things encouraged them to look for good qualities in their captors and to put the horrors of prison into perspective as something that would pass.[15]

One of the most often mentioned reasons for surviving extended torture was inspiration drawn from the Dalai Lama and the belief that he was praying for them. Whether the prisoners came from the monastic or lay community, they believed that by the Dalai Lama's grace they would recuperate. According to a 26-year-old Tibetan in Sangyip, "I did not think of myself in prison....My thoughts were of His Holiness. I kept myself calm and said my prayers."[16]

Patterns of torture are consistent from the Tibetans we interviewed and from other published and unpublished accounts by travelers and human rights groups. The most common pattern is repeated interrogation sessions accompanied by severe beatings and electric shock. If prisoners refuse to state that Tibet is part of China or are suspected of organizing a demonstration or assaulting a policeman or police vehicle, the treatment is much more severe. There is debate over whether the purpose of torture is primarily pragmatic—to extract confessions and gain information—or primarily to intimidate and create fear.[17]

In addition to beatings and electric shock, torture techniques include hanging prisoners by their wrists, thumbs or ankles for prolonged periods, submerging prisoners in tubs of cold water, or dousing them with water. In general, political prisoners are treated much worse than common criminals.[18]

Chinese and Tibetan party officials, as well as official decrees, have called for the "severe punishment of counterrevolutionaries."[19] Martial Law Decree No. 2 [See Appendix V for Martial Law Decrees] issued on March 7, 1989, states that "the judicial departments must immediately investigate criminals referred to in this decree and punish them severely and swiftly." Decree No. 3 says the "personnel on duty have the right to investigate anyone violating these regulations and may take forceful measures on the spot to apprehend them and hold them accountable." The license to use forceful measures is particularly disturbing in light of reports by Westerners in Lhasa at the time that Tibetans were being shot by security personnel on the spot in their homes.

INTERROGATION

Interviewees consistently told us that torture almost always accompanies interrogation, and that interrogation usually takes place within hours of arrest, which is frequently late at night and primarily aimed at uncovering the names of others who were involved in a demonstration or in the underground. The treatment seemed to vary widely depending upon the prisoner's attitude and that of the torturer(s). While most of those interviewed said that they were treated no better even if they gave names, one man stated that he was released quickly after he gave names and said that he admired communism.

A nurse, Yoden Choedak, described her interrogation:

> Ten days after the March 5, 1988, demonstration, the police came to my work place and took me to the police station, where they produced a thick book that, I was told, contained all of my crimes. They never opened the book. At first I tried to tell the police that I had not done anything wrong. Then women police took me to a different room where they kicked me in the chest. They touched my mouth with an electric stick many times, which felt as though my mouth had exploded, and I lost consciousness.
>
> Then I was taken to Drapchi prison where Chinese policemen tried to strip me again. I cried as my clothes were being ripped off, with the help of Chinese women police. Then I was beaten all over my body with the electric stick, many times on my breasts, mouth, and head. I lost consciousness from this many times. The male police were Chinese. The women police were Muslims from Pakistan or Kashmir who had been living in Lhasa for some time.
>
> I did not confess to committing any crimes, other than throwing rocks. Before being released from Drapchi, I was told not to say anything about what had happened to me in prison, and that if I ever participated in another demonstration, I would be treated much worse. Ever since, I have had difficulty remembering things and learning new words. I think this is from the electric sticks.

Most of the interviewees stated that economic incentives were offered to make them talk, such as a high paying job upon release. But a confession, however it was secured, appeared to lead to even harsher punishments and to the breaking of any promises made because the prisoner had confessed to being a counterrevolutionary.

Under Chinese law, "the use of torture to coerce statements and the gathering of evidence by threat, enticement, deceit or other unlawful methods are strictly prohibited."[20]

BEATINGS

According to our interviews, almost no one arrested in Lhasa during demonstrations escapes beating. The severity of the beatings is particularly disturbing—prisoners are often first stripped naked and then beaten until they are unconscious.

Prisoners are routinely beaten with a variety of objects available to the guards: cattle prods, weapons, iron rods, truncheons, clubs with nails driven through the ends, and the guards' fists and feet. Our interviewees said that almost every object in the interrogation room was used as an instrument of torture: telephones, trash cans, chairs, and lamps. Prisoners are also kicked and often have their hands tied or shackled. While prisoners were often forced to beat each other during the Cultural Revolution, there were no reports of this happening now.[21]

When Nima Pasang was arrested on March 8, 1988, and taken to Drapchi prison, he was initially put into a small room by himself. Even before the police began to question Nima, they beat him badly. He described how a Chinese policeman held his hair and beat his face into the concrete floor, which ripped open his mouth and broke several teeth. When interviewed seven months later, Nima had a jagged, four-inch scar on his cheek, consistent with his account.

A former policeman, Thapkey Dorje, confirmed that prisoners were virtually always beaten, and that he himself had tortured his own people. "It was very difficult being a Tibetan and a policeman," Thapkey said. "They put pressure on me in group meetings to do many things I did not want to do." Thapkey explained how he beat prisoners' heads against the wall, used a wooden plank to tie the wrists in unnatural positions behind the head and back, and also administered beatings against the motion of a joint to break an arm or dislocate the joint. "If a prisoner dies during the beatings," Thapkey said, "the police are not responsible because it is the prisoner's fault. The police have the upper hand and are free to beat prisoners to death."

We were often told that guards repeatedly struck tender spots such as the soles of feet, elbows, knees, and abdomens and that prisoners were beaten standing, sitting, or lying on the floor. Geshe Lobsang Wangchuk, a prisoner of conscience adopted by Amnesty International, reportedly lost the use of his hands after they were twisted during torture.[22] Another brutal incident occurred on June 12, 1988, when two Tibetans arrested in front of the Lhasa Dance and Performance Hall were allegedly blinded and their spines broken.[23]

ELECTRIC SHOCK

The use of electric cattle prods against Tibetan detainees and prisoners is widespread. Asia Watch published the first substantive account of their use in a February 1988 report, *Human Rights in Tibet.*[24] Since then, substantive reports of their use have been frequent.[25]

The eight torture victims whom we interviewed had all been shocked repeatedly with electric prods. Sonam Tsering's case is typical. Sonam described the room where he was interrogated and tortured almost every day as an ordinary office outside of the inner compound—a desk, two chairs, and a telephone. The same three Tibetans always interrogated him and electric shock with one long and one short cattle prod always accompanied the interrogation. Every once in a while a Chinese officer came into the room to supervise.

One of the most disturbing allegations is that of electric cattle prods having been forced into the vaginas of women prisoners, including Buddhist nuns. We received a report that a nun was tied to an electrified metal table, that electric cords were tied around her breasts,[26] and that a cattle prod was jabbed into her vagina so many times that she became badly infected. Tinley Chophel, twenty-five years old, said that another monk told him that an electrically charged belt was wrapped around his waist and then pulled tighter and tighter. Many prisoners also reported that electric batons were put into their mouths.[27]

HANGING BY EXTREMITIES

We received many testimonies from victims and others of prisoners being hanged by the thumbs, ankles, or wrists, and with arms tied behind backs—a position known as the "flying airplane." The prisoners hang from roof beams, cell bars, or trees with the toes barely touching or not at all. We are not aware of any accounts of prisoners being hanged by their necks or in a manner causing immediate death.

A monk who had been imprisoned in Gutsa told a *Washington Post* reporter: "I saw people hanging from ropes tied to their arms behind their backs, suspended with their feet off the ground. Two of the people I saw had their shoulders dislocated by the rope. Many became unconscious as a result."[28]

Other reports of hanging prisoners by extremities come from Drapchi. One prisoner released from Drapchi reported that, "four to five people were hanged in midair for a day and a night without any clothes. Some were kept like this until they confessed. They were mostly laypeople. Not many monks received such punishment."[29]

COLD WATER

When Sonam Tsering was moved to Gutsa in the winter of 1988, his captors tied him to a wall, stripped him naked, and poured ice water over him. Sonam saw them do this to many of the prisoners that winter. (Temperatures at night and in the shade in Tibet's high altitude can easily drop below freezing, especially in the winter.) Other prisoners have testified that they have been doused with ice water or held in tubs of cold water and that this practice exists in both Gutsa and Drapchi prisons in winter months.[30]

Although none of our interviewees said that they had been submerged in an ice bath, several Tibetans stated that they knew of others who had experienced such treatment. Submerging prisoners in tubs of cold water, however, has been reported elsewhere as a method of reviving unconscious prisoners.[31]

INJECTIONS

Jigme Norbu, a 34-year-old Tibetan physician who worked in the Mendzekhang, Lhasa's only hospital of Tibetan medicine, described two types of injections used in prisons. One injection makes the prisoner talk freely. Another injection "makes the prisoner go insane, if it did not kill him." The first injection fits the description of what is commonly called "truth serum," or sodium pentothal. One can only guess at the contents of the second type of injection. However, Dr. Norbu had not actually witnessed prisoners receiving injections.

Tinley Chophel, imprisoned for three months in 1988, saw several prisoners who in his words, "became mentally retarded" as a result of prolonged torture or injection. The basis upon which he thought that an injection may have been administered is unclear; nevertheless second and third-hand reports of debilitating injections given in prison are common enough to take seriously. Indeed, two monks treated by Dr. Kerr after the October 1, 1987 demonstration told him that they feared injections that they heard were given in prison more than they feared the torture.

Many Tibetans believe that Lobsang Wangchuk, adopted by Amnesty International, was given an injection the day before his release from Sangyip prison. He died the day after his release at the Mendzekhang.[32]

According to another report, a 22-year-old monk in Sangyip prison was given frequent injections of an unknown substance that caused him to become partially paralyzed. "The paralysis is so severe that he cannot feed himself. When he arrived [at the Tibetan Medical Institute], he could only walk stooped over at a ninety-degree angle to the floor."[33]

TRAINED GUARD DOGS

We received testimony of the use of dogs on prisoners in Gutsa and Sangyip prisons, and two accounts of trained dogs used to attack women prisoners. The incidents in Gutsa have been confirmed by other published reports, including one from Amnesty International.[34] We could not independently confirm the use of attack dogs in Sangyip but believe that the testimony we received is credible, in part because it is so similar to the accounts from Gutsa.

Tenzin Tsering, a 22-year-old monk from Sera Monastery, had a friend named Lobsang who was twenty-six when he was arrested for participating in the March 5, 1988, demonstration. Said Tenzin, "Lobsang was taken the same day to Sangyip prison. After stripping Lobsang, the police tied Lobsang to a stake, hung motor tires around his neck, then let trained guard dogs attack. Lobsang said the Chinese name for the dog is 'Owlie'. They are large, slim dogs, with pointed ears. The dogs tore hunks of flesh from Lobsang's calves and thighs."

The Tibetan policeman, Thapkey Dorje, also confirmed that the Public Security Bureau had dogs trained in China. During the mid-1980s, Thapkey said, "we used the dogs to bark at the prisoners, who often told us many things at this time. The dogs are also trained to bite the prisoners on the command [in Chinese] of the master." Another prisoner also said that the dogs were given and understood orders in Chinese.[35]

NUNS IN PRISON

Reports and allegations of sexual abuse and harassment in Lhasa area prisons filter across the Himalayas. Yoden Choedak told us what a friend, a nun named Ngawang, had told Yoden about her experience in prison.

> Ngawang was released in late July. The first time I visited Ngawang in late March she looked very healthy. When Ngawang came out, she had lost a lot of weight and had difficulty walking. She could hardly walk from the damage to her right hip. She had received daily beatings and torture while stripped naked over a four-month period. They [police] forced women to run for hours while police beat them with cattle prods. Ngawang was tied with an electric cord, beaten with cattle prods, and had dogs attack her many times. For her, the worst problem was the electric cords tied around her breasts. When the electricity was applied, it made her feel like she was going to die.
>
> I saw Ngawang after she was released. The dogs must have had very sharp teeth because there was one place in her right thigh that had a large hunk of flesh missing. Ngawang told me that she decided to be beaten, instead of running and have the dogs eat her, even if they beat her to death.

The following is perhaps the most well-known account of the abuse of a Tibetan nun in prison:

> Upon arrival at Gutsa prison, the nun was stripped of all clothing and placed in a room with two trained dogs and two policemen. The dogs were trained to attack whenever she moved. The policemen proceeded to hit her with rods until she tried to move away, at which time dogs would attack, biting and lacerating her arms and legs. During this

torture, they continually asked her about her involvement in the demonstrations as well as the involvement of others.

After saying nothing, being beaten, and being attacked by dogs, they placed her in a cell at Gutsa where she remained for approximately three months....While in prison, she spoke to another nun who was stripped of all clothing and prodded with an electric rod in the vagina and in the mouth.[36]

Four of our interviewees believed nuns were treated more harshly than other men and women prisoners. Nima Pasang, a 22-year-old from Kham, saw guards come into his cell in Drapchi and start questioning and beating a nun, who was temporarily sharing the cell. When the guards applied the electric prod, she started spitting and yelling "Long Live the Dalai Lama!" Then they put the electric prod in her mouth. Afterwards, her mouth was full of blood and they continued to beat her on her pelvis.

Nuns imprisoned for actual or suspected participation in a demonstration or other unauthorized political activity may be as young as fourteen.

OTHER FORMS OF TORTURE

We found set patterns of torture to exist in Tibetan prisons, but there are certainly also a variety of forms of mistreatment and techniques of torture that do not fit into any discernable pattern. Also, some traditional practices are notably absent, such as "thamzing," or struggle sessions which were very common during the Cultural Revolution.[37]

The 20-year-old Sera monk Sonam Tsering told us that he was forced to eat human excrement in Gutsa. He said it was a joke his captors played on the inmates. Sonam refused to eat it, but they forced him. Once Sonam was brought to a big room full of Chinese and Tibetan prison employees. He was given a plate of food mixed with human excrement and forced to eat it in front of everybody. This practice was corroborated by another prisoner, interviewed inside Tibet, who was also in Gutsa prison between March and July of 1988.

When Nepalese border guards caught Tenzin Samphel they turned him over to the Chinese authorities "in exchange for a carton of cigarettes." His hands and feet were shackled and he was taken to a police station. Later he was tied to two horses and dragged behind them for one and a half hours to a town where the inhabitants and some Nepalese traders gathered to watch the spectacle.

Prisoners have also asserted that guards first placed cattle prods and then chili powder into their mouths, causing edema of the tongue and purulent infections.[38]

Prisoners, including Sonam Tsering, also reported that they were made to stand for long periods of time, for hours or all night, and sometimes outside. Guards put truck tires around their necks and forced them to stand until they collapsed. A special rapporteur from the UN noted an extreme case of this torture in which prisoners "were allegedly kept standing for fourteen days whilst being interrogated."[39]

At least two reports exist of prisoners being forced to inhale the smoke of burning rubbish.[40] Prisoners have also been forced to lie in gutters full of running refuse while being beaten. Being burned with lit cigarettes has also been reported, as have pistols pointed at prisoners' heads under threat of death.[41]

Deaths from Torture

Several of the ex-prisoners we interviewed said that they were aware of prisoners dying in prison. Amnesty International has also reported several cases of prisoners dying as a result of torture, including that of Tenzin Sherap, who is believed to have been tortured to death in prison in mid-March 1988. Pictures of his face when his family came to collect him at the morgue further substantiated this claim.[42] Another ex-prisoner interviewed in Lhasa said that two died in prison on or about March 5 [1988] from severe beatings.[43]

One of the most well known cases of death from torture is that of Geshe Lobsang Wangchuk, who died on November 4, 1987, apparently as a result of prolonged mistreatment and torture during eighteen years in prison.

It is not known how many of the deaths resulting from torture are intentional, although many reports of secret executions now exist.[44] According to sources of the Bureau of the Dalai Lama in Delhi, important political prisoners have been secretly killed without trial since the imposition of martial law in March 1989.

Before he left Lhasa in 1986, ex-policeman Thapkey Dorje accompanied prisoners while they were being paraded through town and to the execution site. He outlined the following scenario, the accuracy or applicability of which we have been unable to confirm:

> Prisoners to be executed get barley beer and good food, not much, the day before the execution. Then they are taken to a special house where they are tied. The next morning, the prisoner is given an injection to become senseless. The injection is similar to the one given before an operation to knock the person out, but only a little. Prisoners are then put in a police truck with a motorcade of at least twenty police vehicles. Five police with guns are in the truck with the prisoner, who is fully tied with his hands behind his back to a plank, while announcements are made to the general population with loudspeakers. Then the prisoner is taken near Phenpo, where a grave is dug. A military jeep comes from a different direction with a person who specializes in executing prisoners. He wears glasses; his face is wrapped so people can't see his face. He shoots the prisoner in the back of the head. If the prisoner does not die, he cuts the nerves in the spine. When they are sure the prisoner is dead, the relatives are told they can come and get the body and give it to the vultures. The prisoner is buried if no one comes for the body.

CONCLUSION

There can be no doubt that the use of arrest, imprisonment, and torture of large numbers of Tibetans continues to be an integral part of China's effort to suppress Tibetan nationalism.

Accurate information is essential for promoting human rights. Although we believe this report to represent the most accurate, detailed, and comprehensive documentation of torture in Tibet to date, human rights documentation in Tibet remains scanty. China's continued denial of human rights abuses in Tibet and its refusal to allow fact-finding missions illustrate the tremendous task that lies ahead. However, significant work can be done now in the Tibetan exile communities in India and also in Nepal. For example, Western and Tibetan physicians have yet to make a concerted effort to document and treat the long term physical and psychological effects of torture suffered by refugees.

We find that the treatment of political prisoners in Tibet is incompatible with international standards of human conduct and decency, and at odds with China's ratification of the United Nations Convention against Torture and Other Cruel, Inhuman, and Degrading Treatment or Punishment in October of 1988. We are gravely concerned that the assault on human rights in Tibet today threatens the very existence of a Tibetan identity. In light of this, we urge the international community to use all available means to encourage China to respect the human rights of the Tibetan people.

---

1. According to "Tibet: The Facts," a report by the Scientific Buddhist Association for the UN Commission on Human Rights, 80% of monasteries and temples were destroyed from 1960 to 1966, before the Cultural Revolution.

2. Xinhua (Official Chinese News Service), "Tibet Sentences March 'Tumult' Participants," August 6, 1989.

3. Asia Watch, Statement on "Human Rights in Tibet," for Hearings of the Subcommittees on Human Rights and International Organizations and on Asian and Pacific Affairs, Committee on Foreign Affairs, House of Representatives, October 14, 1987, p. 8. (Hereafter referred to as "Statement of Asia Watch".)

4. The real population of Lhasa is not known, probably not even by the Chinese. Most informed estimates hover around the 140,000 mark, of which perhaps 70,000 to 100,000 are Chinese.

5. Tai Ming Cheung, "Crackdown on Crime," *Far Eastern Economic Review,* November 3, 1988.

6. Georg Furbock, "Hilft Wien Chinas Sonder-Polizei in Tibet?" *Wiener Kurier,* (Vienna), September 5, 1988.

7. Chinese Criminal Law Procedure Act, Article 3.

8. *Ibid.*

9. Statement of Asia Watch, p. 9.

10. Tibet Information Network (TIN), Int. #5, p. 8. A series of unpublished interviews was made available to us by TIN in London, after deleting names and other identifying information to protect the confidentiality of those still in Tibet. These interviews of torture victims were carried out of Tibet and are considered to be of the utmost reliability as they were all taped and carefully transcribed. We refer to them as TIN, Int.#.

11. For a dated overview of prisons in Tibet see Information Office of His Holiness the Dalai Lama, *Glimpses of Tibet Today* (Dharamsala:1978), pp. 61-66.

12. Statement of Asia Watch, p. 8.

13. TIN, Int. #5, p. 8.

14. Ennals and Hyde-Chambers, "Tibet in China," p. 52. One of our interviewees told us that a Tibetan policeman committed suicide because he had shot a Chinese policeman in the police station on October 1, 1987. We were told that when he realized that he was about to be identified as the assailant, he went home and shot himself in the head with his revolver.

15. For a detailed, fascinating account of how Buddhist practices and teachings helped one prisoner endure years of imprisonment, see "Jiuzhen Prison: A Tibetan Account" by Dr. Tenzin Choedrak in *Seeds of Fire: Chinese Voices of Conscience*, edited by Geremie Barme and John Minford (New York: Hill and Wang, 1989). Another thoughtful account of Dr. Choedrak's mental state in prison can be found in a four part series in *News Tibet* by Dr. Albert Crum, Vol. 22, Nos.1-4.

16. TIN, Int. #2, p. 7.

17. See Ronald Schwartz, "Reform and Repression in Tibet," *Telos*, August 1989, p. 17.

18. This is corroborated by testimony from prisoners included in Asia Watch, *Human Rights in Tibet*, p. 30. See also TIN, Int. #7, p. 5.

19. Text of the Tibet Regional People's Government No. 1 from Lhasa Tibet Regional (radio) Service in Mandarin, reprinted by Foreign Broadcast Information Service, FBIS-CHI-89-044, p. 10, March 8, 1989.

20. Chinese Criminal Procedure Law, Article 32.

21. *Accord*, TIN, Int. #5, p. 7.

22. See Asia Watch, *Human Rights in Tibet*, p. 35.

23. See United Nations, Report by the Special Rapporteur, Mr. P. Kooijmans, p. 7.

24. See also Asia Watch, "Evading Scrutiny: Violations of Human Rights After the Closing of Tibet," Washington, D.C., 1988, p. 25.

25. The U.S. Department of State says that the use of electric prods was "common among those detained following protests in Tibet." See *Country Reports on Human Rights Practices for 1988*, p. 765.

26. Although we heard reports of "electric beds" and wrapping prisoners with electric cords or belts, we were unable to independently confirm them, other than one third hand report of a prisoner tied to a metal wall through which electricity was sent.

27. See Amnesty International (Hereafter referred to as AI.), "Torture and Ill-Treatment," p. 3.

28. Daniel Sutherland, "Tibetan Tells of Torture," *Washington Post*, September 6, 1988. See also AI, "Torture and Ill-Treatment," pp. 5-6 and United Nations, Report of the Special Rapporteur, Mr. P. Kooijmans, p. 7.

29. TIN, Int. #8, p. 9.

30. A prisoner reported to Asia Watch that "In winter one is forced to kneel on ice...the pants are rolled up, one is bound tightly and one's [bare] knees are on the ice for an hour." Asia Watch, *Human Rights in Tibet*, p. 31.

31. See AI, "Torture and Ill-Treatment," *supra*, note 39, p.7 and also, interview transcript published in the *Tibet Press Watch*, Vol. 1, p. 41, International Campaign for Tibet. We are not aware of any allegations that physicians were involved in reviving unconscious prisoners by this method.

32. "Lobsang Wangchuk," *Tibetan Bulletin*, Vol. 18, No. 4 (Nov.-Dec., 1987), p. 29.

33. From interview of a Tibetan who requested anonymity, published in the *Tibet Press Watch*, Vol. 1, p. 43, International Campaign for Tibet. See also AI, "Torture and Ill-Treatment" *supra*, note 39, p. 9.

34. See also AI, "Torture and Ill-Treatment," pp. 4, 8.

35. TIN, Int. #7, p.1.

36. From interview transcript published in the *Tibet Press Watch*, Vol.1, p. 43, International Campaign for Tibet. The interview took place in Lhasa in July 1988. The case of this nun is also reported by AI, "Torture and Ill-Treatment," p. 8.

37. Statement of Asia Watch, p. 10. See also Avedon, *In Exile From the Land of the Snows*, Chapter 9.

38. TIN Int. #2, p. 2. AI, Statement before Subcommittee on Foreign Operations, p. 20.

39. United Nations, Report of the Special Rapporteur, Mr. P. Kooijmans, p. 7.

40. See TIN, Int. #8, p. 9.

41. AI, Statement before Subcommittee on Foreign Operations, pp. 21-22. See also "Some used electric sticks...some beat us with rifles," The *Guardian*, November 8, 1989.

42. AI, "Torture and Ill-treatment," p. 12.

43. TIN, Int. #8, p. 11.

44. On January 19, 1989, China announced the sentencing of twenty-seven Tibetans, one of whom was sentenced to death. See AI, Urgent Action on Yulo Dawa Tsering, Lobsang Tenzin, and Sonam Wangdu, January 27, 1989.

Pig's Swill for Survival:
Report from a Chinese Prison Camp

My name is Adhi and I am fifty-six years old. I was born in Nyarong, and have spent twenty-eight years of my life in prisons. I have come here not only to speak for myself but to inform you of the horrible crimes taking place in my homeland.

When the Chinese began to destroy the values that were important to us Tibetans, it came to the point of resistance, of revolt. One day six Chinese policemen came to my house. They took me and my sister's husband prisoner because we were allegedly the principal instigators of the revolts in Eastern Tibet. At that time I was twenty-five years old. I had two children: a three-year-old son and a daughter less than a year old. The Chinese bound them up in our apartment, hit them and kicked them; my son held onto my ankles and cried "Mother! Mother!" The Chinese showed no feeling in the least. The children were yanked back and beaten, and I tried to say a few words of good-bye to them. I was pulled by the hair and forcibly taken away from my children. This separation from my children was the moment

---

This is an edited transcript of Mrs. Adhi's testimony at the Bonn Hearings, April 1989.

of greatest grief in my life. I still hear today the voices of my children calling after me.

My brother-in-law and I were then brought to a prison. We were supposed to give the names of our co-conspirators and of participants in the revolt. We were told we would be shot if we did not comply.

I would like to pass over for now all the details of the torture and abuse that were everyday occurrences in that place. But you can still see traces of their violence on my body. I agreed with my sister's husband to betray no one, at any price. The two of us were pushed to the floor before a group of questioners. We had to kneel down and look each other in the eye. They hung signs around our necks with Chinese characters that we couldn't read. Then they threatened to shoot my brother-in-law unless we gave them the names they wanted. I had to watch as he was murdered before my eyes with a bullet in the head. Later I also found out that my son had gone insane and killed himself by jumping into a river. In this way, I lost two of the people closest to me.

In the prison to which I was first taken, I saw many monks and lamas chained like animals to one another. They were loaded onto trucks and transported to Dartsedo, where they were kept in a monastery that had been ransacked and converted into a prison.

The conditions in the prison were horrendous. The food was a thin soup of cornmeal, more water than cornmeal, doled out three times a day in cups. If you ran your finger around the inside of the cup after drinking, there was nothing there to stick to your fingers. In this prison, I was fortunate to get a "good" chore assigned to me. Together with four other women I was chosen to take care of the Chinese guards' pigs. Now, in this prison the monks had to go to the bathroom in their cells, and twice a day they could carry out the little pots they had for this purpose. I tried to help the monks by stealing some of the pigs' food and leaving it in certain places where they could find it on these short trips out. For them this food was a delicacy.

In time, we were so weakened physically that we staggered when we walked, as if we were drunk. One question dominated all our thoughts: how can I get something to eat? People began to hallucinate. They would cry out, "Can't anybody give me some *tsampa*? Can't

I get some bread somehow?" Our dreams, too, became like this. Every one dreamed only of eating. I have just mentioned that I had been selected with three other women from a group of about 300 others. This secured a certain privilege for us, but we had to pay dearly for it. We were sexually abused by the Chinese functionaries. What went on in the hearts of the women then can surely be imagined by many women.

Every day anywhere from ten to fifteen prisoners died. On the next day they would simply no longer be there. Finally we were nothing but skin and bones. The corpses were piled up near us and covered with earth. The stench of the corpses was almost unbearable. Some of the survivors, including myself, were then taken to another place to work in a lead factory. We had to walk there, three days' journey on foot. On the way we came to a bridge. The experiences of the recent past had been so horrible for me that I thought, "This is the best opportunity for me to jump into the water." The Chinese must have suspected this, though. They bound us together in groups of six, and guards escorted us across. In that moment I had to struggle powerfully with myself. Shall I jump, I thought, and pull my fellow prisoners with me, or should I keep on, out of consideration for the others?

In the lead factory, I found thousands of other Tibetans present. All had wasted away to their bones. To hold themselves upright, each one carried a stick for support. Everyone was staggering around. It looked like the dance of the dead. We women could do our work in the field, which was somewhat better, inasmuch as we could eat grasses and roots there.

In time we also discovered that everything the pigs ate was, to some degree, tolerable for people also. Some people even ate worms and cockroaches, but I could not bring myself to do that. At meals, naturally, there was crowding and pushing, and you had to drink your cup down all at once for fear of losing it in your feebleness. There were also fights over the few drops that would always be left over in the serving bowl. The Chinese amused themselves delightfully over these scenes. They even made a little game of throwing the leftover tea leaves some distance out on the floor, and watching the greatly-weakened prisoners each try to get there first to grab a few leaves. Many did not get nearly that far, but stumbled and fell in the attempt.

I will tell one more story, about a man named Thubten Dhargye. He was caught when, driven by hunger, he was attempting to bite into the calf of a human body in the heap of corpses. When he was beaten and interrogated by the Chinese, he defended himself by saying that he had not eaten anything because there was only skin left on the corpse; and besides, he was too weak to bite through it.

This place in the vicinity of the lead factory today is called "Place of the Corpses." Once I was so weakened that I could no longer speak and became unconscious. The next day I woke up among the corpses. The people came who had the job of carrying away the bodies, and they noticed that I was still alive. That saved me; otherwise I would be in my grave today.

Of the hundred women with whom I went into captivity, the only survivors were the four women who tended the pigs. All the others died of starvation.

JOHN ACKERLY

Hu Yaobang to Hu Jintao: Persecution of Tibetan Buddhism in the 1980s

The persecution of Tibetan Buddhism by the Chinese government is a natural focus of concern—after all, religion so permeated Tibetan society that many of us—rightly or wrongly—have difficulty thinking about Tibet's identity without focusing on Buddhism. Upon learning of the religious holocaust that China imposed on Tibet, world governments could have reacted resolutely, but by then they had an encompassing alibi: China had become the socialist "good guy." After that came the liberalizing 1980s, and now it is common to hear "conditions have improved," "reconstruction of monasteries is allowed," and "religious freedoms are again permitted." It appeared as if China's "liberal" initiatives had won the day.

This study grew out of an attempt to find out what restrictions on religion the authorities are still keeping in place, and who those authorities are. After a year of interviewing scholars, monks, recent arrivals from Tibet, and tourists, and searching through available literature, a preliminary hundred-page report was written, *Forbidden Freedoms: Beijing's Control of Religion in Tibet*, published by the International Campaign for Tibet (ICT). This paper is a condensation of some of the findings from Forbidden Freedoms.

Whether knowledge and data about current religious restrictions can be effectively used to promote greater freedom of religion in the future, is an open question. As one Tibetologist commented recently, "so total was the repression [in Tibet], that Chinese rule was experienced as monolithic and beyond influence." Since 1987, we have witnessed the monolith quiver and have begun to bring it within the sphere of influence. Accurate and detailed information about the extensive infrastructure the Chinese have built in their attempt to govern religion is a first step towards developing programs to support positive forces inside Tibet and dismantling the structures that are strangling Tibetan Buddhism.

One of the few generalizations that can be made about restrictions on religious freedom in Tibet is that they vary significantly in type and degree depending largely upon geographic factors. In general terms, the state of religion in Tibet today is similar to that of traditional Tibetan culture: it thrives in remote areas where the heavy hands of Chinese administrators are absent. Conversely, those monasteries where the authorities are most actively "promoting" religion with funds and personnel are in fact experiencing the most oppressive restrictions on religious freedom.

Nevertheless, from the rubble of the Cultural Revolution, the roots of a religious revival have taken hold in Tibet. The revival appears to be strongest in parts of Kham and Amdo, Tibetan provinces that lie outside the Tibetan Autonomous Region (TAR). Thus, Tibetan traditions are now being preserved best in areas which China, and much of the world, does not consider "Tibet." The existence of a religious revival in Kham and Amdo is the result of many factors, including more educated officials and a modicum of autonomy from Beijing—things the TAR has never had.

Religious policy is dictated by central authorities in Beijing who know little about Tibet—or religion—and implemented by secular, security-oriented cadres and bureaucrats. In the TAR, many of the cadres and bureaucrats are the same officials who participated in the destruction of the monasteries before and during the Cultural Revolution. For example, Rochi Gumbo was sent to Shekar, near Mt.

Everest, in 1959. As a Red Guard commander in the 1960s, he helped to loot and destroy Shekar Monastery. Today he oversees the monastery, imposing his arbitrary will amidst growing sentiment against him. Another example is Kunjo Thargey, head of the Communist Party-controlled committee which runs Sera Monastery. Thargey, a layperson whose wife and children live with him at the monastery, has usurped many of the traditional roles of the abbot.

Religious restrictions remain in Tibet today partly because of a prevalent Chinese contempt and paternalism toward Tibetans and Tibetan Buddhism. It is still common to hear Chinese in Tibet, as well as official publications, calling Tibetans "backward," "superstitious," and "lazy."[1] The Chinese government insists on trying to micromanage the monasteries out of fear that it will lose control of them and out of a belief that they know what is best for Tibet. As the Chinese government has imposed their often ill-suited economic system on Tibet, it also is imposing its social and cultural systems, making the fabric of a colonial relationship complete. One of the more interesting questions for the future is to what extent the continued economic "development" of Tibet is at the expense of the local Tibetan economy, culture, and religion.

RELIGIOUS COLONIALISM: THE APPARATUS OF CONTROL

Religious policy is managed by both the Communist Party structure and the government structure. The Party's highest authorities, the Central Committee and Politburo, guide and authorize religious policy; the policy is developed and implemented by the United Front Work Department (UFWD), which is also in charge of nationality affairs. On the government side, the State Council is the highest authority and under it are the departments which actually carry out religious policy—the Religious Affairs Bureau (RAB) and the Tibetan Buddhist Association (TBA). However, these departments are closely supervised by, and answerable to, the Party.

Following the 1949 invasion, Chinese authorities built an infrastructure of committees, administrators, and lines of authority, and began suppressing religious and cultural life in a classic colonial manner. In the late 1950s, the Chinese established branches of the RAB and TBA in Lhasa. Initially these bureaus were staffed with some Tibetans appointed by His Holiness the Dalai Lama, although the Tibetans had little actual power. Both of these bodies were closed down during the Cultural Revolution and were reopened in the late 1970s in order to direct and control the new policy of permitting a degree of religious freedom. The policy began in the mid-1970s but did not firmly take hold until 1980 when Hu Yaobang, the General Secretary of the Communist Party, made his historic visit to Tibet. Hu publicly recognized part of the devastation that Chinese policies had wrought on the country and is reported to have said that the situation in Tibet reminded him of "colonialism." His visit presaged the beginning of China's current strategy in Tibet of maintaining political control through economic liberalization on the one hand and carefully managed accommodation of national and religious sentiments on the other.[2]

Most of the restrictions on religion are enforced by the Religious Affairs Bureau.[3] The official functions of the RAB are to oversee the restoration and reconstruction of monasteries, to administer funds allocated by Beijing for these projects, and to screen applicants seeking admission to major monasteries. According to official Party documents: "[A]ll places of worship are under the administrative control of the Bureau of Religious Affairs."[4]

The Tibetan Buddhist Association functions as an advisory body to the RAB and as a conduit between the government and practicing Buddhists.[5] Unlike the RAB, the TBA appears to have no independent authority over the monasteries. The TBA undertakes historical research and forwards suggestions to government offices. Officially, the TBA currently follows the principle of "equal importance to agriculture and faith," as propounded by the CBA.[6]

Within each monastery, religious policy is carried out by the "Democratic Management Committees" (DMC) which have been set up by Chinese authorities in all of Tibet's major monasteries. The DMCs were initially established following the 1959 uprising with the aid of special reform teams. According to official documents, they were given "full powers in routine matters—economy, housing, food, and political study—and in their ranks the poor lamas predominated."[7] Today the DMCs are the highest authority of a monastery and the principle organ charged with overseeing the operation of its affairs.[8] According to official Chinese sources, an important role of DMCs is to "receive guidance and support from relevant government departments in charge of religious affairs, and keep them informed of any problems in implementing state policies."[9] Reports indicate that DMCs range in nature from highly-repressive, government-controlled bodies in larger monasteries to relatively independent, trustworthy bodies, usually in smaller, remote monasteries.

The DMCs have uprooted the monastic hierarchy under the abbot who traditionally enforced discipline, oversaw liturgical acts, organized assembly and prayer meetings, and guided spiritual development. While the DMC may not exert day-to-day control over some of the more religious functions of the monastery, it clearly has the power to intervene in even the most religious matters. The DMCs are solely a creation of the Chinese authorities and often directly collaborate with security forces to arrest and expel monks, but they have drawn surprisingly little attention from Western human rights monitors and the Tibetan Government-in-Exile.

THE POLITICS OF RECONSTRUCTION

The Chinese government widely touts its funding of monastic reconstruction projects. The Tibetan Government-in-Exile asserts that funds claimed to be disbursed to monasteries are often not actually disbursed, and that the amounts are insignificant compared to the value of what China looted and destroyed. It asserts that funding for reconstruction is a cynical gesture amidst the network of religious restrictions and is aimed at impressing foreign tourists.

In order to control the pace of reconstruction, Chinese authorities have often required that Tibetans secure prior approval from the government.[10] As a result, Tibetans must be persistent in their attempts to obtain building approval, and there have been arrests for unauthorized construction activities.[11]

The Panchen Lama incessantly fought for the right of Tibetan communities to rebuild monasteries with some degree of success. Nevertheless, opposition from Beijing to "indiscriminate" building has been strong over the years. An official article in 1983 appearing in *Nanfang Ribao* (Southern Daily) stated:

[We] oppose the indiscriminate building of temples. At present, many localities have engaged in large-scale construction of temples, wasting a lot of manpower, materials, and funds. This is very harmful.[12]

The Tibetan Government-in-Exile claims that there were over 6,200 monasteries in Tibet prior to 1950 and official Chinese sources admit to over 2,400. Both sides agree that by the 1970s only a handful were left standing.[13] Now, Chinese sources say that there are over 200 functioning monasteries, which appears to be reasonable, though lists confirming or rebutting this figure have not been provided by either Beijing or Dharamsala. The number of monasteries reconstructed is an important measure of progress. Yet frequently, a "reconstructed" monastery is only marginally restored, and the number of resident monks is likely to be only five to ten percent of the original number before the destruction of the site.

THE MISSING LINK: MONASTIC EDUCATION

The inability of monasteries to function as genuine centers of learning and transmission of Buddhist teachings is one of the foremost concerns of all the monks interviewed and consulted in preparing this study. A prominent monk now in exile in Dharamsala describes current religious education in Tibet as "similar to allowing children to go to a school where there is no classroom, no teacher, and no books."[14] Nevertheless, monasteries are one of the few places in Tibet today where young Tibetans can get the equivalent of a primary and secondary education in Tibetan language and culture.

The onerous restrictions and control of Lhasa's great monasteries—Drepung, Ganden, and Sera—have an inordinate impact on religious education. These monasteries were not only the Harvard, Oxford, and Sorbonne of Tibet, but they were, with a few exceptions, the only monasteries in Tibet which offered advanced study and the *geshe* (doctorate) degree. The lack of religious freedom in these monasteries, compared to the relative freedoms enjoyed in Kham and Amdo, is thus having a devastating effect on Tibetan Buddhism.

According to monks interviewed for the study, the obstacles to restoring quality religious education in Tibet's monasteries are:

1. Shortage of qualified teachers;

2. Lack of administrative control over monastic education;
3. Insufficient number of students; and
4. Regulations requiring monks to work long hours, leaving insufficient time for studying.

The shortage of teachers is mostly the result of the mass killing and internment of monks between 1959 and 1980. Secondly, most of the few remaining qualified teachers have fled to India where they can freely transmit the teachings and preserve the traditions until they can return. Administrative control over the monasteries is necessary to create an atmosphere conducive to study as opposed to the fear and forced indoctrination sessions prevalent in monasteries today. As for burdensome work requirements, a recent article by a Chinese-backed monk announced the beginning of "a new category of lamas, known as Lalang." This category of monk will be in charge of farming, animal husbandry, commerce, and other productive labor. There is no mention as to whether these monks will receive any religious or educational training or will participate in religious ceremonies.[15]

It is an exaggeration to say that no teaching is going on in Tibet; the advanced geshe degree is now being conferred at Drepung and Sera monasteries, although under very restrictive conditions. Nevertheless, the level of monastic education remains abysmal, far short of meeting the need and demand throughout Tibet.

OBSTACLES TO BECOMING A MONK

Official Party documents stipulate that religious institutions "should hold entrance examinations and admit upright, patriotic young people ... who have reached a certain level of cultural development."[16] The Party's interest in admission decisions is clearly political and security-oriented, although it is unclear to what extent they can implement their policy:

> We must foster a large number of fervent patriots in every religion who accept the leadership of the Party and government, firmly support the Socialist path, and safeguard national and ethnic unity. They should be learned in religious matters and capable of keeping close links with the representatives of the religious masses.[17]

Young Tibetans are admitted to monasteries through a number of procedures, ranging from the relatively traditional agreement between the candidate's parents and his teacher, to an extremely politicized process controlled by Communist Party officials. In Tibet today, candidates must have some, and on rare occasions, all of the following qualifications:

1. The candidate should be at least eighteen years old;
2. The candidate should "love" the country and the Communist Party;
3. The candidate's parents must give their consent;
4. The candidate and the candidate's parents should have a good political background;
5. The candidate must have been raised in a certain geographic area;
6. The candidate must have approval from the monastery's DMC;
7. The candidate must have approval from local authorities;
8. The candidate must have approval from county or provincial authorities; and
9. The candidate must have clearance from the Public Security Bureau.

The requirements that a novice be eighteen years old to enter a monastery[18] contradicts Buddhist scripture which states that children who have reached the age of seven may take monastic vows provided they obtain their parents' permission. This requirement is clearly ignored in some areas and selectively applied in others, but it remains a legitimate and frequently-cited example that the Chinese government remains disrespectful of Tibetan traditions.

Size limits placed on monasteries are another example of oppressive restrictions most commonly cited by Tibetans. While regulations for setting and changing the limits are not exactly known, published regulations for Guangdong province provide us with a good idea of what probably is occurring in Tibet: Buddhist Temples "should set a personnel quota in line with their concrete needs" which "will be approved by the people's government at the county level or above."

Additions to personnel within the specified limits "must be approved by the governmental department in charge of religious affairs."[19] Official government limits are characteristically less than 10% of the original number of monks; however, the limit at Tashilhunpo monastery is reportedly twice that amount, due to the influence of the Panchen Lama.

These methods of suppressing the number of monks in Tibet are effective in some areas. Lhasa, for example, only has around 2,000 monks spread amongst monasteries that used to have ten times that number. There were anywhere from 600,000 to 1,000,000—or even more—monks and nuns in Tibet prior to 1950. It is impossible to determine how many there are today, but there are probably tens of thousands, including those in Kham and Amdo. Chinese sources put the figure as high as 45,000, including Kham and Amdo.[20]

CURRENT RULES FOR SEARCHING FOR REINCARNATIONS

During the first decades of Chinese rule, public recognition of reincarnations was prohibited. In 1985, it was reported that reincarnated monks recognized before 1959 will be treated as such, but no new reincarnations will be recognized.[21] It appears that policy continued to change through the end of the decade to the point that, following the death of the Panchen Lama, Li Peng ordered that the search for his reincarnation be restricted to areas with China's borders and that it be conducted by a government-organized committee. The Panchen Lama's successor must also be approved by the State Council.[22] Tibetan officials-in-exile denounced this move as an illegitimate secular intrusion into an intimately religious matter and a desecration and violation of an ancient religious tradition.[23]

ICT recently received more specific rules from a reliable source inside Tibet. According to this document, the current regulations promulgated for searching for reincarnations are:

1. The search must be conducted under the leadership and guidance of the CCP;
2. The reincarnation must be found within Chinese territory, not in a foreign country;

3. The reincarnation must be determined and recognized by lamas who remain in China. Those who live abroad have no right to either determine or recognize a reincarnation; and

4. Reincarnations must not be found in the families of Communist Party members.

RESTRICTIONS ON LAYPEOPLE

It is often noted that freedom of religion in Tibet consists of the freedom of laypeople to perform a variety of ritualistic observances and that restrictions are aimed at the monks and nuns. Many Tibetans will say that hardly any restrictions are imposed on laypeople. Yet some notable restrictions remain, such as the ability to receive religious teachings.

Preaching religion anywhere other than religious sites is prohibited by law.[24] In Kham's Kanze Prefecture, authorities state that "of course, to undertake religious activities outside the religious site is abnormal and must be forbidden."[25] Traditionally, Tibetans received teachings in their homes and other public and private places outside of the monasteries. The government claims that because people are free to visit places of religious worship, the ban on preaching outside of monasteries "does not discourage religious belief in the least."[26] This policy, however, prevents many laypeople from attending or hosting religious rites in private homes and public areas.

Throughout Tibet, Chinese authorities severely restrict monks from performing public religious rites and teachings. In Lhasa, only a few monks are permitted to give teachings to large groups of laypeople. The Venerable Lamrimpa Ngawang Phuntshog from Drepung and Geshe Senge from Sera are two exceptions.[27] In an attempt to limit the rapid spread of discontent to rural areas in Tibet, authorities are reported to be discouraging and restricting monks from serving nomad populations.[28]

Chinese authorities have always shown outward contempt and animosity toward the amount of resources Tibetans devote to religion. Recent regulations call upon religious leaders to reform outmoded customs and institute new ones—for example, "simple" marriages and funerals are encouraged.[29] In November 1990, a Chinese-backed monk criticized the number of festivals Tibetans hold each year and the amount of roasted barley that is wasted.[30] These are a few blatant examples of how the Party continues to interfere in the religious lives of laypeople.

TOURISM: HELP OR HINDRANCE?

The assertion that the liberalization of religion in Tibet amounts to nothing more than a "facade" for the benefit of tourists is not confirmed by this study. While there is evidence supporting this view, there are many areas of Tibet, particularly in Amdo and Kham, that are experiencing religious revivals even though few, if any, Western tourists frequent the area.

Official Party documents explicitly acknowledge the value of monasteries for tourism. For example, one document calls for "painstaking efforts to safeguard" monasteries, and to keep them in good repair "so that the surroundings are clean, peaceful, and quiet, suitable for tourism."[31] It also seeks restoration of temples and churches which have "international prestige."

There can be no doubt that Chinese authorities promote the monasteries around Lhasa as tourist attractions. Tourists are a mixed blessing for monasteries. On the one hand, tourists bring Chinese administrators, and thus the monastery will be subjected to regulations and restrictions that remote monasteries are not. On the other hand, tourists bring a way for monks and nuns to communicate their grievances with the West, although tour guides try to discourage these interactions. The economic benefits to the monastery are unclear; entrance fees to monasteries go into an account controlled by Chinese authorities which are then spent according to Chinese wishes—not as the Tibetans would spend them. One monk interviewed for this paper reported that Sera monastery took in over 40,000 yuan from tourists in 1987, but it all went to "beautification" projects to make the monastery more photogenic, instead of projects that would improve the quality of life and education of the monks.

Another monk said that it is offensive to charge entrance fees and that donations should be voluntary. The monk thought that entrance fees were a way for the Chinese authorities to ensure that they, and not the monks, received the proceeds. This monk believed that the

Chinese authorities use tourist funds not only for beautification projects, but also to pay the salaries of the members of the Democratic Management Committee as well as to informants and other expenses that were directly inimical to the interests of the monastery. Because Chinese immigrants profit economically from tourism much more than Tibetans, some Tibetans have called upon tourists not to visit Tibet.[32]

There are reports from other monasteries that authorities demand that monks stop their normal routine, put on their robes, and pray in the prayer hall or perform a debate when a tourist bus arrives. Monks at Kumbum report having to put on a religious show when important officials came to visit.[33] One article in the *New Yorker* described how a Chinese tour guide explained that there were no Tibetans visiting the Potala because "if we let them in, there would be so many that tourists wouldn't be able to get through."[34] Another recent article described that tour guides pay monks for their "performances," a humiliation that some monks tolerate and others denounce.[35]

CONCLUSIONS

The policy of limited freedom established in the early 1980s after Hu Yaobang's visit remains basically unchanged, although it has been restricted since the fall of 1987. Hu Jintao, the current Party overlord of Tibet who is considered a "liberal," has yet to firmly align himself as a liberal in the area of Tibetan Buddhism. A positive sign is the growing number of Tibetan cadres. Since the early 1980s, the Chinese government has been trying to diminish some of the more obvious indicators of colonialism by installing Tibetan cadres in place of Chinese ones. While this is superficial in many ways, it is believed that even Tibetans who actively collaborate with the Chinese will have a greater sensitivity and sympathy for Buddhism.

Despite the Chinese efforts to promote their image of Buddhism and suppress Tibetan Buddhism, Tibetans are continuously finding ways of somehow avoiding the restrictions and keeping alive their traditions. Under the current conditions, much of the traditional monastic expression of Tibetan Buddhism will continue to languish, but a religious-based nationalism will prosper. The gains made this decade such as modest amounts of physical reconstruction and an increase in freedom for laypeople to worship appear to have a relatively stable base and could be expanded during the 1990s.

The Panchen Lama and other Tibetans have been able to push the limits of religious freedom set by Beijing. With the death of Panchen Rinpoche, some Tibet watchers believe that His Holiness the Dalai Lama should try to assist, for example, certain monasteries which are trying to overcome particularly harsh restrictions. In the past, the Dalai Lama and the Tibetan Government-in-Exile have focused on building and improving institutions in exile. The Dalai Lama has specifically cautioned that putting too much emphasis on rebuilding monasteries in Tibet is risky because conditions remain unstable and gains could be lost. Rather, he urged, that monks first make sure that the traditions are being kept alive in India, so that they can be transplanted back to Tibet in the future. As one commentator put it:

> Like a species of animal that has become extinct in the wild but can once again be introduced from one of the parks maintained for just such an endangered species, the Dalai Lama and his followers may someday be able to return to their home in Tibet and infuse it with a new, more modern, and relevant strain of Buddhism.[36]

The wisdom of this strategy is unimpeachable yet it should not be seen as exclusive of the efforts by Tibetans inside Tibet to secure greater religious freedom and rebuild their monasteries. As the Chinese Communist Party loses credibility and the ability to govern the country, Tibetans appear to be more prepared to seize opportunities that could have a lasting impact on preserving Tibetan culture and Buddhism. Western governments, support groups, religious organizations, and dharma centers can assist the process of securing increased freedoms either through the Government-in-Exile or other channels. After all, Premier Li Peng recently reiterated that the government supports expanded contacts between religious circles and overseas friends, while guarding against interference through religion by overseas hostile forces.

---

1. A 1985 official report published in the *Peking Economic Research Journal* stated: "They [Tibetans] lack the capacity to absorb advanced technology and are highly imbued with a character of laziness." Quoted in "Masters of the

House." *Far Eastern Economic Review*, July 11, 1985. See also "Lhasa's Lingering Left." *Far Eastern Review*, January 30, 1986.

2. Ronald Schwartz, "The Anti-Splittist Campaign and the Development of Tibetan Political Consciousness," paper presented at the First International Conference on Modern Tibet, London, March 1990, p. 3.

3. In 1985, the RAB merged with the Nationalities Affairs Commission and now it is often called the Nationalities and Religious Affairs Commission.

4. "The Basic Viewpoint and Policy on the Religious Question during Our Country's Socialist Period," Art. VI. Promulgated in March, 1982, "Document 19," as it is commonly called, was directed at Party and state cadres at all levels to provide policy guidelines so that cadres will have "correct and effective methods" for carrying out religious policy. See Donald MacInnis (ed.), *Religion in China Today*. New York: Orbis Books, 1989, p. 2.

5. One of the three original objectives of the TBA's parent organization, the Chinese Buddhist Association, was to "unite government in the movement to love the fatherland." *NCNA*, June 8, 1963. See Richard Bush, *Religion in Communist China*. New York: Abingdon Press, 1970, p. 304.

6. Zhogmi Jambalozhoi, "Tibetan Buddhism: Flourishing Research and Education," in *Tibetans on Tibet*. Beijing: China Reconstructs Press, 1988, p. 134.

7. Israel Epstein, *Tibet Transformed*. Beijing: New World Press, 1983, p. 417.

8. *China Daily*, June 18, 1990.

9. Jing Wei, *100 Questions About Tibet*. Beijing: Beijing Review Press, 1989, p. 61.

10. Religious regulations from Guangdong province require that "any renovation, reconstruction, or extension of churches and temples must be approved by the department in charge of religious affairs of the people's government at the county level or above." See MacInnis, *Op. Cit.*

11. Asia Watch, *Human Rights in Tibet*. New York, 1988, p. 15.

12. "Indiscriminate Building of Temples in Rural Areas Should be Curbed," *Nanfang Ribao*, June 5, 1983. Another article criticized "one period, when religion became almost government policy and practice and on that basis expanded without limits." *Xizang Ribao*, August 7, 1989.

13. "Changing Life of Lamas," *Xinhua*, March 24, 1979, p. 16.

14. Karma Gelek Yuthok, "An Outline of Some Recent Claims by China on Religious Freedom and Development in Tibet," unpublished paper, 1989, p. 1.

15. "Living Buddha on Tibet Human Rights," *Ta Kung Pao*, November 9, 1990. Reprinted in *FBIS*, November 15, 1990.

16. "The Basic Viewpoint and Policy on the Religious Question during Our Country's Socialist Period," *supra* n. 4, Art. VIII.

17. *Ibid.*

18. See Jing Wei, *Op. Cit., supra* n. 13, p. 61; "Monks Feel China's Heavy Hand," *Christian Science Monitor,* November 30, 1989.

19. "Regulations for Guangdong Province," *supra* n. 10, Art. 18.

20. See e.g. United Nations, Report by the Chinese Delegation to the 44th Session of the Commission on Human Rights, December 30, 1988, (E/CN.4/ 1989/44) p. 12; Jing Wei, *Op. Cit., supra* n. 9, p. 61; *Beijing Review,* October 17, 1988; U.S. Department of State, "Special Report on the Treatment of Minorities in China," 1987, p. 15.

21. "Limitations of Religious Freedom," *Tibetan Review,* April, 1985; June Dreyer, "Unrest in Tibet," *Current History,* September, 1989, p. 283.

22. "Monks Clash with China over New Tibetan Leader," *South China Morning Post,* February 24, 1990; "Search for Buddhist Leader Inflames Tibet Debate," *Washington Post,* March 10, 1990.

23. "The Tibetan Tradition of Recognizing Reincarnate Lamas," *Me-Long,* December 1989.

24. "Government Functionary Discusses Religion," *Beijing Review,* August 14, 1989.

25. Ganze Prefecture Propaganda Committee, February 1990, Chapter 5.

26. "Government Functionary Discusses Religion," *Beijing Review,* August 14, 1989.

27. Asia Watch, *Human Rights in Tibet, supra* n .11, p .18.

28. "Tibet: Struggling to Survive," *Third World Week,* October 5, 1990, p. 38.

29. "Party Before God, Religious Leaders Told," *London Observer,* October 31, 1990.

30. "Living Buddha on Tibet Human Rights," *Ta Kung Pao,* November 9, 1990. Reprinted in *FBIS,* November 15, 1990.

31. "The Basic Viewpoint and Policy on the Religious Question during Our Country's Socialist Period," *supra* n. 4, Art. VI.

32. See Jamyang Norbu, *Illusion and Reality,* New Delhi: Sona Printers, 1989, pp. 80-82.

33. Ronald Schwartz, "Religious Freedom and the Monasteries of Tibet," *Cho-yang: The Voice of Tibetan Religion and Culture,* No. 3, p. 114.

34. "Report From China," *The New Yorker,* October 22, 1990.

35. "Tibet: Struggling to Survive," *Third World Week,* October 5, 1990.

36. Orville Schell, "Dispatches from the Tibetan Plateau," *Natural History,* January 1991, p. 66.

MICHAEL VAN WALT VAN PRAAG

Population Transfer
and the Survival of the Tibetan Identity

The immigration of Chinese into Tibet has reached alarming proportions, causing fears that Tibetans will, in the near future, be reduced to an insignificant minority in their own country and will lose their distinct national cultural and religious heritage and identity. The evidence indicates that the government of the People's Republic of China (PRC) is actively encouraging the transfer of Chinese from Chinese provinces to Tibet and establishing Chinese settlements throughout the country, while simultaneously advocating a policy of segregation of Tibetan communities from the more affluent Chinese communities and assimilation of the young Tibetans with the Chinese. The object of this policy is to "resolve" China's territorial claims over Tibet by means of a massive and irreversible population shift.

In pursuing this policy, the Chinese government is violating the fundamental human rights of the Tibetan people. Not only is Beijing violating the universally-accepted rule of international law that prohibits the transfer of citizens to and from occupied territory, a rule

Excerpt from published paper. Second revised edition, January 1988.

to which the PRC is bound by treaty; it is also violating the Tibetan people's right to self-determination. In fact, China's population transfer policy is undermining the Constitution of the People's Republic of China itself, which recognizes the right of Tibetans, and other so-called minority nationalities, to regional autonomy, but only so long as they live in compact communities.[1]

THE RECENT TRANSFER OF CHINESE TO TIBET

To this day, the Chinese have probably sent over seven million civilians into Tibet, in addition to which they maintain at least 400,000 troops in the country (250,000 of them in the Tibet Autonomous Region).[2] Since the Tibetan population is, at most, six million,[3] the Chinese have already outnumbered the Tibetans on the Tibetan plateau. Recent reports from Tibet and from China show a steady and alarming increase in the transfer of Chinese into Tibet,[4] particularly into the so-called Autonomous Region. The principal difficulty in assessing the extent of the Chinese influx into Tibet results from the Chinese authorities' use of population statistics. Only the Chinese who have formally registered as residents in Tibetan areas are included in official immigrant figures.[5] Yet, most recent settlers in Tibet have not registered and, consequently, do not figure in China's Tibet statistics. This problem is most pronounced in the TAR, where large numbers of Chinese settlers have been arriving since 1984.

While few Chinese lived in the Tibetan province of Amdo (renamed Qinghai province and Kanlho Tibetan Autonomous Area) prior to 1950, the Chinese settlers today outnumber the Tibetans three to one. The first wave of settlers was sent to Amdo in the 1950s, the second wave was launched in the early 1980s. The *International Herald Tribune* reported in January of 1983 that Beijing was encouraging young Chinese to move to Qinghai by appealing to their patriotism and by offering higher wages.[6]

Kham, Tibet's eastern province, has also been subjected to Chinese colonization since the 1950s. The number of Chinese settlers in Kham at the present time is conservatively estimated at over two million but less than half of them have registered. Currently there are close to three million Tibetans in the region.[7] The highest concentration of Chinese is found in the cities and towns where they generally constitute the majority of the population. In some places, the percentage is as high as 75%.[8] The lower altitudes of Kham's eastern valleys, and their proximity to the PRC's populous provinces of Sichuan and Yunnan, makes widespread incursion inevitable.[9]

With the arrival of the Chinese, the distinct Tibetan identity is being destroyed, discrimination is practiced openly, and unemployment among the Tibetans is becoming a serious problem.[10] AFP correspondent Pierre Donnet reported from Tibet:

> Tibet's two largest cities, Lhasa and Shigatse,....look thoroughly Chinese with residential districts and administrative buildings indistinguishable from their Beijing counterparts. Colorfully clad Tibetans are hard to spot among the Chinese who crowd the streets and make up more than half the population of Tibet's capital, Lhasa...The overwhelming majority of the merchants are Chinese. In this way, [the Chinese] may quietly but definitely complete the integration of this region called "the roof of the world" with the rest of China.[11]

Radio programs reinforce the penetration of the Chinese language in Tibet and the Central Television Station, recently introduced in Tibetan cities and transmitted by satellite from Beijing, will have an even greater effect. Furthermore, Donnet reports, the education provided in Chinese schools in Tibet is better than that offered in Tibetan schools, and reports reaching India indicate that large numbers of Tibetan children are being taken to China for schooling, away from their families and isolated from their culture.

A correspondent of the *Asian Wall Street Journal* in Lhasa recently warned: "The most significant threat to Lhasa's Tibetan identity comes from recent government efforts to increase the number of Chinese settlers in Tibet—an expression made possible by the new tourist revenue."[12]

THE CHINESE GOVERNMENT POLICY

The government in Beijing officially denies the existence of a policy to relocate Chinese in Tibet.[13] At the same time, Chinese publications, such as *News From China*, issued by the Chinese Embassy in New Delhi, and the official *Beijing Review*, published in Beijing, frequently refer to government encouragement for the settlement of Chinese nationals in Tibet. The urgent need for Chinese personnel to help develop an economically and culturally "backward" Tibet is generally cited as the justification for this policy. The need to relieve excess population and unemployment in China is also given as a reason. Thus, in early 1983, Ren Tao and Yue Bing wrote in *Beijing Review* that "one more outlet that holds immense promise for rural surplus labour lies in China's vast mountainous regions."[14] Two years later, Xinhua news agency reported that "large numbers of peasants" from China's more developed areas "are pouring into remote western areas to earn a living. They have found Qinghai, Tibet, and Xinjiang viable areas for selling goods, building houses and roads, making furniture and clothes, and providing other services."[15] Even Deng Xiaoping admitted that Chinese were being encouraged to move into Tibet because, according to China's supreme leader, the local population "needed Han immigrants as the [Autonomous] region's population of about two million was inadequate to develop its resources."[16]

In order to encourage young people "to dedicate themselves to the construction of border regions," the State Planning Commission, the Ministry of Education, and the Ministry of Labor and Personnel decided in 1983 "to appropriately raise the pay of those graduates who work in the remote areas and countryside." The Chinese government promised further favorable treatment in pay and home leave "to those who go to work in Tibet, Qinghai, and other [Tibetan] plateau areas for a long time."[17] In a later issue of *Beijing Review* (October 10, 1983), it was announced that "the Chinese Government has adopted a series of measures to encourage scientists and technicians from all over China to work in regions inhabited by the minority nationalities." The report explained:

> These regions of Inner Mongolia, Xinjiang, Tibet, Qinghai, Ninxia, Yunnan, Guizhou, Guanxi, and Guangdong make up 60% of the nation's total territory and are inhabited by sixty-seven million minority peoples, or 6.7% of China's total population. Ninety percent of China's grasslands and seven of its ten major forest areas are located in these regions, which also boast a wide variety of cash crops and abundant mineral and water resources... From these facts, it is clear why the government is attaching increasing importance to the development of these regions.

Once again, special wage benefits were promised exclusively to college and secondary technical school graduates moving to the "Tibet-Qinghai plateau." Furthermore, in order to encourage them to *stay* in Tibet, the government announced that "those who wish to stay on after eight years enjoy further pay raises. Those who have worked there for more than twenty years and stay on after retirement will have their pensions increased by 10%."[18] Currently, a special effort is being made to retire Chinese army personnel and their families in Tibet.[19]

The government policies have evidently had some effect, for *Beijing Review* reported on February 27, 1984, that Tibetans were now "fighting shoulder to shoulder with the large numbers of Hans who have sacrificed the comforts of their home towns and dedicated themselves to modernizing the Tibetan areas." *Radio Beijing* announced on May 14, 1984, that over 60,000 workers, representing the vanguard of a large Chinese workforce, were on their way to the Tibet Autonomous Region where they would be employed in the electricity department, in schools, hotels, cultural institutions, and factories. An editorial in *Beijing Review* explained the central government's policy in terms of the need to revitalize the economy of Tibet and "overcome its economic and cultural backwardness."[20]

In October, *Beijing Review* reported that "unsparing help is flowing in steadily from China's more developed regions, bringing the much needed labor, funds and expertise [to the TAR]. Sichuan alone sent 10,000 construction workers. Large numbers of technicians and skilled workers have also arrived from several provinces to join the construction of Tibet's forty-three new projects."[21]

Regarding these "forty-three projects" an earlier issue specified that "All phases of construction including designing, building, and interior decorating are handled by personnel supplied by the cooperative provinces and cities [of China]."[22] In Lhasa alone, 70,000 workers were announced, 50,000 of whom had arrived by the end of the year[23] and thousands more "peddlers and craftsmen from more than twenty provinces" followed.[24] In the Shigatse area, south of Lhasa, 20,000 Chinese construction workers had already arrived in July.

By April 1985, 230,000 new Chinese workers had arrived in the TAR: 100,000 in and around Lhasa and the remainder in the Shigatse, Lokha, and Nagchukha areas. The number has grown since then, but precise figures are not available. This large influx has caused food shortages and put many Tibetans out of work.[25] In 1985, about 30,000 Tibetans reportedly lost their jobs to newly-arrived Chinese settlers in Lhasa and surrounding areas,[26] while some 20,000 Tibetans lost their jobs in other parts of the TAR.[27] In one instance last spring, 3,000 Tibetan construction workers, who had moved to Lhasa in search of work from the Lhoka area south of the capital, were expelled from the city by the Chinese authorities for not having residence permits, while thousands of newly-arrived Chinese construction workers, who also lacked residence permits, were being provided jobs and housing by those same authorities.[28]

As for the future, Chinese predictions speak for themselves. A report entitled "Movement Westward," by the Chinese Embassy in New Delhi,[29] highlights Beijing's intention to "change both the ecological imbalance and the population lack" not just in Tibet but in other "sparsely populated outlying regions" in the western PRC. Chinese migration should be welcomed by the local population, according to the Embassy report, and should result in a population increase of sixty million over the next thirty years in those regions. The report adds: "This is a very conservative estimate. As a matter of fact, the increase might swell to 100 million in less than thirty years."

CHINA'S POLICIES VIOLATE INTERNATIONAL LAW

The transfer of civilians by an occupying power into the territory it occupies is a violation of the fundamental human rights of the people under occupation. This is a universally-accepted principle of international law and one to which the PRC is bound by treaty. The applicable rule of international law and its foundation is concisely formulated by the International Commission of Jurists, as follows:

> Insofar as there existed any doubt about it in the period preceding World War II, the Charter of the United Nations unambiguously rejected the "right to conquest." It was on the basis of this purported right that colonial powers throughout history invaded other territories and settled part of their own population in them. With the right to conquest, the right to create settlements has also disappeared, and what is left is the bare right of temporary military occupation where

necessary in lawful self-defense. This does not include a right to establish settlements of a civilian nature or settlements of a permanent character.[30]

The *Geneva Convention Relative to the Protection of Civilian Persons In Time of War*,[31] generally referred to as the "Fourth Geneva Convention," prescribes rules to mitigate the hardship and suffering that can be imposed on civilian populations, "not only during the hostilities themselves, but also after a cease fire or truce, when civilians could be subjected to military occupation in the absence of a final political settlement."[32]

The overriding aim of the Convention is to ensure that claims of military expediency do not result in the violation of basic political and human rights of the civilians in the territory under occupation. It includes customary law on the subject as well as treaty law and is "human rights law in the most fundamental sense."[33] Professor W.T. Mallison testified before the Committee on the Judiciary of the United States Senate:

> The governments which have created this law have acted on the assumption that even urgent military necessity cannot be allowed to deprive human beings of certain elementary protections. The overriding purpose of the Geneva Conventions of 1949, as reflected in negotiating history, was to avoid a repetition of the atrocities and massive deprivations of human rights which were afflicted upon civilian populations during the second World War by the Nazis in Europe and Russia and by the Japanese militarists in Asia.[34]

Article 49 of the Fourth Geneva Convention expressly deals with population transfers. The last paragraph reads:

> The Occupying Power shall not deport or transfer parts of its own civilian population into the territory it occupies.

Apart from the clear wording of this article, the general principle of international law underlying the rules relating to military occupation requires that the occupying power "administer the [occupied] country, not only in the interest of his own military advantage, but also, at any rate so far as possible, for the public benefit of the inhabitants."[35] The Convention, particularly Article 49, should be given the broadest possible application. "Much of the Convention, including Article 49, is declaratory of pre-existing international law and such provisions in the Convention should be recognized as being of universal applicability and binding in all circumstances upon High Contracting Parties."[36]

The International Committee of the Red Cross' authoritative Commentary to the Fourth Geneva Convention emphasized that:

> ...occupation of territory in wartime is essentially a temporary, de facto situation, which deprives the occupied Power of neither its statehood nor its sovereignty; it merely interferes with its power to exercise its rights...[and] cannot imply any right whatsoever to dispose of territory." The Committee stressed the fundamental principle that "an Occupying Power continues to be bound to apply the Convention as a whole even when, in disregard of the rules of international law, it claims during a conflict to have annexed all or part of an occupied territory."[37]

The protection provided by the Fourth Geneva Convention, again, Article 49 in particular, clearly extends to the people of Tibet.

Tibet was invaded and forcibly occupied by the armies of the People's Republic of China in 1949-50. The so-called Seventeen-Point Agreement for the Peaceful Liberation of Tibet was forced upon the Tibetan government following the invasion of the country by eighty thousand troops and consequently never had any validity. Other attempts by the Chinese to annex Tibet were equally unlawful, so that today Tibet is still a country under illegal occupation.[38] There is general agreement among travelers to Tibet that the region today has all the characteristics of a country under occupation. Besides, Article 47 of the Fourth Geneva Convention provides:

> Protected persons who are in occupied territory shall not be deprived, in any case or any manner whatsoever, of the benefits of the present Convention by any change introduced, as the result of the occupation of a territory, into the institutions or government of the said territory, or by any agreement concluded between the authorities of the occupied territories and the Occupying Power, nor by any annexation by the latter of the whde or the part of the occupied territory.

Thus, irrespective of the de facto status of Tibet today, Tibetans are entitled to the protection of the Geneva Convention at least with respect to population transfers.

The PRC is a Party to the Geneva Conventions, which it ratified in 1956.[39] The PRC does not consider itself an "Occupying Power" because it contends that Tibet has been an integral part of China for centuries and its armies, therefore, neither invaded nor occupied Tibet in 1949-50. Tibetans are not protected by the Convention, the Chinese argue, since it is intended to protect only the "legitimate sovereign," and Tibet was and is not a sovereign state.

As pointed out earlier, the sovereignty argument ignores the fundamental purpose of the Fourth Geneva Convention and the principles of international law it codifies. As Professor Mallison stressed, "the goal of the Conventions was not to respond to claims of sovereignty but to prevent the violation of basic human rights." He continues:

> [In] a number of the post-World War II war crimes trials conducted by the Western Allies, Nazi defendants employed elaborate arguments, including questioning the title to "occupied territory" to avoid the application of the then effective customary and conventional international humanitarian law as criteria for judging the criminality or innocence of their conduct. Although these arguments were rejected by the war crimes tribunals, the four Geneva Conventions of 1949 were written in careful language so as to avoid the possibility of raising these defenses again.[40]

The first two articles of the Convention and the negotiating history make it clear that, just as the lack of a declaration of war is irrelevant, so are questions as to *de jure* titles to territory, for

> ...the Convention must be applied in occupied territory whatever the claims concerning the *de jure* status of that territory....The idea that in order to apply the law of the belligerent occupation it is necessary for the belligerent to recognize the displaced government's title to the territory finds no support in either the text of the Convention or its negotiating history. In addition, it is contrary to the well-established customary law based upon state practice.[41]

China's recognition or rejection of Tibetan claims to sovereignty are consequently irrelevant to the application of the Convention or the rules of law codified therein.

In a similar situation, Israel has consistently claimed that it cannot be regarded as the "occupying power" in the West Bank and Jerusalem—where some 60,000 Israeli settlers live[42]—because neither Jordan nor any other power can be considered the "legitimate sovereign"' of those territories and that Israel has a better title in the territory of what was Palestine than do Jordan and Egypt.[43] The Israeli position, which is similar to that taken by the PRC, has been universally rejected on the grounds that Jordan and Egypt were in *de facto* occupation and control of the West Bank and Gaza Strip at the time of the Israeli occupation.[44] The International Committee of the Red Cross has faced directly the question of the Convention's applicability and from time to time has commented on the issue. In response to the Israeli contention the ICRC has held that "the Fourth Convention is applicable in *toto* to the ... occupied territories"[45] and that "all conditions existed for [its] applicability."[46]

The UN clearly views the Convention as applicable to the Israeli-occupied territories. In particular, the Commission on Human Rights and the General Assembly have repeatedly and consistently reiterated this view virtually since the Israeli occupation began, and the Security Council has endorsed it.[47] Even the Israeli Supreme Court ruled, in a case concerning the Elon Moreh settlement, that

> The decision to establish a permanent settlement intended from the outset to remain in its place forever—even beyond the duration of military government which was established in Judea and Samaria — counts as a legal obstacle which is insurmountable, because the military government cannot create in its area facts for its military need which are designed *ab initio* to exist even after the end of the military rule in that area, when the fate of the area after the termination of military rule is still not known.[48]

The facts in the Tibetan case are similar albeit not identical. The crucial point is that until the Sino-Tibetan conflict is resolved and parties can agree on the future status of Tibet and its relationship with China, the Chinese have no right to colonize Tibet so as to force a "resolution" of the issue by transforming the composition of Tibet's population and destroying the national identity of the Tibetan people. Populations in occupied territories are protected not only during hostilities, but also after they have ceased until a final political settlement has been reached. The Tibetan people consequently have the right, on humanitarian and legal grounds, to be protected by the fundamental principle prohibiting the transfer of civilian populations into occupied territory, codified in Article 49 of the Fourth Geneva Convention. Whether the PRC maintains its political stand that Tibet has always formed a part of China or modifies that attitude is irrelevant in this respect, for the Convention and the principles of law it codifies should apply so long as the question of Tibet's status remains unresolved and China's presence in Tibet continues to be challenged. The United Nations General Assembly and Security Council's determination that the establishment of settlements in occupied territories "constitutes a serious obstruction of efforts aimed at achieving a just and lasting peace in the Middle East"[49] is equally as applicable to the settlement of Chinese in Tibet.

CONCLUSION

The Tibetans' continued existence as a people is severely threatened by the massive influx of Chinese into Tibet. The Tibetan people seek the right to live as a people and to freely determine their own political, cultural and religious destiny. China's attempt to impose its "final solution" on the Tibetans by flooding the country with Chinese settlers is, by any standard, a violation of the Tibetan people's human rights. "Whatever else it may mean," the International Commission of Jurists asserts, "the principle or right of self-determination of peoples must surely include the right of people who inhabit a disputed territory to determine their own future."[50] China's population transfer is therefore not only a violation of the Geneva Convention's prohibition of transfer of civilians into occupied territory, but also inevitably an infringement of the Tibetan people's right to self-determination. The systematic Sinification of Tibet, the discrimination practiced against the native population, and the conversion of the country into an area where Tibetans will in the near future be constrained to live as a minority among Chinese colonizers, is a fundamental violation of the Tibetans' individual and collective human rights and a policy that could be described as genocide.

1. Article 4 of the 1982 Constitution of the PRC.

2. See Heritage Foundation, "Why the World is Watching Beijing's Treatment of Tibet," *supra* note 14; *The Economist*, May 23,1987.

3. In 1951 the population was over six million according to official Chinese statistics and Tibetan government estimates. Since 1.2 million Tibetans died as a result of the Chinese occupation and the birthrate has been relatively low, it is not clear what the exact population is today. Official Chinese statistics put the number at between 3.9 and 4.5 million, but that number does not include groups of persons now classified as belonging to other "minority nationalities" but traditionally considered Tibetan.

4. See Information Office, Central Tibetan Secretariat, *Recent Influx of Chinese Settlers Into Occupied Tibet*, report compiled in November 1985 (hereinafter, Information Office report); John Avedon. *Tibet Today, Current Conditions and Prospects*. London: Wisdom Publications, 1987. See also Radio Lhasa (Xinhua in English), April 11, 1985.

5. See Zhang Tianlu, "Tibet's Population Develops," *Beijing Review*, August 17, 1987.

6. *International Herald Tribune*, January 12-13, 1983.

7. There were close to 3.4 million Tibetans in the area in 1950. The current figure is difficult to determine because a large number, particularly men, perished in Kham between 1956 and 1976. See also U.S. State Department, *Special Report on the Treatment of Minorities in China*, 1987, p. 14. In addition, in statistics the Chinese classify groups of Tibetans living in this area as belonging to other so-called "minority nationalities."

8. Statement by Chen Feng, New Delhi, November 2, 1987. See Elliot Sperling, *Responses to Supplementary Questions Arising Out of the Congressional Hearings on Tibet*, October 14, 1987.

9. Information Office report. See also T. Lhundup, "A Brief Summary of Conditions in Tibet," *supra*, note 17.

10. See F. Steenhuis, *Impressions of My Stay in Tibet*, April 1987; M.C. van Walt van Praag, "Tibet: A 'Colony' of China," *Freedom at Issue*, March-April 1987. This is confirmed by Tibetans from different parts of Tibet interviewed in December 1985. Their names cannot be revealed because these Tibetans fear for their safety.

11. P.A. Donnet, "Tibetan Traditions Slowly Disappearing," South China Morning Post, September 23, 1985.

12. See *The Asian Wall Street Journal Weekly*, June 29, 1987.

13. See e.g. Letter from Yue Junging, Charge d'Affaires, Embassy of the People's Republic of China, London, to Lord Avebury, Chairman of Parliamentary Human Rights Group, November 27, 1986.

14. *Beijing Review*, March 28, 1983.

15. Radio Lhasa (Xinhua in English), April 11, 1985.

16. Deng Xiaoping, during meeting with former President Jimmy Carter, June 29, 1987, reported by Reuters, Beijing, June 30, 1987.

17. *Beijing Review*, September 12, 1983.

18. *Beijing Review*, October 10, 1983, p. 22. See also, *The Economist*, June 15, 1985.

19. Radio Lhasa, July 21, 1986; idem, May 23, 1987.

20. *Beijing Review*, May 27, 1985.

21. *Beijing Review*, October 15, 1984.

22. *Beijing Review*, September 24, 1984.

23. *Intelligence Report*, October 1984; idem, November 1984; idem, December 1984.

24. *Beijing Review*, August 26, 1985.

25. *Intelligence Report*, April 1985.

26. See, *The Economist*, June 15, 1985.

27. 20 *News Tibet* 1, p. 2 (January-April 1985).

28. 18 *Tibetan Bulletin* 3, p. 4 (September-October 1987).

29. *Reference Material No. 2*, New Delhi, February 4, 1985.

30. International Commission of Jurists, "Israeli Settlements in Occupied Territories," in *The Review of the International Commission of Jurists*, No. 19, p. 35 (December 1977).

31. Signed at Geneva, August 12, 1949.

32. United Nations, *The Question of the Observance of the Fourth Geneva Convention of 1949 in Gaza and the West Bank Including Jerusalem Occupied by Israel in June 1967*, p. 1 (New York, 1979).

33. Testimony of W.T. Mallison in "Hearings before the Subcommittee on Immigration and Naturalization of the Committee on the Judiciary, United States Senate, on the Question of West Bank Settlements and the Treatment of Arabs in the Israeli-occupied Territories, October 17 and 18, 1977," p. 47.

34. *Ibid.*

35. L. Oppenheim, *International Law*, ed. H. Lauterpacht, Vol. 2, p. 433 (London, 1952).

36. International Commission of Jurists, "Israeli Settlements in Occupied Territories," *supra*, p. 34.

37. *Commentary: IV Geneva Convention, supra*, p. 275-76.

38. For a full discussion of the subject, see M.C. van Walt van Praag, *The Status of Tibet: History Rights and Prospects in International Law*, p. 142-188. London: Wisdom Publications, 1987.

39. Ratification instrument deposited with the Swiss Federal Council on 28 December 1956. 444 U.N.T.S. No. 973 (1957). The PRC noted in this instrument:

> Although the Geneva Convention Relative to the Protection of Civilian Persons in Time of War of August 12, 1949 does not apply to civilian persons outside enemy occupied areas and consequently does not completely meet humanitarian requirements, it is found to be in accord with the interest of protecting civilian persons in occupied territory and in certain other cases, hence it is ratified [with reservations to Articles 11 and 45].

40. W.T. Mallison, *supra*. See International Commission of Jurists, 1029, "Israeli Settlements in Occupied Territories," *supra*, p. 35.

41. United Nations, The Question of the Observation of the Fourth 1045 *Geneva Convention of 1949, supra*, p. 12-14.

42. International Commission of Jurists, *Op Cit., supra*, p. 29.

43. Y. Blum, quoted in United Nations, *The Question of the Observance of the Fourth Geneva Convention of 1949*, p. 5.

44. The primary method by which the government of Israel encourages settlers to transfer to occupied territories is with subsidies. See, United Nations *Israeli Settlements in Gaza and the West Bank* (New York, 1982).

45. ICRC *Annual Report 1975*, 22 (Geneva, 1976).

46. ICRC *Annual Report 1976*, 11 (Geneva, 1977).

47. United Nations, *The Question of the Observance of the Fourth Geneva Convention of 1949, supra*, p. 12-14.

48. Quoted in *Ibid*. p. 27.

49. General Assembly Resolution 35/122 B of December 11, 1980, and Security Council Resolution 446 (1979) of March 22, 1979.

50. International Commission of Jurists, "Israeli Settlements in Occupied Territories," *supra*, p. 32. Even if the notion that self-determination should apply only to colonized peoples and countries were found to be correct, the Tibetan people have the right to exercise self-determination, for Tibet is in effect a Chinese colony.

Educational Discrimination In Tibet

China's population policies in Tibet, particularly its encouragement of Chinese migration into the region, have generated inequalities that have put the Tibetan populace at a clear disadvantage. It is commonly known that the educational opportunities afforded Tibetans and Chinese in Tibet differ markedly, not least because of the language advantage Chinese have under the current system. Education beyond the elementary level generally requires a good knowledge of Chinese, since most of the instruction offered above that level is in Chinese. Chinese are also at a clear advantage in obtaining employment in positions linked to state-run enterprises, as they have the better language skills when it comes to taking requisite examinations that are generally in Chinese.

In recent years there has been some official recognition given to the lack of sufficient educational facilities in Tibet. In July 1988, Li Tieying, a member of the Communist Party Politburo noted the in-sufficiency of good schools, bilingual education, and trained teachers in Tibetan regions.[1] In December of that year the Panchen Lama

---

Excerpted from *Merciless Repression: Human Rights in Tibet*, an Asia Watch Report, February 1988.

commented that the study and development of the Tibetan language and of Tibetan Buddhism had become "a life and death problem" for Tibetans.[2] Previously the Panchen Lama had noted that resolutions aimed at strengthening the position of the Tibetan language in Tibet had been passed by Tibet's Regional People's Congress, but that no moves to implement them had ever been made.[3]

Official Chinese sources claimed in the fall of 1988 that 70% of school-age children in Qinghai Province were enrolled in schools.[4] Tibetans from the area cannot give specific figures for the number of schoolchildren, but they have noted that elementary education is reasonably widespread, and that in Tibetan areas it is usually carried out in the Tibetan language. This seems to be the case in the TAR, too, and there appear to be Tibetans inside and outside the TAR. It is when one goes above the elementary school level that one finds an increasing decline in the status of the Tibetan language.

In late 1988, China published statistics dealing with the educational situation in the TAR in 1987 and listed 121,000 elementary school students out of which 90% or 109,000 were Tibetan; and three institutes of higher learning with 2,860 students, of whom 66.4% were Tibetan. The same statistics also noted the presence of some 200 students in the region's Academy of Tibetan Buddhism and 5,278 students scattered in middle schools in various provinces and regions of the PRC outside Tibet. The total number of students adds up to 154,398, but the same source also gave the "present" total (that is, as of late 1988) as 166,000, said to be 41.5% of the youth of the TAR.[5]

The decline in the percentage of Tibetans among post-elementary school students in the TAR is clearly due to the decreased emphasis on the Tibetan language in middle and higher educational institutes. As one Tibetan student stated in January 1989, in an official Chinese publication, most middle school teachers in her area are from China proper; that is, they are non-Tibetans who undoubtedly cannot teach Tibetan.[6] Similarly, Punkang Tsering Dhondup, a Tibetan member of the Chinese People's Political Consultative Conference, described the quality of teaching in Lhasa's schools as low. His solution was to call for more Chinese intellectuals to come to Tibet and work in the schools, regardless of the fact that this would constitute a further increase in China's dispatch of Chinese settlers into Tibet.[7]

That the authorities to some extent do acknowledge the inequities in this situation is implied in the promulgation in March 1989, of a set of *Regulations of the Tibet Autonomous Region on the Study, Use, and Development of the Tibetan Language.* Official reports about the regulations noted, among other things:

> Schools in rural areas should concentrate on the Tibetan language, though standard Chinese is also required to be taught.

> Because of an inadequate supply of teaching materials and a shortage of teachers, the regulations pointed out the urgent need to make up this shortfall.

> By 1993 textbooks for middle schools should all be written in Tibetan; by 1997 most of the subjects in senior middle and technical schools should be taught in Tibetan; and after the year 2000, institutes of higher learning should gradually start to use the Tibetan language, the regulations state.[8]

These regulations were drawn up by the TAR government on the initiative, reportedly, of the Panchen Lama and Ngapo Ngawang Jigme. As we have already noted, the Panchen Lama had previously commented on the fact that earlier resolutions aimed at strengthening the position of the Tibetan language had received no more than lip service, so far as the actual situation in Tibet was concerned. Asia Watch's interest in this issue stems from the *de facto* discriminatory conditions that are produced when Tibetans are forced to compete for jobs and positions against native speakers of Chinese on the basis of their abilities in what is at best a second language for most of them. The awareness of the problem implied by the adoption of the regulations in question is laudable. But the extent to which they will be actually implemented, given China's previous track record on the issue and its adoption of harsher policies of control following the period of martial law, remains seriously in doubt. Although the regulations were announced after the proclamation of martial law and the riots that preceded it, they had obviously been prepared before that time, and undoubtedly reflect thinking that may now be considerably altered. More recently, high ranking officials in the TAR have begun to echo an older line linking the issue of access to education at certain levels more tightly to political considerations. They assert for example:

> We must settle the issue of what kind of people should be trained, and this issue carries a special and important significance in Tibet. We must train qualified personnel who love the motherland and maintain national unity, and by no means should we train people who seek to practice splittism. In weighing education in our region, we must see whether the students we train are politically qualified.[9]

The emphasis on Chinese as the language of instruction in Tibetan education and as the primary language for those aspiring to middle and higher level jobs in the TAR's infrastructure acts as an invisible but insuperable barrier to many Tibetans. The results of the Chinese-based educational system were described by a British teacher who went to Tibet as an English teacher at Tibet University in Lhasa from February 1987 to January 1988. She noted that the university's first class of English majors, which graduated in the summer of 1988, had been composed exclusively of Chinese students, the result of a system in which Tibetans must first master Chinese before they can study English (or most other subjects). Although she herself was part of an effort to ameliorate this situation, even in the work of that project resources meant for the advancement of Tibetan education were in fact diverted for the benefit of Chinese students.[10] More recently, the renewed emphasis upon "political qualifications" will undoubtedly cut opportunities even further. In short, Asia Watch considers current educational conditions in the TAR to be biased against Tibetans, and to form part of a situation in which Tibetans are seriously threatened with marginalization within their own areas.

---

1. "Li Tieying Discussed Promoting Tibetan Education," *Xinhua*, July 15, 1988; in *FBIS*, July 19.

2. "Ngapoi, Bainqen Talk About Tibetan Studies," *Zhongguo Xinwen She*, December 6, 1988; in *FBIS*, December 12.

3. *Evading Scrutiny*, pp. 15-16.

4. Cheng Gang, "Qinghai Province's Tibetans," *Beijing Review*, October 17-23, 1988.

5. "Xizang jianqi minzu jiaoyu tixi dazhongxiao xuesheng yiyu shiliu wan," *Renmin Ribao*, December 1, 1988. Most of the same figures for students in the TAR are given in Jing Wei, 100 *Questions about Tibet*, p. 42 but the percentage of school children in schools is given as 54.4%. A *Radio Lhasa* broadcast of April 21, 1989 gave the T.A.R.'s student population as being 165,000: "Editorial Cited on Tibet's Thirtieth Reform Anniversary," *FBIS*, April 27, 1989.

6. Degyisangmo, "Tibetan Student in Beijing," *China Reconstructs*, January 1989.

7. "Tibetan C.P.P.C.C. Member on Reasons for Riots," *Zongguo Xinwen She*, March 22, 1989; in *FBIS*, March 28.

8. "Legislation Encourages Use of Tibetan Language," *Xinhua*, March 17, 1989; in *FBIS* same date. See also "Law on Wider Use of Tibetan Language Promulgated," *Xinhua*, March 16, 1989; in *FBIS*, March 21.

9. "Tibet Secretary Speaks at Educational Forum," *Radio Lhasa*, September 11, 1989, in *FBIS*, September 14.

10. Julie Brittain, "Britain Bows to Chinese in Tibet Teacher Project," *The Hong Kong Standard*, August 6, 1988.

JAMYANG NORBU

On the Brink

We were like people marooned on a dissolving floe of
ice; we dared not think of the moment when it
would melt away.

—Czeslaw Miloz, *The Captive Mind*

It is an amazing thing, this extraordinary feeling of optimism we Tibetans-in-exile have for so long managed to sustain; this hope that, without the need for any effort or sacrifice on our part, we would somehow manage to bumble along to some kind of eventual success; that despite the years of wasted opportunities, fratricidal squabbles, suicidal expediencies, intellectual stupor, and the deliberate entrenchment of some of the most debilitating of political traditions, in the end everything would be put right in the outrageously improbable manner of Bombay films, one detail after another clicking into place like the teeth of a zipper.

Well, that's all over now. To all but the most willfully stupid, it must be painfully obvious that if some cataclysmic change does not occur soon, we can put to rest any last hope for a free Tibet, or even the survival of a living Tibetan civilization.

Since the beginning of our recorded history, we Tibetans have never been confronted with a threat such as we are now facing, as every day more and more Chinese immigrants pour into Tibet in

This article was published in *Illusion and Reality*, October 1986.

search of better opportunities and maybe even an eventual home. In every city and town in Tibet, the Chinese now outnumber the Tibetans; the ratio of Chinese to Tibetans in Lhasa is nearly four to one. These Chinese are not just bureaucrats and soldiers who implemented Chinese rule in Tibet, but the people from every profession and background, who have been enticed to Tibet in the hope of improving their circumstances due to the chronic unemployment in China. Chinese carpenters, masons, tailors, smiths, petty traders, restauranteurs, truck drivers, teachers, electricians, mechanics, barbers, butchers, guides, street entertainers, beggars, and, of course, the myriad ubiquitous functionaries so indispensable to the proper functioning of a totalitarian state, are relentlessly pushing the Tibetans into immediate unemployment and ultimate extinction.

Chinese immigration is even making itself felt in the villages in Tibet, where most of the construction work, previously handled by the village cooperatives or communes, is now being done by Chinese contractors and Chinese labor. Even such desolate and remote areas as Ngari in Western Tibet, are now beginning to receive a considerable influx of Chinese immigrants.

Though the Chinese had, over the centuries, gradually settled in certain parts of Tibet, such as the province of Amdo—where an uneasy demographic balance was maintained between Tibetans, Mongols, Chinese, and the ruling Chinese Muslims (Hui-hui)— Chinese immigration into Tibet in this century began, strangely enough, not so much as a consequence of Chinese government policy, but due to the efforts of European missionaries. In the early 1900s, these missionaries resettled colonies of Chinese Christians in Eastern Tibet in an attempt to bring about the gradual evangelization of Tibet. Since the missionaries relied on the presence of Chinese troops in these places to carry out the Lord's will, the Tibetans, not unnaturally, regarded them as agents of Chinese tyranny and wreaked vengeance on them whenever the Tibetans managed to start up an uprising against the Chinese.

More enlightened Europeans like Sir Erich Teichman, a British Consular officer in China, deplored the activities of the missionaries, and thought that they should confine themselves to helping the people of Eastern Tibet by providing medical and educational services and refrain from trying to convert a people who were quite obviously happy with their own religion.

With the invasion of Tibet by the Communist Chinese came the first large-scale influx of Chinese into Tibet. Although most of these were civil and military personnel, there was a gradual incursion of Chinese farmers into parts of Eastern and Northeastern Tibet, where agriculture was possible. After the Chinese crushed the revolts in these areas and killed or imprisoned a large portion of the indigenous population, more Chinese settlers took over the land thus made available. But even then, it was difficult for Beijing to settle Chinese immigrants everywhere it wanted in Tibet, especially in central and Western Tibet, as these areas were remote and certainly not attractive to the Chinese way of thinking; and the Chinese government did not have the resources to provide incentives and subsidies to immigrants, except for extra hardship pay to officials.

Moreover, since assuming power, the Communists had set their eyes on the great stretches of fertile virgin land in Manchuria to provide them with an answer to China's agricultural problem of feeding its multiplying millions. Millions of prisoners undergoing *Lao Gai*, or "Reform through Labor," were shipped to Manchuria to grow wheat and soya beans and sometimes to perish in the subarctic winters there. Megalomaniac building schemes and campaigns like the Great Leap Forward also created such a demand for labor in Chinese cities that many villages in China suffered from a drainage of farmhands. The consequent famines and many years of political turmoil that followed did not help the Chinese leaders to formulate a long term plan to finalize their hold on Tibet.

But with the death of Mao and the fall of "The Gang of Four," China's new leaders seem to have gradually put together a scheme not only to fill Tibet with Chinese immigrants, but even to make it pay. With typical duplicity, this scheme was launched with the unabashedly insincere announcement that China would greatly *reduce* its administrative and military personnel in Tibet. Ren Rong, the CCP chief in Tibet for ten years, was dismissed in disgrace and conciliatory gestures were made to the Dalai Lama and the Tibetans-in-exile. Transparently spurious admissions were made by Beijing of its "mistakes" in its attitude to Tibetans.

For the Chinese immigrants, the magic wand that has transformed Tibet from an inhospitable place of lonely exile to the land of opportunities is tourism. Tourism provides well-paying jobs, opportunities to open restaurants and small businesses, and many other possibilities. What further sweetens the deal for the immigrants are government incentives like interest-free loans and the knowledge that jobs and opportunities are hard to come by in China. For the Chinese government, tourism in Tibet not only takes a little pressure off its unemployment problems, but also brings in a steady supply of much-needed hard currency.

It would be naïve of us to think that the Chinese will not permanently settle in Tibet because the altitude, the food, and the weather are unpleasant. China will settle anywhere as long as it is economically feasible. Inner Mongolia and East Turkestan (Xinjiang) are as strange and remote to the Chinese as Tibet is, but millions of Chinese have settled there permanently and now greatly outnumber the native inhabitants. Fully 80% of the population of East Turkestan is now Chinese. The Mongols are outnumbered nearly a hundred to one by the Chinese in their own land, and the Mongol language is now an exotic tongue, rarely heard in the capital, Huhehot, except when an occasional nomad dressed in outlandish garb wanders bewilderedly into the city asking for directions.

Aside from the immigrants, what has tourism brought to the Tibetans? Very little, except maybe the opportunity to sell a few items of jewelry and the family heirlooms that the Chinese somehow overlooked and to pester tourists for polaroid shots and pictures of the Dalai Lama. Nearly all the hotels and restaurants in Lhasa are Chinese-owned. Only two boarding houses, the Snowland Hotel and the Banakshol Hotel, belong to Tibetans. The former is owned by a Kathmandu-based Tibetan family, while the latter is owned by a cooperative. Even in the big government-owned hotels, like the 1000-bed Lhasa Hotel and the 220-bed Tibet Guest House, the staff is nearly all Chinese. The Chinese explain this and the generally high percentage of Chinese workers in Tibet with the excuse that most Tibetans are illiterate and have no more than four years of schooling, thus making it necessary for them to be trained by Chinese. But there again is the rub, for the Chinese have devised an educational system whereby a Tibetan can never really become as qualified as a Chinese, unless he is completely Sinicized.

All primary schools in Tibet are either Chinese or Tibetan. The former have, of course, better facilities and teachers, and, most important, a student from a Chinese primary school going to secondary school is permitted to study English as a second language. Therefore, by the time this student graduates from school, he is qualified to join a prestigious university, take select courses, and is eligible for scholarships and fellowships to study abroad. The unfortunate child who studies at a Tibetan medium school is forced to study Chinese as a second language at secondary school and receives no instruction in the English language. Therefore upon graduating from school, his chances of getting a further education are very limited. If Tibetan parents want to give their children the opportunities for further studies and good jobs, they have to enroll them in a Chinese medium school; and the children thereby lose their language, their culture, and gradually their identity as Tibetans. Local educational authorities in Tibet have, I have been told, tried to get Beijing to change its educational policy in Tibet and allow Tibetans in Tibetan medium schools to study English, but to no avail. The Chinese are never going to change such an ideal educational policy, one which manages to combine the advantage of showing to the world China's concern for preserving the Tibetan language in Tibet with the aim of keeping Tibetans as second-class citizens, forever unable to match the Chinese intellectually.

So what does a Tibetan do when he sees millions of Chinese pouring into his country, jeering and sniggering at him for being a barbarian, snatching away his livelihood, eating up his food, and permitting his son only a second-rate education which just about qualifies him to drive a truck? He just sits back and thinks of his father who starved to death in a concentration camp, his elder brother who was tortured and publicly executed for possessing a leaflet that proclaimed Tibet's independence, his invalid mother whose spine is permanently damaged by the blithe ignorance of a barefoot doctor, his monasteries and temples which are in ruins, his own health which is irretrievably damaged by malnutrition and backbreaking labor, and his spirit, which is now broken by denunciations, "struggles," and the secret police. He sits back and thinks about this, and he drinks.

There is a shortage of crockery in Lhasa city, along with a a lot of other things, and the sanitation, as most tourists have had the opportunity to observe, is appalling. But the convoys of trucks that roar into the city every day do not bring in much-needed household items or sanitary fittings; they bring in millions of bottles of hard liquor and beer that the Tibetan now needs to drown his sorrows. Alcoholism is today one of the most severe problems in Tibet; a fact to which the many broken bottles littering the streets of the Tibetan section of Lhasa city will bear partial testimony.

The favorite beverages among hard-core drinkers do not just seem to be the time-honored *chang* and *arak*, but also two vile spirits produced in Sichuan that have the potency of rocket fuel and the smell of nameless chemical by-products. Though *San jiu* is considered more lethal than *Ban jui* by some, both can be used, I understand, to fuel your primus stove when there is a shortage of paraffin in the country, which is a far more likely event than the shortage of alcohol. Moreover, the alcohol is cheap. A friend of mine, who was formerly a police officer in one of the northern Indian states, visited Tibet recently. During his service with the Indian police, he belonged to the excise department, which in this country generally deals with the illegal production of beverages from old car batteries and denatured industrial alcohol. He told me that in all of his experience of such things he had never come across anything so odiferous and vile as the Chinese spirits drunk by Tibetans.

The Tibetans are not only being made into second-class citizens, but are gradually being forced to believe that they are inferior. The fact that many Tibetans are suffering from obvious mental disorders because of their past experiences does not help them to resist this. The Chinese are gradually killing not only the Tibetans' initiative and pride but also their will to survive.

How will this affect the mind of a Tibetan child in the future? Will he understand the true reason for his broken home and the reason his father and many other Tibetans are jobless, alcoholic wrecks, while the energetic and enterprising Chinese collar all the important jobs in the administration and own all the restaurants and shops in

Lhasa and other parts of Tibet? I am sure we all remember how in our childhood even absurdly trivial things like not having the proper kind of school uniform would be an occasion of secret mortification and insecurity. What will a Tibetan child feel when he sees the privileged children of collaborators and of the Chinese studying to go to important universities in China and even abroad, while he attends a poor school which only prepares him to accept a lifetime of subservience?

Whatever the Tibetan people endured before—the executions, tortures, starvation, imprisonment, in fact the entire madness of the Cultural Revolution—does not pose such a threat to their survival as the relatively peaceful immigration into Tibet that China is doing now. Within a few decades the real population of Tibet will be so overwhelmingly Chinese that even an attempt by the few Tibetans left to assert their rights over the country will seem as ridiculous as that of the Native Americans demanding that all Americans go back to their native countries and return America to them.

KATRINA K. MORRIS & ANDREW M. SCOBLE

Tibet and the United Nations

INTRODUCTION

A window of opportunity has opened for Tibetans to present their case to the United Nations. Tibet and the world around it have changed. Renewed demonstrations in Tibet, commencing in 1987, the shocking repression of nonviolent dissent in Tiananmen Square on June 4, 1989, and action by the Tibetan Government-in-Exile and changes in the political structure of Eastern Europe have renewed interest in the problem of Tibet and rekindled hope for the possibility of its peaceful solution.

This article explores the role of the United Nations in the search for such a solution. First, it discusses the chief international legal principles which bear on the systematic violation of the Tibetans' human rights by the People's Republic of China (Section A). Next, it reviews Tibet's record at the United Nations (Section B and C). Finally it offers several recommendations for future activity at the United Nations on behalf of the Tibetan people (Sections D).

The authors wish to acknowledge Tica Broche and Felice Gaer, whose compilations of United Nations actions contributed to the preparation of this summary.

A. CHINA'S RECORD OF HUMAN RIGHTS ABUSE IN TIBET

Self-Determination. Four decades of military occupation by the People's Republic of China (PRC) bear witness to numerous, fundamental human rights abuses in Tibet. The gravest abuse is deprivation of the Tibetan people's right to self-determination—their right as a distinct people to "freely determine, without external interference, their political status and freely pursue their economic, social and cultural development."[1] The importance of the right to self-determination is underscored by the fact that it is considered a peremptory, *jus cogens*, norm. Under international law *jus cogens* norms have a binding, mandatory nature that cannot be ignored or denied. The operation of *jus cogens* voids any conflicting treaty, international instrument, law, or act.[2]

Self-determination is generally viewed as a right of "peoples," not individuals.[3] Peoples have identifiable characteristics, including race or ethnic distinctiveness, language, religion, culture, traditions, customs, and history that set the people apart from others. The Tibetan people meet the relevant tests of peoplehood as defined under international law. It is to be noted, however, that this collective right is inextricably linked with the enjoyment of individual human rights.

Violation of the Tibetan people's right to self-determination is ongoing. Although noted in United Nations resolutions beginning in 1959, the violation might be said to have begun a decade earlier, when Chinese troops entered Tibetan territory with the intent to remain there. Whatever the beginning point, there can be no question that the PRC today denies Tibetans their right to self-determination. The PRC has carved up Tibet, rendering less than half of its territory into a so-called autonomous region and appending the rest to historically Chinese provinces. The PRC has imposed its own political and economic system on Tibet, suppressing resistance with an estimated quarter million troops. It has exploited and exported Tibet's natural resources. It has restricted and in some cases exterminated the indigenous practice of Buddhism, which has become a national characteristic of Tibet. In short, in virtually every detail of their lives, Tibetans are denied the right to "freely determine, without external interference, their political status and freely pursue their economic, social, and cultural development."

Perhaps the cruelest mark of this denial of self-determination lies in the deliberate policy of population transfer of Chinese into Tibetan territory. While appropriating and exporting so much of Tibet's resources, the PRC has been importing settlers and soldiers. They come to stay. Tibetans and outside observers have voiced alarm at this practice, warning that Tibetans may very soon become a minority in their own country. The arrival of large numbers of Chinese has produced "Tibetan ghettos" in the principal cities. It has brought inflation and unemployment. It has resulted in discrimination in housing, education and health care. What the PRC originally obtained by force of arms, it now seeks to secure by force of numbers.

Individual Human Rights Violations. Self-determination is a prerequisite to the enjoyment of other fundamental rights. Linked to the denial of self-determination is a wide array of other reported human rights violations.[4] These include:

> a systematic pattern of discrimination in housing, employment, health care, and education;[5]
>
> denial of freedom of expression;[6]
>
> denial of the freedom of assembly and association;[7]
>
> denial of the freedom of exercise of religion;[8] and
>
> denial of freedom to travel.[9]

There are reliable reports that Tibetans have been arbitrarily detained, tortured in custody, and executed for peaceful protest against the PRC's continued occupation of Tibet.[10] Outside observers report that Tibet's natural resources have been stripped from it for the economic benefit of the PRC.[11]

The imposition of martial law in Lhasa on March 7-8, 1989, failed to deter the Tibetans' willingness to speak out for independence and suffer the consequences. When the PRC nominally lifted martial law on April 30, 1990, it did so without evidence of significant improvement in the human rights conditions or indications that dissent had ceased. To the contrary, reports of unrest, which continue to emerge despite the PRC's clampdown, indicate that the situation continues to deteriorate.

B. RECOGNITION BY THE INTERNATIONAL COMMUNITY OF THE TIBETAN PEOPLE'S CLAIM

In 1959, in 1961, and again in 1965, the United Nations General Assembly passed Resolutions expressing "grave concern" at the "violation of fundamental human rights of the Tibetan people," the suppression of their distinctive cultural and religious life and "the autonomy which the Tibetans had traditionally enjoyed."[12] The most comprehensive of these resolutions, Resolution 1723 (XVI), recognized the right of self-determination for the Tibetan people. From the debates leading up to its adoption it is evident that the resolution was primarily founded upon Articles 1[13] and 55[14] of the United Nations Charter, on the Universal Declaration of Human Rights, and on the Declaration on Granting Independence to Colonial Countries and Peoples.[15]

In the course of discussing Resolution 1723 (XVI), many Member States considered it to be "the minimum pronouncement" that the United Nations should make. Moreover, in 1959, 1960, 1961, and 1963 the Member States debated whether it was even appropriate to discuss Tibet when the PRC was not a member. On each occasion they overwhelmingly voted to leave the item on the agenda, concluding that violation of the fundamental rights and freedoms of peoples is an urgent situation and that it was the obligation of the UN to address the problems facing Tibet.

The delegate from Malaysia stressed that passing Resolution 1723 (XVI) was:

> consistent with the spirit of the resolutions which the Assembly has passed on the elimination of colonialism, such as resolution 1514 (XV). As stated in that resolution, the subjection of peoples to alien subjugation, domination, and exploitation constitutes a denial of fundamental human rights, is contrary to the Charter of the United Nations, and is an impediment to the promotion of world peace and cooperation."[16]

Ireland, a co-sponsor of the resolution, stated that the terms of the 1960 UN Declaration on Granting of Independence to Colonial Countries and Peoples was "just as applicable to Tibet as to any other territory," and reminded the UN Members that the Belgrade Conference of 1961, which endorsed the Declaration, called for the eradication of colonialism in "all its manifestations."[17]

The United States expressed its position in a statement by the Secretary of State, Mr. Christian Herter, on February 20, 1960, as follows:

> While it has been the historical position of the United States to consider Tibet an autonomous country under the suzerainty of China, the American people have also traditionally stood for the principle of self-determination. It is the belief of the United States Government that this principle should apply to the people of Tibet and that they should have the determining voice in their own political destiny.

The United States confirmed this position in the General Assembly debates on December 19, 1961 when it added that "the United States believes that our objectives must include the restoration of human rights of the Tibetan people and their national right of self-determination."[18]

The Republic of China (Taiwan), in arguing for the passage of Resolution 1723 (XVI), said it represented "the minimum that the General Assembly can do for the Tibetan people."[19]

Thailand, which also sponsored the Resolution, concluded that for any state not to support the right of the Tibetans to self-determination "would be tantamount to denying to the Tibetan people the very right that has been advocated for all."[20]

Subsequent to Resolution 1723 (XVI), Tibet was not mentioned again at the United Nations until 1985. A number of factors contributed to the silence. Perhaps chief among them was pressure by the PRC, which gained admission to the United Nations in 1971. During those years of silence by the UN, the Tibetan people struggled with the urgent demands of establishing an exile community. But at no time did they act in any way to abandon their non-derogable right to self-determination or cease resistance to the PRC occupation.

It was only in 1985, at the *Forty-first Session of the Commission on Human Rights*,[21] that the representative of the International Fellowship of Reconciliation, a non-governmental organization (NGO), expressed concern over the inability of PRC officials to implement the Declaration on the Elimination of All Forms of Intolerance and of Discrimination based on Religion or Belief.[22] The PRC delegation replied that religious intolerance could not possibly exist in Tibet. It quoted the Constitution of the PRC and listed religious associations set up by the government.

The following year, at the *Forty-second Session of the Commission on Human Rights*, the International Fellowship of Reconciliation requested the United Nations to offer assistance to the PRC in implementing the Declaration on Religious Intolerance. At the *Forty-third Session of the Commission on Human Rights* in 1987, the International Fellowship of Reconciliation welcomed the appointment of the Special Rapporteur on Religious Intolerance. The NGO representative cited systematic attempts of the PRC government to eradicate Tibetan culture and religion.

Government delegations did not follow the NGO lead. While expressing some interest in the plight of Tibet, they seemed to feel that the overall situation was stable. Tibet had been recently opened to tourists, with more visitors entering the country every year. No one wished to risk accusations of meddling in the PRC's jealously guarded "internal affairs," nor jeopardize Western access to the region.[23] This attitude changed in response to the demonstrations of 1987.

C. REVIVAL OF THE UNITED NATIONS OPTION

In September and October of 1987, Tibetans in Lhasa took to the streets following the public trial and execution of two Tibetans who had peacefully expressed their opposition to the Chinese occupation. At the February 1988 meeting of the *Forty-fourth Session of the Commission on Human Rights*, the question of Tibet was taken up with renewed intensity. In great part the response was due to eyewitnesses who, under the auspices of the International Fellowship of Reconciliation, provided documentation, notarized statements, and testimony regarding the situation in Lhasa.

The Special Rapporteur on Summary or Arbitrary Executions, Mr. S. Amos Wako, included information regarding Tibetan victims in his report,[24] and the Special Rapporteur on the Elimination of

Religious Intolerance, Mr. Angelo Vidal d'Almeida Ribero, listed three instances of non-compliance with the Declaration on Religious Intolerance.[25] Amnesty International, among other NGOs, condemned PRC repression of the Tibetan people. The PRC responded that "order prevailed" and that there would be no recurrence of what it viewed as an isolated incident.

At the *Fortieth Session of the Sub-Commission on Prevention of Discrimination and Protection of Minorities* in August 1988, NGOs, including Amnesty International, Minority Rights Group, and Pax Christi, charged the PRC with continued repression in the wake of the political demonstrations. These NGOs expanded the discussion to include the PRC's colonization of Tibet, discrimination in employment, and systematic destruction of the Tibetan religion and culture. When Sub-Commission expert Louis Joinet requested more information in the plenary meeting and drafted a resolution to that effect, opposition by the PRC delegation became intense. The expert chose to not submit the draft resolution for a vote. But it was clear that the question of Tibet had not escaped scrutiny by members of the Sub-Commission.

Heightened interest in the Tibetan situation was confirmed when Canada and the Netherlands raised the issue of Tibet at the *Forty-fifth Session of the Commission on Human Rights in 1989*. During the meeting, the reports of the Special Rapporteurs on Torture,[26] Summary and Arbitrary Executions,[27] and Religious Intolerance,[28] as well as the Working Group on Enforced or Involuntary Disappearances,[29] all mentioned violations by the PRC in Tibet. During the last week of the Commission, repeated demonstrations and bloodshed in Lhasa culminated in the imposition of martial law on March 7-8, 1989. The ranks of NGOs involved on behalf of Tibet swelled, producing a seventeen-organization appeal to the Commission to address the deteriorating situation in Tibet.

In August 1989, the *Forty-first Session of the Sub-Commission on Prevention of Discrimination and Protection of Minorities* focused its attention on the June 4, 1989 massacre in Tiananmen Square. Support for Tibet continued to grow with statements by four Sub-Commission experts, acceptance of NGO documents for publication on the issues of self-determination (Pax Christi),[30] torture

(International Association of Educators for World Peace),[31] and children in detention (Defence for Children International).[32] Although submitted in a timely manner, written statements on forced abortions (International Commission of Health Professionals) and discrimination (Minority Rights Group) were not published. Fourteen NGOs signed a joint statement addressing the right of the Tibetan people to self-determination. Ten included Tibet in oral statements before the plenary session.

Resolution 1989/5, addressing the situation in the PRC subsequent to the events of June 4, 1989, in Tiananmen Square, passed by a narrow margin. It requested the Secretary General to transmit to the Commission on Human Rights information provided by the PRC and other reliable sources and to make an appeal for clemency for those imprisoned as a result of "recent" events. NGOs supportive of Tibet contributed significantly to the lobbying effort to pass the resolution. Tibetans made it clear that the resolution should not mention Tibet in order to avoid any inference that Tibet is a part of the PRC. While the fact that martial law in Lhasa both resembled and pre-dated martial law in Beijing, and the resolution could have provided an opportunity to address individual abuses, the Tibetan position confirmed the priority of the right to self-determination on the Tibetan UN agenda.

A nine-day hunger strike by one of a group of Tibetans demonstrating outside UN headquarters in Geneva ended when Tseten Gompa addressed the plenary session on behalf of the Movement Against Racism and for Friendship Among Peoples. While he spoke on China's refusal to allow him to enter and leave his own country, the greater significance of his statement lay in the fact that he was the first Tibetan to address the United Nations.

The *Forty-fourth Session of the General Assembly* in 1989 saw the first discussion of Tibet in the General Assembly since 1965. Those speaking included Costa Rica (which addressed the plenary session), Sweden, the Netherlands, Costa Rica, Canada, the United States, and the European Community in the Third Committee. In a related development, the PRC successfully blocked adoption of the *Declaration of Human Responsibilities for Peace and Sustainable Development*, a declaration inspired by His Holiness the Dalai Lama, by exerting its pressure as a permanent member of the Security Council.

At the *Forty-sixth Session of the Commission on Human Rights* in 1990, governments addressing the issue of Tibet included the European Community, the United States, Canada, Sweden, and Australia. Tibet was addressed by the Special Rapporteurs on Religious Intolerance,[33] Torture,[34] and Summary or Arbitrary Executions[35] as well as the Working Group on Enforced or Involuntary Disappearances.[36] Written statements were accepted for publication, including the statement on discrimination by Minority Rights Group which had been refused by the Sub-Commission the previous year,[37] a statement on self-determination by the international Federation of Human Rights,[38] and a document on martial law by the International Fellowship of Reconciliation[39].

Eight NGOs addressed the plenary session on issues ranging from allegations of torture and other abuses to colonial exploitation of Tibet's natural resources. Tsewang Topgyal, on behalf of the International Federation of Human Rights, addressed the plenary session on the issue of self-determination and the PRC's exploitation of Tibet. Twenty NGOs, including the International Commission of Jurists, appealed for the appointment of a Special Rapporteur to address the issue of self-determination and allegations of gross violations of Tibetan human rights by the PRC.[40] The report on the Situation in China,[41] prepared pursuant to resolution 1989/5 of the Sub-Commission, included information from Amnesty International on the situation in Tibet.

On April 27, 1990, the *Fourth Session of the Committee Against Torture* (CAT) examined the PRC's first periodic report. The Committee Against Torture was established in 1987 pursuant to the Convention Against Torture and Other Cruel, Inhuman, or Degrading Treatment or Punishment. Having reviewed communications and other information from UN and NGO sources, the experts in attendance required the PRC to submit an additional report with information on Tibet, including conditions of detention.

On August 9-10, 1990, the *Committee on the Elimination of All Forms of Racial Discrimination* (CERD) reviewed the PRC's third and fourth periodic reports. CERD was established in 1970 to oversee the implementation of the Convention on the Elimination of all forms of Racial Discrimination. The experts asked detailed questions regarding the PRC's record in Tibet. Questions covered a range of topics, including reports of discrimination in restrictions on travel and religious training and practice; in employment, education, housing, and health care; in representation in local government; and in forced sterilization of women. The experts discussed allegations of Chinese racial superiority, vastly disproportionate illiteracy among Tibetans, transfer of Chinese settlers into Tibet, exploitation of Tibet's natural resources, and exportation of Tibetan art and religious artifacts. They noted reports that Tibetan demonstrators had been tortured in custody—despite the PRC's ratification of the Torture Convention. The experts requested supplementary information from the PRC on these issues.

At the *Forty-Second Session of the Sub-Commission* in 1990, Nyima Tsamchoe, a Tibetan schoolgirl representing the International Association of Educators for World Peace, testified about her separate and unequal education and the conditions she faced during several months in detention. Sanggye, a Tibetan who served as a Judge of the People's High Court prior to escaping into exile, stated that because the PRC considered him a member of a minority, he was not allowed to study international law. In his testimony on behalf of the International Fellowship of Reconciliation he described restrictions on his right to travel. Both individuals spoke Tibetan on the plenary floor— a first in UN history.

At this session NGOs addressed the issues of martial law, discrimination, population transfer, and self-determination. Two experts discussed Tibet and one drafted a resolution calling for the assistance of UN Advisory Services to address conditions in Tibet. The Tibetan representatives present declined the resolution on the ground that submission to UN Advisory Services (which would work with the PRC as the member country involved) might imply an admission that the PRC has authority to administer affairs in Tibet. Their position comported with the Tibetans' long-standing refusal to compromise their right to self-determination.

At the *Forty-fifth Session of the General Assembly* in 1990, Sweden, Australia, Norway, Canada, and the European Community criticized the human rights record of the PRC. Before the Third Committee the PRC reiterated its position that in discussing human rights at the UN, non-interference in the internal affairs of Member States is essential and the human rights bodies had exceeded their mandate under the UN Charter in their treatment of country situations. The PRC further stated that collective rights preempt individual rights and that economic, social, and cultural rights prevail over civil and political rights. An initiative led by the PRC in the Third and Fifth Committees to decrease available resources and funding for the UN Human Rights Centre failed.

At the *Forty-seventh Session of the Commission on Human Rights* in 1991, representatives of the European Community, the United States, Norway, Canada, Sweden, and Austria expressed concern over the human rights situation in Tibet. In addition to generally addressing human rights violations, the United States referred to the use of disproportionate force against pro-independence demonstrators. Norway discussed the denial of freedom of expression for Tibetans. Tibet was again addressed by the Special Rapporteurs on Torture,[42] Religious Intolerance,[43] and Summary or Arbitrary Executions,[44] as well as the Working Group on Enforced or Involuntary Disappearances.[45]

Pax Christi addressed population transfer as a means of violating the Tibetan's right to self-determination and proposed that a Working Group on the right to self-determination be formed with active participation of peoples such as the Tibetans who currently have no representation at the UN. The comments drew a rebuttal from the PRC.[46] The International Organization for the Elimination of All Forms of Racial Discrimination, the International League for Human Rights, and Minority Rights Group discussed deaths from torture by prison officials, the use of model prisons for visiting journalists and delegations, and distributed dossiers on twenty cases of prison torture. The PRC responded that the allegations were the work of "separatists and foreigners with ulterior motives," and an appeal was made to allow access by the International Red Cross. Amnesty International reproached the Commission for failing to take action on the situation in Tibet "despite convincing evidence...(and) the long-term pattern of...violations." The International Council of

Voluntary Organizations recalled the UN resolutions on Tibet's right to self-determination and called on the PRC to accept the Dalai Lama's peace plan without preconditions. Other questions addressed by NGOs included religious intolerance, discrimination, and denial of freedom of expression.

D. RECOMMENDATIONS

Since 1987, developments in Tibet and elsewhere have opened a window of opportunity at the United Nations for positive action on behalf of Tibet. In continuing the work of the last several years it is important to keep in mind several considerations:

1. *The United Nations provides an opportunity for Tibetans to put pressure on the PRC.* At the United Nations the PRC has shown a greater willingness to subject its human rights record to international scrutiny. The PRC has ratified or signed at least eight international human rights conventions. Although it has not ratified the International Covenants, the PRC has agreed to their applicability to Hong Kong. It has criticized other nations for their human rights violations and has supported the appointment of Special Rapporteurs to investigate human rights situations in Afghanistan and Chile. The PRC is bound by those international instruments to which it is a party and stopped from protesting outside "interference" in its internal affairs to the same extent that it engages in criticism of its fellow states. The UN is among the most effective fora for integrating fundamental human rights into the PRC's agenda. Efforts should continue to draw China from behind the veil of "internal affairs" into position as a responsible member of the international human rights community.

2. *Tibetans must lead the UN effort.* While the support of non-Tibetans is essential to the process, Tibetans, and only Tibetans, must lead the UN effort. This requires year-round visibility at the United Nations headquarters and active participation in meetings of United Nations bodies. To meet this objective the Tibetan Government-in-Exile recently has created the Tibet Bureau of United Nations Affairs with offices in Geneva and New York headed by Kasur Lodi Gyari.

While non-Tibetans can be useful in preparing background documents and assistance and in encouraging NGOs to raise the issue of Tibet, the attention of the international community will turn more sympathetically to the victims of human rights violations than to outsiders. Moreover, participation of Tibetans at meetings of the UN will open up the possibility of forging ties with developing countries, whose role in the UN is becoming increasingly important.

Non-Tibetans representing the many non-governmental organizations that have expressed concern for the situation in Tibet can continue their efforts by supplying reliable information both to the UN and their home constituencies. They can assist in maintaining pressure on Member States to satisfy their obligations under the United Nations Charter, the Universal Declaration of Human Rights, and international human rights treaties. But it is the Tibetan people who must direct the UN effort whether it be to address an individual violation or seek observer status at the General Assembly. It is the Tibetans who must present their case to the international community and bear the benefits and burdens of the choices they make.

3. *The right of self-determination must continue to be emphasized.* The immediacy of individual human rights abuse require and merit urgent response when lives hang in the balance. But the root of the problem is denial of the right to self-determination. The PRC's illegal occupation of Tibet and practices within the occupied territory constitute a persistent denial of self-determination, which is inextricably linked to individual human rights violations. Moreover, should the focus be diverted from self-determination, the Tibetan people risk an attempt by the PRC to appease the international community by addressing a few individual cases and thereby effectively side-step the issue of its illegal occupation. The Tibetan leadership is well aware of the need to give priority to efforts at achieving self-determination. Non-Tibetans should adhere to this strategic decision.

4. *Grass roots support must be heightened.* Put quite simply, efforts at the United Nations require grass roots pressure back home. Foreign ministries decide the position of their UN delegations on Tibet. Concerns about Tibet raised by citizens to their own governments will have the two-fold effect of driving both domestic legislation and foreign policy decisions at the UN. The importance of concentrating

on developing grass roots support should not be underestimated. Likewise, new bridges spanned between Tibetans and the Chinese Democracy Movement since events in Tiananmen Square should be fortified whenever possible without compromising the Tibetan claim to self-determination.

5. *NGO efforts must be strengthened and coordinated.* In a very real sense, NGOs are the "eyes and ears" of the United Nations human rights bodies. It is crucial that NGOs increase their efforts to provide accurate, credible information on Tibetan issues. Such information may in turn serve as a lever for UN efforts to open up Tibet to outside observers. NGOs thus fill two important functions: they gather information for use by the UN bodies, and they keep the issue of Tibet before the UN. Because of the magnitude of human rights violations occurring, and the multiplicity of available fora at the UN, it is crucial that NGOs coordinate their efforts.

6. *The issue of Tibet should not be raised in isolation.* Human rights are by definition an expression of different peoples' oneness. It is accurate and philosophically appropriate to present the Tibetan situation as one of universal import. It is also advantageous strategically to do so. Tibetans and Tibet-support groups must persuade other peoples to empathize with Tibet's plight—e.g., former colonies to recognize the badges of colonization in the PRC's treatment of Tibet, or other developing nations to feel for the exploitation of Tibet's natural resources, or nations with proud histories of civil and political rights to deplore the loss of free expression in Tibet. Only if they succeed in these efforts can the Tibetans hope to mobilize sufficient pressure to force the PRC to recognize their legitimate claims. Success will, in part, depend on the willingness of Tibet supporters to become knowledgeable about the human rights situations facing other peoples across the globe.

7. *International lobbying efforts should substantially increase.* While maintaining the foothold gained in UN human rights arenas, advocacy of the Tibetan position should be expanded to other UN bodies and skilled representatives should attend meetings of international organizations such as UNESCO, the International Labor Organization, and the United Nations Conference on Environment and

Development presently scheduled for 1992. Tibetans should continue their past efforts while exploring options amongst the vast number of international organizations and governments whose decisions can have an impact on the Tibetan people and their territory.

8. *United Nations advocacy should be viewed as part of a long-term, integrated effort.* While the United Nations makes an effort to address violations of human rights, it is clear that the UN process is not designed to provide a swift remedy in Tibet. Perhaps its greatest potential lies in the opportunity it provides to educate the international community about the current situation in Tibet. Despite its lofty mandate, the UN remains dependent on its members for funding and thus susceptible to political pressures. Nonetheless, work at the United Nations is an area not to be ignored. Tibet must be raised as a topic of debate before the United Nations to be considered a legitimate international issue. As the last several years have clearly shown, work at the United Nations is only one piece of a larger puzzle, dependent on all the many efforts made to realize the legitimate claims of the Tibetan people.

---

1. The collective right of self-determination is so defined in the Declaration on Principles of International Law concerning Friendly Relations and Co-Operation among States in accordance with the Charter of the United Nations (G.A. res. 2625 (XXV) of October 24, 1970). It occupies a prominent position in the United Nations Charter, and is similarly defined in Article 1 of both the International Covenant on Civil and Political Rights and the International Covenant on Economic, Social, and Cultural Rights. It is deemed "a prerequisite to the full enjoyment of all fundamental rights." (G.A. res. 637A (VII) of December 16, 1952).

2. In the International Court of Justice's case on *Namibia*, Judge Ammoun characterized the right to self-determination as a norm of the nature of *jus cogens*, derogation of which is not permissible under any circumstances (1971 I.C.J. 16, 89-90 (Ammoun, separate opinion)). *See also* H. Gros Espiell, The Right to Self-Determination, U.N. Doc. E/CN.4/Sub.2/405/rev.1 (1980) at p. 12: "(N)o one can challenge the fact that...the principle of self-determination necessarily possesses the character of *jus cogens.*"

3. The International Court of Justice emphasized this aspect of the right in the *Western Sahara* case when it referred to "the principle of self-determi-

nation as a right of peoples" (1975 I.C.J. 12, 31). In his report the Special Rapporteur, Hector Gros Espiell, applied the right as "a right of peoples...of a specific type of human community sharing a common desire to establish an entity capable of functioning to ensure a common future." U.N. Doc. E/CN.4/Sub.2/405/Rev.1 (1980) p. 9.

It is to be noted that self-determination is a right of peoples *independent of any issue* of their current legal status. In the case of the Tibetans, there is a powerful argument under international legal principles that Tibet was a sovereign state before the PRC's invasion and occupation, and has remained sovereign since—as is recognized, for instance, in the case of the Baltic States. For a discussion of the legal status of Tibet under international law, see Michael van Walt van Praag, *The Status of Tibet: History Rights and Prospects under International Law (1987)* (Boulder, 1987).

4. See Asia Watch, *Merciless Repression: Human Rights in Tibet* (February 1988); International Campaign for Tibet, *Forbidden Freedoms: Beijing's Control of Religion in Tibet* (September 1990); Physicians for Human Rights, *The Suppression of a People: Accounts of Torture and Imprisonment in Tibet* (November 1989); releases prepared by the Tibet Information Network and the Human Rights Desk of the Office of Information and International Relations, Tibetan Central Secretariat, Dharamsala, India.

5. The PRC is a signatory to the International Convention on the Elimination of All Forms of Racial Discrimination. *See* discussion of the 1990 session of the United Nations monitoring body known as "CERD" *infra*.

6. Article 19 of the Universal Declaration of Human Rights (UDHR) provides:

> Everyone has the right to freedom of opinion and expression; this right includes freedom to hold opinions without interference and to seek, receive and impart information and ideas through any media and regardless of frontiers.

Article 19 of the International Covenant of Civil and Political Rights protects a similar right of free expression, subject, however, to restrictions such as are provided by law and are necessary "for respect of the rights or reputations of others" or "for the protection of national security or of the public order, or of public health or morals." The right "to hold opinions without interference" is not subject to such restrictions. Art.19, para.1.

It should be noted that the PRC is not a party to the International Covenant on Civil and Political Rights nor to the International Covenant on Economic, Social and Cultural Rights, although it has ratified or signed eight other international agreements, including the Convention on the Elimination of All Forms of Racial Discrimination, the Convention on the Suppression and Punishment of the Crime of Apartheid, the International Convention against Apartheid in Sports, the Convention on the Elimination of All Forms of Discrimination against Women, the Convention on the Prevention and Punishment of the Crime of Genocide, the Convention Against Torture and Other Cruel, Inhuman or Degrading Treatment or Punishment, the Convention relating to the Status of Refugees and the Protocol relating to the Status of Refugees. As discussed below, the PRC is legally bound to observe not only those conventions it has signed, but also those others which have assumed the stature of "customary international." See n. 23 *infra*.

The concept of "necessary restrictions" has given the PRC great latitude in defining allowable freedom of expression. Articles 90 and 104 of the Criminal Law of the PRC define crimes of counterrevolution in very broad terms. Article 90 states:

> All acts endangering the People's Republic of China committed with the goal of overthrowing the political power of the dictatorship of the proletariat and the socialist system are crimes of counterrevolution.

The Criminal Law of the People's Republic of China, art. 90, translated in *The Criminal Law and The Criminal Procedure Law of China* (Foreign Languages Press, Beijing, 1st ed., 1984). Other provisions of the Criminal Law proscribe specific kinds of conduct, such as "collu(sion) with foreign states in plotting to harm the sovereignty, territorial integrity and security of the motherland" (art. 91); "plot(ting) to subvert the government or dismember the state" (art. 92); "organiz(ing) or lead(ing) a counterrevolutionary group" (art. 98); and "(t)hrough counterrevolutionary slogans, leaflets or other means, propagandizing for inciting the overthrow of the political power of the dictatorship of the proletariat and the socialist system" (art. 102)(2). Much of the proscribed conduct carries a sentence of life imprisonment or ten years of fixed-term imprisonment. Nonetheless, the death sentence may be imposed "when harm to the state and the people is especially serious and the circumstances especially odious" (art. 103).

7. Article 20 of the Universal Declaration of Human Rights provides:

> 1. Everyone has the right to peaceful assembly and association.
> 2. No one may be compelled to belong to an association.

8. Article 18 of the Universal Declaration of Human Rights provides:

> Everyone has the right to freedom of thought, conscience and religion:

this right includes freedom to change his religion of belief, and freedom, whether alone or in community with others in public or private, to manifest his religion or belief in teaching, practice, worship and observance.

The International Covenant on Civil and Political Rights provides that "(f)reedom to manifest one's religion or beliefs may be subject only to such limitations as are prescribed by law and are necessary to protect public safety, order, health, or morals or the fundamental rights and freedoms of others." Art. 18, para. 3.

Control over religious practice in Tibet rests with the Bureau of Religious Affairs (BRA). The BRA restricts induction of new monks and nuns; controls authorization to restore religious buildings; supervises activities in monasteries; compels monks and nuns to undertake political study illuminating the relationship between Tibet and China; and selects or appoints abbots for the monasteries, as well as political monitors to observe and inform on the monks and nuns. Tsering Shakya, "Religious Freedom in Tibet" (July 1989). See The International Campaign for Tibet, *Forbidden Freedoms: Beijing's Control of Religion in Tibet* (September 1990).

While Article 36 of the PRC Constitution guarantees that citizens "enjoy freedom of religious belief," it also stipulates that nobody "may make use of religion to engage in activities that disrupt the public order, impair the health of citizens or interfere with the educational system of the state." Article 36 further empowers the organs of the state to determine what constitutes "normal religious activities" for purpose of permissible assembly.

In 1982 the Central Committee of the Communist Party issued a set of guidelines entitled, "Concerning Our Country's Basic Standpoint and Policy on Religious Questions During the Socialist Period." Pursuant to these guidelines, the Party's religious policies are to be implemented by patriotic religious organizations; independent religious gatherings are banned; religious activities may take place only in authorized buildings and areas; young religious personnel are to be trained by the state; religion is banned from schools, and cannot be used to interfere in the economic or political administration of the country; unauthorized contacts with outside religious organizations are prohibited.

9. Article 13 of the Universal Declaration of Human Rights states:

1. Everyone has the right to freedom of movement and residence within the borders of each State.
2. Everyone has the right to leave any country, including his own, and to return to his country.

10. Since September 1987, renewed demonstrations in Tibet have drawn worldwide attention. Precise figures of human rights violations are impossible to confirm, as PRC censorship generally excludes the press and human rights monitoring organizations from Tibet. Tibetans maintain that by invoking a policy of "merciless repression" (Statement of Qiao Shi, UPI, reported in *South China Morning Post*, July 20, 1988), the PRC has executed hundreds since the demonstrations of 1989. Eyewitness accounts of the 1989 disturbances suggest that PRC security forces initiated the violence, deliberately provoking the Tibetan crowd (by, for instance, the use of snipers) and responded with vastly excessive force resulting in numerous deaths. *See* Tibet Information Network, "Background Briefing Paper: Summary of Events in Lhasa 5 March to 7 March, 1989" (August 7, 1989). It is widely believed that most Tibetans imprisoned have been detained because of their opposition to the PRC occupation. See Statement of Professor Elliot Sperling, Hearing on "Human Rights in Tibet", before the Subcommittees on Human Rights and International Foreign Affairs, House of Representatives, 100th Congress, 1st Session, Washington, DC, October 14, 1987, p. 8.

11. If accurate, these reports indicate a complex of human rights violations of vast dimensions committed against the entire Tibetan people. Both International Covenants provide:

> All peoples may, for their own ends, freely dispose of their natural wealth and resources without prejudice to any obligations arising out of international economic co-operation, based upon the principle of mutual benefit, and international law. In no case may a people be deprived of its own means of subsistence.

The World Charter for Nature, promulgated by the UN General Assembly, sets out the basic principles of international environmental law. The World Charter obligates states to make an exhaustive examination prior to undertaking any activities likely to pose a significant risk to nature and to show conclusively that the benefits of planned activities outweigh potential damage to the environment. See World Charter for Nature, G.A. res. 37/7 adopted on October 28, 1982, reprinted in 22 I.L.M. 455 (1983); The Charter of Economic Rights and Duties of the States; Environmental Perspective to the Year 2000, G.A. res. 42/186; Declaration of the United Nations Conference on the Human Environment in U.N. Doc A/CONF.48/14 (1972) p. 2 *et seq.*

Environmental questions cannot be addressed without taking into consideration the impact of environmental policy on the right to life as delineated in the Universal Declaration of Human Rights, art. 3. This *jus cogens* norm, extending beyond the definition of deprivation of life, requires that government take affirmative steps to protect the lives of those persons affected by a state's actions. Safeguarding life and protecting human beings from physical danger or environmental hazards are among the most essential obligations and functions of government. Failure to meet these obligations can result in civil or criminal liability under international law. See B. Ramcharan, "The Concept and Dimension of the Right to Life," in *The Right to Life in International Law*, 1, 8 (B. Ramcharan, ed., 1985).

Viewing the right to a healthy and safe environment as a human right has particular application to the Tibetan plateau, where critics charge the PRC with massive deforestation; mining of gold, borax, coal and uranium; nuclear dumping; and nuclear weapons storage. Practices associated with so-called "ecotourism" have aroused grave concern. There is some question, too, concerning the liability of multi-national corporations which engage in practices violating the right to life in association with the PRC.

12. G.A. res. 1353, 14 U.N., GAOR (1959); G.A. res. 1723, 16 U.N. GAOR (1961); G.A. res. 2079, 20 U.N. GAOR (1965). For the full wording of these resolutions, see Appendix II.

13. Article 1(2) of the United Nations Charter provides that a purpose of the United Nations is:

> (t)o develop friendly relations among nations based on respect for the principles of equal rights and self-determination of peoples, and to take other appropriate measures to strengthen universal peace.

14. Article 55 of the United Nations Charter provides:

> With a view to the creation of conditions of stability and well-being which are necessary for peaceful and friendly relations among nations based on respect for the principle of equal rights and self-determination, the United Nations shall promote:
>
> 1. higher standards of living, full employment, and conditions of economic and social progress and development;
>
> 2. solutions of international economic, social, health, and related problems; and international cultural and educational co-operation; and
>
> 3. universal respect for, and observance of, human rights and fundamental freedoms for all without distinction as to race, sex, language or religion.

15. G.A. res. 1514 (XV) of December 14, 1960.

16. G.A. 16th Sess., 1961, Item A/4848, "Question of Tibet," December 19, 1961.

17. U.N. General Assembly, 16th Sess, 1961, Item A/4848 "Question of Tibet", December 19, 1961, Statement of Mr. Aiken.

18. *Ibid.* (statement of Mr. Plimpton, head of the U.S. delegation, on December 19, 1961).

19. *Ibid.* (statement of Mr. Hsueh, head of the Republic of China's delegation).

20. *Ibid.* (statement of Thailand).

21. Copies of statements pertaining to Tibet made at the Commission on Human Rights and the Sub-Commission on Prevention of Discrimination and Protection of Minorities from 1985 to the present are available from the offices of the International Committee of Lawyers for Tibet.

22. G.A. res. 36/55 of November 25, 1981.

23. The PRC routinely protests criticism of its human rights record in Tibet as "interference in its internal affairs". The position does not accord with developments in the international law of human rights, nor indeed with the PRC's own emerging practice of criticizing the human rights records of other nations. For an excellent discussion of the concessions made by the international community to accommodate the position of the PRC see Roberta Cohen, "People's Republic of China: The Human Rights Exception," 9 *Hum. Rts. Q.* 447 (1987).

There is a growing consensus that fundamental human rights are no longer the "internal" affairs of one country. The development of international human rights law since World War II has departed from the classical statist view in two key respects: It is now recognized that individuals have rights *vis-à-vis* their own states, and it is increasingly accepted that every state's human rights record is subject to scrutiny by its fellow states. See, *e.g.,* J. Brierly, *The Law of Nations* 291-96 (6th ed. H. Waldock, ed., 1963); see, R. Lillich & F. Newman, *International Human Rights: Problems in Law and Policy* 1-12, 14-51 (1979).

24. U.N. Doc. E/CN.4/1988/22.

25. U.N. Doc. E/CN.4/1988/45.

26. U.N. Doc. E/CN.4/1989/15.

27. U.N. Doc. E/CN.4/1989/25.

28. U.N. Doc. E/CN.4/1989/44.

29. U.N. Doc. E/CN.4/1989/18.

30. U.N. Doc. E/CN.4/1989/NGO/2.

31. U.N. Doc. E/CN.4/1989/NGO/11.

32. U.N. Doc. E/CN.4/1989/NGO/1.

33. U.N. Doc. E/CN.4/1990/46.

34. U.N. Doc. E/CN.4/1990/17.

35. U.N. Doc. E/CN.4/1990/22.

36. U.N. Doc. E/CN.4/1990/13.

37. U.N. Doc. E/CN.4/1990/NGO/9.

38. U.N. Doc. E/CN.4/1990/NGO/8.

39. U.N. Doc. E/CN.4/1990/NGO/58.

40. Participating organizations included the following: Disabled Peoples' International, Friends of the Earth, Habitat International Coalition, Human Rights Advocates, International Association of Educators for World Peace, International Association for the Defence of Religious Liberty, International Commission of Jurists, International Coalition of Jewish Women, International Fellowship of Reconciliation, International League for Human Rights, International League for the Rights and Liberation of Peoples, International Organization for the Elimination of All Forms of Racial Discrimination, International Union of Students, Liberation, Minority Rights Group, Pax Christi International, Pax Romana, Regional Council on Human Rights for Asia, World University Service, and the World Union for Progressive Judaism.

41. U.N. Doc. E/CN.4/1990/52.

42. U.N. Doc. E/CN.4/1991/17.

43. U.N. Doc. E/CN.4/1991/56.

44. U.N. Doc. E/NC.4/1991/36.

45. U.N. Doc. E/CN.4/1991/20.

46. U.N. Doc. E/NC.4/1991/73.

Tibet's Endangered Environment

photo by Galen Rowell

ORVILLE SCHELL

Chinese Attitudes to Conservation and to Tibet

In the early 1980s, while resting for a day during a trek through the Amdo region of the Tibetan Plateau—a very wild, remote area— several of our expedition's Tibetan guides came galloping into camp. On the back of one of their saddles was a dead snow leopard, which our expedition ate for that day's meal. I thought, at first, that the snow leopard, an endangered species, had been shot solely for that purpose. However, as I began to look more deeply into the incident, I realized that it wasn't the meat of the snow leopard, nor the value of its skin, that our guides had been so excited about. It was the snow leopard's bones that were the most valuable piece of the animal. In Chinese medicine, the bones command a very handsome price as a kidney enhancer and remedy for arthritis.

As it turned out, guides from the Chinese Mountaineering Association who were accompanying our expedition soon bought the bones from the Tibetan guides, took them back to China, and sold them for a handsome profit. This made their entire trip—this

This piece is adapted from comments made at *Endangered Tibet*, an ecology conference held in San Francisco, October 27, 1990.

cold, wet, unpleasant, high-altitude nightmare that we Americans had forced them to endure—quite worthwhile. However, one could not help but be struck by the absurdity and contradictoriness of our guides. They, the supposed custodians of the wilderness, had ended up being its pillagers.

Later, back in Xining, the capital of Qinghai province (formerly known as the Amdo region of Tibet) I saw a sign on a storefront that had pictures of a snow leopard, a blue bharal sheep, a Tibetan brown bear [Ed. Note: the bears are hunted for their paws], and several other exotic and now very scarce species that inhabit the Tibetan Plateau. I was stunned to learn that it was a Chinese government-run store that specialized in purchasing and selling whatever parts of these endangered animals were of value on the Chinese market.

The economics of this one snow leopard's death illustrate the kind of insoluble and often destructive connection that exists between China and Tibet today. The Tibetans would not be hunting with such eagerness if there weren't such a lucrative market in China, where there is little reverence for animal life, endangered or otherwise. Simply put, in Chinese culture, animals are revered primarily as things to eat. These cultural attitudes are one reason why China is such an environmental disaster area today, and such a poor model for Tibet when it comes to wildlife protection.

Compared to the ecological damage China has inflicted upon itself, however, Tibet remains a relatively pristine, untouched wilderness. It would not be too extreme to say that China today is a kind of Dickensian industrial hell, the likes of which are unequalled except perhaps in certain areas in eastern Europe. China is a curious example of a politically-centralized totalitarian country coupled to a growing *laissez-faire* economy at the local level. And it is on the local level that the government has abdicated most control, including over the environment. Although the government still restricts such things as human rights and freedom of expression, it has relaxed its grip on those other mechanisms of control that might enable it to have a salutary effect on things like China's environment.

To put it bluntly, China is an authoritarian country that misapplies its ability to control. When China was much more of a totalitarian state than it is now, under Chairman Mao Zedong, the environmental situation was not nearly as bad as it could have been. The levers of political and adminstrative control were still firmly in the hands of the central government at that point, and when this or that ministry chose to do something, the government could act expeditiously. Had a good environmental policy been on the government's agenda, it could have been implemented quite easily. This is not a polemic for totalitarianism, but simply to acknowledge that dictatorial control can have a beneficial side if it is used to good effect.

Another reason China was not as ecologically devastated then as it is now is that China was not as economically developed. Not only was the power to control all industry still in the hands of the government, but people did not have much money, and industry was producing virtually no consumer goods. The Chinese government did not *want* its people to consume a lot. The cultural revolution under Mao was emphatically not about consumption. It was, instead, about austere struggle, what the Chinese call *jianku fendou*. You were expected to struggle with all your heart to serve the people, not yourself. Owning a washing machine or VCR was unimaginable; a bicycle, a sewing machine—these were the few material objects to which one could aspire. The environmental benefits of this kind of anti-consumerism are obvious.

Paradoxically, then, there was much less environmental destruction going on in China during those early years, when Chinese industry was at a kind of underdeveloped "half-throttle," compared to now. Thus, there was less damage to the natural environment of almost every area under Chinese control.

The situation today, however, has radically changed under Deng's reforms. China's *nouveau* totalitarianism can no longer control things that even democrats might like to see controlled. The burgeoning world of entertainment media is a good example of this. China broadcasts some of the most ghastly television programs in the world today, with absolutely no redeeming political or social importance. The programming is often so bad that you find yourself asking: Why don't they do something about this? Doesn't the government still control the media? Why are they, in effect, shooting themselves in their own feet and subverting their own socialist cause?

For instance, one New Year's Eve I was in my Beijing hotel room, slumped in front of a television set, when a provincial New Year's variety hour special came on. Suddenly, the lights came up on a gazebo, covered with Christmas tree lights, which is China's current idea of being festive. (Every disco in China is plastered with rows and rows of these flashing lights.) And, lo and behold, who was in the gazebo but a young woman, with bright ruby-red lips, spiked heels, a well-tailored People's Liberation Army uniform, and an electric guitar. She sang an amazingly dreadful song called "Foxhole Disco."

Such performances raise the question of how any self-respecting totalitarian government could possibly countenance this sort of thing. The answer has little to do with the tolerance for pluralism and dissent of Li Peng, Yang Shangkun, or Deng Xiaoping. Such Chinese television programs are symptomatic of a far more significant phenomenon: China is out of control. Its government can only control the surface of things. It can shoot people in the streets; it can deny passports; but it often cannot effectively govern in a comprehensive and grass roots way. As a consequence, the lower echelons of the economy are allowed to go pretty much their own way, so that when you come to a provincial city, you enter a smoggy, degraded environment that is essentially a modern industrial hell. It became a hell because the people running the new private enterprises, private cooperatives, and state enterprises at the provincial and county level are obsessed with production and the bottom line. They don't care about the environment. They can't *afford* to care about the environment because of the pressure to increase production. They do not have the wherewithal to be concerned with pollution, nor do they have the regulatory agencies to watch over it.

But equally as important, the government in Beijing no longer has the will nor the power to force them to deal with such problems. As a result, much of China is beyond environmental salvation. This is especially true in the central part of the country, where factories and farms often stand literally side-by-side. It is a depressing sight to see these factories in the countryside, with outfall pipes spewing effluent laden with toxic chemicals and heavy metals into irrigation systems, which flow right into rice fields.

Again, it is China's bastardized and confused system, one that is hamstrung somewhere between socialism and capitalism, centralism and decentralism, that produces this kind of lethal tolerance. The land tenure system presents similar problems. Farmers don't own their land, but with the privatization of agriculture they do have long term contracts to farm it. However, because they are uncertain of their long-term stewardship over their farms, they usually want to maximize their short-term profits. Knowing that they may not have a farm five or ten years from now, they often imagine that it is in their best economic interests to use up the land's fertility without replenishing it. Because there is no long-term relationship between Chinese industry and Chinese natural resources, the overwhelming ethic is to consume the resources as rapidly as possible.

China, then, is caught on the horns of a new and terrible dilemma between production and environmental protection. The government has, in fact, set up a few environmental protection commissions, and you do find a few articles in newspapers, discussing what must be done to save China's ecology. But the bitter truth is that, with its growing population and desperation to produce, China's environment is running downhill at a very, very alarming rate.

Since Tibet is technically part of China, its ecological destruction is ineluctably connected with that of China. Moreover, Chinese are now conducting explorations for oil and other minerals in Tibet, building roads, exporting population, destroying wildlife habitats—all things which are having a profound impact on Tibet's delicate high-altitude ecology. As long as Tibet is under Chinese occupation, we will have to look to Beijing not only to understand why this is happening to Tibet, but to stop it. The political levers are being pulled in Beijing, not in Lhasa, which means local Tibetans have very little control over the future of their land. Tibet is merely a piece of punctuation at the end of a long, complicated Han Chinese sentence of environmental catastrophe.

The Chinese, with all their disregard for their own environment, care even less about that of Tibet. One has only to read Chinese traditional poetry to learn of the abhorrence with which most Chinese have historically looked upon the wild, barbarian hinterlands of Tibet, Mongolia, and Xinjiang. They don't go there for pleasure; they only go to fight or to make money, and neither are particularly salutary ways for the Chinese to be involved in Tibet.

I often wonder why China doesn't just let go of Tibet. Beijing actually sinks enormous amounts of resources into it and, for their efforts, they've gotten nothing but a terrible diplomatic black eye. In fact, one can conceive of a rather good scenario in which they might say "Look, we'll pull out of Tibet, but we'll continue to manage its defense and foreign affairs." This way, they could save face *and* solve any number of major problems for themselves.

The reason they haven't done this, I think, is because of their titanic pride. It is very difficult for a country as insecure as China to consider giving up something to which they have committed so many resources and so much of their ego. One must never under-estimate this sense of insecurity in dealing with China. The Chinese Foreign Ministry has a recurring phrase that appears in many of their statements: "The feelings of the Chinese people have been hurt by X, Y, or Z." It is this feeling of being "hurt," this fear of being made to look weak, that makes them cling so tenaciously to Tibet. From their perspective, to lose Tibet would be a tremendous loss of face.

So Tibet is a sort of tar baby for China, and one doubts that the present leadership will be sufficiently visionary or confident to solve this problem creatively. Indeed, Beijing hardly seems able even to think in terms of the *real* interest of its people, as opposed to all the other interests gravitating around the question of face. Beijing's gerontocrats are living in another era, where they are still struggling against the imputations of old weaknesses. Until there is a change in this leadership, and China's perception of itself, it is doubtful that there will be any kind of real solution to the problem of Tibet.

Sadly, there cannot be an environmental movement in China, or in Tibet, until the political situation changes. Environmental move-ments almost always grow up on the margins of the political and economic mainstream. They are like mosquitoes buzzing around centers of power and rarely grow up within established governments. They represent the nascency of pluralism. China has been singularly unable to purge itself of manifold political, economic, social, and cultural problems precisely because there has been no tradition of pluralism, diversity, or loyal dissent. The government's traditional presumption has been "If you're not with us, you're against us." This traditional attitude was reinforced by the whole orthodox Marxist/Leninist/Maoist canon, which stressed that everyone *must* agree. If one doesn't agree with the government, one is put in prison. Thus, no margins on which people can stand outside the government can develop, and this is the only territory in which a truly independent environmental movement can begin to grow.

By 1989, there was a curious Sherwood Forest growing up in China, outside of the Party. There was a vibrant private economy, where people could make a living outside of state-run enterprises. There was also sort of a proto-Bohemian ethic developing as people began to form rock groups, to write bold, critical pieces of literature, and to set up *avant garde* theater groups that were outside the official ring. One looked to this with great hope for both China and Tibet. There was hope that, out of this new margin of cultural and political life, a host of new groups would arise, groups that could act as checks and balances on the government and keep it honest. But, as everyone knows, this movement died dramatically in Tiananmen Square in June 1989. It was snuffed out before it ever really had a chance to take up the issue of the environment.

The most tragic aspect of China and Tibet's environmental decline is that very few Chinese seem to notice the degradation around them. As more and more Chinese begin to travel abroad—to Europe, the United States, and elsewhere—and begin to come in contact with adversarial environmental groups, this situation may well change. Perhaps they will go home and be able to see the hideous conditions in which most urban people live, and in turn be moved to try and do something about them.

For now, the Chinese government is not about to countenance any kind of political movement that is not completely sanctioned and controlled by it. But, eventually such movements will arise, even though the process may be very painful. We can only hope that Tibet will somehow survive until such a time. The Himalayas are a tremendously fragile environment, however, and the migration of Han Chinese into Tibet is an especially perilous development. No one knows the exact statistics, but they are diluting the Tibetan culture as well as bringing rapacious development to the area.

This migration is being impelled forward by China's most frightening environmental nightmare: namely, its skyrocketing population. Like the periodic plagues of locusts that sweep over the
countryside, China's population is slowly exhausting and devastating the land, and ultimately will overwhelm every available natural
resource in the country. This will, in turn, apply more and more
pressure on the Chinese to move out of China proper and into the
so-called autonomous regions. And if China begins to discover more
and more valuable resources in Tibet, not only will the migration
grow more rapidly, but the despoliation of Tibet will advance as well.

This has created an enormous amount of resentment among the
Tibetan people and nobody knows how that will finally resolve itself.
But once again, it is almost unimaginable that the situation will
resolve itself by Tibetans revolting and overthrowing Chinese rule.
It must, therefore, resolve itself back in Beijing through some kind
of political evolution or revolution at the center. One can only hope
that the Chinese students and dissident intellectuals who are at the
forefront of the democracy movement will not forget Tibet.

His Holiness the Dalai Lama's proposal to turn Tibet into a giant
nature preserve—and a human preserve as well—is a fascinating
idea. He might become the Vaclav Havel of Asia, and Tibet a buffer
zone between India, Pakistan, China, and Nepal—all Asian countries that have histories of tension and border wars.

Is this vision more than just a pipe dream? Well, there are not many
leaders left in the world who have the moral authority of the Dalai
Lama. His powers of moral suasion and his commitment to nonviolence
are very precious commodities in this day and age of hype and deceit.
They are also commodities that could serve the Chinese well, if they
could learn how to put them to good use, rather than to deride and
oppose them. What is important to ask is: Who can help turn Tibet
from being a problem, a land in environmental decline, into something stable and protected? Perhaps the Dalai Lama could play such
a role, but we must not hold our breaths. This will probably not
happen as long as the gerontocrats, who hold the power in Beijing,
endure. I am afraid any kind of real Tibetan autonomy lies down a
long and twisting road. But it is one of those marvelous fantasies that
I nonetheless like to entertain, and I hope that someday it may have
a chance to come to pass.

GALEN ROWELL

The Agony of Tibet

In 1981 I set off to lead the first two American expeditions allowed into the backcountry of Tibet since the Chinese invasion three decades earlier. For a photographer, it was the chance of a lifetime. I thought little of politics or human rights. I simply wanted to climb mountains and take photographs of the mysterious land I had read so much about.

I never dreamed that I would make five visits to Tibet over the next eight years, become the subject of diplomatic complaints, be held by soldiers overnight against my will, and see many of my articles go unpublished in the United States out of fear of Chinese retribution. If I had it to do all over again, there is only one thing I would have done differently. I would not have compromised the story of Tibet's environmental destruction as much as I did. Then, I was worried about going back. Now I simply want to tell the story.

Before 1981 the remote parts of Tibet were shrouded in mystery. All the modern naturalists knew about the region came from reports at least three decades old. "I have never seen so many varieties of birds in one place," wrote British explorer Kingdon Ward in 1920. "One great zoological garden," Joseph Rock wrote in a 1930 *National*

Geographic. "Wherever I looked I saw wild animals grazing content-edly." In the thirties, a German traveler named Dalgleish reported sighting a herd of 10,000 *chiru*, a Tibetan antelope now rarely seen. In the forties, Leonard Clark reported, "Every few minutes, we would spot a bear or a hunting wolf, herds of musk deer, *kyangs*, gazelles, bighorn sheep, or foxes. This must be one of the last unspoiled big-game paradises."

This glory was what I had come to see. For an exorbitant fee—$50,000 to guide several naturalists for three weeks in the Anye Machin mountains of northeast Tibet—our Chinese hosts promised "a wealth of rare birds and animals... thick virgin forests where deer, leopards, and bear thrive, while the grasslands and gravel slopes near the snow line are alive with hordes of gazelles, wild asses, and rare musk deer."

For three weeks, we walked—over a hundred miles in all. We saw virtually nothing. The wildlife had disappeared.

My other trek that year was to the Tibetan side of Mount Everest. I drove through over 1,000 miles of back roads without seeing a single wild large mammal. My negative results confirmed those of Pema Gyalpo, who had led a delegation the previous year that traveled 8,000 miles overland. She made the trip for the Tibetan Government-in-Exile in Dharamasala, India, whose head of state is her brother, the Dalai Lama. "On long journeys," she wrote, "you used to see more gazelles, deer, and antelope than people. Now, in three months of extensive traveling in Tibet, I did not see any of these creatures."

In 1950 Mao's People's Liberation Army invaded Tibet. Nine years later, the Tibetan people rebelled after China's promises of religious and personal freedom proved false. The revolt was brutally crushed, and the Dalai Lama fled into exile in India. More than 80,000 Tibetans were killed in the immediate aftermath, and observers estimate 1.2 million Tibetans have died at the hands of Chinese soldiers or as a result of imprisonment or starvation in the last thirty years. This carnage is just a fraction of the roughly 35,000,000 victims of China's four decades of Maoist rule, but it represents a fifth of the Tibetan population. During the subsequent decade, more than 6,000 monasteries, temples, and historic structures were razed. Alexander

Solzhenitsyn calls China's administration of Tibet "more brutal and inhumane than any other communist regime in the world."

Before the arrival of the Chinese, Tibet had its own separate language, religion, currency, government, and postal system. It also had the most successful system of environmental protection of any inhabited region in the modern world. There were no parks or wildlife preserves in the Western sense. Formal protection of wildlife and wildlands was unnecessary in a land where devout Buddhist compassion for all living beings reigned supreme.

Tibetan Buddhism essentially prohibits the killing of animals. Children are taught from birth that all life is sacred. In his classic work, *Seven Years in Tibet*, Heinrich Harrer wrote of the frustration of working with Tibetans on the dike that to this day protects the capital city of Lhasa from flooding. "There were many interruptions and pauses. There was an outcry if anyone discovered a worm on a spade. The earth was thrown aside and the creature put in a safe place."

The Buddhist ethic pervades all aspects of Tibetan culture. "I have never seen less evidence of hatred, envy, malice and unchari-tableness," wrote British India's Trade Consul in Tibet, Hugh Richardson, after living in Lhasa in the 1940s. "The Tibetan system produced a people who in the upper levels were self-controlled, intelligent, often deeply learned, capable, unpretentious, dignified, humane and friendly. The majority of people made efforts to live as much as possible with nature, not against it."

The 1950 invasion of Tibet, justified on the false grounds that Mao's China was simply restoring historical borders, was in many ways the consummation of China's longstanding desire to gain control of Tibet's natural resources. The Chinese know Tibet as Xizang, which translates as "western treasure house," a name that was born in the ancient myth that Tibet contained gold and other riches. Chinese infiltration into the country had already begun at the turn of the century, when settlers began to deforest the border regions. By 1910 the Chinese had established schools along the border that outlawed the Tibetan language and customs. In 1911 Tibet expelled all Chinese from its borders and was free of foreign control for nearly four decades.

After the invasion, China set out to "liberate" Tibet by systematically destroying its culture. Farmers were forced into collectives and required to grow winter wheat instead of the traditional barley. The policy produced bumper crops for a few years before depleting the soil and ruining the harvest. To make matters worse, China brought much of the wheat home to feed a population cut off from other sources of grains as a result of the 1959 break with the Soviet Union. Tibet was plunged into a famine, the first in recorded history, which lasted through 1963. Another period of famine followed from 1968 to 1973.

The invaders made a sport of shooting indiscriminately at wildlife. In 1973, Dhondub Choedon, a Tibetan now in exile in India, reported that "Chinese soldiers go on organized hunts using machine guns. They carry away the meat in lorries and export the musk and furs to China." Important habitat for vast herds of animals was soon overgrazed as the Chinese forced nomadic families into communes to raise livestock for export instead of their own subsistence. Tibetans, including the children, were forced to kill "unnecessary animals" such as moles and marmots that vied with humans for grain and dug up valuable grazing land. Children were given a quota for small animals to kill that, if not met, resulted in beatings and other forms of punishment.

My first attempts to quantify environmental conditions in Tibet failed. Chinese officials either refused to give me statistics, or interpreters sensed what I was up to and stopped translating. I soon discovered, however, that if I feigned interest in increased productivity under the communist regime, I could glean some alarming statistics. The general secretary of a poor county in the mountains of Amdo province dug out papers and proudly rattled off figures that confirmed my worst suspicions about habitat destruction.

"Before we had communes we had just 7,000 animals. Now the same 700 square kilometers has 70,000 yaks and sheep. Since 1979, many people own their own animals as well. Our comrades are doing very well now. Each makes thirty to forty yuan ($18-$24 at the time) a month, but through personal sales many make 100 yuan a month."

The general secretary admitted that much of the extra income came from the slaughter of wild musk deer. When queried about this apparent violation of Chinese law, he said that special dispensations were granted by the commune leader.

"What happens if a musk deer is killed illegally?" I asked. Such crimes meant a big fine, he responded, although he admitted he could not remember the last time a person had been fined. As it turned out, not one person in recent years had been fined for poaching, but several bounties of fifteen yuan had been paid for the pelts of snow leopards, which are officially protected as an endangered species in China by international agreement. Many ten-yuan bounties had been paid on wolves as well.

At the end of the first two trips in 1981, I joined several of the scientists who had traveled with me at a press conference in Beijing. We laid out the facts for the reporters. "The wildlife of this region has been decimated," said Rodney Jackson, whose snow leopard studies formed the basis of a *National Geographic* cover story in June 1986. "We come to Tibet because of inaccurate information given us by the Chinese about the presence of wildlife in an area they charged us dearly to visit. This, plus attitudes that endorse irresponsible wildlife depletion, can adversely affect China's friendship with other nations if they are allowed to continue."

The Associated Press (AP) bureau chief demanded exclusivity and promised to send me copies of the story. It was never published. An AP correspondent in the United States later told me that they couldn't afford to run "unnecessarily negative China material" that might put their Beijing bureau in jeopardy. When Jackson took his story to several U.S. wildlife organizations that fund research in China, he was again rebuffed. Criticism of China was not allowed in this close-knit scientific community, Jackson discovered. If he continued to threaten the relationship these organizations had cultivated with Beijing, he could not expect to get money for his research.

After I returned home that year, my proposals for articles about the difficulties facing researchers and the environmental holocaust in Tibet were turned down. I was well-connected with many national magazines, and I asked the editors why. "Our readers want upbeat stories," came the chorus. "And besides, China is our friend." The strongest motive, future press access, went unspoken. I began to see how the Chinese could censor the American press almost as successfully as their own.

My first major article appeared in the February 1982 *National Geographic*. I wanted to focus on the false promise of Tibet's "wildlife," but I didn't have the photographs to support such a story. I had no direct documentation of the killing, except for a picture of Rodney Jackson examining a fresh snow leopard pelt hanging on a commune wall. The editors and I agreed that shots of empty plains are not only inconclusive, but rather boring. The focus of the article was thus tightened into "Nomads of China's Wild West," a cultural profile of an armed and surprisingly independent Tibetan tribe called the Goloks. But I held out, bravely I thought, for at least one photo caption that mentioned the environment.

Beneath my photo of an overgrazed landscape ran a quote from me about the promise of "blue sheep, gazelles, bears, wolves, and deer—a richness of animal life touted to me by the Chinese authorities in Beijing. The Chinese also spoke of dense virgin forests. In fact, we saw almost no wildlife and...no forests at all."

Upon publication, the Chinese embassy lodged a formal complaint: I was guilty of an intentional political act that jeopardized Sino-American friendship. As I was planning to return to Tibet the following year as climbing leader of the first American expedition permitted to attempt Mount Everest's West Ridge, I heeded the Chinese authorities' demand that I write a letter of self-criticism. Beneath a haze of murky Latin-based words, I confessed how unwise I had been to say what I did if I ever planned to return to Tibet again.

For the next six years, I wrote with a split personality. For my own book, *Mountains of the Middle Kingdom*, published by the Sierra Club in 1983, I wrote a tell-all account, but for periodicals that might reach Beijing, I omitted all strong personal observations and opinions.

Despite this self-censorship, I again incurred the wrath of the Chinese authorities. My *National Geographic* assignment in 1988 was to document the Tibetan side of a proposed joint Chinese-Nepalese national park surrounding Mount Everest. My wife, Barbara, and I traveled with representatives of the Woodlands Mountain Institute of West Virginia, which had been working with both governments to create the park. As we left the United States in May 1988, we were told that China would announce the establishment of the park within days.

We were accompanied during our three weeks in the field by Yin Binggao, Director of Forests for Tibet, along with several of his employees. Despite Tibet's high altitude, large forests are nurtured by monsoon rains in parts of southeastern Tibet and also along the Nepalese border, where river valleys cut through the rain shadow of the Himalayas.

One of these valleys is on the east side of Mount Everest. While the rest of my group stayed in a 14,000-foot camp, I crossed a high pass and hiked into the fabled Valley of Flowers, discovered by the first British Everest expedition in 1921. Here, amidst twenty colors of native rhododendron blossoms, I was shocked to see trees being felled by the thousands. I photographed a convoy of Tibetan women carrying fresh hundred-pound beams over the pass directly through our camp. The operation appeared to be centrally organized. Lumber was cut on the spot and piled into four-cornered stacks that formed orderly rows across the valley.

Yin Binggao said he knew nothing about the timber operation. He suggested it must be Tibetans cutting wood on their own. A day later, we saw Chinese trucks in the village of Kharta loaded with the same wood bound for towns on the treeless plains to the North. There, virtually all new construction is undertaken by Chinese residents or officials. Embarrassed now, Yin Binggao promised to report the situation immediately to the closest forest official. I later found out the nearest office was in Shigatse, hundreds of miles from any forest.

The entire forestry department of Tibet employs just thirteen people. According to official documents, $54 billion of timber has been cut within the borders of old Tibet since 1959. As Tibetans do not use much wood for fuel or to frame ordinary houses, the majority of this timber is destined for China. The deforestation is aided by the forced labor of thousands of Tibetan prisoners in the southeastern part of the country. In Amdo, nearly 50 million trees have been felled since 1955, and millions of acres at least seventy percent cleared, according to the Dalai Lama's exiled government in India. Roughly 70,000 Chinese workers have been brought to the region or have traveled there voluntarily, in large part to cut down the rich stands of trees.

My colleague assigned to cover the Nepalese side of Everest and I reached the same conclusion: the environment on both sides of the mountain was being destroyed. Neither government indicated they were planning to declare a joint park, although the Nepalese had long maintained the rather ineffectual Sagarmatha National Park at the core of the proposed area.

National Geographic had hoped for an upbeat story, but instead of killing it entirely, they ran it as "Heavy Hands on the Land," a litany of wildlife and land-use problems surrounding a seemingly immutable mountain. Soon after publication, the Woodlands Institute informed me that, according to the Chinese government, my article was in error. I had stated that the park would not be created in the near future, but a document contradicting my claim had been forwarded to *National Geographic* by the institute.

In typically vague phrases, a Chinese official stated it was indeed the government's intention to proceed toward the goal of creating a natural preserve near Mount Everest, someday. I was surprised, since I had been present at meetings with the top two officials in the Tibetan government, both of whom refused to sign any letter of intent. Scanning the letter, I noticed that their names were indeed absent. It was signed by Yin Binggao. As of this writing, the intent to create the park remains on paper only.

But that was not the end. Upon my return to the United States, I was notified that I had been tried and convicted in absentia for "sedition." During my trip I had given a picture of the Dalai Lama to the patriarch of a nomad family that gave us splendid hospitality for three days and opened up his family's lives for us to photograph. This was, using phrases that commonly issue from Beijing, "wanton intrusion in China's internal affairs and overt support for the separatist Dalai-clique."

As I had become accustomed to doing, I sat down and wrote the obligatory letter to the Chinese Embassy explaining that I had no political motivation in giving the photo and apologized for any trouble I might have caused. It was simply a gift, I explained, to a man who invited me into his home and allowed me to photograph his family. But as I did this, I felt humiliated and compromised in a way I never had before. Something inside of me finally snapped. Whatever the consequences, I vowed then that I would no longer just stand by and watch the power of my work be diluted.

Since my last journey to Tibet in 1988, much has happened. There are fewer wild animals and trees, more prisoners and paper promises, but still no parks or real progress toward environmental protection. Peaceful demonstrations for Tibetan independence in Lhasa in 1987 became riots after Chinese soldiers fired into unarmed crowds, killing Buddhist monks and nuns. Observers estimate that at least 600 Tibetans have been killed and thousands of Tibetans imprisoned and tortured in the subsequent crackdown. The Chinese government instituted martial law in Tibet in March 1989, and as of this writing it has not been lifted [Ed. note: martial law was lifted on April 30, 1990]. Three months later, the government in Beijing unleased its tanks on the students occupying Tiananmen Square. And in December 1989, the Dalai Lama was awarded the Nobel Peace Prize.

The most bizarre manifestations of China's ideological rule, such as the killing of all "unnecessary" animals, have disappeared. What remains is a steady consolidation of China's domination of the country, aided by naked political oppression. As Tibet's animal and plant resources are destroyed, Beijing is now gearing up to extract gold and minerals, including uranium. China's armed forces have established nuclear missile bases on Tibet's high plateau and are now rumored to be preparing a high-level nuclear waste dump that would accept nuclear reactor fuel from China as well as Western Europe.

Despite the attention focused on the plight of Tibet in the last year, no country has gone on record as supporting Tibet's right to independence for fear of angering Beijing. In the wake of the Nobel Committee's decision to award its peace prize to the Dalai Lama, China has made it as difficult as possible for any nation extending support to the exiled leader. The government in Beijing even threatened to cut all economic ties to Norway if its king attended the prize ceremony. Although the United States Congress passed a resolution condemning China's treatment of Tibet, President Bush refused to meet with the Dalai Lama, preferring instead to send emissaries on a secret mission to China. To this date, no U.S. President has ever shaken hands with the exiled head of state.

In May 1989, I traveled to Dharamsala with my wife to meet the Dalai Lama and discuss a book we were preparing together called *My Tibet*, published by the University of California Press. After several hours of interviews about the past, present, and future of Tibet's environment, we found him to be deeply concerned, well-versed in the natural history of his country, and surprisingly hopeful and compassionate in his outlook. The Dalai Lama believes that behind every apparently bad event lurks some hidden goodness. With the right attitude, he avows, one's worst enemies aid us in becoming clear and strong. Despite the desperate situation in his country, the Dalai Lama consistently argues against taking up arms against the Chinese. He remains confident that Tibet will emerge from Chinese oppression with greater compassion and unity than ever before.

It came as no surprise to us that a few months later, the Nobel Committee made special mention of the Dalai Lama's commitment to the environment, the first time a Nobel citation has made specific reference to the ecological crisis. As he looked at some of my pictures of Tibet's last remaining wildlife that I planned to include in the book, he commented on the way his people used to coexist with humans and animals before the invasion. "Some of that harmony remains in Tibet today," he told me, "and because it happened in the past, we have some genuine hope for the future."

ELMAR R. REITER

Tibetan Deforestation and Possible Climate Effects

For me, there are three "Tibets": The first is the one that I dreamed about in my early teens, devouring the books by Sven Hedin and Heinrich Harrer describing a forbidden and forbidding country full of strange customs and fascinating people. Then there is the Tibet that lives in the hearts of the thousands who left their homes, monasteries, and temples to find refuge in Nepal, India, and around the world, trying to preserve its identity amidst the onslaught of alien cultures. Finally, there is the Tibet of stark realities that I first saw in 1980, and then again in 1983 and 1986. It is the latter one that I will try to describe.

Tibet already meets you in Chengdu, the capital of Sichuan Province. Here the Min River empties its grey waters into numerous canals dug from the fertile soil many centuries ago in one of the world's largest and oldest irrigation projects. The Min brings its waters, and the fertilizing silt it carries, from the eastern slopes of the Tibetan Plateau, formerly known as the province of Kham. It was not

This piece is adapted from Reiter's presentation at *Endangered Tibet*, an ecology conference held in San Francisco, October 27, 1990.

so much the river itself that fascinated me, but the massive hardwood tree trunks that floated haphazardly, by the dozens and hundreds, in its churning waters. Here and there small working parties along the shoreline used long grappling hooks to salvage these wooden treasures. These trees had been cut on the steep slopes of Kham and had been entrusted to the wild glacial waters for a journey. The woodchoppers did not know where this journey would end, nor did the salvage crews know where it began. How many of these precious trees were cut, but never reached a useful destination?

Flying at 30,000 feet from Chengdu to Lhasa reveals only little of the man-made devastation. The deep river gorges and steep mountain sides are dark green, but it is hard to tell from the scratched windows of a turbo-jet what is primeval forest and what is brush and vines left over after the tall giants have been felled. Making our final exit from Tibet by car through the narrow gorge of the Bo Qu River, forcing its way through the Himalayas between Nyalam in Tibet and Zham on the Nepal border, brought the human effects closer to our minds: First, our 1980 exit journey was delayed for three days in Xigaze (Shigatse), because a landslide blocked the road south of Nyalam. Finally, in Xegar (Tingri) word was received that the road would be open by next afternoon. As we descended from the windswept and barren Yagru Xongla high plains northeast of Qomolangma Feng (Mt. Everest) and Cho Oyu, into the terraced fields around Nyalam, the summer monsoon enveloped us. As we crossed the slide area, it became evident that the mud from the mountainside had not simply blocked the narrow road—the road itself had found a new resting place in the abyss at the bottom of the river. Tibetan work crews waved at us, as our caravan crawled along the newly-carved track. Anxiously, I watched rivulets of mud and gravel cutting new scars into the hillside, wondering if the mountain would be stable enough to let us pass unharmed.

It was not only our excursion tour that was blocked by the mudslide. There was a convoy of northbound trucks, loaded to capacity with heavy timber, that nature tried to immobilize.

The signature of deforestation was everywhere. While on the west side of the Bo Qu River the mountain sides abounded with lush hardwood forests, the east side, where the road wound its way towards Nepal, was covered with stumps, bushes, and vines. Man's heavy hand on nature did not stop at the border. In Nepal, north of Kathmandu, even the steepest mountain slopes were terraced into rice paddies. I wondered how much top soil would be lost in one monsoonal deluge that broke through the fragile dams of these paddies.

So much for the evidence. How about the consequences?

Of course, there is the obvious one: As mountainsides are denuded of their forest protection, erosion in these subtropical climates of monsoonal downpours carries the thin topsoil layer into the muddy rivers that empty through narrow gorges to the plains beyond the foothills. It took millennia to build these soils. Once gone, these forests will not come back on their own, even if man should realize his folly. There are large areas in Yunnan Province where deforestation and subsequent erosion have already bared the earth down to bedrock.

Forests and their ecosystem serve as delaying buffers in the hydrological cycle. Much of the moisture that is deposited as rain or, in higher regions, as snow is retained by the spongy humus soil and given off to slowly trickling brooks. Even the flooding effects of monsoonal downpours are delayed and spread over days, instead of hours. Not, however, when the forests and water-retaining soils are gone.

Most climate atlases indicate about 200 to 600 mm of precipitation for Tibet, less in the west, and more in the east where the headwaters of some of Asia's largest rivers are found. But these values have to be viewed with suspicion, in the absence of long measurement records. Of more importance is the cycle of precipitation and evaporation which constitutes the life-supporting water budget of any region.

As the forests of eastern and southern Tibet are depleted and the soil is washed away, there will be a marked reduction of evaporation. The moisture, formerly retained in the soil, will not have time to stay there until warm sunshine and vegetation send it back to the atmosphere. Instead, it will seek its shortest path to creeks, streams, and rivers, to be lost to the sea. Some of this moisture, by not re-evaporating, will be missed in the air streaming farther into the dry heartland of Tibet, raising concerns about desertification.

There are much more subtle, yet equally alarming, potential side effects of human interference in the balance of Nature in Tibet. The sharp increase in population during recent years, mostly by immigration, has brought about a dramatic surge in grazing activities. While most of the natural wildlife seems to have withdrawn to high altitudes and remote regions, out of harm's way and the iron sights of hunters' rifles, herds of domesticated yak, sheep, and goats dot the mountain slopes of the high plateau. The average elevation of the Tibetan Plateau of 4500 m (13,000 ft) above sea level does not support lush vegetation carpets that would heal easily from man-made wounds. Short grasses prevail, with long roots reaching more than 40 cm deep to tap moisture during the dry season. The hillsides near permanent settlements show deep, crisscrossing scars from thousands of hoofs that have walked the steep slopes over decades. And then there are the sand dunes, even along the sides of the fertile Lhasa River valley. Were they here forever, or are they a further sign of progressing desertification in a fragile ecosystem? During summer of 1986 we measured the surface temperatures of some of these dunes. They exceeded 60° centigrade (140° F) during the noon hours. There is not much that could entice natural vegetation to come back to such hostile environments.

Noble discussions have been held about the need to reforest denuded landscapes in Tibet and China, and token efforts have been launched in this direction. It is one thing, however, to cut century-old hardwood forests, and another to replace them with "trash" vegetation, such as poplar and eucalyptus trees. Man always seems quick in cutting wounds, slow in helping to heal them, but never short of proposals for "Band-Aid" fixes.

By cutting the vast forests in the Tibetan river gorges, and the even vaster ones in the Brazilian and African jungles, humanity may shoot itself in the foot. The recently proposed Gaia Hypothesis only spells out knowledge that has been around for quite a while: life is operating to keep the planet's livable conditions. The present balance between carbon dioxide and oxygen is a product of life forms that have developed over eons. This balance controls temperatures within a range that makes life possible. We can extend the notion of the earth-atmosphere-ocean system behaving almost like a living organism even further. What happens during the monsoons of Asia, including Tibet, is not merely a matter of local concern over there. For years we have studied so-called "teleconnections," i.e. the seeming relationship of weather and climate anomalies in widely distant regions. We know that abnormal sea-surface temperature regimes in the tropical East Pacific are linked to rainfalls during the Indian summer monsoon, upon which millions stake their livelihood. We know that the Indian and Tibetan monsoons are linked. There have been speculations about the vagaries of late-season snow in Tibet causing advances or delays in the heating of the Plateau—that heating having an effect on the surge of moist monsoon air seeking to rise and precipitate over the continent. There are compelling signs, however, that both the Tibetan snow cover and the Indian summer monsoon may be linked to ocean temperatures in the Pacific and the Atlantic.

Thus, it appears that none of the "limbs" that make up the complicated "body" of our environment—air, water, and land—can lead a separate existence. We can punish one part of this body by burning it, by turning lush green into barren desert, but surely the rest of this body of Nature will feel the pain. Lest we forget: We—the people of this planet—are part of this body, whether we like it or not.

TENZIN PHUNTSOK ATISHA

The Tibetan Approach to Ecology

For centuries Tibetans have lived with nature, always seeking to learn and understand its nuances and rhythms. Our religion, Buddhism, which was introduced to Tibet in the second or third century, has played a role in this respect. A general taboo against exploiting the environment was a direct result of our Buddhist knowledge and belief in the relationship of all plants, animals, and other elements of nature. This close relationship between nature and our religion means the principles which maintain balance in the natural world have become a part of our daily lives. And after living like this for hundreds of years, it has become difficult for any Tibetan to differentiate between the practice of religion and concern for the environment.

Furthermore, we Tibetans have always been aware of the inter-dependent nature of this world. We know that our large country, with its diverse flora and fauna, its primal forest cover, and above all the many great rivers which rise in Tibet, is a source of life to an area many times larger than Tibet itself. For most of Asia, Tibet's environment has always been of crucial importance. And so for

This piece is adapted from Atisha's presentation at *Endangered Tibet*, an ecology conference held in San Francisco, October 27, 1990.

centuries Tibet's ecosystem was kept in balance and alive out of a common concern for all of humanity.

In the Horse Water Year (1642) His Holiness the Great Fifth Dalai Lama, Ngawang Lobsang Gyatso, became the spiritual and political mentor of Tibet. From this date, in the tenth month of every year, a Decree for the Protection of Animals and the Environment was issued in the name of the Dalai Lama.[1] One of the Decrees (or "Tsatsigs") issued by the Great Thirteenth Dalai Lama states:

> From the first month of the Tibetan calendar to the 30th of the seventh month, with the exception of tigers, leopards, bears, hyenas, rats, and *Rishu* (no translation available), nobody will hurt, let alone kill, the different birds of the air, animals of the hills and forests, or fish and otter of the water. In fact nobody, noble or humble, should do violence to or harm any animal of the land or water or air, no matter how big or small.[2]

And a few decades later, His Holiness the Fourteenth Dalai Lama writes in his widely-read *Human Approach to World Peace*:

> All beings primarily seek peace, comfort, and security. Life is as dear to the mute animal as it is to any human being: even the simplest insect strives for protection from dangers that threaten its life. Just as each one of us wants to live and does not wish to die, so it is with all other creatures in the universe.[3]

The monks and nuns, farmers, nomads, and other lay Tibetans had their own prescribed practices and conventions which showed concern for the environment. For three months in the summer, monks and nuns—one fifth of Tibet's entire population—went into retreat. Such retreats served to prevent the killing or accidental crushing of worms, insects, larvae, etc. which develop during the summer, and to protect the plant life. Instead, the monks and nuns would pray for the well-being of all sentient beings.

The farmers had their own traditions. They would get together and make their own laws concerning the preservation of their environment for the current year.

The anthropologists Melvyn Goldstein and Cynthia Bell have documented how, before 1959, the nomads carefully divided their regions into sections in a "pasture book." The number of animals allowed in each pasture was carefully regulated, and penalties were quickly enforced on offenders. Livestock censuses were taken every three years, and areas carefully guarded against overgrazing. By following this system, the nomads managed to conserve the health of these grasslands through centuries of continuous use.

RESOURCES

For centuries, the rich mineral resources of Tibet were not extracted except for some gold. Tibetans believed that mining the natural resources of the country would diminish the natural strength of the land, invite the displeasure of the deities, and bring harm to society.

For instance, gold was mined near Lake Manasorover in Western Tibet in the 1900s. But following an outbreak of smallpox attributed to the wrath of the presiding deity of the mine, the Tibetan government stopped the mining.[4] Similarly, Khenrab Kunsang Mondrag, a Tibetan trained in mining, surveyed some parts of Dakpo and Lokha in the 1920s and found petrol in large reserves. But the government did not give permission to extract the petrol on the grounds that this would effect the ecosystem.[5]

However, since the Chinese invasion and occupation of Tibet, the situation has completely changed. China is rapidly exploiting the virgin mineral resources of Tibet. So far, they have been able to identify more than sixty types of minerals including alum, antimony, asbestos, asphalt, borax, boron, chromium, cobalt, coal, copper, diamond, gold, graphite, gypsum, iron ore, jade, lead, lithium, magnesium, mercury, molybdenum, nickel, natural gas, oil, oil shale, iodine, potassium, radium, silver, sodium chloride, tin, tungsten, uranium and zinc.

The deposits of uranium and borax are the biggest in the world.[6] The deposits of lithium constitute half the world's supply.[7] Tibet's copper deposit is the second largest in Asia,[8] and its reserves of iron and chrome are larger than any in China.[9]

Central Tibet alone has more than 5,760 varieties of plants of which 3,000 have an economic value. In addition, there are over 1,000 varieties of medicinal herbs. Many of them are of high economic value and easy to collect because of their concentrated growth.[10]

DEFORESTATION

Tibet's forests constitute the largest forest reserve at China's disposal. Their devastation has been widely documented and up to 1980 an estimated $54 billion worth of trees have been felled and taken to China. With such colossal and deliberate deforestation, Tibet's ecosystem has rapidly deteriorated.[11]

Tibet is the principal watershed for the Asian continent. Four rivers, all with descriptive names, rise near Mount Kailash in the west. The Sengye Khabab (meaning "out of the lion's mouth") flows through Kashmir to become the Indus in Pakistan. The Langchen Khabab ("out of the elephant's mouth") flows southward to become the Sutlej in Western India. The Mapcha Khabab ("out of the peacock's mouth") becomes the sacred Ganges (though Gangotri in India is the accepted source for Hindus). And the Tachok Khabab ("out of the horse's mouth") flows eastward and, joining the Kyichu River south of Lhasa, forms the Brahmaputra, which winds through Assam and Bengal.

Tibet is mountainous and much of the terrain is very steep, so that many rivers have enormous drops in elevation. The potential hydro-electric power was never harnessed. The geothermal energy, solar energy, and wind power were also not exploited.

In addition there are more than fifteen hundred lakes scattered all over Tibet. These lakes, teeming with fish and surrounded by grasslands, provided ideal areas for animal husbandry.[12]

RESPECT FOR NATURE

As a result of their upbringing, Tibetans have a great respect for all forms of life. Traditionally Tibetans have always lived in harmony with nature. They obey the environmental decrees issued by the government. Through their religion, Tibetans strive to improve the vitality of the earth and protect life on earth.

As for the future policy, His Holiness, the Fourteenth Dalai Lama, announced a Five-Point Peace Plan for Tibet, on September 21, 1987, at the Congressional Human Rights Caucus in Washington, D.C. The fourth point of the plan addressed the environmental issue, saying that "what little is left in Tibet must be protected and efforts must be made to restore the environment to its balanced state."

On June 15, 1988, at the European Parliament in Strasbourg, His Holiness again declared:

> The Government of Tibet would pass strict laws to protect wildlife and plant life. The exploitation of natural resources would be carefully regulated. The manufacture, testing, and stockpiling of nuclear weapons and other armaments must be prohibited as well as the use of nuclear power and other technologies which produce hazardous wastes. It would be the government of Tibet's goal to transform Tibet into our planet's largest natural preserve.

And on December 11, 1989, in his acceptance spech for the Nobel Peace Prize, His Holiness stated:

> It is my dream that the entire Tibetan plateau should become a free refuge where humanity and nature can live in peace and in harmonious balance. It would be a place where people from all over the world could come to seek the true meaning of peace within themselves, away from the tensions and pressures of much of the rest of the world. Tibet could indeed become a creative center for the promotion and development of peace.

---

1. Regent Rading Rinpoche's Tsatsig issued in 1939.

2. The Tsatsig issued by the Thirteenth Great Dalai Lama in 1901.

3. The Dalai Lama, *A Human Approach to World Peace* (London, 1984).

4. Shankhawa Gurme Sonam, *Tibetan Government's Political and Religious Ceremonies* (Dharamsala, 1984).

5. Interview, N.17.

6. *Tibet: A General Survey* (Beijing, 1988).

7. *Ibid.*

8. *Ibid.*, p. 62.

9. *Ibid.* Questions and Answers About China's National Minorities (Beijing, 1985). P.S.

10. *Ibid.*

11. *Present Conditions in Tibet* (Dharamsala, 1990), p. 20.

12. Tsepon W. D. Shakyapa. *A Political History of Tibet* (New York, 1967), p. 211.

TYRONE DANLOCK

Tibet's Changing Ecology

Before the Chinese occupation of Tibet, conservation was the natural expression of a peace-oriented social system. Laws, education, and cultural events gave highest priority to generating a social consciousness in which people, of any social niche, would behave with kind-heartedness. The fundamental expression was not humanly chauvinistic but extended towards all of nature; the majority of people made efforts to live as much as possible with nature. Consequently, Tibet's ecosystem was kept in balance and alive.

WILDLIFE

There was a general taboo against encroaching excessively on the natural environment, which was a direct result of Buddhist knowledge about the interdependence of all living things, about interrelationships among the whole spectrum of plant and animal life, including human beings, as well as the "non-living" elements of nature which such mountains, valleys, lakes, rivers, air, sky, and sunshine. Buddhist teachings were also lessons in ecology, their effect being visible to foreign visitors. H. Deasy, exploring western Tibet about 1900, wrote:

It is unusual to travel for a day without seeing antelope and kyand (a sort of wild donkey). The former of these animals is a valuable friend to travelers and is seldom found at elevations under 15,000 feet. He is in many places remarkably tame, remaining close to the caravan and watching it with evident curiosity...I must refer to the enormous numbers of antelope seen near camps No. 19 and No. 20. For many miles in every direction except west, in fact as far as the human eye aided by powerful binoculars could see, there were thousands of antelope in large herds scattered about irregularly wherever there was plenty of grass. In a few places on lofty ground in Tibet we found wild yak in herds numbering from ten to thirty and sometimes more. Most of the animals were black, brown specimens being very rare. These roving herds move with agility over the steep and stony ground, apparently enjoying the snow and frost and wind which seldom fail. At about the distance of two marches east of Charol Cho, I observed a very large herd resting on the top of a high ridge covered with snow, where it was evident that a strong, cold wind was blowing. They sought no shelter, not even that which they could easily have found on the lee side of the ridge.

VARIETY OF BIRDS

Around 1920, English explorer of southern Kham province F.K. Ward gives this description:

Most beautiful of all were the forests below the upper temple, with the sunlight splashing between trembling leaves and dancing with the shadows on the carpet of pale blue irises beneath. Here were maples and oaks, lindens, birch trees....I have never seen so great a variety of birds in one place. One had only to sit still under a tree for a few minutes and the curious little creatures came in numbers to look and chirp. One day I saw a troop of short-tailed monkeys—fancy monkeys at 10,000 feet! A little above the lower temple there stepped out onto the path to meet us a black Himalayan bear, but he quickly plunged into the forest where it was impossible to follow.

And J. Hanbury-Tracy, also traveling in Kham, during the 1930s, says:

The Salween valley is a haunt of wild birds, even in winter; daily we saw flocks of the great white pheasants; they have a comic little crouching run....There were partridges, eagles, and hawks of a dozen varieties, rose-finches, orange-beaked choughs, crows, rock pigeons, and numerous small dun-colored birds....All were extraordinarily tame on account of the rigidly enforced ban on hunting. It was no uncommon sight to see a covey of partridges scratching happily in a backyard. Monasteries, housing from six to three hundred monks, are ubiquitous in the Salween valley and the peasant dare not violate their laws.

During the spring of 1943, while about halfway between Lhasa and Koko Nor, the American mission was impressed with the abundant wildlife of the region, of which Lieutenant Colonel Ilia Tolstoy says:

> We camped at an attractive little monastery called Zuru Gompa. Unmolested by the monks, large flocks of blue sheep, or bharal, ranged the hills....We passed the beautiful valley and the plain of Nima Runghsha where hundreds of wild asses and gazelle were grazing. The mountain slopes were thickly forested and we saw musk deer jumping high through the underbrush. Riding along a stream, we jumped a small flock of Lhasa stag.

NOMADS AND FARMERS LIVE WITH NATURE

From the preceding observations, it is clear that nomad herders and farmers had minimal negative impact on the natural environment throughout the country. Traditional methods of agriculture were in unison with climate conditions, soil conditions and terrain; although not highly technological, their ways were both intelligent and resourceful, adapting to local conditions. Early this century, Dr. A.L. Shelton became well-acquainted with Tibetans while living for seventeen years in the Kham-China borderland. He writes:

> The nomads live the year round in their tents, seldom even entering a house. When the lower slopes of the mountains become free from snow in the spring, they begin their upward pilgrimage with their herds, closely following the receding snow-line until in the summer they are living far up in the highlands and on the sides of the peaks. When winter begins to set in they make the reverse journey, going down to the valleys only as fast as the descending snow-line drives them. In this way they are able to use the supply of grass to better advantage. The herders remain close to the snow also because their yak thrive best in a cold temperature....The agricultural people of the lower valleys live in substantial houses of mud, with flat roofs. In constructing the mud walls the Tibetans use forms of parallel boards not unlike the forms used in

the United States for molding walls of concrete. The mud is beaten into the forms until it is puddled, and when dry, it is very hard....The harvested grain is carried to the tops of houses, where it is threshed on the flat roofs by means of flails. 'Primitive' mills are set up along the streams, where the grain is ground raw into flour....The mills are of a simple type common in many lands, consisting of a stationary lower stone and an upper stone revolved on the lower by means of a shaft extending upward through a central hole in the fixed stone. The shaft is attached to a water-wheel below.

They were self-sufficient enough, with staples from the cool-climate barley and yak products, that no Tibetan ever starved or suffered from lack of clothing or shelter. Content with this, they had no desire to "exploit" the land's resources more.

HUNTING BRIGADES

All that has changed since the arrival of the Chinese army. They are the "knife-point" in China's thrust to "exploit," or rather steal, the abundant resources. One woman, Dhonduh Choedon, who worked several years in a commune before escaping in 1973 to India, says:

> Now everything in Tibet is the private property of a few Chinese rulers in Peking: the hills, forests, rivers and green fields, the animals, precious minerals and even human beings—to do as they [the Chinese] please, without fear of judgment....Not only the Tibetan people but even the wild animals have no freedom. In the past we used to see big herds of hundreds of various kinds of wild animals. Now even though their own 'rules' forbid the killing of females, Chinese soldiers from the military camps go on organized hunts using machine guns. In local areas there are special hunting brigades who kill wild animals indiscriminately. They carry away the meat in lorries and export valuables like musk and fur to China.

For some time, the army killed every cat or dog in sight, considering them useless and a burden on the food supply. Most of the nomads' big mastiff guard dogs were killed, in spite of the nomads' advice; soon after, wolves began decimating the livestock which had no protection. Nomads are now allowed to breed mastiff dogs.

KILLING OF ANIMALS, BIRDS AND INSECTS

The same persecution was rendered to small animals, birds, and insects, which also were considered useless and harmful to agriculture since they nibble or peck seeds, grass, or crop. The other motive was: Keep the old Tibetan society torn to shreds, since one basic structure of that society was kindness for all sentient beings. Recently Zong Rinpoche, a high Tibetan lama, gave this account:

> The Chinese forced monks, especially the higher Lamas, and children, to kill animals, birds, and insects on their way to work in the fields and on the way back. They were given a quota to kill and had to show evidence of the number killed, such as legs or wings. Failure to fulfill the quota would invite severe punishment. Some children were better than others at catching, so would help others reach their quotas, thus sparing them a beating after the day's work in the fields.

The ecological consequence of this relentless slaughter of small birds began during the 1970s, with swarms of insects plaguing crops, since their natural predators, insect-eating birds, were almost totally decimated.

Lack of ecological awareness in agriculture has brought destruction of grassland by tilling all the available land. The Second Delegation visiting Tibet during the summer of 1980, states:

> Disregarding and ignoring the local Tibetans' expertise in farming, the Chinese policy for a number of years was to introduce winter wheat crops and to cultivate all available land, including grasslands which were used for grazing by nomadic herds. In the first year, the crop yields were dramatically increased, then gradually they began to drop. Winter wheat sucked the soil dry of nutrients and the soil was soon exhausted and useless. Traditionally in Tibet, sections of farmland were left to lie fallow for at least a year before the next crop was planted.

SOIL EROSION AND FLOOD

Owing to extreme inflexibility of Han ideology, such mistakes are inherent within the system; so, the longer they dictate policy, the more havoc will result. Their mania for resource exploitation requires that all natural resources be consumed or used in some material way, be they wildlife, land, mountains, rivers, lakes, minerals or forests. There are also known mineral bodies of chromium, iron, zinc, lead, copper, silver, gold, uranium, antimony, mercury, coal, oil, and sulfur. What habitat damage and pollution will result from mining and use of these! Forests of fir, hemlock, spruce, larch, pine, cypress, juniper, walnut, birch, poplar, and rhododendron, covering a vast expanse of mountains and valleys, are the living biological water attractors and purifiers— the vital habitat for continuity of all living things, including human beings. These forests as a 'resource' are worth much more alive and standing than cut, floating down the Yangtze or Huang Ho; excessive logging has been in progress for some time, already resulting in extreme soil erosion and downstream floods. If continued, the ecological result will eventually be a drying of climate and land into desert. Without the living forests, all else will die because living things are biologically interdependent.

But above all, the essential factor that is absent from the Han system is the kind-hearted attitude that respects all living things for what they are. The old Tibetan society had this vital quality which made it civilized in the true sense. Lama Anagarika Govinda, a German Buddhist who over the years became well-acquainted with Tibetan culture wrote:

> Tibet has chosen to go a different way: to renounce the conquest of the forces of nature. . . . Instead she chose to cultivate and develop the powers of inner perception, which are the very source of all human culture, knowledge, and achievement. . . . This is the way the Tibetans viewed the problem of the future of humanity, a problem that now faces us on a global scale.

LUDMILLA TÜTING

"Life Was Harder, But It Was Easier To Live."

I understand "ecology" to mean a complete system and a complete mode of thinking. Ecology is the constantly changing relationship between nature, technology, human beings, and human culture. But we are drilled, under the instruction of many scientists and technical experts, to divide everything into separate pieces, to analyze and, in the process, to lose sight of the whole system of relationships. A very distressing example of this process is the case of Tibet.

Until a few years ago, there was hardly any outsider who tried to see the country, the living conditions, the people, and the religion of Tibet as a necessary whole. We rationally-thinking Westerners, in particular, seem largely incapable of understanding or even tolerating the crucial element of spirituality—a spirituality that had developed over millenia in Asia, and whose realizations we have mostly been unable or unwilling to develop for ourselves.

I confess that I was at first also very uncertain on reading these reports, and for lack of corroborating information, I took the horror stories of Tibetans-in-exile for great exaggerations. But since 1974, I have had the privilege of considering Nepal my second home. A great many Tibetans live in Nepal, around 10,000 of them refugees. And these people were quite different from the Tibetans described in these books: not an inferior race, not parasites, not barbarians.

Of course, there are Tibetans who look dirty. But who will be surprised if hygiene falls short of the Western urban sense at a mean elevation of 14,000 feet, in icy cold and fierce wind? Tibetans in the countryside, which is most of them, have no water faucets, no warm water, often in fact no water at all in their houses, and rooms are unheated. The only warmth available is around the hearth. The nomads, in particular, dress in wild-looking sheepskins and rub their skin with butter to help retain body heat. Dust sticks to the butter, and the result looks unmistakably like a dirty person. Yak butter plays an important role in the Tibetan eco-system.

Over many centuries, this system has developed as an adaptive way of life, which works in harmony with the natural world to make the best out of the existing conditions. The Chinese characterize these survival techniques as "uncivilized" and "backward," although it is these techniques that have made it possible for human beings to live well in this hostile climate and under difficult conditions. This point will be clearer from a few examples of this adaptation:

> *Food* is salted butter tea, roasted barley flour (*tsampa*), dried yak meat, and dried cheese;
>
> *Butter* is used as food, to protect the skin against the wind and cold temperatures, and fuel for butter lamps;
>
> *Yaks*—their manure is used as fuel, they provide milk and meat, and are used for transport, riding, and as draught animals;
>
> *Dwellings*—the nomads live in tents or huts made of stamped clay or sun-dried clay bricks mixed with *chaff* (adobe)—they have no heating facilities;
>
> *Marriage*—there is widespread polyandry where a woman marries two to three husbands (always brothers)—the result is fewer children and hardly any division of property; and
>
> *Death*—since there is no wood for burning the dead, and the ground is frozen hard, the dead are thrown to the vultures and returned to the natural cycle.

A Tibetan accurately described the times before Tibet was occupied by the Chinese when he said: "Life was harder, but it was easier to live like that."

The greatest mistakes made since the occupation of Tibet in 1949/50 have been in the field of agriculture. Suddenly there were famines, a phenomenon Tibet had never known before. "It was not just an economic fiasco, it was genocide,"a high-ranking monk said, "the family clans who had just managed to make ends meet over the centuries, since they had always been self-sufficient, starved in the thousands because the people's communes had ruined their property."

The cultivation of food, particularly of grain, was directed towards the needs of the Chinese occupation forces and was, moreover, exported to China. It was the fact that the Tibetans were forced to cultivate mainly winter wheat rather that the traditional mountain barley, as well as the fact that the nomad economy was collectivized, that brought unprecedented famines to Tibet.

Although the so-called reform policy of 1979 exempted all farmers and nomads from the obligation to hand over supplies and pay taxes for fifteen years and once again promoted private property and the private economy, the effects of the earlier mismanagement are still visible everywhere. Tourists should, therefore, not be astonished if hordes of men, women, and children sometimes grab the leftovers from their plate. Because they are too proud to beg, even Khampas wait patiently beside the table until people have finished eating.

A Tibetan woman living in exile in India saw a woman from Nagchu (north of Lhasa) trying to sell her five-year-old son in Lhasa. She was expecting another child and did not know where to get enough food and clothes. It is fortunate that this desperate woman is not aware that 55,000 tons of yak meat are exported to Hong Kong each year. Yak meat from Qinghai (Amdo) has become very popular with the 500,000 inhabitants of Xining, the capital of the province.

Animals in the wild have, according to many concurring eyewitness reports, been drastically reduced in number. Great herds of antelopes, gazelles, wild asses, yaks, and sheep are now a rarity. Tibetans are punished for killing these animals, but Chinese settlers hunt them for their meat and hide. And wealthy tourists are permitted, at least in Qinghai (Amdo) province, to hunt for trophies.

Nor do things look good in the case of forests. Although woods only make up 4.1% of the entire Qinghai-Tibet plateau, these are still the second-largest natural wooded areas in China. They are located mainly in the East and Southeast below 4,300 meters. According to official information, the timber stocks of the autonomous region of Tibet amounted to over 668 million cubic yards in 1984.

Radio Lhasa reported several times, stating exact figures, that large woods in Tibet had been cleared and that the timber had been transported to China. By contrast, there is no mention of afforestation in Tibet, except for a few attempts made by some villages.

In the meantime, the autonomous region of Tibet has been connected to China by means of four large highways that make it easier to transport the tree trunks. It is via these hazardous routes that Tibet is supplied with all goods from China, nowadays coming mainly from the North. Since May 1984, there has been a railway line to Golmud (from Xining), from where a strategically important asphalt road leads to Lhasa (and, since 1967, from Lhasa to Nepal). In 1987 there were approximately 13,400 miles of roads in Tibet.

Petrol stations are rare. Oil resources and refineries are unknown in Tibet. Thirty percent of the entire transport capacity is required for fuel, all of which has to be imported, naturally almost exclusively for the troops stationed there, for the Chinese, and for the tourists. There are no private vehicles, and public transport is rare. However, the cold region of Tibet has the world's largest resources of geothermal energy, underground sources of heat which come to the surface as boiling hot, steaming, or salty springs. In other places, steam comes out of the hot ground, and on the periphery of the geothermal area of Yangpachen (Yangbaijing), which is 62 miles from Lhasa, there is even a hot lake with a temperature of 117 degrees Farenheit. With a depth of seventeen and a half yards and an area of 7,658 square yards, it is the deepest and largest hot water lake in China.

In the question of energy resources, great hopes have been placed on solar and wind energy; the temperatures are too low for biogas. Although in China around 40% of country-dwellers have no access to electricity, in Tibet the numbers are much greater. Most of the 1.4 million small farmers and 400,000 nomads in the Tibetan Autonomous Region make use of yak dung, laboriously gathered juniper scrub (also used for incense), and—if it is available at all—with firewood. The power cables along the highways should not lead those on such tours and expeditions to believe that all Tibetan

villages have electricity. In reality, there is electricity only where
Chinese people live or work. Though the cables may lead through
Tibetan villages, they do not supply them with electricity.

Even in Lhasa hardly any of the approximately 120,000 inhabitants (of whom only 30,000 are Tibetans) cook with electricity, but
mainly with wood. In the hotels in and around the old town, anyone
can observe the enormous additional amounts of wood being used
by tourists to heat water (for tea, showers) and for meals in restaurants. The wood is brought in from far away by lorry.

The Lhasa Holiday Inn is even equipped with central heating
facilities (oil?). And since October 1987, the most striking example of
progress has been a swimming pool, the first in the history of Tibet,
which is constantly heated to a water temperature of 81 degrees
Farenheit. Johnny Erling, a foreign correspondent, said in this
connection: "What absurd misunderstandings there must be between
those responsible for planning in Beijing and the Tibetans!" The
luxury pool is only one of numerous examples of how plans and
developments fail to take Tibetan interests into account. While
Chinese officials and publications like to pride themselves on having
brought considerable progress to Tibet since its liberation, the
question arises: for whose benefit? Experts and Tibetans agree that
the modernizations introduced, including schools and jobs, benefit
almost exclusively the Chinese and that most of the money invested
is being used up by the administration of the occupation forces and
the 300,000 to 500,000 soldiers of the People's Liberation Army.

Development experts are in agreement that the so-called modernization of Tibet can only occur very slowly and cautiously.
Progress can never be accomplished through destruction. Whoever
wished to deny Tibetans a self-reliant development process in which
cultural and ethnic identity can remain intact should study the case
of the Himalayan kingdom of Bhutan. The inhabitants of Bhutan are
for the most part of Tibetan descent. Although it has been ruled for
centuries as a theocracy, always looking to Tibet as its spiritual home,
it is today the only country in the world that is following a consistent,
ecological, complete course of development. An essential basis for
this path has been the country's deep spirituality, drawn from
Tibetan Buddhism.

TENZIN GYATSO

An Ethical Approach to Environmental Protection

Peace and survival of life on earth as we know it are threatened by human activities which lack a commitment to humanitarian values.

Destruction of nature and natural resources results from ignorance, greed, and lack of respect for the earth's living things.

This lack of respect extends even to earth's human descendants, the future generations who will inherit a vastly degraded planet if world peace does not become a reality and destruction of the natural environment continues at the present rate.

Our ancestors viewed the earth as rich and bountiful, which it is. Many people in the past also saw nature as inexhaustibly sustainable, which we now know is the case only if we care for it.

It is not difficult to forgive destruction in the past which resulted from ignorance. Today, however, we have access to more information, and it is essential that we re-examine ethically what we have inherited, what we are responsible for, and what we will pass on to coming generations.

Clearly this is a pivotal generation. Global communication is possible, yet confrontations more often than meaningful dialogues for peace take place.

Our marvels of science and technology are matched if not outweighed by many current tragedies, including human starvation in some parts of the world, and extinction of other life forms.

Exploration of outer space takes place at the same time as earth's own oceans, seas, and fresh water areas grow increasingly polluted, and their life forms are still largely unknown or misunderstood.

Many of the earth's habitats, animals, plants, insects, and even micro-organisms that we know as rare may not be known at all by future generations. We have the capability and the responsibility. We must act before it is too late.

This message is dated June 5, 1986, in recognition of World Environment Day and that day's 1986 theme, Peace and the Environment.

Tibet Under Siege

Above: A young Tibetan Boy from Golog China, wearing a Chinese military uniform hat. *Below:* A Tibetan man wearing a traditional *chuba* is arrested in the Barkhor market by the People's Armed Police.

photo by Galen Rowell

photo from Tibetan Information Network

MICHAEL ALEXANDER

Nuclear Weapons on the Roof of the World

It is widely known that today more than 300,000 Chinese soldiers are stationed in Tibet and that roads are built for strategic/military reasons. It is about time to draw attention to less well-known aspects of Tibet's military occupation that are not mentioned by the media but which are of far-reaching importance for the geo-political situation of all of Asia.

The People's Republic of China has worked for many years at developing atomic weapons. This effort was not even interrupted during the years of the Cultural Revolution. China developed further generations of missiles from the first SS-2 it received in the 1960s from the Soviet Union. In 1966 China first tested a nuclear missile developed from the Soviet SS-4, which was launched from Shuang Cheng Tsu testing station in Inner Mongolia to Lob Nor in Zinjang in Eastern Turkestan. Later, China tested countless intermediate range missiles of different kinds in Golmu, located in the Tibetan province of Amdo, renamed Xinghai by the Chinese.

The first intercontinental missile (ICM), the CSS-3, was tested in the Wuzhai desert in Shanxi province, and eight of these missiles are currently stationed in valleys at the border between Amdo province and the so-called "Autonomous Region" of Tibet. On September 20, 1981, three satellites were successfully launched into orbit. This enabled the Chinese to begin the development of the MIRV with multiple warheads. On October 12, 1982, the first sea-based ballistic missiles (ICBMs), the CSS-X, were tested. The CSS-4 missile, first tested in 1980, is currently the most advanced among missiles of similar types. It is even superior to Soviet missiles (with the exception of the SS-18) as far as its multiple warheads and launching capacity are concerned. These missiles are manufactured in Baton, Xian, and Shengyang. Their outer shells and motors are produced in Shengyang, Xian, Ransu, and Chengdu.

Seventy ICMs and twenty IRBMs of varying ranges are stationed approximately ten km outside the small town of Nagchu, 320 km northeast of Lhasa. From that location they are able to reach northern India and other countries in southern Asia. Yet other missiles, the twenty-five-meter-long Dan-Tan-Chi-Ze, are stationed in Golmu, located at the coordinates of 94 degrees East and 36 degrees North. Another large base can be found in the desert northeast of Tsaidam.

There are also ICBM bases at Kongpo Nyitri and Powo Tamo in Tibet. These ICBMs were originally stationed on Lob Nor directed at the USSR. Today, in their new locations, they are directed at the Indian cities of New Delhi, Ludhiana, Kanpur, and Amritsar. But Sikkim, Burma, Kampuchea, and Vietnam are also within their threatening range. Since the Chinese also have two submarines of the "Han" class, equipped with sea-launched CSS-4 missiles (SLBM), they can operate in the waters of the Indian Ocean. The range of CSS-4 missiles is currently 750 miles. The PRC has successfully developed an Excocet missile, called C-801, which can be launched from air, sea, or land.

At Gonggar airport, sixty miles southwest of Lhasa, the Chinese have stationed a squadron of J-7 fighter bombers, the Chinese version of the Soviet Mikoyan MiG-21. These planes are equipped with two PL-2 air-launched missiles and 800 liter tanks, allowing for the flight range of 900 miles. Moreover, there are seven Sikorsky S-70C Black Hawk helicopters in Gonggar, which were also used to monitor the unrest in and around Lhasa.

It is clear that from Tibet, the roof of the world, China is capable of militarily threatening southern and parts of Southeast Asia. This fact necessitates a radical rethinking of the geo-political situation. With the continuing Chinese policy of population transfer, millions of Chinese are living in Tibet; the Tibetans are a minority in their own country; and the Chinese armies are at India's doorstep, backed by already existent missile bases.

An independent Tibet, protected by the Himalayan mountain ranges, had played the role of a buffer state between China and India until the Chinese invasion. Today this is no longer the case. China's expansionist policies resulted already in border conflicts in 1962. In subsequent years, China intensified its policy with the political and, at times, military assistance of Pakistan, Nepal, and Sri Lanka in order to isolate India.

China did not recognize the border, the McMahon Line of 1912, between India and Tibet. Having occupied Tibet, China today is in a position to threaten India's border directly. In June 1986, border skirmishes and transgressions were reported in Arunachal Pradesh in Northeast India and earlier on in Ladakh. According to the most recent information (March 1987), in the winter months several hundred Chinese soldiers had been flown by helicopter into Wang Tung in the Indian Sumdurong Chu valley. There are detailed reports of Chinese influence in Nepalese diplomatic, as well as military, circles. So far, there have been seven rounds of negotiations between Delhi and Beijing, each of which broke down [Ed. note: as of October 1987]. A similar situation can be observed along the Chinese-Vietnamese border.

China is in the process of strengthening its position of power, unnoticed by Europe, but with the help of the U.S. as well as the Federal Republic of Germany. A few examples:

1. The Chinese received $500 million in advanced and highly sophisticated electronic equipment from the U.S. and $62 million of radar installations, types ANTPQ-37 and ANVRC-46. The latter serve to detect enemy artillery and are for precision targeting. Radio sets for tanks were also delivered.

2. Among military experts, the German 120 mm (Glattrohr) cannon is considered to be the best of its kind. Aviatest, a subsidiary company of Duesseldorf's Rheinmetall, delivered to China all the necessary technology and equipment to manufacture it there.

3. The PRC has purchased, for $91.5 million, two Crotale surface-to-air missile systems from France that were delivered in 1988. One of these systems has been assigned to the Navy for frigates of the Jian-Dong class; the other to a destroyer currently being built at the Shanghai shipyard. The basic system consists of eight missiles launched by an eighteen missile magazine. Their range is eight miles, and they are guided and traced by radar.

The domination of Tibet is the key to the military and political expansion of China. Only by means of the military occupation of Tibet, can China threaten or dominate or, at least, influence the surrounding Asian countries. For these reasons, all peace-loving nations of the world should pressure China to restore the sovereignty of Tibet.

In accordance with the wishes of the Dalai Lama, Tibet should be a nuclear-free country, a country of peace, not subjected to expansionist ambitions. China's policies, a threat to peace and security, should be discussed in international and national fora, such as the European Parliament, the UN, and national parliaments, because what happens in Asia today will affect the entire world tomorrow in one form or another.

CHRISTA MEINDERSMA

Eyewitness Report:
Tibet, December 10, 1988
(International Human Rights Day)

I would like to report as an eyewitness what happened in Tibet on December 10, 1988. It is very easy to accuse us all of being agents of the Dalai Lama or to say that we only wish to draw attention to ourselves in the mass media. I can only speak on the basis of my own experiences, and this is what I will do here. I was in Tibet a fairly long time. But I was not officially employed there; I had a tourist visa.

Before December 10, tensions in and around Lhasa had already been on the rise. We asked people why there were so many more Chinese police; why were more and more being flown in? We were told that December 10 would be the fortieth anniversary of UN Human Rights Day, and people were planning demonstrations to draw attention to the human rights violations in Tibet. Tibetans were meeting with their neighbors and warning one another about the Chinese. The story was that anyone taking part in the demonstrations would lose one month's pay. There was even some danger of

Transcript of Christa Meindersma's testimony at the Bonn Hearings, April 1989.

being shot. Children were told not to come home after school, and everyone was to steer clear of the Jokhang Temple.

On December 10, there were many people there at the Jokhang. Around 11:30 a.m., a small group of people assembled—not only monks and nuns, but also some young laypeople. They seemed very much afraid. They carried a flag with them, which was held by a monk. Onlookers did not participate in the demonstration, but many broke down in tears; the whole situation was very emotional. The demonstraters crossed the Ring Road and took up a stand on the square in front of the Jokhang Temple. A few foreigners were looking on from nearby streets.

We were not far away as the group came into the square; we could see them very clearly. Up to this point there had been no violence, and apparently no intention of violence. At this moment Chinese policemen came running towards the demonstration in front of the temple. The police chief then aimed and fired, and fatally wounded the monk with the flag. That seemed to be the signal for the other police officers to open fire. No warning shots were fired. They fired on the group, and they fired on people not taking part.

Suddenly policemen seemed to come from everywhere, and people ran in panic in all directions. We were all afraid they would shoot at us. I myself was wounded by a bullet. People ran for cover, fell down, lay bleeding. We didn't know whether they were dead or wounded. The whole thing happened on a marketplace, and many people were taking cover behind overturned tables. I also tried to take cover, but found no place available. We were ten feet from the police, who were still firing into the crowd with automatic weapons.

Another foreigner helped me to get away from them. We were pursued by the police, who were now using tear gas.

When we reached the main street, there were military checkpoints everywhere. We pretended we were a happy couple. I leaned on his arm in pain. A friend who had a car brought me back to my hotel. There were many Chinese doctors there, but they seemed to have no interest in treating me or anyone else. There were also many police officers from the foreign ministry there who threatened us. Even when the doctors saw my wound, they refused me any medical attention. They poked at my bullet wound, and laughed when I cried out in pain. Other people were brought or carried in. They were taken to a different room, perhaps because the Chinese were afraid of us talking to each other. I assume the others received treatment similar to ours. Finally they took X-rays, but they would not tell us if the bullets were still in our bodies. Fortunately someone whispered to me that everything looked all right, and that I should try to get out as fast as possible. The Chinese medical system was no help to me. I'm sure it was like this or worse for many Tibetans as well.

If Tibetans are fired on in a demonstration, they are considered guilty by the Chinese government. This accounts for the lack of medical care. For those wounded, it is practically impossible to go to the hospital, since they know that they will not receive medical attention but will instead be transported directly to prison. Therefore, people play a kind of "hide-and-seek." Tibetans take into hiding those people who have been shot, and hide the bodies of those killed. For this reason it is very difficult to give exact figures about the dead and wounded. I have heard that there were eighteen people killed, and between seventy and eighty wounded. But many of those wounded surely died later, since they received no medical care.

I would like to add an observation. These people were not killed because they were a threat. They were only a small crowd, which could have been easily dispersed or arrested without the use of guns. The police were following the orders of the government. Everything happened within a few seconds of the group reaching the square. It was quite obviously planned to shoot at Tibetans and at foreigners (many of the approximately fifty foreigners present were wounded). The Dalai Lama says the Tibetans must not use force, but this stands in flagrant contrast to the behavior of the Chinese.

SUSANNE MAIER

Impressions of Lhasa, March 1989

On February 28, 1989, I arrived in Lhasa. The first three days passed quietly. On the first of March, the first peaceful incident occurred in the form of a demonstration of about thirty Tibetans carrying signs and walking around the Jokhang Temple.

SUNDAY, MARCH 5, 1989

On this day I take a bicycle tour of the outskirts of Lhasa. When I return to the old city around 1:30 p.m., the main street is barely passable. Chinese police have made a line of barricades. Shots and cries can be heard. Wisps of smoke are rising in the area; no one dares break through the barricades. In spite of great fear, I push my bicycle past the barricades and head for my hotel. The hotel seems to be the only safe place. All along the way, masses of people throng around me, and their feverish, oppressed mood increases my panic still more.

Finally reaching the hotel, I find the gate locked. I can still hear shots. Despairing, I beat against the wooden gate, imagining every moment that the next bullet will hit me. My whole body is shaking.

Transcript of Susanne Maier's presentation at the Bonn Hearings, April 1989.

When finally I am admitted and meet up with the rest of the tourists in the hotel's inner courtyard, I find out what has happened.

The first demonstrations began about noon at the Barkhor (the marketplace around the Jokhang Temple). The ranks of demonstrators stretched along the main street. Three Swedish tourists who are also staying in my hotel were on the roof of the Jokhang Temple at the time the demonstration started. The Swedes saw Chinese police throw bottles from the roofs of nearby buildings to provoke the demonstrators. Some of the police used video cameras to record the demonstrators' reactions and later to identify them.

Without warning, the police opened fire on the crowd. The many eyewitnesses say unequivocally that the Tibetans in no way provoked the police, but only reacted to the police's harassment.

Policemen suddenly caught sight of the Swedes, and they were promptly taken back to the hotel, where their passports, cameras and film were immediately confiscated. The hotel staff was yelled at for letting people leave the hotel. Later the tourists get their passports back, but not their cameras or film. The film will be developed to identify demonstrators, who will then be arrested in "purges."

When, towards 3 p.m., the demonstrators march for the second time down the main street and move towards the police line, the police hurl tear gas into the crowd. The Tibetans first defend themselves with stones before fleeing from machine-gun fire.

Outside, there are thousands of people, old men and women, children, mothers with babies on their backs. The Chinese fire indiscriminately into the crowd. It is a massacre. From our hotel, which we may not leave, we observe the events on the street below.

MONDAY, MARCH 6, 1989

In the morning we are permitted to leave the hotel.

It is a scene of devastation: everywhere there are stones, window panes are shattered, many Chinese restaurants have been destroyed and partly burned. Their furniture has been piled up into barricades and set burning. Some buildings are now no more than blackened walls. This morning, B.B.C. radio delivers the Chinese official announcement: "Certain Tibetans made an armed assault on the Chinese police, who only defended themselves."

Towards noon the demonstrations begin again. Again the same course of events as on the previous day. Police throw tear gas bombs into the crowd; women try with buckets of water and wet rags to alleviate the burning in their eyes. Again merciless shooting, screams, fleeing demonstrators. This time a gas bomb lands directly in front of our window. We flee to the interior of the hotel. When the gas has dissipated, we continue watching the demonstration on the street. There are still hundreds of people on their feet. Some go by carrying the bodies of dead Tibetans.

Our first, much-wished-for contact to the outside world is a journalist from Chengdu, who calls on the hotel telephone to ask for reports on the events in English. He works for the Associated Press. Contact with journalists seems to us to offer our only hope of helping the Tibetans. Already, on the B.B.C. Radio Evening News, the statements of the Chinese news agency are being refuted by eyewitness accounts. We listen to the news, and the phone rings off the hook. The U.S. ambassador in Chengdu asks about our condition, and journalists are constantly calling for the latest information.

TUESDAY, MARCH 7, 1989

In the morning I go out on the street. The same frightening picture as the day before. The staff calls out to me that I should return at once, the military police might be on the march, you never know. Towards noon the demonstrations begin once again.

The Tibetans have wrapped their heads in cloth to escape identification by police video cameras. The number of demonstrators has significantly shrunk. Some Tibetans report that during the preceding night hundreds had been arrested and taken away in trucks. A young Tibetan woman was gruesomely killed by a shot in the head.

In late afternoon the demonstrations continue. A military squad passes our window. One of the soldiers notices us at the window and immediately aims his machine gun at us. We throw ourselves to the ground. It is clear that the Chinese want no eyewitnesses. The mass arrests are still taking place, only at night. A journalist informs us by telephone late that evening that martial law begins at midnight.

WEDNESDAY, MARCH 8, 1989

Around 2:30 a.m., two soldiers storm their way into the hotel, force the tourists to get up and into a group, and give us notice that we have until Thursday noon to leave Lhasa, either overland by bus to Kathmandu or by air to Chengdu.

In the morning there is hardly anyone on the street. A few children gather stones together. The military has set up checkpoints everywhere. Towards noon, two Chinese policemen come to the hotel and inform us that at 2 p.m. we must hand over our passports and money for air tickets. We are not permitted to go to the bank; those without enough money must borrow it from other tourists. Then we wait.

In order not to let the time go by uselessly, we assemble all the medical supplies we have brought in our luggage. Tibetans are not treated in Chinese hospitals. A Tibetan with a bullet wound is immediately handed over to the police. Arrested Tibetans end up in prison or work camps, where many die from torture or starvation.

By the afternoon we are still waiting for our tickets. Suddenly there is tumult on the street. Three Chinese soldiers pull a Tibetan from his bicycle and shatter his kneecap with an electric cattle prod. He remains prostrate and bloody in the street. They approach him. The bloody bundle is thrown onto a pickup truck. Around 10 p.m., two Chinese soldiers come with two employees of the Chinese travel agency who have our plane tickets.

The Tibetan hotel staff asks us not to show sympathy or friendship toward them, since our departure will be carefully watched. Any Tibetan who seems too close to foreigners is arrested for treason.

THURSDAY, MARCH 9, 1989

The bus drives into the inner courtyard of the hotel. Silently we get on, at pains to keep our eyes on the ground so as to cast suspicion on no one, and to hide our own emotions.

Suddenly a Tibetan woman comes running to us and hangs a *kata* (a white scarf, a Tibetan traditional farewell) around each of our necks. We all have lumps in our throats as we get on the bus. The Tibetan woman presses her hands against the window and cries, "Please help us. You are the only hope we have. When you have gone, we will have no one."

AMNESTY INTERNATIONAL

One Year under Martial Law: Update on Human Rights in Tibet

CONTINUING POLITICAL UNREST IN TIBET

During the year since the March 7, 1989, imposition of martial law in Lhasa, the capital of the Tibetan Autonomous Region (TAR) of the People's Republic of China (PRC), Tibetans have continued to be detained for peacefully exercising their right to hold and express opinions. Over a thousand people were believed to have been arrested in the days after martial law was declared and in subsequent months. Many are still held in incommunicado detention without charge or trial. Some, including prisoners of conscience, are known to have been sentenced to periods of imprisonment through administrative proceedings without charge or trial while others were sentenced after trials that fell far short of international standards for fairness. Torture and ill-treatment have continued to be reported in use in at least three of Lhasa's prisons and detention centers.

Excerpt from Amnesty International, *People's Republic of China: Tibet Autonomous Region*, Compilation Document, March 1990.

Amnesty International has in the past been concerned by reports of arrests, untried detention, and unfair trials in Tibet. The organization documented cases of torture and ill-treatment of Tibetans in a paper published in February 1989 (see *People's Republic of China: Torture and Ill-Treatment in Detention of Tibetans*, AI Index ASA/17/04/89). The present document summarizes reports of arrests, administrative detention, and trials of Tibetans involved in pro-independence protests since martial law was decreed in March 1989.

Martial law was imposed at midnight on March 7, 1989, following pro-independence demonstrations and violent confrontations with police forces from March 5-7, 1989. The security forces were reported to have carried out indiscriminate beatings and shootings to suppress the protests. Sixteen civilians and one armed police officer are officially acknowledged to have been killed during the unrest, although eyewitnesses in Lhasa estimated the civilian death toll to be above sixty and said that at least 200 people were injured. Unofficial sources have reported police killings of unarmed civilians during and after the March demonstrations and of severe beatings of demonstrators and detainees by police. A senior Tibetan official has acknowledged that police brutalities had occurred in March. The official *Tibet Daily* newspaper quoted Ngapoi Ngawang Jigme, an ethnic Tibetan vice-chairman of the National People's Congress (NPC), China's legislative organ, as saying in August that "during the riots, some members of the armed police failed to obey discipline and prior instructions and opened fire on innocent people."

Whereas martial law imposed in parts of Beijing in June 1989 was formally lifted in December, martial law remains in Lhasa. [Ed. note: martial law was lifted on April 30, 1990.] Tanks were reportedly moved into the city in early March and public celebrations of the *Monlam* prayer festival, a major event in the Tibetan Buddhist calendar, were banned. Under martial law, according to travelers and journalists, guard posts are placed at almost all crossroads and checkpoints are set up before party and government offices, temples, and monasteries. Political controls over Tibetan religious activities have been sharply increased: "work teams" have been dispatched to monasteries. Political controls over Tibetan religious activities have been dispatched to monasteries to screen monks and nuns for their political attitudes; the enrollment of Buddhist novices has reportedly been restricted as were the activities of Buddhist teaching institutions which had been allowed to re-open during the 1980s after their forced closure during the previous two decades.

Since the imposition of martial law in Lhasa, pro-independence demonstrations by Tibetans have taken place mostly on the octagonal pilgrimage path known as the *Barkhor*, which circles the Jokhang Temple. Most have been small, although one on October 25, 1989, reportedly drew about 1,000 protesters.

PATTERNS OF INTIMIDATION

According to the official *Tibet Daily*, city police authorities indicated at a mass sentencing rally held on September 24 that those who "dare to test the law by themselves" and "persist in being enemies of the people" will be "resolutely dealt with and shown no mercy." The police described a demonstration held on September 22 as "counter-revolutionary" and "aimed at splitting the motherland."

Monks and nuns are subject to "screening" procedures aimed at "assessing" and "remolding" their political stand. Students at Lhasa's No. 1 Middle School have been ordered, on pain of expulsion, not to support or take part in any "unusual event" they may witness. Monks in a temple in Gyantse, a town southwest of Lhasa, have been warned by political study officials that independence should be renounced. They were told that they needed to study to "clarify" their thinking. Monks in Gyantse and Lhasa have reported that their living quarters had been searched for unauthorized literature.

The official *Tibet Daily* argued in an editorial comment on August 7, 1989, that the current wave of unrest in Tibet was caused, among other factors, by past laxity towards religious activities. This comment appearing after the crackdown on pro-democracy demonstrators in Beijing in June 1989, was part of a nationwide drive to reassert the primacy of central policies, including that of tolerating only a limited role for religious bodies in China.

The degree of autonomy to be granted TAR government authorities appears to be an issue with some bearing on the implementation of legal provisions on the tolerance of religious activities in the TAR. Ngapoi Ngawang Jigme, in an interview published in November, expressed dissatisfaction with the attitude of some central administrative departments in Beijing. He seemed to suggest they do not sufficiently take into account Tibet's nominal autonomy, enshrined in the Regional Autonomy Law of the PRC promulgated in 1984 and in the Basic Law of the Xizang Tibetan Autonomous Region of the PRC. These provide, among other things, for the freedom to use and develop the Tibetan language and to ensure that Tibetans are adequately represented in the civil service. The implementation of the law appears, however, to be defective. Ngapoi Ngawang Jigme apparently suggested that other Beijing authorities than those normally involved in work on minority nationalities issues should take their special character into account. The interview noted that:

> The phenomenon of [Chinese central authorities] failing to take into account the reality of national autonomous areas and regarding resolutions, decisions, decrees, and instructions for these areas as the same as for ordinary areas is still a grave problem...The [Regional Autonomy] Law is not effective..... The State Council and its departments have not yet formulated rules and provisions to implement the law....It is wrong to think that nationalities work should be done only by minority nationalities areas and departments in charge of minorities.

Martial law regulations have been set out in decrees of the TAR People's Government published on March 7 and 8, 1989. (See Appendix V for complete text of Martial Law Decrees.) TAR People's Government Decree No. 1 of March 7, 1989, Article 2, prohibits "all assemblies, parades, workers' and students' strikes, petitions, and other gatherings." Decree No. 2 of March 1989, Article 1, also prohibits "instigation of separatist actions against the country, instigation of riots, and gatherings which seek to attack State organs, destroy public property, or engage in such sabotage acts as beating, smashing, and looting in any place."

Under Decree No. 2, Article 2, law enforcement personnel in the region are given the "right to take the necessary forceful measures to expeditiously put an end" to acts prohibited under martial law. The same Article also states that "people committing such acts can be detained immediately. In case of resistance, [law enforcement personnel] may take action against them in accordance with the law." Decree No. 1, Article 6, gives law enforcement personnel " the right to search people suspected of causing riots, places where criminals may be concealed and other suspicious places" without securing search warrants.

Decree No. 6 of March 8, 1989, provides that all personnel responsible for enforcing martial law, including agents of the Public Security Bureau, Armed Police officers, and People's Liberation Army soldiers, shall "strictly observe the regulations on the use of arms and police weapons by the people's police. This provision appears to subject all personnel, both civilian and military, to regulations on the use of firearms to which only Public Security Bureau officers are normally subjects. Amnesty International is concerned, despite this provision, that other martial law provisions, especially Decree No. 2, Article 2 and Decree No. 1, Articles 2 and 6, may encourage the use of unnecessary force, including the use of firearms, by law enforcement personnel.

Amnesty International is further concerned at provisions, under martial law Decrees No. 2 and 5, which increase the likelihood that prisoners may be given unfair trials and be denied the opportunity to present an adequate defense. Decree No. 2, Article 4, provides that "criminals" under the Decree's provisions shall be "punished severely and swiftly" under the provisions of various "Decisions" passed by the NPC in 1983. These allow for summary trial procedures and require more severe punishments, including the death penalty, of a variety of offenses that are normally provided for by the Criminal Law. Courts are to inform prisoners of charges against them only three days prior to trial and to reduce the time allowed for appeals to three days following sentencing.

ARRESTS AND ADMINISTRATIVE SENTENCES

Since March 1989, at least fifty-three people, some of them aged under eighteen, have been given administrative sentences of two or three years' "reeducation through labor," or detained pending such sentencing, on charges of taking part in demonstrations or engaging in "counter-revolutionary activities." People thus sentenced do not appear before a court and are unable to present a defense. One Tibetan member of an official political consultative body has been detained on political charges stemming from his alleged unwillingness to accept official pronouncements concerning the political situation in Tibet.

Municipal authorities in Lhasa confirmed in October 1989, that over 400 people had been arrested since March and said that "almost all" of those who took part in riots before May 19, 1989, had been released as of October 1989, because "they had confessed their mistakes." However, about 250 people arrested since March 1989, are believed still to be held without trial. Some people who had been arrested after demonstrations in 1987 and 1988 and subsequently released, in what was described as a measure of leniency, have been re-arrested and formally charged with "counter-revolutionary activities."

There were reportedly around 600 prisoners in Lhasa's Sangyip prison as of mid-1989. Sangyip, together with two other main prisons in Lhasa, Drapchi and the Gutsa detention center, are believed to have a total capacity of 1,700 and to have been full following the March 1989 demonstrations, although not all prisoners were said to have been arrested in connection with the unrest. Amnesty International is unable to confirm these numbers, but it has received numerous reports since March 1989, of people being arrested at their homes following night house searches.

POLITICAL TRIALS

Since January 1989, at least twenty-nine people have been sentenced to prison of "reform through labor" terms ranging from four years to life on charges of counter-revolutionary crimes, espionage or using violence during demonstrations. According to TAR regional chief procurator, Yang Youcai, 29.7% more major and serious cases of separatist activities occurred in 1989 compared to 1988. Some of those imprisoned are prisoners of conscience held solely for the nonviolent exercise of their right to freedom of opinion and their right to freely seek and impart information.

ROBBIE BARNETT

Martial Law without Checkpoints

The lifting of martial law on April 30, 1990, was acclaimed by Hu Jintao, the Tibetan Autonomous Region (TAR) Party secretary, as "a major victory in our region's struggle against splittism." However, as stated in a July 13, 1990, televised report by Jintao, "Tibet is still facing an arduous task in carrying out an in-depth struggle against splittism and in further stabilizing the situation in the next five years."

Since April 1990, the streets of Lhasa have been described by several visitors as "martial law without checkpoints." Soldiers of the People's Liberation Army are reported to have changed into uniforms of the People's Armed Police. Especially during "alert periods" around anniversaries when demonstrations are expected, security forces patrol the Barkhor; military convoys regularly parade through the streets; monasteries are sealed off and pilgrims searched; non-Lhasa residents are prohibited from entering the city and monks and nuns banned from leaving their monasteries; Tibetans are warned that if they demonstrate they will be shot or imprisoned for life; and tour groups are restricted from entering the TAR.

This piece is excerpted from "Tibet: Defying the Dragons" in *Lawasia-Tin*.

PICO IYER

Unhealed Wound

Every year at the beginning of the eighth month of the Tibetan calendar, the citizens of Lhasa, the capital, collect each night by star-light at the Kyi Chu, or Happy River, to wash themselves and their clothes—a symbolic way, they believe, of cleansing themselves of passion and rage. This year, however, after just four of the Golden Star Festival's seven nights, the Chinese-run government in Tibet abruptly canceled the festivities, for fear that the gathering might turn into an anti-Beijing demonstration.

That decision, suggesting the demon of anger would go unexorcised in the year ahead, seemed too perfectly symbolic. For Tibet feels like a wound with no prospect of healing. The hidden land that was long a Lost Horizon model of unworldly calm is in a state of tense expectancy, a disturbance waiting to erupt.

Armed soldiers man rooftops around the Jokhang Temple, the holiest site in Tibet, and tanks occasionally clatter down Lhasa's main street. All day long, squads of riot police, helmet visors down and truncheons ready, march counterclockwise around the temple and the octagonal street that rings it, in the face of pilgrims walking in

---

This piece is reprinted with permission from *Time Magazine*, International Edition, October 1990.

a clockwise direction. Nearly all vehicles in the center of town are military. Not long ago, a dozen monks and nuns gathered outside the Jokhang and called for a free Tibet; within minutes they were arrested, and within hours twenty-five trucks filled with armed soldiers were conspicuously asserting their presence downtown.

Five years ago, when China first opened Tibet to the world, the blue-sky, flower-filled city almost 12,000 feet above the sea was vibrant with cafes, rainbow-awninged hotels, and many young travelers from abroad. Today Lhasa's mood is sullen and recalcitrant. Thirty-one years after the Chinese drove Tibet's ruler, the Dalai Lama into exile in India and effectively claimed control over the Land of the Snows, Tibetans remain determined to express their resentment of their rulers. Eager to bring their cause to the world, the protesters are willing to throw self-protection to the winds; recently signs were plastered all around the Barkhor, or free-market area, giving the Chinese two weeks notice of a demonstration to be held on the anniversary of the first recent uprising, three years ago.

Though that day apparently passed relatively quietly last week, neither side was prepared to relax. For three years, Tibet has been the focus of agitation so intense that martial law was imposed in March 1989, two months before it went into effect in Beijing. During the first year of martial law, Tibetans claim 450 of their compatriots lost their lives in violence (the Chinese admit to about a dozen). An observer who witnessed the crackdowns in both Lhasa and Tiananmen Square maintains the violence has been more unrelenting in Tibet.

LHASA UNDER SIEGE

Lhasa is a city under siege, perpetually on maximum alert. Though martial law officially ended in April, it remains in all but name. One of the shops in the main square outside the Jokhang has been turned into an army post, ringed by jeeps and sentry boxes. The roughly 400,000 People's Liberation Army soldiers stationed in Tibet have been joined by units of the People's Armed Police. Roadblocks check every visitor into the City of Gods, and monks, in the past the leaders of the demonstrations, are kept under house arrest.

The Potala palace, once the symbol of Tibetan sovereignty, is under scaffolding; it opens only two mornings a week, and then, often, only to foreigners. The Jokhang is sometimes closed altogether. In the sunlit quiet of an afternoon stroll through the grounds of the summer palace, the silence is suddenly broken by gunfire—Chinese soldiers at target practice. One day, a group of monks set up an impromptu prayer hall in the main square, filling the juniper-scented air with low-voiced chants and the summons of ceremonial long horns; the next day, six PLA soldiers were sitting in their place.

PRAYER FLAGS STILL FLUTTER

The more forceful the Chinese presence, in fact, the more defiant the resistance. Prayer flags still flutter from almost every Tibetan home, and huge portraits of Buddha adorn rocks along the roadside. Young Tibetans in sweatshirts and sneakers join the dozens of votaries prostrating themselves outside the Jokhang. Every shop, cafe, even billiard hall has as its centerpiece a framed portrait of the Dalai Lama reverently draped in white silk or a picture of his former residence, the Potala. A hobbled crone comes up to a visitor and, motioning to her rheumy eyes, gestures that she does not want to be given a picture of the Dalai Lama, as most of her compatriots do, but merely to look at one. Another has an even stranger request: that a foreigner bless her on the head with a set of Tibetan postcards.

PACKAGED TOURISTS

The few foreigners who reach Lhasa find themselves, therefore, at the center of the struggle: over the past five years China has opened Tibet as its unease about letting visitors witness the unrest has sometimes overwhelmed and sometimes deferred to its hunger for tourist dollars. Last year, owing to the disturbances, fewer than 4,000 tourists visited Lhasa, down from some 40,000 the year before. Visitors are once again officially allowed entrance to Tibet, provided they come in organized groups (even if they are "groups" of one) and stay in the Holiday Inn on the Chinese side of town; a few resourceful travelers, however, still slip across the border and crowd into the cheap hostels in the Tibetan quarter. Two weeks ago, officials burst into the Tibetan-run Yak Hotel and told foreigners there on their own that they should leave Tibet; $200-a-day "packaged" tourists were told they could stay and were diverted with opera and dance performances in a faraway park but forbidden to visit the center of town. Both sides know that in the absence of foreign witnesses, the Tibetans would be shouting their protest into the wind.

Though China made claims on Tibet as early as 1720, the issue of Tibetan self-determination has recently turned upon an ambiguous, unratified 1914 agreement moderated by Britain, which called for Tibetan autonomy with Chinese suzerainty. The Chinese, stressing the latter part, claim they are trying to bring Tibet into conformity with the rest of their nation; the Tibetans, holding the former, contend that their occupiers are seeking to destroy their culture.

DISTANT RULE

In the past five years, the clean, modern blocks of the Chinese part of Lhasa have taken over much of what was once the dusty, many-colored maze of the Tibetan area; the six million Tibetans are a minority in their own land. And the practical difficulties of ruling a vast mountainous region from Beijing make for all kinds of improbable anomalies. Last month early-rising peasants were harvesting barley in the pre-dawn dark. Why? Because Lhasa, 1,600 miles to the west, must observe Beijing standard time, leaving a situation in which the sun does not rise until after 8:30 a.m.

"Now Lhasa's good," says a foreign diplomat. "A year ago we couldn't even walk along the road." But the state of relative calm feels highly tentative. Many devout Tibetans no longer go to pray in the outlying monasteries, preferring to remain near the Jokhang, so that they will be ready for action should a demonstration start up. Every day brings new rumors, new restrictions. From dawn to dusk, scores of Tibetans mill about the main square; sturdy bandits with jeweled daggers, wild-eyed medicine men furiously spinning prayer wheels, gold-toothed nomads in sheepskin rags, monks in traditional cowboy hats from distant lands. Soldiers and plainclothesmen slip in and out of the crowds, walkie-talkies at the ready.

In such an atmosphere, it does not take much to set off an incident. One bright afternoon there is a sudden scuffle, and twenty frightened, boyish-looking soldiers race across the square. Instantly, a group of Tibetans gather menacingly around them. This time it is a false alarm. Next time, maybe not.

Political Initiatives and Strategies

photo by M. Kellermann

Above: The Dalai Lama with Li Bo, a representative of the Chinese Student Democracy Movement. *Below:* The Dalai Lama with President Vaclav Havel in Prague, Czechoslovakia, February 1989.

photo by G. Bastian

M.L. SONDHI

The Return of Tibet to World Politics

POLITICAL OPPORTUNISM
AND THE THEME OF TIBET AS A LOST CAUSE

The government of India, by stifling discussion of Tibet in the General Assembly of the United Nations in 1950, swung the political pendulum away from any serious resistance to Chinese encroachment and expansionism. New Delhi's opposition to adding the Tibetan issue to the agenda of the General Assembly was a short-sighted and opportunistic posture which, under the guise of seeking a peaceful solution, strengthened the inclination to sweep the matter under the rug. India's abdication of its role, as a country with strategic interests intimately connected to Tibet, was highly anachronistic. The British, who had a greater understanding of Tibetan history and culture than any other Western country, lacked the leverage to accomplish anything meaningful once they had decided to downplay the hegemonic tendencies in Communist China. Britain opportunistically contoured its tactical moves on Tibet to Indian compromises, and by its refusal to help strengthen the legitimacy of basic Tibetan interests.

This piece was adapted from Sondhi's presentation at the International Convention on Tibet and Peace in South Asia, August 1989.

While New Delhi and London both prevented each other from adopting more assertive policies on Tibet, the distinctive characteristics of their respective political opportunisms fused into a common thesis that Tibet was a lost cause. The Indo-British policy of backing China in denigrating Tibetan freedom had serious international consequences. It effectively prevented the rest of the world from seeing Beijing's policy towards Tibet as imperialist. It prevented the Tibetans from finding other countries who also rejected the misnomer of "liberation" to Chinese imperialist actions in Tibet.

Apart from the abdication of responsibility by India and Britain, other trends in international politics kept the Tibetans from achieving their political goals in the international community.

1. *The illusion of the "success" of the Chinese Revolution.* The flaws in the revolutionary strategies of the Chinese Communists are only beginning to be understood. It is becoming clear that there were different, deep-seated perspectives about regional and minority problems, and the Maoist regime did not enjoy more than a fragile policy consensus. The inherent contradictions of the Chinese revolution, however, were generally ignored by the world. There was little debate on the consequences for immediate victims of Chinese Communist aggression and violence. The incentive to ignore Tibet was strong.

2. *Interventionism of the superpowers.* During the Cold War, when worst case scenarios prevailed and both the Soviets and the Americans had renewed their geopolitical interest in interventionism, there was a reluctance to focus sharply on Chinese misconduct in Tibet.

3. *Underestimation of the strategic significance of Tibet.* With the new approach to coexistence through disengagement, Tibet's significance for arms control and disarmament becomes crucial, but it was not a core issue in the maintenance of global equilibrium among the superpowers under confrontationist pressures.

4. *The erosion of human rights in Asia.* The worsening of the human rights situation in the Soviet Union, Eastern Europe, and South Africa led the international community to propose radical measures to cope with the situation. The contribution of the international community to the maintenance of human rights in Asia, however, remains

modest. The Chinese version of apartheid in Tibet has been ignored by governments more confident in dealing with Moscow or Pretoria.

5. *The normative connotation of Tibetan nonviolent resistance.* The lack of a violent strategy by the Tibetan leadership in exile was misinterpreted as a political vacuum by the international community, which is accustomed to dealing with violence and military preparations by exile organizations like the PLO. Unless a new international mentality favoring nonviolence arises, the Dalai Lama, with his persistent desire to practice Buddhist nonviolence, is at a disadvantage.

CHANGES IN THE INTERNATIONAL SYSTEM: TAKING TIBET SERIOUSLY

From its inception, the Dalai Lama's diplomacy in exile has stressed the interdependence of national interests and universal human goals in accordance with a Buddhistic rejection of military conflict. He did not accept the wisdom of the nuclearized bi-polar world, and identified Tibetan ethos with improvements in global and regional security through a demilitarized and de-nuclearized status for Tibet. His readiness to search for solutions—even with China, which had indulged in horrendous repressive and destructive activities against the Tibetans—signifies a rare intellectual awareness of the need to improve the world political climate in the interests of human survival.

With the two superpowers now moving away from confrontation to a normalization of relations, their proposals for global cooperation provide Tibet with a unique opportunity to become an inalienable component of an interdependent world. The Tibetan leadership in exile was among the first in the world to reject a zero-sum concept of international relations. It is not unreasonable to hope that Tibet will play a major part in environmental and humanitarian issues that now need urgent attention from the UN.

DIMINISHING RETURNS TO CHINESE IMPERIALISM IN TIBET

Most scholars agree that Tibet would provide diminishing returns to any imperialism. Only through coercive power is China able to maintain some semblance of political stability over the Tibetan Plateau. The Tibetans continue to stubbornly resist Chinese overlordship, and—apart from a handful of collaborators—the vast majority of the Tibetan people regard themselves as implacable enemies of the Han Chinese. This mentality is not likely to change anytime soon. The Tibetan people, in their common frustration and suffering, have become ever more loyal to the Dalai Lama and show no receptivity whatsoever to Chinese indoctrination. Even a stance of moderation will not lead to a sophisticated political policy in the absence of a *modus vivendi* between the Chinese and the Dalai Lama. The Chinese thesis of "national liberation" has prevented Beijing from developing enough political imagination to achieve or even define realistic objectives in Tibet. They have brought neither freedom nor economic prosperity to the Tibetans, and have failed to convince the outside world that the People's Liberation Army did not use "national liberation" as a pretext to enslave another nation. The denial of political participation to the Tibetans shows that Chinese policy is oriented towards colonialism, and lacks a genuine peace strategy.

CHOICES ON TIBET

Much of the conventional analysis of international law is inapplicable to the Tibetan situation. The idea that Tibet can no longer realistically sever its ties with the Chinese is not supported by the facts. There are new constraints on Chinese policy which need to be carefully analyzed. A gradual shift is occurring in the perceptions and interests of other countries in response to the criticism of Chinese behavior in Tibet by legislators and concerned citizens. An important development is India's increasing realization that its strategic interests cannot be served by risks involved in the continued military occupation of Tibet by China. In the absence of confidence-building measures which would actively involve the Tibetans, India is not prepared to freeze the status quo, which the Chinese would like to do. A South Asian detente could produce options favorable to Tibet on the part of most of the SAARC countries. U.S. Congressional initiatives in the have laid the groundwork for a changed U.S. attitude to Tibet.

STRUCTURAL FACTORS AND PROCESSES IN THE INTERNATIONAL SYSTEM: DISMANTLING CHINESE HEGEMONY IN TIBET

The Chinese perception that Tibet is their bilateral concern is part of their persistent effort to maintain their hegemonic position. The truth is the structural factors and processes in the international system do not encourage this hegemonic role. The Chinese would be wise to count the number of shifts all over the globe to multilateralism. Having used their military capacity for an illegal armed intervention against Tibet, the Chinese take a less sanguine view of the limits of hegemonic integration. They are also reluctant to introduce political changes in their domestic system, and have, in a specific and particularly inhumane way, used their military capacity against their own citizens. The dismantling of the Chinese hegemony in Tibet will not be the result of manipulation from outside. The Chinese have driven themselves into a rigid position in which they oppose Tibetan autonomy and refuse to recognize the internal causes of social and political change in Tibet. Chinese expansionism not only has come up against the interests of the people of Tibet, but has sought to preserve a hegemonic role which is inconsistent with the rules of the international game. Tibetan interests can be pursued more energetically in the current transitional stage of the political organization of the international system.

THE RELEVANCE OF THE DALAI LAMA'S PEACE STRATEGY

At the begining of this article, I drew attention to the political opportunism of India and Britain—the direct consequence being the marginalization of the Tibet issue in world politics. The international system of the 1980s provides an opportunity to mend these injustices. Moreover, the Dalai Lama's peace strategy is harmonious with other efforts to stabilize international relations. The proposals of the Dalai Lama cannot be dismissed as "utopian"; they challenge the role of Chinese hegemonic power through the joint efforts of the international community in a multilateral diplomatic process. The Dalai Lama has provided a coherent concept for real measures towards a more independent Tibetan position at a time when the hegemonic position of the two superpowers is in decline and the conflict potential in the Chinese system needs to be contained. While the Chinese continue to violate the rules of detente with their domestic and foreign policy actions, the Dalai Lama has used his international experience and Buddhist insights to address the central problems relating to the new character of international relations.

ROBBIE BARNETT

Tibet: The Effectiveness of Parliamentary Initiatives

The last two years have seen a flurry of Parliamentary actions throughout the world on the subject of Tibet. This paper attempts to look at these initiatives and to assess their effectiveness. In particular it aims to examine the shortcomings and inconsistencies that can erode the apparent achievements of these initiatives. In addition, it asks why it was that the last phase of interest in Tibet was followed by twenty years of silence.

PARLIAMENTARY INITIATIVES 1987-89: RESOLUTIONS

The first parliamentary initiative in this period was the resolution passed by the U.S. Congress in June 1987. Three months later the Dalai Lama presented his own initiative, the Five-Point Peace Plan, in Washington. Since then the Congress has passed five more resolutions, one of them binding on the Executive, and at least one passed unanimously. Two others are being tabled at this moment. [Ed. note: see U.S. *Congressional Action* for up-to-date information.]

This piece is adapted from Barnett's presentation at the Bonn Hearings, April 1989.

Other resolutions broadly supporting the Tibetans have been passed in Europe—two by the European Parliament and one by the West German Bundestag. These are the key indicators of parliamentary interest in the West, and reflect the efforts of the lobby groups in those countries as well as the breadth of concern amongst the politicians who supported them.

DEBATES AND PETITIONS

Other forms of parliamentary action are less spectacular but present alternative strategies for improving the political and humanitarian conditions of life in Tibet.

A debate in the Upper House of the Irish Parliament, for example, did not lead to a resolution. But it was significant because Ireland was one of the original sponsors of the UN resolutions on Tibet in the 1960s: lobbyists there consider that it may therefore be moved more readily to take action again, especially since the Republic was itself born out of a long struggle against foreign occupation.

In India, the key player in the strategic debate over Tibet, over 200 MPs including a Government Minister presented a parliamentary petition in support of the Dalai Lama's proposals. Similar petitions have been endorsed by ninety-five Parliamentarians, including three Ministers, in Australia, and by 169 Members of the Swiss Parliament. In Britain some fifty MPs have signed what are called there Early Day Motions, one of them worded in uncompromising terms.

OPEN LETTERS AND FACT-FINDING MISSIONS

Two other mechanisms besides petitions have been used in Britain and the U.S.—letters and missions. Nearly 100 U.S. Congressmen have signed three open letters to the Chinese leadership—one of them as early as 1985—criticizing their policies in Tibet. As for missions, in April last year the British Parliamentarian Lord Ennals went on a fact-finding mission to Lhasa in which he succeeded in circumventing attempts to discourage him from meeting Tibetan dissidents. Congressional assistants visited refugee settlements in India and Nepal, and three Senators from the U.S. Congress Agricultural Committee visited Tibet in 1988—a visit notable for its definition of the right of foreigners to enquire about human rights: "China has obligations under the United Nations Charter and under international law to protect basic human rights. The Delegation consistently took the point of view that the world human rights community has a legitimate basis to raise concerns about human rights matters in China, including Tibet."

Strategically, missions have the advantage that the visitors might actually meet dissident Tibetans, if they can escape the attentions of their hosts. But missions can be easily manipulated, since any official visitors can be exposed only to official views—a tactic used already with foreign government officials like former Australian Foreign Minister Bill Hayden.

We can expect to see, in the near future, the Chinese inviting Parliamentarians disposed towards their case to Tibet. This is a tactic for which the human rights community should be well-prepared.

ASSESSING EFFECTIVENESS:

1. IMPACT ON THE EXECUTIVE

Are these initiatives effective? In the short term we can only guess at this. But some criteria can be suggested. Firstly, there may have been a knock-on effect on the executive arms of governments. The British and American governments have issued statements of concern, with the British putting particularly strong emphasis on the Chinese commitment to hold talks. But the Dutch, who were the first in nearly twenty years to raise the issue of Tibet at the UN, were not under visible pressure from their parliament. Still less so was the Canadian government, who also spoke out at the UN this year, or the French, who on March 13 went way beyond other governments when they called for China to admit UN and NGO observers to Tibet. On the other hand, the Australian, Indian, Irish, Swiss, and German governments have not acceded to the demands of their parliamentarians.

2. IMPACT ON THE CHINESE

It is hard to assess the political impact of a parliamentary action on the Chinese Government. Several observers have noted that the foreign remarks which set off the loudest Chinese complaints are not always those which might actually cause the Chinese most concern. However, study of the content of parliamentary statements indicates that those statements have generally been politically vague. If we take three criteria which could be said to be typical of strong political statements, it is clear that most recent statements about Tibet are relatively weak.

1) *Specificity.*

Most statements, reflecting the nervousness of those who are reluc-tant to "awaken the sleeping dragon," are broad and generalized. They usually refer to vague and abstract notions of moral values and human rights. The Chinese often describe these as amounting to "grave" or "intolerable" interference in their internal affairs, but in reality the political threat they offer is small. The grievances they imply can easily be appeased by a carefully arranged fact-finding mission, or by vague promises for future reform. This happened several times with propos-als for language reform—as with the latest proposal on March 16, 1989, to introduce Tibetan in the University of Tibet "for the most part by the year 2,000." Broad gestures also serve to conceal possible lack of commitment amongst those who might wish to show concern but who are not actually looking for any kind of change in the Tibetan situation.

Significantly, the Chinese themselves rejected vague Western criticisms of their actions in Lhasa on March 5 this year. The criticisms were, they said, veiled attacks on their country, and the perpetrators of these statements should stand up and say exactly what they meant. They implied that these criticisms were superficial gestures that politicians lacked the will and muscle to pursue. So far, no government has publicly responded to this challenge.

There have been some instances of detailed demands for action, and it can be argued that these are more politically significant than broad expressions of concern. Such things as providing funds or scholarships for Tibetan refugees may seem trivial, but they are much harder for a foreign Government to refuse. The proposals put forward by the group of Congressional assistants after their trip to India and Nepal in November 1988, included several small, specific, and politically sharp demands, such as giving more funds to VOA for Tibetan language broadcasts, and, more dramatically, linking arms sales to China's record on human rights. There have been few if any such specific demands outside the United States by either parliaments or lobby groups.

2) The Use of International Legal Standards.

The Chinese have gone to great lengths to present themselves as responsible members of the international community, particularly at the UN. This is implicit in China's acceptance, in 1989, of the position of vice-chair of the UN Commission for Human Rights. In this context any allegations that specific international laws have been breached by the Chinese are relevant, as they could be damaging to China's credibility in the UN and other international fora, unlike general remarks about the commitment to democratic values and human rights.

China has not signed either of the International Covenants on Human Rights, an omission which has also not attracted wide attention. But it has in the last two years acceded to the Convention on Torture, thus exposing itself to any well-documented allegation of breaches of that Convention. So far no one has cited this law, breaches of which it is the responsibility of foreign governments to pursue. Other legal instruments, such as those relating to employment practices and forced transportation of peoples, have also not been cited. Cases of racial discrimination are covered by international agreements and are particularly significant because last December the Chinese, a signatory to the Convention for the Elimination of Racial Discrimination, admitted that racial discrimination was a legitimate cause for foreign involvement in another nation's affairs.

In this context it is noteworthy that, as with specific or practical demands, few parliamentary groups have referred to breaches of specific legal instruments which China has signed. This is also true of foreign lobby groups campaigning about Tibet.

3) Other Countries and Conflicts.

Allegations of human rights abuses are not in themselves threatening to a country. But in the wider arena they can take on a much larger political significance, as they have in South Africa and Palestine. Politicians could have compared the Tibetan situation to the conflicts in those and other countries, particularly to national liberation struggles. They could also have referred to East Turkestan (Xinjiang) and Hong Kong, areas where discontent with Chinese rule or with the prospect of Chinese rule could lead to political unease. This would have allowed them to have viewed the issue in a framework which the traditional Western human rights approach does not on its own provide. It has not, for example, been presented in a regional context. If Nepal, for instance, where Tibetan refugees have recently been repatriated to the Chinese authorities, had been treated in this manner, the issue would have widened and it would have been harder for the issue to be regarded as a small, internal affair. So far these kinds of considerations have not formed part of public statements on Tibet.

WILL PARLIAMENTARY INTEREST LAST?

Since 1987 these and other initiatives have changed the pattern of foreign parliamentary attitudes towards China, a pattern which until then saw China as what Roberta Cohen in her definitive study of the subject called "The Human Rights Exception." This shift in attitudes towards Tibet was partly brought about by the Dalai Lama's own political initiative in 1987. It was also fueled by the press coverage of the demonstrations that followed the Chinese rebuttal of the Dalai Lama's proposals. What we need to examine here, however, is not so much why this sudden change in attitudes came about, but whether they are likely to last. Some indicators can be seen by comparing the current international activity about Tibet with earlier surges of interest.

In the 1960s there was also a certain amount of activity, including a significant resolution at the UN in 1961 calling for the protection of the Tibetans' right to self-determination. But by 1971, when the U.S. finally allowed the People's Republic to take its seat at the UN, international silence over the issue of Tibet was total. That silence continued until March 1989—eighteen years without a mention of human rights atrocities that occurred in China or of the situation in Tibet.

Clearly, that change in policy reflected changes in U.S. concepts of geo-strategy. But the earlier interest in the Tibet issue was different in a number of ways from the current phase. Three aspects of the situation can be singled out as having, for the most part, changed.

1. LACK OF GRASS ROOTS INVOLVEMENT

As has been pointed out by others, the actions of those years were motivated by ideological concerns. They were very much part of cold war politics and were initiated not by parliaments but by executive arms of government as part of their complex strategies of alliance and attack. The governments who supported Tibet in the 1960s dropped the issue when they found that they needed China as an ally and as a potential marketplace. They had no need to explain this change of policy since their electorates and newspapers had not taken up the issue.

Today the initiatives are coming from the parliaments, reflecting a wider concern based not on strategic postures amongst the influential but on information and sympathy at the grass roots level. If this basis were to be built upon, it is likely to prove more durable and effective than the earlier campaigns, which appear to have been dominated by the shifting allegiances of political rulers.

2. GOVERNMENT EXCUSES FOR INACTION—LACK OF INFORMATION

Secondly, we should take note of the reasons put forward by governments of the time to explain their reluctance to criticize China. The most extraordinary of these was the idea that the Chinese people had no notion of human rights in their indigenous moral tradition, and so did not need it now. This fit in with the idea that the Chinese were not quite individuals in the Western sense. It was an argument of convenience, historically without basis and morally indefensible. Documentation of it exists in learned papers presented at hearings held by the U.S. Congress in 1970. It was also an argument which the Chinese Communist Party itself was happy to use to justify its policies.

But the principal justification presented by the reluctant governments of those years to explain their inaction was the claim that they lacked information. They argued that they simply did not know enough about what was happening in China or Tibet to make any judgment on allegations of human rights atrocities, or, it seemed, on any other matter. This was not an apt defense in the early sixties, given the number of refugee accounts and the reports of the International Commission of Jurists (ICJ), but it was nevertheless accepted as a valid excuse. What they probably meant at the time was that nobody else knew enough about conditions in Tibet or China with which to challenge their claim to ignorance. In any case, they used their apparent lack of information to justify inaction. Several governments, including the British, are still using this argument.

This is an area in which Westerners have a role to play because governments and journalists find it harder to ignore information received from their own nationals. For reasons that are not always clear or above question, the stories carried over the mountains by Tibetans themselves have not generally been believed by foreigners, particularly by foreign governments. It is possible that this may have been partly because some of these accounts were presented in ways that were exaggerated and polemical. But that was in fact in keeping with the standards of the Tibetans' foreign allies at the time, who were themselves encouraging the spread of anti-Communist propaganda for their own ideological purposes. The ICJ reports were later discredited on the grounds that they had been influenced by CIA involvement, an accusation that seemed sufficient to make governments ignore their findings.

Foreign governments are now less likely to be able to claim ignorance as an excuse for inaction, as there has recently been an increasing flow of relatively well-documented and non-polemical information about Tibet, gathered by both Tibetans and non-Tibetans. In these ways the current interest in Tibet could be seen as having a longer political life expectancy than earlier phases of foreign interest. These characteristics offset to some extent the relative weakness of most parliamentary initiatives so far.

3. FUNERALS & DYNASTIES: THE SENSING OF POLITICAL CHANGE

Thirdly, there are a cluster of causes for that period of international silence about Tibet which can be broadly grouped together under the notion of the political. Usually these are discussed in terms of geopolitics and strategy, and seen as reflections of the Sino-American need to counterbalance the Soviet threat. But there is another political interpretation of that sudden change of heart by erstwhile supporters of the Tibetan cause. This is the Western sense of collapsing dynasties: when China is politically strong and ideologically coherent, foreign governments do not support its critics. When the machinery of power in Beijing is being destroyed or reconstructed, those governments are not afraid to voice adverse opinions of the outgoing system.

This is not entirely a form of foreign opportunism. The paramount need of governments is to be on the side of whoever is a rising force or a future power. Simply put, governments don't like to criticize a regime or an ideology unless they see that indigenous forces in that country are already threatening its survival. In the case of modern China, this reluctance is self-evident: the first country in the world to criticize the excesses of the Cultural Revolution was China itself. The rest of the world merely followed suit.

What interests governments and journalists are incidents and statements that may themselves be quite small but which suggest a challenge to the ruling system. The sea-change in modern Chinese history, for example, when the reformist movement first emerged as a viable force, was signalled by a funeral, that of Premier Zhou Enlai. On that day, April 5, 1976, thousands of students and workers gathered in Tiananmen Square apparently to lament the death of a leader; hundreds are believed to have been killed or wounded on that occasion. But in fact their actions led to the passing of one dynasty and the promotion of another. It was clear that although their demands were for human rights and more democracy, their real impact would be on the government itself and on its right to rule.

It was only after this funeral that the international community began to show even a passing interest in Chinese human rights. April 22, 1989, saw in Beijing another funeral, that of Hu Yaobang—incidentally the first supreme Chinese leader ever to visit Tibet. Students who demonstrated in Beijing that day demanded such apparently trivial concessions as a ban on the import of luxury motor cars. Governments across the world who watched that funeral carefully waited to see not if luxury cars would be banned, but if the demonstrators' demands and deeds would indicate not merely circumstantial grievances but, as they had done in 1976, a political challenge to the powers that be and the death knell for an outlived dynasty. We now know that the funeral did indeed come near to toppling the *régime*.

Before speaking out about human rights in Tibet, the outside world also waited for a funeral, or at least for deaths: in this case the deaths of those demonstrators shot by police on the morning of October 1, 1987. At that time only parliamentary bodies took initiatives. But the deaths on December 10, 1988, and on March 5, 1989, finally brought statements from governments as well.

Their statements may have talked about human rights, but the impulse that seemed to move them was political, not moral. What made those incidents different from previous disturbances was not just that tourists witnessed them, but that they came after the Dalai Lama had re-emerged as a political force, and after the Chinese had staked their right to rule on their policy of liberalization. It was a policy that the demonstrators by their actions implicitly rejected and the legitimacy of which the police by opening fire exposed as void. Clearly the demonstrations in Tibet posed a political and ideological threat to Chinese rule in its present form. Recent events have proved that this is so in the eyes of the Chinese too: no serious observer could suggest that martial law was imposed, and some 20-30,000 troops deployed, merely to control a couple of thousand unruly but unarmed demonstrators.

If what really motivates foreign governments in daring to criticize the dragon is the perception of imminent political change, then those who wish to see the Tibet issue addressed with more than token deference will need to emphasize its political significance. The current trend has been to say "the Chinese police are being nasty to Tibetans": this is essentially the tone of existing public statements on Tibet. Politically, the Tibetan issue will change its character when its proponents start to emphasize that the Tibetan people are rejecting not just the abuses and excesses of Chinese rule but the authority and legitimacy of that rule.

It was the first of these perceptions which characterized Western interest in Tibet in the 1960s, when the Chinese state was not seen as threatened by the Tibetan opposition; it did not sustain their interest for long. For there to be long-term interest among politicians the political nature of the Tibetan challenge would need to be made clear. Even if future parliamentary resolutions do not include the issue of national independence, they will have indicated a major development in the Western view of Tibet if they start to identify what may appear to foreigners to be merely questions of human rights as, in this context, deeply political demands.

THREATS TO A SOLUTION: APPEASEMENT VS. SUPPORT

I have looked at some ways in which Western governments have avoided the responsibility of taking up the Tibetan issue, as well indicating other conditions under which they are more likely to be impelled to move. But if foreign parliamentarians and powers do endorse the issue of Tibet, other dangers follow, some of which may be no less prejudicial to Tibetan interests than silence.

Since governments are motivated primarily by the need to appease, many of their statements on an issue like Tibet will be designed to calm not only their electorates, but also the Tibetan dissidents. If in some way they can help to end unrest without disrupting the Chinese government they will place the Chinese in their debt. This is not bad in itself, but it means that Tibetans could again find themselves abruptly deprived of support once the threat of disruption has abated. If negotiations take place and the unrest subsides, the mediating gestures of foreign powers and individuals could evaporate, just at the time when the Tibetans will be looking for support in order to press the Chinese for political concessions.

The vagueness of most parliamentary statements makes it hard to judge at this stage if their authors are motivated more by the need to help the Chinese placate the situation in Tibet than by the wish to protect and advance the rights of the Tibetans. The call for talks, for example, does not in itself signify concern for Tibetans at all. It could equally well signify a dignified attempt to quieten Tibetan truculence. What would make such a demand less equivocal would be support for the right of Tibetans to state their own demands. The motives behind parliamentary initiatives can only be assessed by their closeness to the specific demands raised by the Tibetan people themselves, or to the specific rights to make and enforce those demands.

THE TENDENCY TO INTERFERE

There is another hidden agenda attending foreign claims to support Tibetans. It is the tendency of non-Tibetan groups and organizations not only to be seen to support the Tibetans, but also to advocate, pressurize or influence them on the making of their own policy. A lot of what is behind support for the Tibetans may not be support for the Tibetans, but unconscious support for Western ideas of what is right for the Tibetans. This tendency is a continuation of historical beliefs of racial or cultural superiority amongst people, especially those in countries with recent or continuing imperial traditions.

It is not clear to what extent these habits underlie Western statements of concern about Tibet, but it is a criticism raised regularly by both Tibetans and non-Tibetans of other foreign supporters. In almost all cases the criticism conceals a history of factional in-fighting between different support groups or personality cliques, and often stems from personal or class jealousy amongst non-Tibetan supporters. Nevertheless, the political consequences of the tendency to interfere are detrimental to the Tibetan issue because they threaten to link Tibetan policy-formation to a particular Western culture, usually that of a superpower or regional power, and because in effect they negate the claim of Tibetans to practice self-determination. This in turn gives the impression that Tibetans lack a coherent or evolving sense of collective political will, an impression that directly undermines the post-1987 sense that protest in Tibet represents a genuine political challenge to the Chinese state.

In addition, policy formulated by non-Tibetans tends to always reflect non-Tibetan interests, few if any of which are identical in the long-run to Tibetan interests. Both the non-Tibetan factions which pressurize Tibetans to seek independence and the non-Tibetan factions which encourage Tibetans to pursue compromise solutions can be shown to reflect deep-seated interests which are quite different than those of the Tibetans themselves.

Such manipulation is one of the more obvious sub-texts that can be contained within broad statements of support. Careful scrutiny of the wording of statements would no doubt elucidate more.

THE QUESTION OF STATUS

Generally governments and parliaments have so far confined themselves to matters of human rights. This has dangers and limitations, which have been touched upon above. But in some cases there is scope for a potential political debate as well, and even a potential discussion of the status of Tibet. I would like to mention this possibility even though there is no sign of such a thing occurring any time soon.

To see an example of it, we should look at the British position. At the moment there appears to be no real debate over Tibet's status at a governmental level. Most lobby groups regard Tibet as independent and assume that all foreign governments regard Tibet categorically as part of China. No common ground is perceived between them, and as a result there is no dialogue over this issue: the debate between these two positions, such as it is, amounts to either aggressive rhetoric or extraction of minute symbolic concessions. This absence of dialogue is reflected in the studious avoidance of the issue by parliamentary bodies.

But in fact, it is not true to say that all governments have accepted China's rights to sovereignty. In fact, several countries have equivocated over the issue, saying only that Tibet is "effectively" or "in present reality" part of China. The Tibetans in any case were granted explicit recognition as an independent state by the Mongolians in 1913. More complex variants exist, as, for example, in Britain, where Tibet has never actually been described as part of China. This position is not without international significance since the British, being the last treaty-makers with Tibet, are in an authoritative position from which to comment on the situation.

They have used this formula: "Successive British governments have consistently regarded Tibet as autonomous while recognizing the special position of the Chinese authorities there." It is based on an understanding reached with the Tibetans in 1914 by which the British would give China not absolute but only conditional recognition of the rights it claimed over Tibet. The condition was that China must allow Tibet to practice autonomy. At the time the statement was first made, autonomy probably meant the state of effective independence that Tibet enjoyed before the Chinese invasion. Clearly that condition has not been fulfilled and therefore, strictly viewed, the British do not, in theory, recognize China's claim to suzerainty, let alone sovereignty.

There are, therefore, grounds which parliamentarians could use to push their governments to consider their position on the status of Tibet, since even the official British position does not provide clear support for the Chinese claim. Although in the short-term foreign interest is focused on the question of human rights, it is possible that the Tibetans and their supporters might pursue the political implications of those demands for human rights in the future.

CONCLUSION

Although there has been a marked increase in the number of parliamentary initiatives concerning the question of Tibet, the phraseology and style of those statements generally suggest a low level of political will or clarity. In themselves these statements therefore do not suggest that the current level of political support for Tibetans is likely to last longer or prove more effective than the abortive wave of international interest twenty years ago.

However, other more general characteristics of the current wave of activity indicate that it is more sharply defined in its political role than its predecessors, and less subject to the interests of regional forces or superpowers. Recent political and dynastic developments in Tibet and China have now given the Tibetans another window of political opportunity, and it seems possible that they could be served, this time, by a more effective body of foreign support.

POSTSCRIPT

FEBRUARY 1991

Since this was first written, a number of important developments have taken place. The Nobel Peace Prize, awarded to the Dalai Lama in December 1989, allowed parliaments and some governments to ignore with impunity Chinese orders that they should not meet the Tibetan leader; in addition, the Prize citation specifically defined him as a political as well as a religious leader. This has led to a slow politicization of the issue, with the most concrete result being the

Australian Senate's unanimous resolution on Tibet on December 6, 1990 [See Appendix III]. The Australian resolution was a breakthrough because it referred specifically to the UN resolutions on Tibet of 1961 and 1965. Both of these affirmed the Tibetans' right as a people to self-determination. A major foreign parliament had, for the first time in recent years, confronted the question of the Chinese invasion as well as the question of its human rights abuses.

It was not a development without parallel. Parliamentary groups were formed in Norway, Italy, France, and the United Kingdom to gather together parliamentarians concerned about Tibet; the Norwegian and French groups include around one hundred members already. In May 1990, the European Parliament's Political Affairs Commission appointed a Rapporteur to consider issues of human rights in Tibet. Like the Parliamentary Groups, he is unlikely to accept governmental or Chinese arguments which in effect deny that self-determination is a right equal to individual rights such as freedom of expression and belief.

The invasion of Kuwait means, above all, that the concept of self-determination cannot be marginalized; at least in the eyes of the public, the case of Tibet is likely to gain from the anti-Iraqi rhetoric of 1990, as from the emergence of the new democracies, and of the Baltic States, in Eastern Europe in 1989. The developments are sure to encourage parliamentarians to stronger rhetoric and broader views of what constitutes a people's inalienable right.

But at the same time, China has won its own victories. By recruiting multi-lateral and non-governmental aid for Tibet, it has begun a powerful campaign to regain credibility for its presence in the Himalayas. As it moves swiftly away from the language of absolute sovereignty to the rhetoric of economic and social development, the arguments about status and abuses become more complex. In the eyes of governments eager to cooperate with China, those arguments become redundant, as they strive to bypass dissent and complexity by offering aid and cooperation to China's Tibet. As China follows through its declared aim for its foreign policy in Tibet for 1991—to encourage foreign cooperation—parliamentarians and Tibetan lobby groups in other countries may find the grounds of the argument shifting yet again.

TENZIN GYATSO, THE FOURTEENTH DALAI LAMA

Five-Point Peace Plan for Tibet

The world is increasingly interdependent, so that lasting peace—national, regional, and global—can only be achieved if we think in terms of broader interest rather than parochial needs. At this time, it is crucial that all of us, the strong and the weak, contribute in our own way. I speak to you today as the leader of the Tibetan people and as a Buddhist monk devoted to the principles of a religion based on love and compassion. Above all, I am here as a human being who is destined to share this planet with you and all others as brothers and sisters. As the world grows smaller, we need each other more than in the past. This is true in all parts of the world, including the continent I come from.

At present in Asia, as elsewhere, tensions are high. There are open conflicts in the Middle East, Southeast Asia, and in my own country, Tibet. To a large extent, these problems are symptoms of the underlying tensions that exist among the area's great powers. In order to resolve regional conflicts, an approach is required that takes into account the interests of all relevant countries and peoples, large and

This is a transcription of a speech the Dalai Lama made to members of the United States Congress in Washington, DC, September 21, 1987.

small. Unless comprehensive solutions are formulated, that take into account the aspirations of the people most directly concerned, piecemeal or merely expedient measures will only create new problems.

The Tibetan people are eager to contribute to regional and world peace, and I believe they are in a unique position to do so. Traditionally, Tibetans are a peace-loving and nonviolent people. Since Buddhism was introduced to Tibet over one thousand years ago, Tibetans have practiced nonviolence with respect to all forms of life. This attitude has also been extended to our country's international relations. Tibet's highly strategic position in the heart of Asia, separating the continent's great powers—India, China and the USSR—has throughout history endowed it with an essential role in the maintenance of peace and stability. This is precisely why, in the past, Asia's empires went to great lengths to keep one another out of Tibet. Tibet's value as an independent buffer state was integral to the region's stability.

When the newly formed People's Republic of China invaded Tibet in 1949-50, it created a new source of conflict. This was highlighted when, following the Tibetan national uprising against the Chinese and my flight to India in 1959, tensions between China and India escalated into the border war in 1962. Today large numbers of troops are again massed on both sides of the Himalayan border and tension is once more dangerously high.

The real issue, of course, is not the Indo-Tibetan border demarcation. It is China's illegal occupation of Tibet, which has given it direct access to the Indian sub-continent. The Chinese authorities have attempted to confuse the issue by claiming that Tibet has always been a part of China. This is untrue. Tibet was a fully independent state when the People's Liberation Army invaded the country in 1949-50.

Since Tibetan emperors unified Tibet over a thousand years ago, our country was able to maintain its independence until the middle of this century. At times Tibet extended its influence over neighboring countries and peoples, and, in other periods, came itself under the influence of powerful foreign rulers—the Mongol Khans, the Gorkhas of Nepal, the Manchu Emperors, and the British in India.

It is, of course, not uncommon for states to be subjected to foreign influence or interference. Although so-called satellite relationships are perhaps the clearest examples of this, most major powers exert influence over less powerful allies or neighbors. As the most authoritative legal studies have shown, in Tibet's case, the country's occasional subjection to foreign influence never entailed a loss of independence. And there can be no doubt that when Beijing's communist armies entered Tibet, Tibet was in all respects an independent state.

China's aggression, condemned by virtually all nations of the free world, was a flagrant violation of international law. As China's military occupation of Tibet continues, the world should remember that though Tibetans have lost their freedom, under international law Tibet today is still an independent state under illegal occupation.

It is not my purpose to enter a political/legal discussion here concerning Tibet's status. I just wish to emphasize the obvious and undisputed fact that we Tibetans are a distinct people with our own culture, language, religion, and history. But for China's occupation, Tibet would still, today, fulfill its natural role as a buffer state maintaining and promoting peace in Asia.

It is my sincere desire, as well as that of the Tibetan people, to restore to Tibet her invaluable role, by converting the entire country—comprising the three provinces of U-Tsang, Kham and Amdo—once more into a place of stability, peace, and harmony. In the best of Buddhist tradition, Tibet would extend its services and hospitality to all who further the cause of world peace and the well-being of mankind and the natural environment we share.

Despite the holocaust inflicted upon our people in the past decades of occupation, I have always strived to find a solution through direct and honest discussions with the Chinese. In 1982, following the change of leadership in China and the establishment of direct contacts with the government in Beijing, I sent my representatives to Beijing to open talks concerning the future of my country and people.

We entered the dialogue with a sincere and positive attitude and with a willingness to take into account the legitimate needs of the People's Republic of China. I hoped that this attitude would be reciprocated and that a solution could eventually be found which would satisfy and safeguard the aspirations and interests of both parties. Unfortunately, China has consistently responded to our efforts in a defensive manner, as though our detailing of Tibet's very real difficulties was criticism for its own sake.

To our even greater dismay, the Chinese government misused the opportunity for a genuine dialogue. Instead of addressing the real issues facing the six million Tibetan people, China has attempted to reduce the question of Tibet to a discussion of my own personal status.

It is against this background and in response to the tremendous support and encouragement I have been given by you and other persons I have met during this trip, that I wish today to clarify the principal issues and to propose, in a spirit of openness and concili-ation, a first step towards a lasting solution. I hope this may contribute to a future of friendship and cooperation with all of our neighbors, including the Chinese people.

The peace plan contains five basic components:

1. Transformation of the whole of Tibet into a zone of peace;

2. Abandonment of China's population transfer policy which threat-ens the very existence of the Tibetans as a people;

3. Respect for the Tibetan people's fundamental human rights and democratic freedoms;

4. Restoration and protection of Tibet's natural environment and the abandonment of China's use of Tibet for the production of nuclear weapons and dumping of nuclear waste;

5. Commencement of earnest negotiations on the future status of Tibet and of relations between the Tibetan and Chinese peoples.

Let me explain these five components.

1. *I propose that the whole of Tibet, including the eastern provinces of Kham and Amdo, be transformed into a zone of "Ahimsa," a Hindi term used to mean a state of peace and nonviolence.*

The establishment of such a peace zone would be in keeping with Tibet's historical role as a peaceful and neutral Buddhist nation and buffer state separating the continent's great powers. It would also be in keeping with Nepal's proposal to proclaim Nepal a peace zone and with China's declared support for such a proclamation. The peace zone proposed by Nepal would have a much greater impact if it were to include Tibet and neighboring areas.

The establishing of a peace zone in Tibet would require withdrawal of Chinese troops and military installations from the country, which would enable India also to withdraw troops and military installations from the Himalayan regions bordering Tibet. This would be achieved under an international agreement which would satisfy China's legitimate security needs and build trust among the Tibetan, Indian, Chinese and other peoples of the region. This is in everyone's best interest, particularly that of China and India, as it would enhance their security, while reducing the economic burden of maintaining high troop concentrations on the disputed Himalayan border.

Historically, relations between China and India were never strained. It was only when Chinese armies marched into Tibet, creating for the first time a common border, that tensions arose between these two powers, ultimately leading to the 1962 war. Since then numerous dangerous incidents have continued to occur. A restoration of good relations between the world's two most populous countries would be greatly facilitated if they were separated—as they were throughout history—by a large and friendly buffer region.

To improve relations between the Tibetan people and the Chinese, the first requirement is the creation of trust. After the holocaust of the last decades in which over one million Tibetans—one sixth of the population—lost their lives and at least as many lingered in prison camps because of their religious beliefs and love of freedom, only a withdrawal of Chinese troops could start a genuine process of reconciliation. The vast occupation force in Tibet is a daily reminder to the Tibetans of the oppression and suffering they have all experienced. A troop withdrawal would be an essential signal that in the future a meaningful relationship might be established with the Chinese, based on friendship and trust.

2. *The population transfer of Chinese into Tibet, which the government in Beijing pursues in order to force a "final solution" to the Tibetan problem by reducing the Tibetan population to an insignificant and disenfranchised minority in Tibet itself, must be stopped.*

The massive transfer of Chinese civilians into Tibet in violation of the Fourth Geneva Convention (1949), threatens the very existence of the Tibetans as a distinct people. In the eastern parts of our country, the Chinese now greatly outnumber Tibetans. In the Amdo province, for example, where I was born, there are, according to Chinese statistics, 2.5 million Chinese and only 750,000 Tibetans. Even in the so-called Tibet Autonomous Region (i.e., central and western Tibet), Chinese government sources now confirm that Chinese outnumber Tibetans.

The Chinese population transfer policy is not new. It has been systematically applied to other areas before. Earlier in this century, the Manchus were a distinct race with their own culture and traditions. Today only two to three million Manchurians are left in Manchuria, where 75 million Chinese have settled. In Eastern Turkestan, which the Chinese now call Sinkiang, the Chinese population has grown from 200,000 in 1949 to 7 million, more than half of the total population of 13 million. In the wake of the Chinese colonization of Inner Mongolia, Chinese number 8.5 million, Mongols 2.5 million.

Today, in the whole of Tibet, 7.5 million Chinese settlers have already been sent, outnumbering the Tibetan population of 6 million. In central and western Tibet, now referred to by the Chinese as the "Tibet Autonomous Region," Chinese sources admit the 1.9 million Tibetans already constitute a minority of the region's population. These numbers do not take the estimated 300,000 to 500,000 troops in Tibet into account—250,000 of them in the so-called Tibet Autonomous Region.

For the Tibetans to survive as a people, it is imperative that the population transfer is stopped and Chinese settlers return to China.

Otherwise, Tibetans will soon be no more than a tourist attraction and relic of a noble past.

3. *Fundamental human rights and democratic freedoms must be respected in Tibet. The Tibetan people must once again be free to develop culturally, intellectually, economically, and spiritually and to exercise basic democratic freedoms.*

Human rights violations in Tibet are among the most serious in the world. Discrimination is practiced in Tibet under a policy of "apartheid" which the Chinese call "segregation and assimilation." Tibetans are, at best, second class citizens in their own country. Deprived of all basic democratic rights and freedoms, they exist under a colonial administration in which all real power is wielded by Chinese officials of the Communist Party and the army.

Although the Chinese government allows Tibetans to rebuild some Buddhist monasteries and to worship in them, it still forbids serious study and teaching of religion. Only a small number of people, approved by the Communist Party, are permitted to join the monasteries.

While Tibetans in exile exercise their democratic rights under a constitution promulgated by me in 1963, thousands of our countrymen suffer in prisons and labour camps in Tibet for their religious or political convictions.

4. *Serious efforts must be made to restore the natural environment in Tibet. Tibet should not be used for the production of nuclear weapons and the dumping of nuclear waste.*

Tibetans have a great respect for all forms of life. This inherent feeling is enhanced by the Buddhist faith, which prohibits the harming of all sentient beings, whether human or animal. Prior to the Chinese invasion, Tibet was an unspoiled wilderness sanctuary in a unique natural environment. Sadly, in the past decades the wildlife and the forests of Tibet have been almost totally destroyed by the Chinese. The effects on Tibet's delicate environment have been devastating. What little is left in Tibet must be protected and efforts must be made to restore the environment to its balanced state.

China uses Tibet for the production of nuclear weapons and may also have started dumping nuclear waste in Tibet. Not only does China plan to dispose of its own nuclear waste but also that of other countries, who have already agreed to pay Beijing to dispose of their toxic materials.

The dangers this presents are obvious. Not only living generations, but future generations are threatened by China's lack of concern for Tibet's unique and delicate environment.

5. Negotiations on the future status of Tibet and the relationship between the Tibetan and Chinese peoples should be started in earnest.

We wish to approach this subject in a reasonable and realistic way, in a spirit of frankness and conciliation and with a view to finding a solution that is in the long term interest of all: the Tibetans, the Chinese, and all other peoples concerned. Tibetans and Chinese are distinct peoples, each with their own country, history, culture, language and way of life. Differences among peoples must be recognized and respected. They need not, however, form obstacles to genuine cooperation where this is in the mutual benefit of both peoples. It is my sincere belief that if the concerned parties were to meet and discuss their future with an open mind and a sincere desire to find a satisfactory and just solution, a breakthrough could be achieved. We must all exert ourselves to be reasonable and wise, and to meet in a spirit of frankness and understanding.

Let me end on a personal note. I wish to thank you for the concern and support which you and so many of your colleagues and fellow citizens have expressed for the plight of oppressed people everywhere. The fact that you have publicly shown your sympathy for us Tibetans, has already had a positive impact on the lives of our people inside Tibet. I ask for your continued support in this critical time in our country's history. Thank you.

U.S. Congressional Action on Tibet: 1987-1990

1987

September 21: The Dalai Lama presents his Five-Point Peace Plan before the Congressional Human Rights Caucus in Congress.

September 22: House passes a Concurrent Resolution HJ 191 unanimously welcoming His Holiness the Dalai Lama to the United States.

December 22: Congress passes and the President signs into law, Section 1243 of the Foreign Relation Authorization Act, Fiscal Years 1988-89, linking defense sales to human rights abuses and providing for financial aid and scholarship for Tibetan refugees.

1988

May 1: The Congressional Human Rights Caucus holds hearing on human rights violations perpetrated by the Chinese against Tibetans in Tibet.

May: Congress presents an art exhibit featuring Tibetan artwork with opening ceremony sponsored by the Congressional Human Rights Caucus and Tibet House.

September 16: Congress passes Senate Concurrent Resolution 129 expressing the support of Congress for His Holiness the Dalai Lama's proposal to promote peace, protect the environment, and gain democracy in Tibet.

October 11: Senate Delegation led by Senator Patrick J. Leahy (D-VT) reports on fact-finding visit to Tibet; confirms allegations of serious human rights violations in Tibet. Senator Leahy publishes a list of over one hundred Tibetan political prisoners with the hope that every member of the U.S. Senate would adopt a prisoner.

1989

March 3: Congressional Staff Delegation issues a report on its visit to Tibetan refugee settlements in India and Nepal; recommends plan for Congressional action.

March 15: Congress passes S.R. 82 on human rights abuses in Tibet; condemns China's imposition of martial law in Lhasa and its environs; and calls upon the United Nations and U.S. Administration to address the situation.

April 17: Congressman Ben Gilman (R-NY) introduces legislation prohibiting export to China of defense articles used to violate human rights and enforce martial law in Tibet. Provisions of this bill were included in Congress' China sanctions package following the Tiananmen massacre.

May 4: Senator Claiborne Pell (D-RI), Chairman of the Senate Foreign Relations Committee, introduces S.928 and establishes a "Voice of America" Tibet Service and Fulbright scholarships for Tibetans to study in the U.S. This provision became law and is currently underway.

May 16: Congress passes H.R. 63 urging China to lift martial law, admit foreign journalists and human rights monitors to Tibet, allow access to prisons, and to support His Holiness the Dalai Lama's initiative to resolve the Tibet situation through the process of negotiations.

June 29: House unanimously passes an amendment to H.R. 2655 which proposes specific sanctions to be taken by the U.S. Government against the Government of the People's Republic of China

(PRC). In this amendment, it was determined that sanctions taken against the PRC government also be explicitly linked to the situation in Tibet.

1990

May 13: Congress Passes S.J. Res. 275 designating May 13, 1990 as the "National Day in Support of Freedom and Human Rights in China and Tibet."

May-June: Bills entered regarding Most Favored Nation (MFN) status for China include: House Resolution 5260 denying China non-discriminatory trade treatment; H.R. 5252 seeking to impose additional conditions of the extension of MFN treatment to the products of the PRC; H.R. 2613 suspending further operations by the Overseas Private Investment Cooperation in the PRC until that country recognizes and protects fundamental human rights; H.J. Res. 578 disapproving of the extension of MFN status to the PRC; H.J. Res 586 disapproving of granting MFN status to China; H.R. 4939 making extension of MFN to China in 1991 conditional upon improvements in China's human rights and foreign policies; H.J. Res. 581 reversing the extension of MFN benefits to China; H.J. Res. 576 requiring the President to submit a report to Congress on human rights conditions in China six months after the enactment of MFN status.

June 21: Congressman John Miller (R-WA) introduces House Resolution 5129 to encourage ethical business practices in the PRC. This legislation sets up nine guiding human rights principles for American businesses to follow while conducting business in the PRC and in Tibet.

October 27: A one-million dollar humanitarian aid package for Tibetan refugees, introduced by Congressman John Porter (R-IL) as part of the Foreign Aid Bill, passes both House and Senate and is signed into law by President Bush.

October 28: An amendment to the Immigration Bill (H.R. 4300) introduced by Congressman Barney Frank (D-MA) that provides 1,000 immigrant visas for Tibetans living in India and Nepal, passes both House and Senate. The Bill was subsequently signed into law by the President.

German Parliamentary Action on Tibet: 1985-1990

1985

Summer and Fall 1985: Protest letters of Gert Bastian, MdB, and Petra K. Kelly, MdB, to Foreign Minister Genscher and visiting Chinese Foreign Minister on Tibet and the Human Rights Situation in Tibet.

1986

June 16: Minor Interpellation submitted by Petra K. Kelly, MdB, and Parliamentary Group of the Green Party on international law and human rights policies concerning Tibet.

October 8: Reply of the Federal Government (10/6127).

November 7: Minor Interpellation submitted by H. Rusche, MdB, and Parliamentary Group of the Green Party on humanitarian aid for Tibetan refugees and insufficient answers of Government to questions put by Petra K. Kelly, MdB.

November 13: Reply of the Federal Government

1987

July 10: Written Questions to German Federal Government by Petra K. Kelly, MdB, concerning Chancellor Kohl's visit to Tibet and the rejection of contacts with exile Tibetan Government; Answer given July 10, 1987 (11/608).

August 12: Study made by German Federal Parliament's Research Service at the request of Petra K. Kelly, MdB, on "What arguments support the contention that the intergration of Tibet into the Chinese State is not valid in international law?" (WF II-163/97). Study came to the conclusion that at the time Tibet was forcefully annexed by China it was an independent state.

August 14: Minor Interpellation submitted by Petra K. Kelly, MdB, on Tibet's status on visits of Western governmental representatives to Tibet and on contacts between German Government and H.H. the Dalai Lama.

September 16: Reply of the German Federal Government (11/814).

September 16: Gert Bastian and Petra K. Kelly, as former and present MdBs, invite His Holiness the Dalai Lama to reception and discussion with Parliamentarians from the Green Party, SPD, and FDP in Bonn.

October 8: On request of Green Parliamentary Group, German Federal Parliament discussed as a matter of urgency (Aktuelle Stunde) the position of the German Government vis-a-vis human rights violations in Tibet.

Autumn 1987: Written Questions to German Federal Government of Dr. Penner (SPD) concerning attempt of the Dalai Lama to speak with Federal Government (11/880) of Dr. Hamm-Brücher (FDP) concerning Five-Point Peace Plan (11/880), of Dr. Daniels (Green Party) on radioactive waste storage in Tibet (11/1109), and of Ms. Geiger (CSU) on human rights in Tibet (11/4279).

October 14: Petra K. Kelly, MdB, submits motion on human rights violations in Tibet supported by the Parliamentary Groups of CDU/CSU SPD, FDP and Greens, calling on People's Republic of China to respond positively to the Dalai Lama's efforts to bring about a constructive dialogue (11/953).

October 15: German Federal Parliament adopts this motion unanimously (Chinese Embassy protests with official letter to Parliament).

November 19: Minor Interpellation submitted by Petra K. Kelly, MdB, on adopted motion and steps taken to implement motion on German economic assistance for Tibet.

December 30: Written questions of Petra K. Kelly, MdB, concerning fate of Tibetan Monk G.L. Wangchuk (11/1586).

1988

February 12: Reply of the Federal Goverment to Minor Interpellation of November 19, 1987 (11/1917).

June 16: Introduction of German edition *Tibet—a Violated Country* edited by Petra K. Kelly and Gert Bastian together with His Holiness the Dalai Lama in Stuttgart.

1989

April 21-22: First international, independent hearing on Tibet and Human Rights, initiated by Petra K. Kelly and Gert Bastian in the Parliament House in Bonn with over forty experts.

May 2: Petra K. Kelly, MdB, submits far-reaching motion on human rights violations and martial law in Tibet calling on PRC to acede to the human rights covenants of the UN; welcoming the Dalai Lama's resepcted calls for the Tibetan conflict to be resolved by nonviolent means, calling on China to respond constructively to the Dalai Lama's negotiating offer (11/6956).

Summer 1989: Petra K. Kelly, MdB, and Green Parliamentary Group submit two urgent motions on economic sanctions against China after the massacre in Peking together with CDU/CSU, SPD, and FDP (also mentioned in Tibet) which were adapted unanimously by the Federal Parliament.

August 14: Minor interpellation submitted by Petra K. Kelly, MdB, on Development-Aid projects in Tibet.

August 25: Reply of the German Federal Government (11/5101).

December 6: Petra K. Kelly, MdB, and Gert Bastian initiate together with East German citizen action movement first meeting between GDR Opposition and His Holiness the Dalai Lama in East Berlin (permission obtained from GDR Government).

December 8: Petra K. Kelly and Gert Bastian initiate reception and luncheon with His Holiness the Dalai Lama and members of SPD and Green Parliamentary Groups as well as exile members of Chinese Democracy Movement in Bonn.

His Holiness the Dalai Lama also met with Willy Brandt, SPD, and unofficially with Rita Süssmuth, CDU (President of German Parliament) and Otto Graf Lambsdorff, FDP.

December 10: German Parliament sends Petra K. Kelly, MdB, as representative to Oslo to Nobel Peace Prize Ceremony with His Holiness the Dalai Lama.

December 2: Minor Interpellation submitted by Petra K. Kelly, MdB, on treatment of the Dalai Lama during his stay in Federal Republic of Germany.

1990

February 8: Reply of the German Federal Government (11/6392).

September 14: Minor interpellation submitted by Petra K. Kelly, MdB, on economic sanctions and China; human rights situation in China and Tibet.

October 4-6: Introduction of German edition of Tibet Hearing Book of Petra K. Kelly and Gert Bastian together with His Holiness the Dalai Lama in "Evangelische Akademie" in Tutzing, Bavaria.

October 31: German Federal Government adopts unanimously the motion submitted by Petra K. Kelly, MdB, on May 4, 1989 on human rights violations in Tibet and martial law (11/6956).

November 14: Reply by German Federal Governemtn to minor interpellation of September 14 (11/8447).

TENZIN GYATSO, THE FOURTEENTH DALAI LAMA

The Strasbourg Statement: An Address to Members of the European Parliament

We are living today in a very interdependent world. One nation's problems can no longer be solved by itself. Without a sense of universal responsibility, our very survival is in danger. I have, therefore, always believed in the need for better understanding, closer cooperation, and greater respect among the various nations of the world. The European Parliament is an inspiring example. Out of the chaos of war, those who were once enemies have, in a single generation, learned to co-exist and to cooperate. I am, therefore, particularly pleased and honored to address this gathering at the European Parliament.

As you know, my own country, Tibet, is undergoing a very difficult period. The Tibetans—particularly those who live under Chinese occupation—yearn for freedom and justice and a self-determined future, so that they are able to fully preserve their unique identity and live in peace with their neighbors.

This amendment to His Holiness' "Five-Point Peace Plan"—known as "The Strasbourg Statement," was delivered in a speech by His Holiness to the European Parliament.

For over a thousand years, we Tibetans have adhered to spiritual and environmental values in order to maintain the delicate balance of life across the high plateau on which we live. Inspired by the Buddha's message of nonviolence and compassion and protected by our mountains, we sought to respect every form of life and to abandon war as an instrument of national policy.

Our history, dating back more than two thousand years, has been one of independence. At no time, since the founding of our nation in 127 B.C., have we Tibetans conceded our sovereignty to a foreign power. As with all nations, Tibet experienced periods in which our neighbors—Mongol, Manchu, Chinese, British, and the Gorkhas of Nepal—sought to establish influence over us. These eras have been brief, and the Tibetan people have never accepted them as constituting a loss of our national sovereignty. In fact, there have been occasions when Tibetan rulers conquered vast areas of China and other neighboring states. This, however, does not mean that we Tibetans can lay claim to these territories.

In 1949 the People's Republic of China forcibly invaded Tibet. Since that time, Tibet has endured the darkest period in its history. More than a million of our people have died as a result of the occupation. Thousands of monasteries were reduced to ruins. A generation has grown up deprived of education, economic opportunity, and a sense of its own national character. Though the current Chinese leadership has implemented certain reforms, it is also promoting a massive population transfer onto the Tibetan plateau. This policy has already reduced the six million Tibetans to a minority. Speaking for all Tibetans, I must sadly inform you, our tragedy continues.

I have always urged my people not to resort to violence in their efforts to redress their suffering. Yet I believe all people have the moral right to peacefully protest injustice. Unfortunately, the demonstrations in Tibet have been violently suppressed by the Chinese police and military. I will continue to counsel for nonviolence, but unless China forsakes the brutal methods it employs, Tibetans cannot be responsible for a further deterioration of the situation.

Every Tibetan hopes and prays for the full restoration of our nation's independence. Thousands of our people have sacrificed their lives and our whole nation has suffered in this struggle. Even in recent months, Tibetans have bravely sacrificed their lives to achieve this precious goal. On the other hand, the Chinese totally fail to recognize the Tibetan people's aspirations and continue to pursue a policy of brutal suppression.

I have thought for a long time on how to achieve a realistic solution to my nation's plight. My cabinet and I solicited the opinions of many friends and concerned persons. As a result, on September 21, 1987, at the Congressional Human Rights Caucus in Washington, D.C., I announced a Five-Point Peace Plan for Tibet. In it I called for the conversion of Tibet into a zone of peace, a sanctuary in which humanity and nature can live together in harmony. I also called for respect for human rights and democratic ideals, environmental protection, and a halt to the Chinese population transfer into Tibet.

The fifth point of the Peace Plan called for earnest negotiations between the Tibetans and the Chinese. We have, therefore, taken the initiative to formulate some thoughts which, we hope, may serve as a basis for resolving the issue of Tibet. I would like to take this opportunity to inform the distinguished gathering here of the main points of our thinking.

The whole of Tibet known as Cholka-Sum (U-Tsang, Kham, and Amdo) should become a self-governing democratic political entity founded on law by agreement of the people for the common good and the protection of themselves and their environment, in association with the People's Republic of China.

The Government of the People's Republic of China could remain responsible for Tibet's foreign policy. The Government of Tibet should, however, develop and maintain relations, through its own Foreign Affairs Bureau, in the fields of religion, commerce, education, culture, tourism, science, sports, and other non-political activities. Tibet should join international organizations concerned with such activities.

The Government of Tibet should be founded on a constitution of basic law. The basic law should provide for a democratic system of government entrusted with the task of ensuring economic equality, social justice and protection of the environment. This means that the Government of Tibet will have the right to decide on all affairs relating to Tibet and the Tibetans.

As individual freedom is the real source and potential of any society's development, the Government of Tibet would seek to ensure this freedom by full adherence to the Universal Declaration of Human Rights, including the rights to speech, assembly, and religion. Because religion constitutes the source of Tibet's national identity, and spiritual values lie at the very heart of Tibet's rich culture, it would be the special duty of the Government of Tibet to safeguard and develop its practice.

The Government should be comprised of a popularly elected Chief Executive, a bicameral legislative branch, and an independent judicial system. Its seat should be in Lhasa.

The social and economic system of Tibet should be determined in accordance with the wishes of the Tibetan people, bearing in mind especially the need to raise the standard of living of the entire population.

The Government of Tibet would pass strict laws to protect wildlife and plant life. The exploitation of natural resources would be carefully regulated. The manufacture, testing and stockpiling of nuclear weapons and other armaments must be prohibited, as well as the use of nuclear power and other technologies which produce hazardous waste. It would be the Government of Tibet's goal to transform Tibet into our planet's largest natural preserve.

A regional peace conference should be called to ensure that Tibet becomes a genuine sanctuary of peace through demilitarization. Until such a peace conference can be convened and demilitarization and neutralization achieved, China could have the right to maintain a restricted number of military installations in Tibet. These must be solely for defense purposes.

In order to create an atmosphere of trust conducive to fruitful negotiations, the Chinese Government should cease its human rights violations in Tibet and abandon its policy of transferring Chinese to Tibet.

These are the thoughts we have in mind. I am aware that many Tibetans will be disappointed by the moderate stand they represent. Undoubtedly, there will be much discussion in the coming months within our own community, both in Tibet and in exile. This, however, is an essential and invaluable part of any process of change. I believe these thoughts represent the most realistic means by which to re-establish Tibet's separate identity and restore the fundamental rights of the Tibetan people while accommodating China's own interests. I would like to emphasize, however, that whatever the outcome of the negotiations with the Chinese may be, the Tibetan people themselves must be the ultimate deciding authority. Therefore, any proposal will contain a comprehensive procedural plan to ascertain the wishes of the Tibetan people in a nationwide referendum.

I would like to take this opportunity to state that I do not wish to take any active part in the Government of Tibet. Nevertheless, I will continue to work as much as I can for the well-being and happiness of the Tibetan people as long as it is necessary.

We are ready to present a proposal to the Government of the People's Republic of China based on the thoughts I have presented. A negotiating team representing the Tibetan Government has been selected. We are prepared to meet with the Chinese to discuss details of such a proposal aimed at achieving an equitable solution.

We are encouraged by the keen interest being shown in our situation by a growing number of governments and political leaders, including former President Jimmy Carter of the United States. We are also encouraged by the recent changes in China which have brought about a new group of leadership, more pragmatic and liberal.

We urge the Chinese Government and leadership to give serious and substantive consideration to the ideas I have described. Only dialogue and a willingness to look with honesty and clarity at the reality of Tibet can lead to a viable solution. We wish to conduct discussions with the Chinese Government bearing in mind the larger interests of humanity. Our proposal will therefore be made in a spirit of conciliation and we hope that the Chinese will respond accordingly.

My country's unique history and profound spiritual heritage render it ideally suited for fulfilling the role of a sanctuary of peace at the heart of Asia. Its historic status as a neutral buffer state, contributing to the stability of the entire continent, can be restored. Peace and security for Asia as well as for the world at large can be enhanced. In the future, Tibet need no longer be an occupied land, oppressed by force, unproductive, and scarred by suffering. It can become a free haven where humanity and nature live in harmonious balance; a creative model for the resolution of tensions afflicting many areas throughout the world.

The Chinese leadership needs to realize that colonial rule over occupied territories is today anachronistic. A genuine union or association can only come about voluntarily, when there is satisfactory benefit to all the parties concerned. The European Community is a clear example of this. On the other hand, even one country or community can break into two or more entities when there is a lack of trust or benefit, and when force is used as the principal means of rule.

I would like to end by making a special appeal to the honorable members of the European Parliament and through them to their respective constituencies to extend their support to our efforts. A resolution of the Tibetan problem within the framework that we propose will not only be for the mutual benefit of the Tibetan and Chinese people but will also contribute to regional and global peace and stability. I thank you for providing me the opportunity to share my thoughts with you.

EDWARD LAZAR

Accommodation or Independence?

The vast majority of the Tibetan people, both within Tibet and in exile, favor independence for Tibet. They do not support accommodation with the People's Republic of China, an occupying foreign nation which has laid Tibet waste for forty years. The demonstrations by monks, nuns, young people, and other laypeople within Tibet are for independence. The Tibet Youth Congress and many international Tibet supporters are dedicated to independence and not accommodation. But the official position of the Tibetan Government-in-Exile and the Dalai Lama, as re-stated in the Strasbourg Statement of June 15, 1988, is for accommodation with China. And most writing about Tibet serves to obscure the fact that the goal for Tibet is not defined as independence, with the result that there is no clear overall strategy for change.

The word itself, "independence," is avoided in official Tibetan pronouncements and is avoided at meetings. "Independence" is not one of the hundreds of index entries in the Dalai Lama's new autobiography. The idea of independence is so dangerous that it is only referred to as the "I" word in some Tibet circles.

Why do over one hundred countries recognize the PLO and not one country in the world recognizes Tibet? A major part of the reason for international tolerance of China's occupation of Tibet is that the Tibetan leadership has maintained a consistent pattern of accommodation with the Chinese occupiers, and that this spirit of accommodation is currently maintained from exile.

It is often noted that after the 1949-50 Chinese invasion the Seventeen-Point Peace Agreement between China and Tibet was signed under duress, did not involve consultation with the Tibetan government in Lhasa, and that the treaty used false Tibetan seals. This is undoubtedly true—but then why did the Tibetan government work within the framework of an unauthorized anti-Tibet agreement for the next ten years? Why didn't the Tibetan leadership, which had left Lhasa, go into exile and rally the world community to the cause of Tibet when the act of colonialism was freshly committed and had the attention of the world? The shameful fact that Britain and India did not come forward to champion Tibet's cause is hardly reason to come to such an accommodation with an invading force.

With ten years lost through this stance, the Dalai Lama, the Tibetan leadership, and 100,000 Tibetans finally went into exile in 1959. This next period is marked by Tibetans working hard to survive as individuals and as a people in exile. The hardships endured and achievements of Tibet-in-exile are very great. But in the political realm there has been less success. Besides three very brief and ineffectual Tibet-related UN resolutions in 1960, 1961 and 1965, there were not any major international Tibet initiatives until 1987. Thus international political efforts for Tibet were a wasteland for thirty-seven long and, for Tibet, very destructive years.

On September 21, 1987, the Dalai Lama issued a comprehensive Five-Point Peace Plan for Tibet. This plan was excellent and presented a positive vision of what Tibet can be if the Chinese leave—a vision of Tibet as an environmentally harmonious zone of peace. As originally stated, the peace plan could have been the centerpiece of a nonviolent independence struggle. But with the issuance of the follow-up Strasbourg Proposal, which was presented as a clarification of the original plan's fifth point concerning negotiations on the future status of Tibet, the peace plan was transformed from being a beacon of independence into a new offer of accommodation. In the Strasbourg addendum it is stated that China can "remain responsible for Tibet's foreign policy," and can "maintain a restricted number of military installations in Tibet," and finally calls for "association with the People's Republic of China." The Strasbourg Statement was a surrender of the most important Tibetan concerns (independence and an end of the Chinese occupation) before negotiations with the Chinese even began. It would be hard to recall so much being given up, not for so little, but for nothing, in the annals of diplomacy.

In the Strasbourg Statement there is acceptance of Chinese foreign control over Tibet and acceptance of limited internal Tibetan autonomy. Ironically, Tibetans already know too well that China does not respect internal autonomy, and there can never be any realistic guarantee that China would respect internal autonomy in the future. The official policy of accommodation translates into a legitimatization of colonial status, a kind of national suicide.

The Strasbourg Statement was intended to calm Chinese fears that the peace plan favored separation of Tibet from China — it was said that the Chinese had an incorrect reading of the original peace plan if they thought it involved separation. Although even this offer of a surrender of sovereignty did not elicit a positive Chinese response, the Strasbourg statement did serve to dampen the hopes of many Tibet supporters who had thought that the original five-point plan did indeed point to separation and independence. A look at the record shows that the Strasbourg Statement was not an aberration, rather it was the logical conclusion of a policy of accommodation.

What is the basis of this policy? Some oft-cited reasons are the enormous population and military strength of the occupying power, the relative isolation of Tibet, and the lack of strong international response to Chinese aggression. One little explored aspect of accommodation is the Dalai Lama's relationship to Marxism, Communism, and China. In his latest autobiography, *Freedom in Exile*, the Dalai Lama states that in 1954 "during the first few weeks of our stay in China, the main topic of conversation amongst all of us Tibetans was naturally how we could best reconcile our needs with China's desires." He then continues:

> I began to get very enthusiastic about the possibilities of association with the People's Republic of China. The more I looked at Marxism the more I liked it. Here was a system based on equality and justice for everyone, which claimed to be a panacea for all the world's ill. From a theoretical standpoint, its only drawback as far as I could see was its insistence on a purely materialistic view of human existence. This I could not agree with. I was also concerned at the methods used by the Chinese in pursuit of their ideals. I received a strong impression of rigidity. But I expressed a wish to become a Party member all the same. I felt sure, as I still do, that it would be possible to work out a synthesis of Buddhist and pure Marxist doctrines that really would prove to be an effective way of conducting politics.

The Dalai Lama goes on to say "it was true that I wanted to modernize Tibet in line with the People's Republic and true also that my cast of mind is basically scientific." Later, in his autobiography, the Dalai Lama, bringing us up-to-date, writes "However, inasmuch as I have any political allegiance, I suppose I am still half Marxist." This was written in 1990, after Stalinist revelations, the Berlin wall, Hungary, Czechoslavakia and numerous atrocities in the cause of Marxism throughout Eastern Europe, China, and Tibet.

The Marxist system denies the value of a spiritual life, and promotes class warfare, violence, and the use of any means to reach a desired end. To talk of a synthesis of Buddhism with "pure Marxist doctrines" is a philosophical exercise which has no relation to dealing with the human rights violations and aggression of totalitarian communist governments. The Dalai Lama's half-Marxism is a result of an improbable philosophic accommodation which contributes to an overall policy of accommodation with China with resultant tragic consequences for Tibet and the Tibetan people.

The Dalai Lama is a world-renowned spiritual leader and respected advocate of world peace. And the Dalai Lama has been a great advocate of the democratization of the Tibetan government. The establishment of a democratic system in which political leaders can be criticized for their actions and can be held accountable for their political actions is the best way for the Tibetan cause to leave behind accommodation. Before Tibet can achieve independence its leadership needs to publicly advocate independence—only then can a unified nonviolent struggle be possible.

Most of the world community united to express outrage over the Iraqi occupation of Kuwait. The outrage of China occupying Tibet parallels and dwarfs what occurred in Kuwait. With a clearly expressed goal of Tibetan independence, the world community can hopefully respond, not with bombs, but with full recognition and support of Tibet and with full pressure on China to end their occupation.

LODI GYALTSEN GYARI

Prospects for Sino-Tibetan Dialogue

I am speaking today about Tibetan-Chinese dialogue, and I would like to consider three points: Why do we advocate dialogue, what forms can it take, and can dialogue be successful at all?

On the first point: Why do we advocate dialogue? We support fundamentally a nonviolent, peaceful settlement. To solve a problem peacefully, dialogue is essential. There are many grounds for seeking a peaceful solution, and all those who have had the chance to meet His Holiness the Dalai Lama know this. The Tibetans are a peaceful people. Perhaps this may not apply to each and every individual, but His Holiness, our greatest personage, has devoted his whole life to peace. Therefore, we wish to negotiate.

Naturally, we Tibetans have not always been blameless. There have been times in which we were a military power and exercised force. In the past we proved that we were in a position to fight. Today we are only six million people, or a little more. According to Chinese statistics, in fact, we are only half that number. What chance then could we have against a billion Chinese?

There have been times when I, too, would have preferred to fight, but we must be realistic. We have had some bad experiences and have been left in the lurch. I don't wish to go into this matter more fully now; it's all in the past. But in our memory, it is still living.

Today we are grateful for any support in dialogue. We desire no support for armed combat. We ourselves bear the responsibility for our deeds, and we do not wish to burden anyone else with them.

I come now to my second point: What form can dialogue take? What is the topic at stake? His Holiness made a proposal before the European Parliament with which many of us are not in agreement. He is well aware of that fact. Representatives of our youth came to him with tears in their eyes and declared their opposition to the proposal. Why then do we strive for a solution that the Tibetan people plainly do not want? Not because we ourselves are opposed to independence. There is probably not a single Tibetan who would be opposed to independence. Even His Holiness gave clear expression to our historical right to independence before the Tibetan Youth Congress and before the European Parliament. His Holiness pointed out that in the eyes of the Chinese it is already treason and a punishable offense to maintain this. But His Holiness is first of all a monk. This status is more important to him than being the Dalai Lama, or being the leader of the Tibetans. And as a monk he may not lie, not even for reasons of state.

The Chinese, however, will never accept our independence. Therefore, we must be prepared to accept compromises. Our proposals of compromise are all on the table, and it is necessary to explain them, from my own personal point of view.

In 1982 the Dalai Lama called on me to participate in a three-person delegation which would travel to Beijing and conduct talks there. For me this meant the first task that I really did not want to take on. There are probably no Tibetans who have gladly negotiated with the Chinese. Of course there are Chinese who are friendly to us, but the mere thought of sitting and eating at a table with Chinese officials was very hard for me. I come from the eastern part of Tibet. Half my family died in the Chinese invasion. The Chinese deliberately allowed two of my brothers to starve to death because they were physically handicapped. My older brother, who loved me very much, always gave me some food out of his own bowl, but died of hunger himself, along with my mother. Among the dead in my family were some very great scholars. So even the thought of speaking in China with the people responsible for these crimes was very difficult for me. Although it is a great honor for any Tibetan to be charged with a responsibility by the Dalai Lama, I did not like this task.

Nevertheless I went to Beijing. I spoke with the Chinese; I argued with them. All along I knew that people like myself will perhaps go down in Tibetan history as traitors, since even if we concluded a treaty with the Chinese, anything we might achieve would be far below the expectations of Tibetans. But we have no other choice.

A young Tibetan woman once went to visit her parents' homeland in the province of Amdo. It seemed to her that she was in China. And even as we speak here today, thousands of Chinese are immigrating into Tibet. For this reason, the Dalai Lama says, we *must* negotiate. Whoever does not trust the statistics of the Tibetan exile government can listen to Radio Lhasa, or to Ngapoi Ngawang Jigme, the highest-ranking Tibetan under the Chinese. In a speech before the National Congress, broadcast on March 23 by Radio Beijing, he criticized the massive resettlement of Chinese into Tibet, and he spoke at that time of over 100,000 Chinese. Thus, it is not a matter of the Dalai Lama's propaganda when Ngapoi Ngawang Jigme reports this. There are further examples. I will cite the mayor of Lhasa, a high-ranking Tibetan, who also works for the Chinese. He says that Tibet is a very sparsely populated region. We want no family planning. And what do we get? Family planning! If representatives of the Chinese regime in Tibet direct these kinds of reproaches to the government, even in Beijing, then it should be clear to everyone what the situation in Tibet really looks like. I will mention one even more convincing proof: the Panchen Lama, who, as we know, is no longer with us. I had the honor to meet him on several occasions. His Holiness said that always, whenever we sent a delegation to Tibet, we should consult the Panchen Lama before negotiating with the Chinese government. In 1984, on our second visit, the Chinese were decidedly hospitable. Our food and lodging were good; there was no cause for complaint. Immediately upon our arrival we were told that we would meet with high officials the next day. We declined, explaining that we first had to meet with the Panchen Lama. Naturally the Chinese did not like this, and so as punishment they let us wait three or four days for the official meeting. But we did not allow ourselves to be dissuaded, and insisted on meeting with the Panchen Lama.

He was a great nationalist and spoke out for an independent Tibet, although he knew that under the present circumstances this could hardly be realized. On his last trip abroad to Central America, our government met with him for the last time. He was returning through Tokyo, where our representatives received him. His message to us was: I support unreservedly the proposal of His Holiness the Dalai Lama. But he made it clear that the situation is difficult and compared it with British policies in Northern Ireland. His last appearance before his death and the manner of his death make it clear that he kept his word; and I, as a Tibetan, believe in rebirth.

The Panchen Lama lived under hard conditions. Although he was designated a national leader, he could not return to Tibet. He did so nonetheless, held religious ceremonies, and rebuilt the tombs of his predecessors, which was forbidden. Moreover, he called together in Shigatse Tibetans from all three provinces and openly declared, "We have suffered more than we have gained from the presence of the Chinese." With this unambiguous message he left us, and therefore his name is beyond reproach. He stressed that the Chinese propaganda machine cannot cite him to document their credibility.

I come now to my third point: Can there be a solution through negotiation? I think that it is possible, although I too have had doubts. When I saw on the television the faces of the thousands of young Chinese demanding freedom and democracy, then I thought, perhaps there is a hope for us all. But I also see Chinese in whom I can recognize no human feelings. That worries me, for if in fact Mao created a generation of unfeeling, inhuman Chinese, then I lose all hope for a peaceful solution. His Holiness believes unshakably in the human heart and believes that even the Chinese can be persuaded.

People in the West should know that China needs them more than they need China. The myth that prevails in the West regarding China really fascinates me, and I often wonder where it comes from. But more and more I have the impression that this myth will be of little profit to China in the long run. The myth, and friends like Dr. Wickert, contribute to China's inability to grow up. The new, revolutionary China is already 40 years old and no longer a baby. We cannot therefore treat it as one, but rather as an adult. People in the West have committed themselves to certain principles, but they must continue to represent these principles in dealings with China. We too have principles from which we cannot draw back.

For people in the West themselves it is better to be for Tibet than against it. We are a poor nation, but we are attempting to speak with the Chinese on a level of equal rights. But they do not accept us as equals. Our Chinese friends have always loved walls. There is the famous Great Wall of China, and every sizable city is encircled by big walls. But when I saw the faces of the thousands of young people, I recognized for the first time the will to pull down the walls. We must help them in this struggle. For this reason it is possible, with help from outside, to move China to the negotiation table and to ratify an agreement. Of course there is no call for euphoria. Even in 1951 we ratified a treaty under similar circumstances. We had to accept it under compulsion, and nonetheless we tried to abide by the treaty. In time, it was the Chinese who violated the treaty. There are no guarantees for us. They can sign anything, and in the next moment they can tear it up. Nonetheless, we will continue our efforts, and for that we need support.

There are further problems, like those with respect to Taiwan, or problems with internal critics who are pleading emphatically for independence, and who maintain that the Dalai Lama is trying to sell out Tibet. This point of view is, of course, false. His Holiness the Dalai Lama recently met with representatives of several governments. Moreover he had a productive talk with Mrs. Mitterand. Through these initiatives, and above all through the engagement of India, a negotiated settlement is possible.

Epilogue

photo by M. Kellermann

Above: Petra K. Kelly and Gert Bastian celebrate with Tibetans after the Bonn Hearing. *Below:* Dr. Palden Tawo, Tibetan activist and composer, translating at the Bonn Hearing.

photo by M. Boller

PETRA K. KELLY & GERT BASTIAN

Epilogue: We've Set the Wheels Turning

The international, non-partisan hearing on Tibet initiated by us in Bonn, West Germany, on April 20 and 21, 1989, were the first large-scale attempt to break the silence existing for decades regarding the ruthless oppression of Tibet. The hearing featured forty speakers from eight countries—including eleven Tibetans—and 400 committed participants from all over the world.

The huge organizational and financial input required by a small group of us was worthwhile—not only because it proved possible to confront the public with previously concealed facts about the suffering of the Tibetans in their own country and about the systematic destruction of their very existence by the Chinese occupying power, but also because the hearing induced dedicated friends of Tibet throughout the world to carry out activities of their own. As a result, more and more people in many countries are being persuaded to protest against the suppression of Tibet by the People's Republic of China.

The most immediate result of the hearing in Bonn was the unanimous adoption of a resolution on the situation in Tibet [see Appendix IV]. The intention expressed in the declaration was more than an empty phrase, as soon became evident. In the subsequent months, Tibet support groups emerged across Germany with the aim of informing the public about the current situation in Tibet by means of events, bookstands, flyers and media activities, and encouraging protest against the human rights violations committed there.

The immediate media response in West Germany, however, was quite disappointing. Television stations refused to report on the hearing because it was allegedly of no interest to the public; by and large the print media was also very reticent. They were evidently very afraid of unfriendly reactions by China and the Chinese Embassy in Bonn. Indeed, these reactions soon occurred. Mr. Mei Zhaorong, the PRC's ambassador in Bonn, held a press conference at the Embassy on April 24, 1989, where he read a seven-page statement condemning the hearing as an insult to China and as a mass of lies, gross falsehoods and vicious distortions. His accusations and depiction of Tibet's situation were so absurd that they are included here:

Press statement made by the Chinese ambassador on April 24, 1989, concerning the International Hearing on Tibet and Human Rights:

> On April 20 and 21, a so-called International Hearing on Tibet and Human Rights was held in the conference room of a certain parliamentary party. It was initiated and chaired by the MPs P. Kelly and Mr. Bastian. The initiators even invited members of the so-called Tibetan Government-in-Exile, various Tibetans who have left their native country, and people with perfidious ideas from several other countries. At the hearing they beat the drum for the partition of China, circulated a host of lies and falsehoods regarding Tibet, and attacked and maliciously distorted the policies of the Chinese government. They adopted a so-called Bonn Declaration accusing China of violating human rights and illegally occupying Tibet. All of this constitutes blatant interference with China's internal affairs. I can but express my indignation and deep regret.
>
> As is generally known, Tibet has been an inseparable part of China's sacred territory since the thirteenth century, and the Tibetans belong to the large family of the Chinese nation comprising fifty-six nationalities. This is a fact recognized by the governments of all countries in the world, including the Federal Republic Germany. It goes without saying that all affairs pertaining to Tibet are internal affairs of China. No foreign government, organization, or individual has the right to

interfere. Any attempt to interfere with China's internal affairs under the guise of human rights and to prise Tibet out of the Chinese union of states is doomed to failure. The Chinese people, including the Tibetans, fought hard for over a century until they succeeded in driving the imperialistic forces out of the country forty years ago. They rose up from absolute degradation and took charge of the country. The wheel of history definitely cannot be turned back.

At the hearing some people used human rights as a pretext for demagoguery and tried in this way to pressure the Chinese government. This was a wholly futile undertaking. If human rights are at all involved, then it should be stated that our conception of human rights is far broader and deeper than those people believe. As far as human rights in Tibet are concerned, we Chinese and especially the Tibetans are the ones most entitled to judge. As you no doubt know, a feudal system of serfdom prevailed in Tibet thirty years ago, a system even more sinister and barbaric than the European one in the Middle Ages. From generation to generation, 95% of the Tibetans were deprived not only of all means of production, but also of the most fundamental right to individual freedom and development. Human rights did not at all exist for them. Only after the democratic reform were they able to rid themselves of the yoke of serfdom, enjoy democracy and freedom that had never existed before, and become masters of their own destiny. The support of the Chinese central government for the Tibetans' demand for the abolition of serfdom was the greatest contribution to securing human rights for the Tibetans. Over the last ten years the Chinese central government has granted the Autonomous Region of Tibet a number of specific privileges, enabling Tibet to make generally recognized progress in economic, cultural, educational, and other fields. The living standards of the Tibetans have risen appreciably. Under the constitution they have national territorial autonomy and enjoy full democratic rights and freedom of religion. Separatists, who in the past suppressed the serfs and now long for their former privileges, talk a great deal about human rights. By means of unrest and foreign forces, they seek to separate Tibet from China and restore their lost "paradise." This is what the so-called Tibetan question is really about.

It needs to be pointed out that the unrest which started roughly a year ago did not concern ethnic or religious matters nor human rights, but constituted acts of violence deliberately staged by a few separatists in order to divide the country. Incited by certain foreign forces and by separatists living abroad, they engaged in fighting, destruction, pillage, and arson under the motto of independence for Tibet. During the unrest in March of this year, they even used weapons that they had smuggled in from abroad. This seriously endangered the safety and property of the population. Under these circumstances the central government was compelled to impose a state of emergency. It is not only a sovereign country's legitimate right but also its downright duty to protect the life and property of the population, maintain public order, and preserve the authority of the law.

Furthermore, I wish to point out that the Chinese government's stance on negotiations with the Dalai Lama has always been clear and unequivocal: It is willing to negotiate with the Dalai Lama as soon as he abandons his activities aimed at Tibet's independence and declares his readiness to help preserve the unity of China, promote national cohesion, and advance the development of Tibet. There can be no independence for Tibet, no semi-independence, or disguised independence. Negotiations are an internal affair concerning the central government and the Dalai Lama alone. It is inadmissible for any foreign government, organization, or individual to interfere.

Finally, I would like to state this: I am convinced that the remarks made at the hearing, which constitute blatant interference with China's internal affairs and gravely injure the feelings of the Chinese people, do not reflect the attitude of the population of West Germany. The Chinese people have always had feelings of friendship for the German people. Ties between China and West Germany have developed satisfactorily since the establishment of diplomatic relations in 1972. They should be appreciated and developed further. The consolidation and advancement of these friendly relations and cooperation serve the interest of both nations. We sincerely hope that the friendly ties and good cooperation achieved by the efforts of both sides will not be impaired or jeopardized.

This slander campaign proved to be useful because it induced foreign press to report on the hearing and to rate China's criticism as a sign of insecurity and nervousness. The German press again refrained almost completely from any reaction. But this reticence did not affect the international repercussions of the hearing. These first became evident in India, where George Fernandes, who had been a speaker at the Bonn hearing, organized an International Conference on Tibet and Peace in South Asia in August 1989.

The three-day event was strongly criticized by the Indian government, which evidently feared that its relations with China would be impaired. This not deter Indian independent newspapers from reporting on this conference and its results at length, regardless of Chinese sensitivities. The final resolution adopted by the roughly 250 participants was also widely published. [See Appendix IV]

Another large-scale hearing on Tibet was held at Copenhagen on November 19, 1989, by the Tibet Support Group Denmark. Michael Alexander, head of Tibet Information Service at Langenfeld, West Germany commented, "The hearing was an outstanding success of this Tibet Support Group, as regards to both the perfect organization and the high standard of the contributions. At the end the participating speakers unanimously adopted a resolution calling upon the Danish government to give His Holiness the Dalai Lama an official reception on the occasion of his next visit." [See Appendix IV]

The Netherlands parliament at The Hague hosted a Tibet conference on January 20-21, 1990. It was organized by the Tibet Support Group in the Netherlands and was chaired by Dr. D. Dolman, formerly vice-president of the second chamber of the Netherlands parliament. The general view was that the event marked a turning point in the Netherlands' stance on Tibet, with the following being demanded by the participants:

1. the Tibetan question again be brought before the United Nations,

2. independent observers be sent to Tibet, and

3. Sino-Tibetan talks be sought on the basis of the Dalai Lama's Five-Point Peace Plan.

Further meetings dealing with Tibet were held by the European Parliament at Brussels in February 1990 and by the International Alert Tibet and China Committee in London from July 6-8, 1990, the latter event being chaired by Lord David Ennals and devoted to the theme of self-determination for Tibet. As Lord Ennals pointed out in a letter, this international meeting was a direct consequence of the hearing in Bonn in April 1989, which, in his view, inspired many to put the Tibetan question on the international agenda.

A conference took place in Tokyo from May 23-29, 1990, on the subject of "Peace in Asia, with Particular Regard for the Situation in

Tibet." This event extended to the Far East the protests against China's suppression of Tibet.

Another remarkable consequence of the Bonn hearing is the fact that it proved possible to mobilize solidarity with Tibet in a country that, under Erich Honecker's government, was one of the most devoted vassals of China, namely the German Democratic Republic (East Germany).

As is well known, the East German rulers up to November 1989 were not ashamed to congratulate the Chinese government after the slaughter of the pro-democracy movement in Beijing in June 1989 on its "victory over the counter-revolution." After the peaceful revolution of the East Germany population, our friends in the independent peace and human rights groups, who had already collected signatures in the spring of 1989 for our appeal for a hearing on Tibet in Bonn, invited us to a Tibet meeting in a community center in Berlin. There we had an opportunity on November 17, 1989, to describe in detail the oppression in Tibet. This event led to the spontaneous formation of a Tibet action group in East Berlin. In addition, we suggested to our friends in the independent opposition groups "New Forum," "Democracy Now," and "Initiative for Peace and Human Rights" that they invite the Dalai Lama to visit the capital of the East Germany during his envisaged visit to West Berlin on December 5-6, 1989. This was done, the letter was sent to Dharamsala, and the Dalai Lama immediately accepted the invitation. However, it was initially doubtful whether the East German authorities would permit him to enter East Germany and thus incur the displeasure of China.

Yet despite Chinese protests, permission was granted with the approval of Egon Krentz, chairman of the Council of State. We were thus able to accompany the Dalai Lama to East Berlin on the morning of December 6, 1989. A very frank and sincere exchange of views then took place between people who had toppled the repressive regime in their own country with a peaceful revolution, and the spiritual and political leader of the Tibetan people, whose forty-year peaceful struggle for freedom and self-determination is still going on.

The Dalai Lama subsequently described this discussion at Dietrich Bonhoeffer House as one of the most moving meetings in his life. It made a substantial contribution towards increasing and deepening understanding in the East Germany for Tibet and solidarity with the oppressed Tibetans.

In his New Year's address Vaclav Havel, freely elected by the people as President of Czechoslovakia on December 29, 1989, invited the Dalai Lama to visit Prague in the first half of 1990. This invitation indicates a breakthrough in the attitude of a democratic government towards the Dalai Lama and the Tibetan question. [Ed. note: His Holiness visited Prague in early February 1990, where he and President Havel made a joint appeal to the politicians of the world "...to rid themselves of the restrictions of particular private or group interests, and to lead their minds by their conscience, and their feeling and responsibility for truth and justice."] It is no coincidence that the hitherto oppressed Czech people, who boldly secured their freedom, are the first ones willing to set new standards of solidarity with people still suffering oppression. This reflects poorly on the self-righteous governments of complacent Western countries, but perhaps it also induces them to reconsider their stance.

On December 8, 1989, following the Dalai Lama's stay in East Berlin, we had the pleasure of welcoming His Holiness at a reception in his honor at the Parliamentary Association in Bonn. On that occasion we also attempted to arrange for him to meet with representatives of the Chinese students' movement. Li Bo and other Chinese students now living in West Germany accepted our invitation and graphically described to the Dalai Lama how the massacre in Beijing on June 4, 1989 had radically changed their assessment of the Tibetan question and convinced them that the reports of Chinese atrocities in Tibet were in fact true.

"We apologize for our former ignorance," a Chinese student told the Dalai Lama and added that they would henceforth make every effort to bring about a fundamentally different attitude towards Tibet on the part of an ultimately democratic China. Nobody who was present is ever likely to forget the noble gesture of friendship and reconciliation with which the Dalai Lama responded to this assurance, and how he embraced the young Chinese student.

This particular incident mirrors a new consciousness of the Tibetan question that has arisen in the Chinese pro-democracy movement. In fact, the Manifesto of the Federation for a Democratic China states:

The Federation for a Democratic China (FDC) has reflected self-critically on the longstanding neglect by China's democratic forces of the Tibetan people's quest for liberal and democratic rights and holds the view that the problem of Tibet and of the other nationalities can only be solved on the basis of democratic principles, the rule of law, and respect for individual freedom and human dignity.

Professor Yan Jiagi, formerly chief adviser to the ousted Communist Party leader Zhao Ziyang and now one of the leading members of the FDC, said in an interview on October 27, 1989:

As we also experienced repression by the Communist Party, we can now understand the injustice suffered by the Tibetans and the Dalai Lama in 1989 and 1988. We know that freedom of religion is one of the essentials for Tibet. If freedom of religion does not exist in Tibet, Tibet itself will not exist. I also believe that Tibet should not be ruled according to the same political principles as other parts of China. In my view, Tibet's problems can be resolved in a federal system. But the nature of such a system as well as Taiwan's and Hong Kong's membership of it are matters to be decided by the people themselves in Tibet, China, Hong Kong, and Taiwan.

Judging from these responses, there can be little doubt that we, the friends of Tibet, have progressed towards the common goal of motivating ever more people in an increasing number of countries to display solidarity with the oppressed Tibetans deprived of their rights. Our aim is to generate stronger protests worldwide against the oppressors in Beijing and on the Roof of the World until politicians can no longer ignore the issue of Tibet when framing their policies towards China.

We received thousands of letters from all over the world after the Bonn hearings, expressing support for the Tibetans in their peaceful struggle for survival. The silence of past decades about the misery in Tibet has been broken and will not recur. Headway is being made on the Tibetan question. The wheels are turning! This means we must fully maintain our commitment to obtaining a free Tibet, bringing about an end to the suppression by the government of the PRC, and ensuring that our governments no longer ignore this suppression. We must continue to strive for direct, constructive talks between Beijing and the Tibetan Government-in-Exile.

Appendices

Appendix I

Nobel Peace Prize

NORWEGIAN NOBEL COMMITTEE
PEACE PRIZE ANNOUNCEMENT
OSLO, OCTOBER 5, 1989

The Norwegian Nobel committee has decided to award the 1989 Nobel Peace Prize to the Fourteenth Dalai Lama, Tenzin Gyatso, the religious and political leader of the Tibetan people.

The Committee wants to emphasize the fact that the Dalai Lama in his struggle for the liberation of Tibet consistently has opposed the use of violence. He has instead advocated peaceful solutions based upon tolerance and mutual respect in order to preserve the historical and cultural heritage of his people.

The Dalai Lama has developed his philosophy of peace from a great reverence for all things living and upon the concept of universal responsibility embracing all mankind as well as nature.

In the opinion of the Committee the Dalai Lama has come forward with constructive and forward-looking proposals for the solution to international conflicts, human rights issues, and global environmental problems.

UNITED STATES CONGRESS
S. CON RES. 75
WASHINGTON, DC
OCTOBER 5, 1989

To congratulate His Holiness the Fourteenth Dalai Lama of Tibet for being awarded the 1989 Nobel Peace Prize.

For the Senate: Mr. Pell (for himself and Mr. Helms, Mr. Biden, Mr. Pressler, Mr. Simon, Mr. Sarbanes, and Mr. Stanford) submitted the following concurrent resolution;

For the House: Mr. Rose (for himself, Mr. Levine of California, Mr. Gilman, Mr. Lantos, Mr. Porter, Mr. Levin of Michigan, and Mr. Douglas) submitted the following concurrent resolution; which was referred to the Committee on the Post Office and Civil Service.

Whereas His Holiness the Fourteenth Dalai Lama of Tibet is the spiritual mentor to millions of Buddhists throughout the world and the leader of the Tibetan people;

Whereas His Holiness the Fourteenth Dalai Lama of Tibet has persistently promoted justice, offered hope to the oppressed, and upheld the rights and dignity of all men and women regardless of faith, nationality, or political views;

Whereas His Holiness the Fourteenth Dalai Lama is a world leader who has admirably and with dedication advanced the cause of regional and world peace through adherence to the doctrines of nonviolence and universal responsibility;

Whereas His Holiness the Fourteenth Dalai Lama has, through his example, his teachings, and his travels, furthered mutual understanding, respect, and unity among nations and individuals; and

Whereas the Norwegian Nobel Committee has awarded His Holiness the Fourteenth Dalai Lama of Tibet the 1989 Nobel Peace Prize; Now, therefore, be it

Resolved by the Senate (the House of Representatives concurring),

That the Congress commends His Holiness the Dalai Lama for furthering the just and honorable causes that he has championed, expresses its support for those causes, and congratulates him for being awarded the 1989 Nobel Peace Prize.

Appendix II

United Nations Resolutions

UNITED NATIONS GENERAL ASSEMBLY
RESOLUTION 1353 (XIV)
NEW YORK, 1959

THE GENERAL ASSEMBLY,

Recalling the principles regarding fundamental human rights and freedoms set out in the Charter of the United Nations and in the Universal Declaration of Human Rights adopted by the General Assembly on December 10, 1948,

Considering that the fundamental human rights and freedoms to which the Tibetan people, like all others, are entitled include the right to civil and religious liberty for all without distinction,

Mindful also of the distinctive cultural and religious heritage of the people of Tibet and of the autonomy which they have traditionally enjoyed,

Gravely concerned at reports, including the official statements of His Holiness the Dalai Lama, to the effect that the fundamental human rights and freedoms of the people of Tibet have been forcibly denied them,

Deploring the effect of these events in increasing international tension and embittering the relations between peoples at a time when earnest and positive efforts are being made by responsible leaders to reduce tension and improve international relations,

1. *Affirms its belief* that respect for the principles of the Charter of the United Nations and of the Universal Declaration of Human Rights is essential for the evolution of a peaceful world order based on the rule of law;

2. *Calls* for respect for the fundamental human rights of the Tibetan people and for their distinctive cultural and religious life.

UNITED NATIONS GENERAL ASSEMBLY
RESOLUTION 1723 (XVI)
NEW YORK, 1961

The General Assembly,

Recalling its resolution 1353 (XIV) of October 21, 1959 on the question of Tibet,

Gravely concerned at the continuation of events in Tibet, including the violation of the fundamental human rights of the Tibetan people and the suppression of the distinctive cultural and religious life which they have traditionally enjoyed,

Noting with deep anxiety the severe hardships which these events have inflicted on the Tibetan people, as evidenced by the large-scale exodus of Tibetan refugees to the neighboring countries,

Considering that these events violate fundamental human rights and freedoms set out in the Charter of the United Nations and the Universal Declaration of Human Rights, including the principle of self-determination of peoples and nations, and have the deplorable effect of increasing international tension and embittering relations between peoples,

1) *Reaffirms its conviction* that respect for the principles of the Charter of the United Nations and of the Universal Declaration of Human Rights is essential for the evolution of a peaceful world order based on the rule of law;

2) *Solemnly renews* its call for the cessation of practices which deprive the Tibetan people of their fundamental human rights and freedoms, including their right to self-determination;

3) *Expresses the hope* that Member States will make all possible efforts, as appropriate, towards achieving the purposes of the present resolution.

UNITED NATIONS GENERAL ASSEMBLY
RESOLUTION 2079 (XX)
NEW YORK, 1965

THE GENERAL ASSEMBLY,

Bearing in mind the principles relating to human rights and fundamental freedoms set forth in the Charter of the United Nations and proclaimed in the Universal Declaration of Human Rights,

Reaffirming its resolutions 1353 (XIV) of October 21, 1959 and 1723 (XVI) of December, 1961 on the question of Tibet,

Gravely concerned at the continued violation of the fundamental rights and freedoms of the people of Tibet and the continued suppression of their distinctive cultural and religious life, as evidenced by the exodus of refugees to the neighboring countries,

1) *Deplores* the continued violation of the fundamental rights and freedoms of the people of Tibet;

2) *Reaffirms* that respect for the principles of the Charter of the United Nations and of the Universal Declaration of Human Rights is essential for the evolution of a peaceful world order based on the rule of law;

3) *Declares its conviction* that the violation of human rights and fundamental freedoms in Tibet and the suppression of the distinctive cultural and religious life of its people increase international tension and embitter relations between peoples;

4) *Solemnly renews* its call for the cessation of all practices which deprive the Tibetan people of the human rights and fundamental freedoms which they have always enjoyed;

5) *Appeals* to all States to use their best endeavors to achieve the purposes of the present resolution.

Appendix III

International Parliamentary Resolutions

UNITED STATES
FOREIGN RELATIONS AUTHORIZATION ACT
FISCAL YEARS 1988 AND 1989
WASHINGTON, DC

[EXCERPT]

This act was approved and signed by President Ronald Reagan of the United States of America on the 22nd of December, 1987.

The committee of conference on the disagreeing votes of the two Houses on the amendment of the Senate to the bill (H.R. 1777) to authorize appropriations for fiscal years 1988 and 1989 for the Department of State, the United States Information Agency, the Voice of America, the Board for International Broadcasting, and for other purposes, having met, after full and free conference, have agreed to recommend and do recommend to their respective Houses as follows:

That the House recede from its disagreement to the amendment of the Senate and agree to the same with an amendment as follows:

In lieu of the matter proposed to be inserted by the Senate amendment insert the following:

SECTION 1. SHORT TITLE AND TABLE OF CONTENTS

a) SHORT TITLE: This Act may be cited as the "Foreign Relations Authorization Act, Fiscal Years 1988 and 1989."

b) TABLE OF CONTENTS: The table of contents for this Act is as follows:

TITLE 1—THE DEPARTMENT OF STATE

PART A: Authorization of Appropriations; Allocations of Funds; Restrictions

Sec 105- Other Programs.

SEC 1243—HUMAN RIGHTS VIOLATIONS IN TIBET BY THE PEOPLE'S REPUBLIC OF CHINA.

(A) FINDINGS: The Congress finds that—

(1) on October 1, 1987, Chinese police in Lhasa fired upon several thousand unarmed Tibetan demonstrators, which included hundreds of women, children, and Tibetan Buddhist monks, killing at least six and wounding many others;

(2) on September 27, 1987, a peaceful demonstration in Lhasa calling for Tibetan independence and the restoration of human rights in Tibet, which was led by hundreds of Tibetan monks, was violently broken up by Chinese authorities and 27 Tibetan Buddhist monks were arrested;

(3) in the wake of His Holiness the Dalai Lama's five point peace plan, which was presented to Members of the United States Congress during his visit to Washington in September 1987, Chinese authorities in Tibet staged, on September 24, 1987, a mass political rally at which three Tibetans were given death sentences, two of whom were executed immediately;

(4) beginning October 7, 1950, the Chinese Communist army invaded and occupied Tibet;

(5) since that time, the Chinese Government has exercised dominion over the Tibetan people, who had always considered themselves as independent, through the presence of a large occupation force;

(6) over 1,000,000 Tibetans perished from 1959 to 1979 as a direct result of the political instability, executions, imprisonment, and wide scale famine engendered by the policies of the People's Republic of China in Tibet;

(7) after 1950, particularly during the ravages of China's Cultural Revolution, over 6,000 monasteries, the repositories of 1,300 years of Tibet's ancient civilization, were destroyed and their irreplaceable national legacy of art and literature either destroyed, stolen, or removed from Tibet;

(8) the exploitation of Tibet's vast mineral, forest, and animal reserves has occurred with limited benefit to the Tibetan people;

(9) Tibet's economy and education, health, and human services remain far below those of the People's Republic of China as a whole;

(10) the People's Republic of China has encouraged a large influx of Han-Chinese into Tibet, thereby undermining the political and cultural traditions of the Tibetan people;

(11) there are credible reports of many Tibetans being incarcerated in labor camps and prisons and killed for the nonviolent expression of their religious and political beliefs;

(12) His Holiness the Dalai Lama, spiritual and temporal leader of the Tibetan people, in conjunction with the 100,000 refugees forced into exile with him, has worked tirelessly for almost thirty years to secure peace and religious freedom in Tibet, as well as the preservation of the Tibetan culture;

(13) in 1959, 1961, and 1965, the United Nations General Assembly called upon the People's Republic of China to end the violations of Tibetans' human rights;

(14) on July 24, 1985, ninety-one Members of the Congress signed a letter to President Li Xiannian of the People's Republic of China expressing support for direct talks between Beijing and representatives of His Holiness the Dalai Lama and the Tibetans-in-exile, and urging the Government of the People's Republic of China "to grant the very reasonable and justified aspirations of His Holiness the Dalai Lama and his people every consideration;"

(15) on September 27, 1987, the chairman and ranking minority member of the Senate Foreign Relations Committee, the chairman and ranking minority member of the House Foreign Affairs Committee, and the Co-Chairman of the Congressional Human Rights Caucus signed a letter to his Excellency Zhao Ziyang, the Prime Minister of the People's Republic of China, expressing their "grave concern with the present situation in Tibet and welcome(d) His Holiness the Dalai Lama's (five point) peace proposal as a historic step toward resolving the important question of Tibet and alleviating the suffering of the Tibetan people...(and) express(ing) their full support for his proposal;" and

(16) there has been no positive response by the Government of the People's Republic of China to either of these communications.

(B) STATEMENT OF POLICIES: It is the sense of the Congress that—

(1) the United States should express sympathy for those Tibetans who have suffered and died as a result of fighting, persecution, or famine over the past four decades;

(2) the United States should make the treatment of the Tibetan people an important factor in its conduct of relations with the People's Republic of China;

(3) the Government of the People's Republic of China should respect internationally-recognized human rights and end human rights violations against Tibetans;

(4) the United States should urge the Government of the People's Republic of China to actively reciprocate the Dalai Lama's efforts to establish a constructive dialogue on the future of Tibet;

(5) Tibetan culture and religion should be preserved and the Dalai Lama should be commended for his efforts in this regard;

(6) the United States, through the Secretary of State, should address and call attention to the rights of the Tibetan people, as well as other non-Han-Chinese within the People's Republic of China such as the Uighurs of Eastern Turkestan (Xinjiang), and the Mongolians of Inner Mongolia;

(7) the President should instruct United States officials, including the United States Ambassadors to the People's Republic of China and India, to pay greater attention to the concerns of the Tibetan people and to work closely with all concerned about human rights violations in Tibet in order to find areas in which the United States Government and people can be helpful; and

(8) the United States should urge the People's Republic of China to release all political prisoners in Tibet.

(C) TRANSFER OF DEFENSE ARTICLES: With respect to any sale, licensed export, or other transfer of any defense articles or defense services to the People's Republic of China, the United States Government shall, consistent with United States law, take into account the extent to which the Government of the People's Republic of China is acting in good faith and in a timely manner to resolve human rights issues in Tibet.

(D) MIGRATION AND REFUGEE ASSISTANCE: Within 60 days after the date of the enactment of this Act, the Secretary of State shall determine whether the needs of displaced Tibetans are similar to those of displace persons and refugees in other parts of the world and shall report that determination to the Congress. If the Secretary makes a positive determination, of the amounts authorized to be appropriated for the Department of State for "Migration and Refugee Assistance" for each of the fiscal years

1988 and 1989, such sums as are necessary shall be made available for assistance for displaced Tibetans. The Secretary of State shall determine the best means for providing such assistance.

(E) SCHOLARSHIPS: For each of the fiscal years 1988 and 1989, the Director of the United States Information Agency shall make available to Tibetan students and professionals who are outside Tibet no less than 15 scholarships for study at institutions of higher education in the United States.

UNITED STATES CONGRESS
S. CON. RES. 129
WASHINGTON, DC
SEPTEMBER 16, 1988

The concurrent resolution (S. Con. Res. 129) expressing the support of the Congress for the Dalai Lama and his proposal to promote peace, protect the environment, and gain democracy for the people of Tibet, was considered and agreed to.

Resolved by the Senate (the House of Representatives concurring),

SECTION 1. FINDINGS

The Congress makes the following findings:

(1) The Congress has previously expressed its concern regarding the policies of the People's Republic of China in Tibet, including the violation of Tibetan human rights, and has called on the Chinese Government to ameliorate the situation.

(2) The Dalai Lama presented a five-point peace plan for the restoration of peace and human rights in Tibet during his visit to the Congress in September 1987. This peace plan has received considerable international support.

(3) The Dalai Lama has now prepared a proposal for a democratic system of government for the people of Tibet founded on law, by agreement of the people of Tibet, for the common good and protection of themselves and their environment.

(4) The proposal of the Dalai Lama recognizes that the primary responsibility for the conduct of the foreign affairs, and the exclusive responsibility for the

defense, of Tibet will remain with the Government of the People's Republic of China, [which] in order to fulfill its defense responsibility, will be permitted to maintain a restricted number of military bases in Tibet, but these bases must be located away from population centers.

(5) The proposal of the Dalai Lama contains important measures to ensure and enhance the human rights of the Tibetan people to include the following:

(A) Specific steps will be taken to fulfill the goal of transforming the Tibetan plateau into a peace sanctuary. These steps include convening a regional security conference to determine ways to reduce regional tensions and eventually to demilitarize the Tibetan plateau and bordering regions.

(B) Tibet will be founded on a constitution, or basic law, which will provide for a democratic form of government, with an independent judiciary, and a popularly elected chief executive and legislative assembly. The basic law will contain a bill of rights which will guarantee individual human rights and democratic freedoms as expressed in the Universal Declaration of Human Rights.

(C) The basic law of Tibet will ensure the protection of the natural resources of the plateau by requiring the passage of strict laws to protect wild life and plant life and by effectively converting almost the entire area of Tibet into national park lands or biospheres.

(D) During an interim period, following the signing of an agreement based on the proposal, Tibet will be governed according to a transitional agreement providing for a gradual reorganization of the administration of Tibet, the restoration of human rights to Tibetans, and the return of the People's Republic of China of Chinese recently settled through inducement and involuntary placement by the People's Republic of China in Tibet.

(E) In order to create an atmosphere of trust conducive to fruitful discussions, the Government of the People's Republic of China should respect the human rights of the people of Tibet and not engage in a policy of transferring Chinese persons to Tibet.

(F) Before ratification of any agreement, the proposal will be submitted to the Tibetan people in a popular referendum.

(6) The Dalai Lama has asked the Government of the People's Republic of China and other concerned governments to study carefully, and respond constructively to, the substance of the proposal.

SECTION 2. EXPRESSION OF CONGRESSIONAL SUPPORT
FOR THE DALAI LAMA AND HIS PROPOSAL
FOR TIBETAN DEMOCRACY

The Congress:

(1) *Commends* the Dalai Lama for his past efforts to resolve the problems of Tibet through negotiation with the People's Republic of China, and for dissuading the Tibetan people from using violence to regain their freedom;

(2) *Commends* the Dalai Lama for his new proposal in his continued quest for peace, and expresses its support for the trust of his proposal;

(3) *Calls on* the leaders and the Government of the People's Republic of China to respond positively to the proposal of the Dalai Lama, and to enter into earnest discussions with the Dalai Lama, or his representatives, to resolve the question of Tibet along the lines proposed by the Dalai Lama; and

(4) *Calls on* the President and the Secretary of State to express the support of the United States Government for the thrust of the proposal of the Dalai Lama, and to use their best efforts to persuade the leaders and the Government of the People's Republic of China to enter into discussions with the Dalai Lama, or his representatives, regarding the proposal of the Dalai Lama and the question of Tibet.

UNITED STATES CONGRESS
S. RES. 82
WASHINGTON, DC
MARCH 15, 1989

Expressing the concern of the Senate for the
ongoing human rights abuses in Tibet

Mr. Pell (for himself, Mr. Helms, Mr. Murkowski, Mr. Kennedy, Mr. Kerry, Mr. Simon, Mr. Moynihan, and Mr. Chaffee) submitted the following resolution; which was ordered to be placed on the calendar;

Expressing the concern of the Senate for the ongoing human rights abuses in Tibet.

Whereas for the past four decades, repressive actions by the Chinese have resulted in the deaths of as many as one million Tibetans, the destruction of a large part of Tibet's unique cultural heritage, the flight of the Dalai Lama and tens of thousands of Tibetans from their homeland;

Whereas despite a short period (1978-1982) when a Chinese policy attempt was initiated to address the grievances of the Tibetan people, recent reports issued by credible human rights organizations, including Asia Watch and Amnesty International, and the international press confirm mounting human rights violations in Tibet, including arbitrary arrest and detention, the use of excessive force on peaceful demonstrators, restrictions on religious freedoms, torture, and a systematic pattern of discrimination;

Whereas Congress passed, and President Reagan signed into law on December 22, 1987, legislation stating that "the Government of the People's Republic of China should respect internationally recognized human rights and end human rights violations against Tibetans . . . and should actively reciprocate the Dalai Lama's efforts to establish a constructive dialogue on the future of Tibet;"

Whereas on September 16, 1988, the United States Senate unanimously passed S. Con. Res. 129 commending the Dalai Lama for his efforts to resolve the problems of Tibet through negotiations, supporting his proposal to promote peace, protect the environment, and gain democracy for the people of Tibet, and calling on the Government of the People's Republic of China to enter into discussions to resolve the question of Tibet along the lines proposed by the Dalai Lama;

Whereas on September 21, 1988, the Chinese Government welcomed negotiations with the Dalai Lama and stated: "the venue of the talks can be Beijing, Hong Kong, or any of the Chinese embassies and consulates abroad. Should the Dalai Lama find these places inconvenient, he can choose any place at his discretion provided that no foreigners participate in the talks,"

Whereas the Chinese Government has yet to accept negotiations with representatives of the Dalai Lama, and no such negotiations have taken place;

Whereas Tibetans continue to demonstrate in support of human rights and democratic freedoms in Tibet. On March 5, 6, and 7, 1989, at least thirty and, according to some reports, as many as sixty people died and hundreds were injured when Chinese authorities fired on unarmed Tibetan demonstrators in Lhasa;

Whereas Chinese officials in Beijing have declared martial law in the Tibetan capital of Lhasa and its environs. Western tourists in Lhasa during these demonstrations have reported random mass arrests and mistreatment of Tibetans by Chinese authorities; Now, therefore, be it

Resolved, That the Senate

(1) *Condemns* the recent use of violence against unarmed Tibetan demonstrators on March 5, 6, and 7, 1989;

(2) *Expresses* sympathy for those Tibetans who have suffered and died as a result of Chinese policies in Tibet over the past four decades;

(3) *Urges* the People's Republic of China to respect internationally recognized human rights and end human rights violations in Tibet;

(4) *Urges* the People's Republic of China to lift the government-imposed restrictions on foreign press and human rights monitoring groups in Tibet;

(5) *Urges* the Administration to propose that a United Nations observer team monitor the situation in Tibet;

(6) *Urges* the United States to make the treatment of the Tibetan people an important factor in its conduct of relations with the People's Republic of China;

(7) *Urges* the United States, through the Secretary of State, to address and call attention to, in the United Nations and in other international fora, the rights of the Tibetan people;

(8) *Supports* the efforts of the Dalai Lama and others to resolve peacefully the situation in Tibet; and

(9) *Calls upon* the Government of the People's Republic of China to meet with representatives of the Dalai Lama to begin initiating constructive dialogue on the future of Tibet.

UNITED STATES CONGRESS
H. CON. RES. 63
WASHINGTON, DC
MAY 16, 1989

Whereas on March 5, 6, and 7, 1989, Tibetans engaged in peaceful demonstrations in Lhasa were fired on by Chinese authorities, reportedly killing thirty to sixty persons and injuring hundreds;

Whereas on March 8, 1989, martial law was declared in Lhasa and its environs, and there were subsequent reports of mass arrests and mistreatment of Tibetans by Chinese authorities;

Whereas despite some Chinese efforts to address the grievances of the Tibetan people, reports issued by the International press and credible human rights organizations, including Asia Watch and Amnesty International, confirm mounting allegations of very serious violations of human rights in Tibet, including arbitrary arrest and detention, the use of excessive force on peaceful demonstrators, restrictions on religious freedoms, torture, and a systematic pattern of discrimination;

Whereas the government of the People's Republic of China has endorsed the Universal Declaration of Human Rights and has expressed its concern about human rights conditions in other countries, including South Africa and the United States;

Whereas Congress passed, and President Reagan signed into law on December 22, 1987, legislation stating that "the Government of the People's Republic of China should respect internationally-recognized human rights and end human rights violations against Tibetans ... and should actively reciprocate the Dalai Lama's efforts to establish a constructive dialogue on the future of Tibet."

Whereas although both the Government of the People's Republic of China and the Dalai Lama has declared an intention to enter into negotiations concerning the situation in Tibet, no talks yet have taken place; and

Whereas the Dalai Lama has called on Tibetans to refrain from violence; "There is no justification for violence—to use guns, or to stone people, or to burn houses,": Now therefore, be it

Resolved by the House of Representatives (the Senate concurring), That the Congress—

(1) *Condemns* the use of excessive and lethal force by the Chinese authorities in Tibet against individuals engaged in the peaceful expression of their political beliefs;

(2) *Urges* the People's Republic of China to exercise restraint in response to future peaceful demonstrations, to respect internationally recognized human rights, and to end human rights violations in Tibet;

(3) *Urges* the People's Republic of China to lift martial law in Lhasa and its environs at the earliest possible date and to admit foreign journalists and human rights monitors to Tibet;

(4) *Urges* the People's Republic of China to allow representatives of respected international humanitarian organizations to have access to prisons in Tibet;

(5) *Consistent with* section 1243 of Public Law 100-204, urges the President to continue to make respect for human rights (including the treatment of Tibetans) an important factor in United States conduct of relations with the People's Republic of China;

(6) *Urges* the executive branch, through the Secretary of State, to call attention to violations of human rights in Tibet; and

(7) *Supports* all efforts, including those of the Dalai Lama, to peacefully resolve the situation in Tibet and urges both sides to pursue a constructive dialogue for a peaceful resolution of the situation as early as possible.

WEST GERMAN BUNDESTAG
BONN, OCTOBER 15, 1987

TRANSLATION OF WEST GERMAN PARLIAMENTARY RESOLUTION ON TIBET:

Deutscher Bundestag

(West German Parliament) no. 11/953 of 14-10-87

The parliamentary parties of the CDU/CSU (Christian Democrats), SPD (Social Democrats), FPD (Liberals), and DIE GRUENEN (Green Party) propose a motion on Human Rights Violations in Tibet which was initiated by Petra K. Kelly, MdB.

Parliament may pass the following:

> Despite some liberalizing steps on the part of the Chinese Government, which are to be commended, there are still violations of Human Rights on the part of the Government of the People's Republic of China going on.

> With growing concern the German Parliament notes that the situation in Tibet has changed for the worse during the last weeks.

The German Parliament asks the Federal Government to support that:

1) The Government of the People's Republic of China should respect internationally accepted Human Rights and should put an end to violations of Human Rights towards Tibetans,

2) The Government of the People's Republic of China should react positively to the efforts of the Dalai Lama to come to a constructive dialogue,

3) The significant wishes of the Tibetan People should be recognized to preserve Tibetan culture and religion and find out ways to enable the German people and the Government to help,

4) All political prisoners in Tibet should be freed,

5) The Federal Government, in Consultation with the High Commissioner for Refugees of the United Nations, should find out what active help may be necessary and appropriate to specially preserve cultural identity of Tibetan refugees,

6) A fair number of scholarships be given to Tibetan youth, students and scholars in German schools, universities, and other institutes of learning.

[THE ABOVE MOTION WAS PASSED BY THE HOUSE UNANIMOUSLY ON OCTOBER 15, 1987]

WEST GERMAN BUNDESTAG
BONN, MARCH 28, 1990

TRANSLATION OF WEST GERMAN PARLIAMENTARY RESOLU-
TION ON TIBET:

Deutscher Bundestag

(W-German Parliament) no. 11/4264 of 28-3-90

Recommendation for a resolution and report of the Committee on Foreign Affairs concerning the motion tabled by Petra Kelly, Member of the German Bundestag and the parliamentary group of THE GREENS.

HUMAN RIGHTS VIOLATIONS AND MARTIAL LAW IN TIBET

A. Problem

In a resolution unanimously adopted on October 15, 1987, the German Bundestag expressed its concern about human rights violations in Tibet. It must now be stated that, as a result of further human rights violations and the imposition of martial law in parts of Tibet by the Government of the People's Republic of China on March 8, 1989, the situation of the Tibetan people has deteriorated further. Chinese security forces used force to combat peaceful demonstrations.

B. Solution

The Federal Government is called upon to use its influence to induce the Government of the People's Republic of China to accede to the human rights covenants of the United Nations, to lift the martial law imposed in parts of Tibet and to acknowledge that suppression and the use of force are not suitable means of solving political conflicts. The German Bundestag welcomes the Dalai Lama's calls for a nonviolent solution to the Tibetan conflict and the fact that the interests and rights of the Tibetan people are being taken into consideration in the Federal Government's contacts with the Chinese leadership.

RECOMMENDATION FOR A RESOLUTION

The Bundestag is called upon to adopt the following resolution:

I. The German Bundestag states that:

The German Bundestag first expressed its concern about human rights violations in Tibet in a resolution unanimously adopted on October 15, 1987; it is dismayed to note that the situation in Tibet has since deteriorated even further. Not only do fundamental human rights of the Tibetan people continue to be systematically violated, but the martial law imposed by the Chinese Government in parts of Tibet on Wednesday, March 8, 1989, is still in force as well. This measure was preceded by peaceful demonstrations which, according to all independent sources of information, escalated into violence on both sides only after Chinese security forces had opened fire on the Tibetan demonstrators. The number of victims is still unknown. Several eyewitnesses speak of several hundred dead. Further bloodshed is to be feared.

In an urgent appeal on March 6, 1989, the Dalai Lama called upon politicians, parliaments, and governments throughout the world to help put an end to the continuing human rights violations in Tibet and to encourage the Chinese Government to find a peaceful solution to the Tibetan conflict. Parliaments, governments, and the United Nations are responsible for international peace and respect for human rights all over the world. This responsibility includes using peaceful, political means to defend the rights of the Tibetan people *vis-à-vis* the Government of the People's Republic of China.

The German Bundestag regards the right of every individual to inviolability of his person, worldwide protections of internationally-recognized human rights and the preservation of internal and external peace to be the most important basis of the Federal Republic's foreign policy. This human rights aspect must of course also play a major role in the further development of relations between the People's Republic of China and the Federal Republic of Germany.

II. The German Bundestag

Calls upon the Government of the People's Republic of China to accede to the human rights covenants of the United Nations;

Calls upon the Government of the People's Republic of China to recognize that political conflicts cannot be solved by suppression and the use of force, without delay to lift the martial law imposed in parts of Tibet and to guarantee freedom of reporting in Tibet;

Welcomes the Dalai Lama's repeated calls for the Tibetan conflict to be resolved by nonviolent means;

Welcomes the fact that the Government of the People's Republic of China has expressed it s willingness in principle to engage in direct talks;

Calls upon the Government of the People's Republic of China to furnish evidence of its willingness to enter into negotiations by lifting martial law, respecting human rights, and stopping the further transfer of Chinese citizens to Tibet, and to respond in an equally constructive manner to the Dalai Lama's constructive negotiating offer and not to procrastinate by continually expressing new reservations, so that in this way the talks can be brought to a peaceful conclusion acceptable to both sides as soon as possible;

Supports the efforts being made by human rights organizations, in the light of the *de facto* ban on reporting imposed in Tibet, to send an independent international commission of inquiry to Tibet to hear, on the spot, eyewitnesses of the recent unrest and to look into the current human rights situation.

Welcomes the fact that in its contacts with the Chinese Government the Federal Government has paid greater attention to the interests and rights of the Tibetan people;

Calls upon the Federal Government to urge the Government of the People's Republic of China to lift, without delay, the martial law imposed in parts of Tibet and respect human rights, with Tibet's cultural identity being preserved;

Calls upon the Federal Government to follow the example of Canada and the Netherlands and to raise the subject of the human rights situation in Tibet in the bodies of the United Nations, particularly in the UN Commission on Human Rights, and to make greater use of the bodies and resources of the United Nations to improve the human rights situation and the political and ecological situation in Tibet;

Calls upon the Federal Government to support in an appropriate manner efforts to send an independent international commission to investigate the human rights situation in Tibet.

Report submitted by Members of Parliament, Dr. Volkmar Köhler, Freimut Duve and Petra Kelly

At the 151st sitting on June 1, 1989, the motion tabled by Petra Kelly, Member of the German Bundestag and the parliamentary group of THE GREENS—printed paper 11/4262 (rev.)—was referred in a simplified procedure without a debate to the Committee on Economic Cooperation as the committee asked for an opinion.

As a result of the amendment moved by Petra Kelly, Member of the German Bundestag, on October 5, 1989, and the Subcommittee on Human Rights and Humanitarian Aid of the Committee on Foreign Affairs on February 14, 1990, and was taken into consideration in their statements.

The Subcommittee on Human Rights and Humanitarian Aid of the Committee on Foreign Affairs proposed this recommendation for a resolution, which was unanimously approved by the Committee on Foreign Affairs at its 66th meeting on March 28, 1990.

[THE WEST GERMAN BUNDESTAG PASSED THE ABOVE RESOLUTION UNANIMOUSLY, OCTOBER, 1990.]

THE AUSTRALIAN SENATE
DECEMBER 6, 1990

SENATE MOTION ON TIBET

THAT THE SENATE:

a) Expresses its deep concern about the current situation in Tibet;

b) Recognizes that human rights abuses have been committed in Tibet by the People's Republic of China since 1959, and that human rights abuses are reportedly continuing;

c) Endorses Resolutions No. 1353 of 1959, No. 1723 of 1961, and No. 2079 of 1965 of the United Nations General Assembly;

d) Endorses the call for the cessation of practices which deprive the Tibetan people of their fundamental human rights and freedoms;

e) Commends the Dalai Lama and his representatives for consistently rejecting the use of violence, and notes that this was acknowledged in the awarding of the 1989 Nobel Peace Prize to the Dalai Lama;

f) Endorses the representations made by the Australian Government and by members of this Parliament to the People's Republic of China on alleged human rights abuses, generally and in Tibet;

g) Calls on the Chinese Government to:

i) Recognize the fundamental human rights and freedoms of the Tibetan people as set out in the Universal Declaration of Human Rights and the International Covenants, including the right to practice their cultural and religious traditions without fear of persecution, arrest, or torture;

ii) Enter into earnest discussions, without preconditions, with the Dalai Lama and his representatives with a view to reducing tensions in Tibet; and

iii) Respond to representations made by the Australian Government and by members of this Parliament on allegations of human rights abuses, and the human rights situation in general in Tibet; and

h) Calls on the Australian Government to continue to make representations to, and seek responses from, the Government of the People's Republic of China on allegations of human rights abuses in Tibet.

Appendix IV

Excerpts from Declarations
of International Hearings on Tibet

BONN INTERNATIONAL AND NON-PARTISAN HEARING
"TIBET AND HUMAN RIGHTS"
BONN, WEST GERMANY, APRIL 1989

We, the participants of the Hearing on Tibet and Human Rights, have come together from all parts of the world and have listened to the testimonies of Tibetans, some of whom have recently fled their country, and reports from scholars, eyewitnesses, Parliamentarians, and other concerned people on all aspects of the Tibetan situation.

We *condemn* the continued illegal occupation of Tibet, the gross and systematic violations of human rights, the destruction of the environment, and the overwhelming military presence in Tibet.

We *insist* that the People's Republic of China immediately lift martial law and release all those who have been imprisoned in the course of their struggle for human rights and freedom.

We *affirm* our belief in the freedom of Tibet and the inalienable right of the Tibetan people to assert this freedom and call upon the People's Republic of China to respect the right of the Tibetan people to determine their own future, free of foreign interference, in accordance with the UN General Assembly Resolution 1723 of 1961 and to allow free access to Tibet to independent international human rights organizations and press.

We *strongly endorse* the Five-Point Peace Plan as presented by H.H. the Dalai Lama.

We *urge* the People's Republic of China to enter into sincere and substantive negotiations with representatives appointed by H.H. the Dalai Lama.

We *call* upon governments, political leaders, and all concerned persons to take all possible measures to further the cause of the Tibetan people.

We, the participants of this hearing, confirm that we will join in our efforts to draw attention to this resolution, to approach Parliamentarians and Governments to take up the issue of Tibet and to hold similar hearings and conferences.

THE INTERNATIONAL CONVENTION
ON TIBET AND PEACE IN SOUTH ASIA
NEW DELHI, INDIA, AUGUST 1989

THE CONVENTION:

Expresses its belief that historically and legally Tibet has been a free country with its distinct culture, language, and history;

Condemns the continuing illegal occupation of Tibet by China and calls upon the Chinese to respect the UN Declaration contained in the Resolution of the General Assembly, No.1514 that "The subjection of peoples to alien subjugation, domination, and exploitation constitutes a denial of fundamental human rights;"

Expresses its outrage at the brutality perpetrated against the Tibetan people by the Chinese government and the systematic efforts to destroy the Tibetan identity by taking recourse to infanticide and population transfer;

Calls upon the People's Republic of China to acknowledge the right of the Tibetan people to decide their own future, free of any foreign interference in accordance with the Resolution of the UN General Assembly No. 1723 of 1961;

Demands that the People's Republic of China at once lift the martial law imposed on Tibet in March 1989 and release all those who have been detained with or without trial in the course of their struggle for human rights and freedom;

Seeks a more active involvement of the United Nations on the issue of Tibet and urges the UN to grant observer status to the representatives of the Dalai Lama;

Endorses the Five-Point Peace Plan of His Holiness the Dalai Lama and urges the Chinese government to open negotiations with the representatives of the Dalai Lama on the basis of this Peace Plan;

Asks the governments of India and China to take positive steps to demilitarize the Himalayan region and ensure that Tibet becomes a zone of peace in accordance with the wishes of its people;

Appeals to the free peoples of the world to extend their support to the cause of the Tibetan people both in the matter of their human right and their right to live as the free people of a free country;

Urges the government of India to acknowledge its responsibility for Tibet and appreciate the importance of a free Tibet to ensure peace between India and China and generally in South Asia; and

Calls upon the governments of the world to use their moral and political power to persuade the People's Republic of China [to] respect the wishes of the Tibetan People.

THE INTERNATIONAL CONSULTATION ON TIBET
LONDON, JULY 1990

NOTING WITH ANXIETY:

the critical situation in Tibet where the Tibetan people's inalienable right to self-determination continues to be denied and where the fundamental individual human rights and freedoms of the Tibetan people, including both civil and political rights and economic, social, and cultural rights continue to be violated by the People's Republic of China;

SOLEMNLY DECLARE THEIR SUPPORT:

for the full implementation of the rights of the Tibetan people throughout Tibet, not only in the recently created "Autonomous Region of Tibet," but in all areas historically part of Tibet;

for the acknowledgment of the Tibetan Government-in-Exile and His Holiness the Dalai Lama, Tibet's exiled Head of State, as the sole legitimate representatives of the Tibetan people;

for the Tibetan effort to regain freedom by means of nonviolent action under the leadership of His Holiness the Dalai Lama, Nobel Peace Prize Laureate;

CALLS UPON THE PEOPLE'S REPUBLIC OF CHINA:

to start, without further delay, genuine negotiations with the representatives designated by His Holiness the Dalai Lama for a peaceful transfer of power leading to independence for the Tibetan people in accordance with their inalienable rights and based on the Five-Point Peace Plan;

to cease all practices which deny the Tibetan people their individual human rights and freedoms, including the right to life, movement, religious belief, free speech, and assembly;

to cease all practices which violate the rights of the Tibetan people to self-determination and in particular to the policy of population transfer.

URGES THE GOVERNMENTS OF THE WORLD:

Call for the cessation of all executions and the release of all political prisoners;

Take the necessary measures in their relations with the People's Republic of China to advance the demands set out in the above paragraphs of this Declaration to secure the implementation of the Tibetan people's rights;

Actively pursue the question of the rights of Tibet at the United Nations and in the European Community, the Non-Aligned Movement, the Organization of African Unity, the Organization of American States, the South Asian Association for Regional Cooperation (SARC), and the Association of South East Asian Nations (ASEAN).

Acknowledge and where consistent with state practice, recognize the Tibetan Government-in-Exile and His Holiness the Dalai Lama as the sole and legitimate representatives of the Tibetan people;

Adopt other appropriate measures to support the nonviolent Tibetan struggle;

THE INTERNATIONAL CONVENTION ON ASIAN PEACE
TOKYO, MAY 1990

The years 1989 and 1990 have witnessed major democratic and economic changes worldwide. Peoples and nations in all continents are in the process of exercising their right to self-determination.

The situation in Asia gives cause for serious concern. Of particular concern is China's repressions of the democratic movement in China and of the legitimate demands of Tibet, the peoples of East Turkestan, and Inner Mongolia for self-determination.

The concern shown for the plight of Tibet by an ever-increasing number of governments, political parties, statesmen, and other people the world over is very encouraging. Yet, the level of concern shown for what is undoubtedly one of the most tragic situations in our time and one which seriously threatens the peace and stability of Asia, is till insufficient to bring about the necessary change there.

The delegates to the Convention resolve:

Whereas regional and world peace must be founded on mutual respect of nations and peoples and can result only from the recognition and realization of the legitimate aspirations of nations and peoples for freedom and human rights including, in particular. the right to self-determination;

Whereas, the repression of a people and violation of its dignity and human rights, including the right to self-determination by an other people or its government poses a serious threat to peace and stability and is a violation of international law, including the Charter of the United Nations;

Whereas, Tibet has, during its long history of independent statehood, greatly contributed to the heritage of humankind by its rich and unique culture and spiritual tradition and by its pursuit of the values of Peace and Humanity;

Whereas, the continued military occupation of Tibet and repression of the Tibetan people by the People's Republic of China as well as the mass population transfer implemented by the Chinese authorities in areas inhabited by Tibetans for centuries constitute a serious violation of the human rights of the Tibetan people, in particular the right to self-determination, and a threat to peace in Asia.

Demands that the Government of the People's Republic of China

- cease practices which deny the Tibetan people fundamental human rights and freedoms including the right to free speech, assembly, movement, religious belief, and self-determination;
- reverse the policy of population transfer which is reducing Tibetans to a minority in their own country;
- restore to the Tibetan people control and ownership of all political, economic, social, religious, and cultural institutions and resources;

Appendix V

Martial Law Decrees

Issued by Dorjie Ceiring, Chairman of the People's Government of the Tibet Autonomous Region

ORDER NO. 1 OF THE PEOPLE'S GOVERNMENT OF THE
TIBET AUTONOMOUS REGION, MARCH 7, 1989

In accordance with the martial law issued by the State Council, the People's Government of the Tibet Autonomous Region has issued the following orders:

1. Start from zero hour of March 9, 1989, a martial law will be enforced in Lhasa city proper and in the area west of Lhamo Township, Dazi County and east of Dongga Township, Duilong Deqing County.

2. During the time of the enforcement of the martial law, assemblies, demonstrations, strikes by workers, students and other people, petitions, and other get-togethers are strictly forbidden.

3. Traffic control measures will be implemented in the martial-law-enforced-area. People and vehicles entering and going out of the area must go through formalities according to the regulations and receive security inspections.

4. Without permissions, foreigners are not allowed to enter the martial-law-enforced-area. Foreigners who are now in the martial-law-enforced-area must leave within a definite time, except those who have permissions.

5. Firearms and ammunition possessed illegally should be taken over. People who are not entrusted with the task of enforcing the martial law are not allowed to carry firearms, ammunition, and other dangerous articles.

6. Public security organs and people entrusted with the task of enforcing the martial law have the right to search the riot-creating suspects and places where criminals are possibly hidden.

7. Those who resist to carry out the martial law and instigate others to do the same will be severely punished according to the law.

ORDER NO. 2 OF THE PEOPLE'S GOVERNMENT OF THE TIBET AUTONOMOUS REGION, MARCH 7, 1989

In order to safeguard the unity of the motherland, ensure the safety of citizens and personal property and protect public property from violation, the People's Government of the Tibet Autonomous Region specially issues the following orders:

1. It absolutely bans anyone, in any case and in any form, to instigate split of the country, create riots, group people to attack government offices, damage public property, [or] undertake such sabotaging actions as lighting, smashing, robbing, and arson.

2. Once the above-mentioned action happens, public security and police force and the PLA men on patrol have the right to take necessary and strong measures to put the action down at once. Those who make above-mentioned action will be detained right on the spot, and if resistance occurs, police and armymen on duty can deal with them according to the law.

3. Any government institutions, units, mass organizations, and citizens must immediately send criminals either found in operation or detected afterwards to judicial organs.

4. The judicial organs should make investigations of the crimes as soon as possible, handle cases without delay and give them heavy punishment in accordance with relevant decisions and articles of "The Decision of the Standing Committee of the National People's Congress on Heavy Punishment to Criminals Who Seriously Violate Public Security" and "Criminal Law."

ORDER NO. 3 OF THE PEOPLE'S GOVERNMENT OF THE TIBET AUTONOMOUS REGION, MARCH 7, 1989

In accordance with the martial law of the State Council, the People's Government of the Tibet Autonomous Region has decided that traffic control will be enforced during the time of martial law. It specially issues the following orders:

1. All kinds of motor-driven vehicles cannot pass without the special permit or provisional passes issued by the traffic police brigade of the Lhasa Public Security Bureau. The persons who have the provisional pass must go through the designated way and within the fixed time.

2. Cadres and staff members must have identity cards or certificates issued by their units; the officials and soldiers of the People's Liberation Army and the police force must have armyman's permits; the officials and soldiers of the public security departments must have employees' cards or the identity cards on patrol duty; students in schools must have their students' identity cards or schools' certificates; monks and nuns must have the certificates issued by the democratic management committees of their monasteries; the preschool children should move about with adults.

3. All kinds of motor-driven vehicles on entering the martial-law-enforced-area must show certificates issued by the people's government of county level or above, and apply for provisional passes; persons from out of Lhasa on entering the martial-law-enforced-area must have certificates issued by the people's government of county level or above and must go through formalities for temporary residence within five hours after entering the area; cadres, workers, and staff members of the Tibet Autonomous Region back from holidays and official business can enter the area with certificates which establish their identities.

4. Motor-driven vehicles and persons leaving the martial-law-enforced-area must be approved by leaders of county level or above and have their unit's certificates.

5. Motor-driven vehicles and persons passing within the martial-law-enforced-area or entering and going out of the area must receive security inspection by police and armymen.

6. If any persons violate the above-mentioned orders, the people on patrol duty have the right to examine them according to the different cases, adopt mandatory measures on the spot and even look into responsibility for a crime.

ORDER NO. 4 OF THE PEOPLE'S GOVERNMENT OF THE TIBET AUTONOMOUS REGION, MARCH 8, 1989

In order to ensure the security of aliens in the martial-law-enforced-area, the People's Government of the Tibet Autonomous Region issues the following orders:

During the time of the enforcement of the martial law in Lhasa City, aliens cannot enter the area without permission. Aliens now in Lhasa must observe "martial law" issued by the State Council of the People's Republic of China and Orders of the People's Government of the Tibet Autonomous Region.

Foreign guests to Lhasa invited by the People's Government of the Tibet Autonomous Region and by other government organs must show "the Pass of the People's Republic of China" (which is called "Pass" for short below) issued by the Foreign Affairs Office of the People's Government of the Region when entering and going out of the area.

Foreign specialists and foreign staff members of joint ventures working in Lhasa must show "Pass" issued by public security authorities when entering and going out of the area.

Aliens who have obtained the right of residence in Lhasa must show valid residence identity cards when entering and going out of the area.

Foreign tourist groups organized by tourist agencies now staying in the Region can enter and go out of the area, only if they are accompanied by Chinese guides with "Pass" issued by the public security authorities.

Unorganized foreign tourists now staying in Lhasa must leave in the time fixed by the public security authorities.

The "Pass" will be obtained at the Foreign Section of the Lhasa Public Security Bureau with "Residence Identity Card for Alien" issued by the public security authorities.

ORDER NO. 5 OF THE PEOPLE'S GOVERNMENT OF THE TIBET AUTONOMOUS REGION, MARCH 8, 1989

In order to fully reflect the policy of "leniency towards those who confess their crimes and severe punishment to those who refuse to do so, atone for a crime by good deeds and render outstanding service to receive awards," and to resolutely crack down [on] the separatists and those who have committed serious crimes of fighting, smashing, robbing, and arson, the People's Government of the Tibet Autonomous Region has issued the following orders:

Those who have plotted, created and participated in riots, committed fighting, smashing, robbing, and arson, and given shelter to criminals and booty must surrender themselves to the police at once, so that they can receive leniency.

Those who know the facts of separatists' activities and crimes of fighting, smashing, robbing, and arson should expose and report the cases to their units or to the public security authorities. Those people should be protected. Those who retaliate people who inform against them shall be severely punished.

Appendix VI

Organizing a Tibet Support Group

The International Campaign for Tibet and the U.S. Tibet Committee urge universities, communities, and concerned individuals to form groups to promote awareness of the Tibetan cause. The guidelines outlined here are designed to provide concrete, attainable goals for small or large groups and for groups already formed.

Tibet support groups have an unprecedented opportunity to further raise the level of awareness and concern about the struggle going on inside Tibet. Since October 1987, the continued demonstrations in Tibet against Chinese rule have aroused world concern about arbitrary arrests, detention, and imprisonment without trial, the routine torture of political prisoners, forced abortions and sterilization of Tibetan women, and China's devastating impact on Tibet's environment, culture, and education. In the 1980s, the massive transfer of Chinese settlers into Tibet reduced Tibetans to a second-class minority in their own land. Today, despite the Chinese claim of greater leniency, there is little religious or political freedom in Tibet, and the drive to impose Chinese culture and values on the Tibetan people is being carried out with renewed fervor. The result is the annihilation of the Tibetans as a distinct people through the destruction of a rich and spiritual culture. Thousands of Tibetan men, women, and children have been arrested in recent years for their opposition to Chinese rule.

FORMING A GROUP

Gathering a nucleus of people is the first step to forming a Tibet support group. Choose a name, a statement of purpose and, for university groups, apply for official recognition. Groups formed to promote human rights in countries such as South Africa serve as good examples for organization and activities. Many of these organizations are eager to help a new group start up and provide information and support.

Plan monthly or bimonthly meetings in a public place such as a university classroom. Establish a telephone number with an answering machine and keep a current message which gives the time and place of the next meeting. Let people find their strengths and take responsibility for areas in which they are interested—media, political contacts, ecology, fund-raising, or organizing events. Make certain newcomers are made to feel welcome and oriented as to what is going on in your group.

LETTER WRITING

Letter writing is one of the most effective and time-efficient activities to raise the awareness of your Congressional representatives, administration officials, writer and editors of newspapers and magazines, and many others to Tibet's plight. Letters to your own elected representatives are the most important. But don't hesitate to write to a legislator who does not directly represent you if he or she chairs or serves on a committee considering legislation of importance. As few as five to ten letters from concerned constituents to a Congressional representative may be perceived as a significant number. By setting up a table in a highly visible location you will accomplish several purposes: getting many letters written and names signed on a petition, educating people about Tibet, distributing literature, heightening visibility of your group, and potentially raising some funds.

Letters to Congress should stress the need for hearings and legislation on Tibet. In response to your letters, if members of Congress do not state their position on Tibet, ask them directly. Also, identify the legislative aide who handles foreign affairs. This is actually the person who is responsible for informing the Congressperson, responding to constituents as well as drafting legislation. Try to meet your Representative when he or she is in the district and develop a working relationship with the staff. The International Campaign for Tibet has an Action Alert! network to whom it sends emergency appeals. These appeals, which your group will periodically receive, request that you promptly write letters on behalf of a Tibetan prisoner or a certain incident.

SPEAKERS & EVENTS

Hosting a speaker, a cultural event, or a movie provides a forum to educate, organize, and raise funds. Universities, churches, community centers, and museums are excellent locations for events. Members of your group can also offer to give a talk or show slides to community groups, high schools, nursing homes, and then encourage them to write letters and sign petitions. Co-sponsoring events with other campus, local, or national organizations will cut costs, increase turnout and develop alliances with well-established, larger organizations.

NETWORKING

The goal of networking is to involve the members and leaders of other organizations by supplying them with information and proposing some concrete action that they can take. Co-sponsoring an event, including an article about Tibet in their magazine or newsletter, getting their leaders and members to write and sign petitions to Congress, are examples of mutually-beneficial projects. The importance of developing relationships with groups who already support or would be willing to address Tibetan issues should not be underestimated.

If possible, become a member of local human rights, peace, environmental, religious, medical, or legal groups and start a Tibet project or committee for them. Outreach to Chinese-American communities, and particularly to Chinese nationals studying in the U.S. is vital. With 36,000 Chinese nationals now studying in the U.S., we have a tremendous opportunity to exchange views and information on Tibet. The "Tibet Forum," a new Chinese language newspaper, is an excellent tool for this outreach. Some members of your group or people in the community may be interested in providing assistance to Tibetan exiles in India and Nepal. Pamphlets are available which outline how you can sponsor a Tibetan monk or student in India. You can also adopt a prisoner or be a pen-pal with a Tibetan in exile. Tibetans living in exile are also in need of books, school, and science supplies.

MEDIA

Working with the media is an exciting and important function to any cause. The key here is developing personal contact with writers and editors. Find out the appropriate names of people and contact them to get acquainted. If you are hosting an event, invite them. Provide them with information and/or ask if they would accept an article or opinion/editorial on Tibet. College, local, and state-wide papers are often amenable to freelance submissions. Articles can be condensed from school papers or developed and researched from the "Tibet Press Watch." Be very straightforward and professional in letting writers and editors know what you want and why they should cover this issue. Whenever a paper carries an article relating to Tibet, or fails to mention it when they should, write a letter to the editor applauding, criticizing, or adding to it. (The Campaign for Tibet would appreciate receiving articles for inclusion in the "Tibet Press Watch.") A "press kit" will not only assist and encourage the media to write articles, but also serve as a future reference. A "press kit" can be as simple as a cover letter from your group and a few relevant articles to one loaded with reports from Amnesty International, Asia Watch, UN and Congressional Resolutions, and books.

BOYCOTTS, VIGILS, AND DIRECT ACTION

Many different forms of nonviolent protest are developing spontaneously around the world. Every March 10 there are marches, demonstrations, and vigils in New York, San Francisco, Los Angeles, Washington, DC, and many other cities. Grace Springs began standing outside the Chinese Embassy in Washington, D.C. every Friday with a Tibetan flag and literature for people passing by. The idea spread to Tibet support groups worldwide to have a weekly vigil at every Chinese embassy or consulate around the globe.

Create your own media event: candlelight vigils around a building where a Chinese official is addressing a college or community group; guerilla theater in widely-accessible, public places; mock funerals and processions with flags; and picketing. Holding your event on or near an auspicious date may help increase media attention (October 1, Chinese National Day; first new moon on the lunar year, usually in early February; Tibetan New Year; March 10, anniversary of the 1959 uprising; July 6, His Holiness' birthday). Ten mayors and governors in Arizona, California, Florida, Maine, Massachusetts, Minnesota, New Jersey, New York, Rhode Island, and Wisconsin have already proclaimed March 10th to commemorate the Tibetan national uprising of 1959. Consumer boycotts of goods originating in the PRC are developing in many communities. Let companies, investment brokers, and socially responsible investment groups know that you don't want your money going to companies who do business in China. Request that China be included in their negative screens (lists of countries to avoid investing in and companies who do business with these countries). Ask your Congressperson to support legislation that ties the sale of arms and high technology to improvements of human rights in Tibet.

Whenever you hold an event, be certain to give people the opportunity to add their names to your mailing list. Your mailing list will be a key tool for fund-raising and disseminating information.

Fund-Raising

Fund-raising possibilities range from sponsoring events, annual dues and selling t-shirts to working with a fund-raiser and direct mail. While some groups will not need many funds, larger and more ambitious groups will need funds for copying, postage, phone calls, speakers, and for opening office space. Groups have sponsored fund-raising dinners and benefits with speakers or entertainment at a local restaurant or club. College groups have the advantage of funds available for student activities. Many groups have successfully solicited moderate donations from individuals in their communities. Be creative. Don't be afraid to think big.

Additional Resources

Resources are available to keep your group informed and to distribute to others. The three organizations listed below will regularly send you mailings, provide speakers, films and petitions and assist with volunteer and student research projects. The International Campaign for Tibet is a non-profit organization based in Washington, D.C. that monitors and publicizes current human rights conditions in Tibet and works toward a negotiated solution to the Tibetan problem. The International Campaign for Tibet actively works with human rights groups, the U.S. Congress, and the media. The Campaign also publishes the "Tibet Press Watch," a bimonthly compilation of articles on Tibet from papers around the world.

The U.S. Tibet Committee is a network of grass roots Tibet support groups whose primary focus is to transform people's compassion and understanding of Tibet's religion, history, and culture into political action. New groups that become official chapters of the U.S. Tibet Committee may have the advantage of soliciting tax-exempt donations.

The Office of Tibet represents His Holiness the Dalai Lama and the Tibetan Government-in-Exile, based in Dharamsala, India. It is the official liaison between the Government-in-Exile and Tibetan communities in North America. In addition to publishing "News Tibet," a bimonthly newsletter, the Office of Tibet has an extensive bookstore, a library of video tapes and current documentaries from inside Tibet, and films on Tibetan culture and history. The Office of Tibet also is a network center for Tibetan Buddhist centers in North America. Literature and resources available from the above groups at no cost include copies of the "Tibet Press Watch," "The Tibetan Review, "News Tibet," and an assortment of handouts, pamphlets, and reports from human rights groups and others. A box of books is also available from the Office of Tibet at cost, which can be resold, such as John Avedon's *In Exile From the Land of Shows*, and Michael van Walt van Praag's *The Status of Tibet*.

Taken from a document created through the combined efforts of the International Campaign for Tibet and the New England Regional Office of the U.S. Tibet Committee.

Appendix VII

Ethical Guidelines for Travel to Tibet

There are those who feel that traveling to Tibet in itself is not ethical because it is mainly the Chinese who benefit from tourism. On the other hand, tourists been a conduit for information from and to the Tibetans.

If you decide to travel in Tibet, as is the case in every country, there are certain dos and don'ts that travelers should follow. In general, Tibetans are very easygoing, accommodating, and quick to laugh. However, because Tibetans are struggling to regain their independence from China and to restore freedom of expression and religious belief, they ask foreigners to follow certain principles. Here are some of those principles along with other helpful hints.

RELIGION AND CULTURE

• *Observe Customs.* Tibetans are an extremely religious people and appreciate foreigners respecting a few simple customs: always walk clockwise around temples, religious sites and within monasteries. Take hats off when visiting monasteries (even when it is cold!). Don't smoke.

• *Support Religious Freedom.* Donations left on altars or donation boxes in the large monasteries will go to a committee controlled by the Chinese authorities. Donations can be made directly to individual monks or given in-kind. Clothing, food, film, or books are much appreciated. Donations to smaller, out of the way monasteries will be used properly, according to traditional Tibetan custom since they are not so regulated by Chinese authorities.

SHOPPING

• *Buy From Tibetans.* If you want to support Tibetans, Tibetan culture, and the Tibetan economy, buy from Tibetan shops and stalls. You will notice a large influx of Chinese immigrants in Lhasa who are now taking over Lhasa's economy and putting Tibetans out of work. The

Dalai Lama has called this influx possibly the greatest threat to the survival of Tibetan culture.

• *Do Not Buy Antiques.* Most of Tibet's artistic treasures have already been destroyed or plundered by Chinese forces and immigrants. Please leave antiques in Tibet. Since it is difficult to tell what is antique and what is not, a good rule of thumb to follow is that if someone tries to sell you something secretly, don't buy it. Stick to the public stores and stalls.

ECO-TOURISM

• *Help Protect Tibet's Wildlife.* Do not buy animal products made from wild animals, especially from endangered species (i.e. pelts of the snow leopard, the common leopard and tiger; horns of Tibetan antelopes; paws of the Himalayan brown bear). If you see these items, please take a photograph and notify World Wildlife Fund or the International Campaign for Tibet.

• *Leave Only Footprints.* The Himalayan eco-system is fragile. If you go trekking use kerosene even where wood is available. Wet trash should be buried (100 feet from streams), paper burned and cans and bottles packed out with you to a hotel or large town. (Do not leave this up to your guide since environmental awareness is often low.)

GROUP TRAVEL

• *Use Knowledgable Tibetan Guides.* Travel to Tibet is only permitted in groups at present and all travel companies must work through a travel operator in Lhasa. It is important to select a company which works with a Lhasa-based operator run and staffed by Tibetans as opposed to Chinese. To quote one experienced tour guide, "When you go to France you don't want a German tour guide; when you go to Tibet you don't want a Chinese one." Moreover, using Tibetan-staffed companies promotes Tibetan culture and employs Tibetans. The recommended companies are Lhasa Travel and the Chinese Workers Travel Service (CWTS); the ones to avoid are China International Travel Service (CITS) and China Youth Travel Service (CYTS). Ask your travel agent which one they use.

• *Break Away From the Group.* Almost all the people who visits Tibet say that the best part was their interaction with Tibetans. Photos of your family and neighborhood are great "conversation pieces"— don't worry about the language barrier.

WHAT TO BRING (AND NOT TO BRING!)

• *Be Prepared for Border Crossings.* The best presents for Tibetans are photos and postcards of the Dalai Lama. However, postcards with his signature may be confiscated at the border. Also, books by the Dalai Lama (and sometimes about the Dalai Lama) are often confiscated.

• *Be Informed.* The best guidebook to Tibet is *The Tibet Guide* by Stephen Batchelor. Also good are *Power Places of Central Tibet* by Keith Dowman, and *Tibet: A Complete Guide* by Elisabeth Booz. Since you are likely to be on a tour with an official government guide, do not expect accurate answers to historical or political questions. Educate yourself before you leave.

Appendix VIII

Organizations That Support Tibet

TIBETAN GOVERNMENT OFFICES

Rep. Kasur Tashi Wangdi
Bureau of H.H. The Dalai Lama
10 Ring Road
Lajpat Nagar IV
New Delhi, 110024, INDIA

Paljor Tsering
Gadhen Khangsar
P.O. Box No. 310
Lazimpat
Kathmandu, NEPAL

Sonam Topgyal
Information Office
Central Tibetan Secretariat
Gangchen Kyishong - 176215
Dharamsala, H.P., INDIA

Kalon Tenzin Tethong
The Kashag
Central Tibetan Secretariat
Gangchen Kyishong - 176215
Dharamsala, H.P., INDIA

Kasur Tenzin Geyche Tethong
Office of HH the Dalai Lama
Thekchen Choling, 176219
Mcleod Ganj, Dharamsala
Himal Pradesh, INDIA

Rep. Thubten Norbu
Office of Tibet
Sukaisu Kerepa 205 (2F)
Oyamadae 2 Shome 19-14
Denenchobu, Setiagaya - KV
Tokyo, JAPAN

Dicky Y. Tsün/Buchen Tsering
Office of Tibet
Waffenplatz Straße 10
CH-8002 Zurich, SWITZERLAND

Kesang Takhla
Office of Tibet
Linburn House
342 Kilburn High Road
London NW6 2QJ
UNITED KINGDOM

Rinchen Dharlo
Office of Tibet
107 E. 31st St.
New York City, NY 10016 U.S.A.

TIBETAN ORGANIZATIONS

Central Institute of Higher Studies
P.O. Sarnath
Varanasi, U.P., INDIA

Charitable Trust
16, Jor Bagh
New Delhi - 110003, INDIA

Library of Tibetan Works & Archives
Gangchen Kyishong
Dharamsala - 176215
District Kangra, H.P., INDIA

SOS - Tibetan Children's Village
Dharamsala Cantt. - 176216
District Kangra, H.P., INDIA

Tibetan Homes Foundation
Gadenling
Happy Valley
Mussorie, U.P., INDIA

Tibet House Cultural Centre
of His Holiness the Dalai Lama
1, Institutional Area, Lodi Road
New Delhi - 110003, INDIA

Dorji Lama
Tibetan Association of Northern
   California
33220 Sandpiper Place
Fremont, CA 94555 U.S.A.

Tibetan Institute of Performing Arts
McLeod Ganj
Dharamsala - 176215
District Kangra, H.P., INDIA

Tibetan Medical Institute
Khara Danda Road
Dharamsala - 176215
District Kangra, H.P., INDIA

Tibetan Wormen's Association
McLeod Ganj
Dharamsala - 176215
District Kangra, H.P., INDIA

Tibetan Youth Congress
Office of the Central Executive
   Committee (CENTREX)
McLeod Ganj
Dharamsala - 176215
District Kangra, H.P., INDIA

HUMAN RIGHTS ORGANIZATIONS

Amnesty International
International Secretariat
1 Easton St.
London WC1X 8DJ
UNITED KINGDOM

Mike Jendrzejczyk
Asia Watch
1522 K St., NW, #910
Washington, DC 20005 U.S.A.

Congressional Human Rights
   Foundation
901 31st St., NW
Washington, DC 20007 U.S.A.

Aryeh Neier
Human Rights Watch
485 Fifth Ave.,
New York City, NY 10017 U.S.A.

Edward Lazar
Humanitas International
Human Rights Committee
P.O. Box 818
Menlo Park, CA 94026 U.S.A.

Michele Bohana/John Ackerly
International Campaign for Tibet
1511 K St., NW, Suite 739
Washington, DC 20005 U.S.A.

Katrina Morris/Andrew Scoble
International Committee of Lawyers
   for Tibet
347 Dolores Street #206
San Francisco, CA 94110 U.S.A.

International Human Rights Law
   Group
1601 Conn. Ave., NW, Suite 700
Washington, DC 20009 U.S.A.

Lawyers' Committee for Human Rights
330 7th Ave., 10th Floor
New York City, NY 10001 U.S.A.

Refugees International
2201 I St., NE, Suite 240
Washington, DC 20002 U.S.A.

CULTURAL & BUDDHIST ORGANIZATIONS

American Himalayan Foundation
909 Montgomery Street #400
San Francisco, CA 94703 U.S.A.

Buddhist Peace Fellowship
P.O. Box 4650
Berkeley, CA 94707 U.S.A.

Robert Thurman
Center for Buddhist Studies
623 Kent Hall
Columbia University
New York City, NY 10027 U.S.A.

Warren Smith
Cultural Survival Tibet Project
103 Warren St.
Medford, MA 02156 U.S.A.

Tibetan Cultural Center
P.O. Box 2581
Bloomington, IN 47402 U.S.A.

Pema Gyari
Tibetan Cultural Center
Rm. 401,
Gotanda Lilas Hi-Town
15-12-2 Nishi Gotanda,
Shinagawa-Ku
Tokyo 141, JAPAN

Stichting Ontmoeting met Tibetaanse Cultuur
De Beaufortlaan 12
NL-3768 Mt. Soest
THE NETHERLANDS

ENVIRONMENTAL ORGANIZATIONS

Nancy Nash
Buddhist Perception of Nature
5 H Bowen Rd., 1st Floor
HONG KONG

Justin Lowe
Earth Island Institute
300 Broadway, Suite 28
San Francisco, CA 94133 U.S.A.

Susan Bachelder
Eco-Tibet
23 E. 20th St. #7
New York City, NY 10003 U.S.A.

Eco-Tibet, California
347 Dolores Street #206
San Francisco, CA 94110 U.S.A.

Greenpeace
1436 U St., NW
Washington, DC 20009 U.S.A.

MEDIA & PUBLICATIONS

Pat Aiello
Parallax Press
P.O. Box 7355
Berkeley, CA 94707 U.S.A.

Tenzin Choedak
Potala Press
107 East 31st St.
New York City, NY 10016 U.S.A.

Sidney Piburn
Snow Lion Publications
P.O. Box 6483
Ithaca, NY 14851 U.S.A.

Dr. Jan Andersson
Tibet Forum
Pfauengasse 12
D-7900 Ulm, WEST GERMANY

Tsering Wangyal, Editor
Tibetan Review
c/o Tibetan SOS Youth Hostel
Sector 14 Extn, Rohini
Delhi - 110 085, INDIA

TIBET SUPPORT GROUPS

Actie Comite Tibet (ACT)
Albert Termotestraat 77
2552 WC Den Haag, HOLLAND

Australia Tibet Council
22 Mariana Crecent
Lethbridge Park
NSW 2770, AUSTRALIA

Bay Area Friends of Tibet
347 Dolores Street #206
San Francisco, CA 94110 U.S.A.

Canada-Tibet Friendship Society
PO Box 6588
Station A
Toronto, Ontario
M5W 1X4, CANADA

Capital Area Friends of Tibet
P.O. Box 66373
Washington, DC 20035 U.S.A.

Mr. Tony Karam
Casa Tibet - Mexico
Orizaba 93 - A
Col Roma
CP067000, Mexico City, MEXICO

Anne de La Celle
Comite de soutien au Peuple Tibetain
B.P. 175 - 75062
Paris, Cedex 02, FRANCE

Piero Verni
Italia-Tibet Association
Via C. Ravizza, 11
20149 Milano, ITALY

Petra K. Kelly/Gert Bastian
P.O. Box 410 154
D-5300 Bonn 1
West Germany

Tsewang Norbu
Fritz Pulligstraße 28
D-5202 St. Augustin 2
WEST GERMANY

Paljor Thondup
Project Tibet
403 Canyon Rd.
Santa Fe, NM 87501 U.S.A.

Peter Kedge
SFE Systems Ltd.
1602 Cambridge Hse
26-28 Cameron Rd.
P.O. Box 98650, HONG KONG

TACO
Apartado Postal 573
E - 20080 San Sebastian, SPAIN

Dr. Palden Tawo
Hardenbergstraße 17
D-5880 Lüdenscheid
WEST GERMANY

Thubten & Gwen Kesang
Tibet Group
52 Lancaster Road
Beachhaven
Auckland 10, NEW ZEALAND

Anna Souza
Tibet House
636 Broadway
New York City, NY 10016 U.S.A.

Robert Barnett
Tibet Information Network
7 Beck Road
London, E84RE,
UNITED KINGDOM

Tibet Initiative
P.O. Box 2531
D-5300 Bonn 1
WEST GERMANY

Kunzang King
Tibet Rights Campaign
4833 151st Place SE
Bellevue, WA 98006 U.S.A.

Ed Bednar
Tibet U.S. Resettlement Project
Walker Center
144 Hancock Street
Newton, MA 02166 U.S.A.

Paula de Wijs-Koolkin
Tibetan Affairs
Coordination Office
Postbox 1276
3500 Bg Utrecht,
THE NETHERLANDS

Tibetan Cultural Association
4675 Coolbrook Ave.
Montreal, Quebec H3X 2K7
CANADA

Migmar Raith
Information Service
TYAE
Nonnenweg 7
4055 Basel, SWITZERLAND

U.S. Tibet Committee
107 East 31st St.
New York City, NY 10016 U.S.A.

Appendix IX

Author Biographies

JOHN ACKERLY serves as Projects Director and Legal Counsel for the International Campagin for Tibet. Prior to joining ICT, he practiced civil rights law in Mississippi and worked in Washington for a Ralph Nader organization. In 1987, Mr. Ackerly witnessed and photographed demonstrations in Lhasa and his pictures have appeared widely. He is the co-author of "Suppression of a People" published by the Physicians for Human Rights and "Forbidden Freedoms" published by ICT.

MRS. ADHI comes from Nyarong in Kham. The area where her family lived was inhabited by both nomads and farmers. Her family belonged to one of the leading clans of the region. In 1958 she was arrested and charged with belonging to the reactionary upper classes and further charged with having protested against the Chinese occupation. Altogether she was incarcerated for over twenty-six years in prisons and work camps, from 1964-1979 in severe solitary confinement. In 1986 she was released, and in 1987 she succeeded in fleeing to Nepal.

PAT AIELLO is a co-founder of Snow Lion Publications. She has been actively working for the Tibetan cause for twelve years and is presently a member of the Advisory Board for the International Campaign for Tibet and Coordinator for the International Year of Tibet in the San Francisco Bay Area.

MICHAEL ALEXANDER is the founder and director of the Tibet Information Service, which works to bring to public attention the situation of the Tibetans-in-exile. He has made many extended visits to India, Pakistan, Australia, and East Africa and is a member of the Sextant Journalists' Cooperative in Bonn.

TENZIN PHUNTSOK ATISHA is the Tibetan Government-in-Exile's ecology coordinator and is research officer of the *Tibetan Bulletin*.

JOHN F. AVEDON is a longtime journalist at Newsweek magazine and an expert on Tibet. He is the author of the books *An Interview with the Dalai Lama* and *In Exile from the Land of Snows*.

ROBBIE BARNETT is a journalist and has written for the *Independent*, the *Times*, and the *Guardian* in London on issues related to politics and human rights in China and in Tibet. He has taught on the subject of China's national minority policies at London University. After visiting Tibet in 1987, he set up the Tibet Information Network to maintian a flow of independent and detailed information from Tibet.

GERT BASTIAN became an officer in the German armed forces (Bundeswehr) in 1956. In 1980 he retired from active military sevice and from 1983 to 1987 he was a member of the German National Parliament and member of the Green Party's Parliamentary Group. He is the author of the well-known "Krefelder Appell," an appeal against the deployment of medium-range missles in Europe, which was signed by over five million people. He is also co-initator of the Bertrand Russell Campaign for a nuclear-free Europe. In 1981, he co-founded the group "Generals for Peace and Disarmament," a group of fourteen highranking retired NATO generals and admirals. In 1981 he received the Carl-v.Ossietzky Prize.

MICHELE BOHANA has spent over ten years monitoring the situation in Tibet and networking with other human rights groups and is responsible in bringing the Tibet issue to Capitol Hill in Washington, D.C., in the 1980s. She now serves as Director for Human Rights of the International Campaign for Tibet, based in Washington, DC.

T.L. DANLOCK has minors in Sociology, Mathematics, and Zoology from University of British Columbia and Simon Fraser University, B.C., Canada and is a member of Canada Tibet Committee.

PEMA DECHEN is the vice-president of the Central Executive Committee of the Tibetan Women's Association. She has served as a teacher and headmistress in the Tibetan Homes Foundation and the Tibetan Children's Village in India and was an active member of the Tibetan Youth Congress.

LORD DAVID ENNALS is a peer of the British House of Lords and the Chair of the Tibet Committee of the human-rights organization *International Alert*.

GEORGE FERNANDES was a member of the Indian Parliament from 1967-70 and 1977-83. In 1974 he led the biggest railway strike in Asia. He is Chairman of the New India Cooperative Bank and Editor of the journals *The Other Side* and *Pratipaksh*. He is the General Secretary of the newly-formed Jananta Dal and the Chairman of its Natiuonal Campaign Commitee.

GYALTSEN GYALTAG has been a resident of Switzerland since 1960. He has been a lecturer since 1986 in Pestalozzidorf in Trogen, Switzerland. A co-founder of the Tibetan Youth Association in Europe, Gyaltag has been a representative of the Dalai Lama in the Office of Tibet in Zürich since 1985 .

TENZIN GYATSO, THE FOURTEENTH DALAI LAMA is the temporal and spiritual leader of the Tibetan people. He and his government are now in exile in Dharamsala, India. His Holiness was awarded the Nobel Peace Prize in 1989.

LODI GYALTSEN GYARI was born in the eastern Tibetan province of Kham in 1947 and received a traditional monastic education. After his escape to India, he worked as an editor of *Voice of Tibet* and founded *Tibetan Review*. Former Minister of Information and International Relations of the Tibetan Government-in-Exile, he is now the Tibetan representative of the Bureau of UN Affairs for the Tibetan Government-in-Exile, President of the International Campaign for Tibet and special envoy at-large of H.H. the Dalai Lama..

DR. THOMAS HEBERER is a university lecturer. From 1967-73 he studied Ethnology, Sinology, and Politics. From 1977-1981, he was a reader and translator at the Foreign Literature Press in Beijing and has written numerous publications on China, including many on minority issues.. He currently teaches Chinese policy at the University of Duisburg, Germany, and is Chair of the Society for German-Chinese friendship.

PICO IYER is a writer for Time Magazine. He first went to Tibet in 1985 and has known His Holiness the Dalai Lama for seventeen years.

PETRA K. KELLY is co-founder of the German Green Party and and was a member of West German Parliament from 1983-1991. She was Party Spokesperson from 1980-82 and 1983-84. Kelly was the recipient of the "Alternative Nobel Prize" in 1982. She has been active many years in the international peace, environmental, and human rights movements.

BLAKE KERR, M.D. traveled in Tibet for three months to help organize a medical expedition with U.S. and Tibetan doctors. He has extensively interviewed Tibetan refugees in India.

EDWARD LAZAR is co-director of Humanitas International Human Rights Committee. He has organized national conferences in support of Tibetan independence, human rights, and the environment.

SUSANNE MAIER was born in 1964. She studied Near Eastern Archaeology and was an eyewitness of the 1989 Lhasa riots.

CHRISTA MEINDERSMA was an eyewitness of the December 1988 riots and herself the victim of a bullet injury. She spent fourteen months in Tibet, of which three and one-half were spent working for the Swiss Red Cross. She is fluent in Tibetan and works as a medical translator.

KATRINA M. MORRIS is a partner in the law firm of Schmit, Morris, Bittner and Schmit in Redwood City, California. She is President of the International Committee of Lawyers for Tibet and a Board Member of Human Rights Advocates, an NGO with consultative status at the United Nations. She has assisted the Tibetan effort at the UN since 1989.

JAMYANG NORBU has worked for the Tibetan Government-in-Exile in various posts and is also a former member of the Tibetan Resistance Force at Mustang. Norbu was one of the conveners of the first Tibetan Youth Congress in 1970. Besides having written many articles of political and ethnological nature, he is the author of *Warriors of Tibet*.

ELMAR REITER is Emeritus Professor of Atmospheric Science and Civil Engineering at Colorado State University. He has been involved with the issues of Tibetan Ecology and Climatology since 1980.

HUGH RICHARDSON, who was in the civil and foreign services in India, taught Tibetan History and Language at the University of Washington (Seattle), the University of California (Berkeley), and the University of Bonn.

GALEN ROWELL is America's pre-eminent nature photographer. He is the author of several books on the earth's wild places and has recently co-authored the book *My Tibet* with His Holiness the Dalai Lama.

ORVILLE SCHELL is an internationally-known chronicler of the Chinese Democracy Movement. He is the author of eight books on China including, *Discos and Democracy: China in the Throes of Reform* and *To Get Rich is Glorious*

ANDREW M. SCOBLE is an attorney practicing in San Francisco, California. He is a member of the Board of the International Committee of Lawyers for Tibet and the Board of Human Rights Advocates. He serves as Vice-Chair of the San Francisco Bar Association Human

Rights Sub-Committee. He is the author of "Enforcing the Customary Law of Human Rights in Federal Courts," 74 Cal.L.Rev 127 (1986).

PROF. M.L. SONDHI is a professor of International Relations and Head of the Institute for International Relations at Jawaharlal Nehru University in New Delhi. For many years, Sondhi served in the diplomatic corps of the Indian Foreign Ministry and was a longtime member of the Indian Parliament. He is a member of the Parliamentarians for Tibet.

DICKY Y. TENLEY is vice-president of the Tibetan Youth in Europe and a leading member of the Tibetan Youth Congress. She visited Tibet two years ago and now lives in Switzerland.

LUDMILLA TÜTING, a freelance journalist, lives in Berlin and in Kathmandu, Nepal. She has made several extended visits to Tibet and is the author of numerous publications on Nepal, Tibet, the Himalaya, the environment, tourism, and racism. She is the founder of Society of Workers Against Racism, which campaigns against discrimination and racism in tourism.

MICHAEL VAN WALT VAN PRAAG, an attorney, is a member of the delegation appointed by the of Tibetan Government-in-Exile to negotiate with the Chinese government. Since 1973, he has been active in the cause of Tibet and has organized numerous tours for the Dalai Lama in Europe. He is the author of the standard work *The Status of Tibet: History, Rights and Prospects in International Law*, the comprehensive legal history of Tibet, and of other scholarly articles on Tibet.

DR. ERWIN WICKERT is a Former Ambassador and Chair of the Advisory Board of the German-Chinese Friendship Society.

Appendix X

Bibliography

Ackerly, John, and Dr. Blake Kerr. *The Suppression of a People: Accounts of Torture and Imprisonment in Tibet.* Boston: Physicians for Human Rights, 1989.

Addy, Premen. *Tibet on the Imperial Chessboard.* New Delhi: Academic Publishers, 1984.

Amnesty International. *Tibet Autonomous Region: Compilation Document.* New York: March 1990.

Andrugtsang, Gompo Tashi. *Four Rivers, Six Ranges (A True Account of Khampa Resistance to Chinese in Tibet).* Dharamsala: Information Office of H.H. the Dalai Lama, 1973.

Asia Watch. *Human Rights in Tibet.* Washington, D.C., February 1988.

———. *Evading Scrutiny: Violations of Human Rights After the Closing of Tibet.* Washington, D.C., July 1988.

———. *Merciless Repression.* Washington, D.C., May 1990.

Avedon, John. *An Interview with the Dalai Lama.* New York: Littlebird Publications, 1980.

———. *In Exile from the Land of Snows.* Boston: Wisdom Publications, 1985.

———. *Tibet Today: Current Conditions and Prospects.* Boston: Wisdom Publications, 1987.

Bass, Catriona. *Inside the Treasure House.* London: Collanez, 1990.

Batchelor, Stephen. *The Tibet Guide.* Boston: Wisdom, 1987.

Bell, Sir Charles. *Portrait of the Dalai Lama. The Life and Times of the Great Thirteenth.* Boston: Wisdom Publications, 1987.

———. *Tibet, Past and Present.* Philadelphia: Coronet Books, 1990

Booz, Elizabeth. *Tibet: A Complete Guide.*

Chapman, Spencer F. *Lhasa, The Holy City.* Salem: Ayer Co., 1940.

Choedon, Dhjondub. *Life in the Red Flag People's Commune.* Dharamsala: Information Office of H.H. the Dalai Lama, 1978.

Clarke, Graham. *China's Reforms of Tibet and Their Effects on Pastoralism.* Sussex: IDS,1987.

David-Neel, Alexandra. *Initiations and Initiates in Tibet.* New York: University Books, 1959.

——. *With Mystics and Magicians.* London: Penguin Books, 1959.

de Riencourt, Amaury. *Roof of the World, Key to Asia* , 1950.

Dhondop, K. *The Water Bird and Other Years.* New Delhi: Rongwang Publishers, 1986.

Dowman, Keith. *Power Places of Central Tibet.* New York: Penguin, 1988.

Ennals, The Rt. Hon. Lord David and Frederick R. Hyde-Chambers. *Tibet in China.* London: An International Alert Report, August 1988.

Epstein, Israel. *Tibet Transformed.* Beijing: New World Press, 1983.

Gashi, Tsering Dorje. *New Tibet: Memoirs of a Graduate of Peking Institute of National Minorities,* Dharamsala: Information Office of H.H. the Dalai Lama, 1980.

Goldstein, Melvyn C. *A History of Modern Tibet.* Berkeley: University of California Press, 1989.

Gyatso, Tenzin, The Fourteenth Dalai Lama. *A Policy of Kindness,* Ithaca, Snow Lion Publications, 1990.

——. *Freedom in Exile: The Autobiography of the Dalai Lama,* San Francisco: Harper Collins, 1990.

——. *Kindness, Clarity, and Insight.* Ithaca, Snow Lion Publications, 1984.

——. *My Land and My People.* New York: Potala Press, 1983.

——. *My Tibet,* Berkeley: University of California Press, 1990.

——. *Ocean of Wisdom,* Santa Fe: Clear Light Publications, 1981.

——. *Proposals for a New Tibet: Five Point Peace Plan.* 1987.

————. *Proposals for a New Tibet: Strasbourg Proposal.* 1988.

————. *The Opening of the Wisdom Eye.* Wheaton: The Theosophical Publishing House, 1974.

————. *Universal Responsibility and a Good Heart.* Dharamsala: Library of Tibetan Works and Archives, 1980.

Harrer, Heinrich. *Return to Tibet,* New York: Schocken, 1987.

————. *Seven Years in Tibet.* Los Angeles, J.P. Tarcher, 1981.

Hicks, Roger. *Hidden Tibet.* Dorset: Element, 1988.

Hoffman, Helmut. *Tibet: A Handbook,* In Collaboration with Stanley Frye, Thubten I. Norbu, Ho-chin Yang, Bloomington, 1975.

Information Office of His Holiness the Dalai Lama. *Collected Statements, Interviews, and Articles of His Holiness the Dalai Lama.* Dharamsala, 1982

————. *From Liberation to Liberalization.* New Delhi: 1982.

————. *Glimpses of Tibet Today.* Dharamsala, 1978.

————. *Tibet under Chinese Communist Rule, A Compilation of Refugee Statements.* Dharamsala. 1958-1975, 1976

————. *Tibetans in Exile.* Dharamsala, 1981

International Campaign for Tibet. *Forbidden Freedoms: Beijing's Control of Religion in Tibet.* Washington, D.C., 1990.

International Commission of Jurists. *The Question of Tibet and the Rule of the Law.* Geneva, 1959.

Kewley, Vanya. *Tibet: Behind the Ice Curtain.* London: Grafton, 1990.

Lamb, Alistair. *Tibet, China and India: A History of Imperial Diplomacy.* Roxford, 1989.

Ledger, W.P. *The Chinese and Human Rights in Tibet: A report to the Parliamentary Human Rights Group.* London, April 1988.

MacInnis. *Religion in China Today.* New York: Orbis Books, 1989.

Michael, Franz. *Rule by Incarnation: Tibetan Buddhism and its Role in Society and State,* Boulder: , 1982.

Minority Rights Group. *The Tibetans: Two Perspectives on Tibetan-Chinese Relations*. London, Report No. 49, 1983 edition.

Norbu, Dawa. *Red Star Over Tibet*. London: Collins, 1974.

Norbu, Jamyang. *Illusion and Reality*. Dharamsala: Tibetan Youth Congress, 1989.

———. *Warriors of Tibet: The Story of Aten and the Khampas Fight for the Freedom of their Country*. Boston: Wisdom Publications, 1986.

Norbu, Thupten Jigme. *Tibet is My Country*. As told to Heinrich Harrer. Boston: Wisdom Publications, 1987.

Richardson, Hugh. *Tibet and its History*. Boston: Shambala, 1984. Second edition.

Richardson, S.D. *Forestry in Communist China*. Baltimore: John Hopkins University Press, 1966.

Sakya, Jamyang and Julia Emery. *Princess in the Land of the Snows*. Boston: Shambhala, 1980.

Schwartz, Ronald D. "Reform and Repression in Tibet." *Telos*, August, 1989.

Shakaba, W.D. *Tibet: A Political History*. New York: Potala Publications, 1984.

Singh, Amar Kaur Jasbir. *Himalayan Triangle*. London: British Library, 1988.

Snellgrove, David and Hugh Richardson. *A Cultural History of Tibet*. Boston: Shambhala, 1980.

Stewart, Whitney. *To the Lion's Throne*. Ithaca, Snow Lion Publications, 1990.

Taring, Rinchen Dolma. *Daughter of Tibet*. London: Wisdom Publications, 1987.

Thomas, Lowell. *Out of this World*, 1950

Trungpa, Chögyam. *Born in Tibet*. London: George Allen & Unwin, 1987.

Tucci, Giuseppe. *The Religions of Tibet*. Berkeley: The University of California Press, 1988.

United Nations, "Report by the Special Rapporteur, Mr. P. Rooijmans, pursuant to Commission on Human Rights resolution 1988/32." E/CN.4/1989/15.

United States House of Representatives, Committee on Foreign Affairs, Hearing on "Human Rights in Tibet," before the Subcommittee on Human Rights and International Organizations, and on Asian and Pacific Affairs. 100th Congress, 1st Session, Washington, D.C., October 14, 1987.

van Walt van Praag, Michael C. *Population Transfer and the Survivial of the Tibetan Identity*. New York: The U.S. Tibet Committee, 1986.

———. *The Status of Tibet*. London: Wisdom Publications, 1987.

Wei, Jing. 100 *Questions About Tibet*. Beijing: Beijing Review Press, 1989.

Yuthok, Dorje Yudon. *House of the Turquoise Roof*. Ithaca: Snow Lion Publications, 1990.

Zhogmi, Jambalozhoi. *Tibetans on Tibet*. Beijing: China Reconstructs Press, 1988.